The 464th Bomb Group in World War II

The 464th Bomb Group in World War II

In Action over the Third Reich with the B-24 Liberator

Mike Hill & Betty Karle

Schiffer Military History
Atglen, PA

Book Design by Ian Robertson.

Library of Congress Catalog Number: 2002109106

Printed in China.
ISBN: 0-7643-1628-1

We are interested in hearing from authors with book ideas on related topics.

Published by Schiffer Publishing Ltd.
4880 Lower Valley Road
Atglen, PA 19310
Phone: (610) 593-1777
FAX: (610) 593-2002
E-mail: Schifferbk@aol.com.
Visit our web site at: www.schifferbooks.com
Please write for a free catalog.
This book may be purchased from the publisher.
Please include $3.95 postage.
Try your bookstore first.

In Europe, Schiffer books are distributed by:
Bushwood Books
6 Marksbury Avenue
Kew Gardens
Surrey TW9 4JF
England
Phone: 44 (0) 20 8392-8585
FAX: 44 (0) 20 8392-9876
E-mail: Bushwd@aol.com.
Free postage in the UK. Europe: air mail at cost.
Try your bookstore first.

Contents

Acknowledgments

The men who served with the 464th Bomb Group in Italy during the Second World War are the men who lived and made the history of the group. It is only fitting that they also helped to place on the printed page the history of the 464th so that future generations will be able to remember their valor.

A special thank you to Merlon Bailey. It was his hope and dream that a history of the 464th Bomb Group would be written. During the early sixties he started trying to contact as many former members of the group as possible. Through his efforts, many memories of service with the 464th were preserved for posterity. Sadly, many of those who responded to Merlon's efforts have passed on. Their contribution to this project is because of Merlon's groundwork. Merlon joined his comrades before he could see the end result of what he started.

Betty and I wish to express a grateful thank you to the following individuals for the loan of photos, stories, diaries, letters, and unpublished memoirs, along with permission to quote from material that has been published:

William Millar; John Graham; Al Karow; Glenn Gunn; Robert Rector; Duane Buckmaster; Thomas Mills; John Porter; Robert De Lawder; Robert Sundlof; Francis Magill; Robert Roy Jr.; David Preller; William Cook; LeRoy Marsh Jr.; Theodore Moldenhauer; Herman Moldenhauer; Robert Gorder; John Rucigay; Donald Takes; Don Sherard; Verl Fielding; John O'Hara M.D.; Gordon Broadhead; Robert Wingfield; Robert Holcomb; Charles Preston; Anthony Schneider; Roman Kruty-Slovakia; John Gordon; Robert Garlock; Felix Rameder; Rod Binger; Marshall Stephenson; John Baker; William Barron; George Carney Jr.; Neal Cobb; Talmadge Callison; Fredrick DeMatteis; Don Dickson; George Drew; Rev. John Eastwood; George Eckhart; Robert Fowler; Walter Freeman; Edward Gaspari; John Gottschalk; Edmund Grochowski; Willard Gustafson; Samuel Handsman; Stilman Harding; Merle Hoffman; Frank Kinberger; John Klika; Norbert Kustka; Douglas Lambert; Ernie Latham; Virgil Leverett; Dorothy Maxson; Arden Mattice; Elmer Miller; Joseph Miniter; Allen Orton; Lewis Perkins; Alvin Platt; Thomas Potts; Harold Reeck; Franklin Rickenbach; Robert Rose; Joseph Santkuyl; Wlliam Schneider; Thomas Scott; Donald Tate; Francis Tuohy; Phillip Turner; Sharon Waggoner; Lester Watkins; William Watkins; Roy Wehman; Robert Weinberg; Richard Wolfe; Don Hayden; Edwin Cane Jr.; Robert Hoskinson; Paul Lester; Robert Larson; Betty Miller; Drew Thompson; John Dersch; Patrick Carr; Harris Frausel; Evo Lucchinn; Cecil Scott; Harold Smith; Sam Parker; John Ryan; William Loughlin; Bruce Callander; Talmadge Callison; Robert Garlock; Charles Houlihan; Warren MacDonald; John McGovern; and Karl Walker.

Special thanks:

John Campbell, friend and wingman on several projects.

Arlen D. Smith, my friend and "brother."

My wife, Linda, for her support in all of my book projects past, present, and future.

J.R. Beitling for his help "above and beyond" in helping to prepare the listing of aircraft used by the 464th.

Foreword

It has been more than fifty years since we served our country in Italy. During these many years, there have been times in motion pictures that I have seen Hitler strutting with his troops and exulting his power. How arrogant he was! As I watched, I found great satifaction in knowing that we had a small part in bringing him down in defeat. We demolished his oil fields; and when there was no more oil, his planes could not fly. We had lots of help, but we did our share; we helped to win the victory, and our efforts were not in vain.

The men we want to remember and honor most are those who gave their lives—the last full measure of devotion. May God bless their souls, and may we so live that their sacrifices will not have been in vain.

As the years have passed, our memory of those days has become less and less clear, and in many cases has passed beyond recall. I am sure that all of us are delighted to learn that Michael Hill and Betty Karle have written a history of the 464th Bomb Group, and will be anxious to secure a copy and live those heartbreaking tradgedies and heart warming victories over again, which we are in danger of forgetting.

Rev. John Eastwood
Chaplain, 464th Bomb Group

Introduction

They have been called the generation of the century. They have also been referred to as the Millennium generation. Either of the titles are rightly bestowed on the men and women who served our country during World War II.

This generation laid aside their future aspirations, families and, if needed, their very lives to serve this great country in a time of armed conflict. Never before or since September 11, 2001, has there been such a spirit of nationalism as this country experienced after the outbreak of the war. Everyone pulled together against the common enemy and did whatever was needed to win the war against the Axis Powers.

From across the length of our country, men and women heard the call to duty. To them, duty and honor were more important than life itself. Everyone began to do their part in the war effort.

Throughout the armed forces of the United States, recruits were brought together and trained for specific duties and to fight the common foe of democracy. Some fought from the deck of a ship, while others fought from a foxhole.

This is the history of men who helped win the war from the air. It is the history of the 464th Bomb Group, who flew the B-24 Liberator through the war torn skies of Europe. The 464th was assigned to the 15th Air Force and flew from Pantanella Army Air Field near Canosa, Italy. The 464th was only one of the 15th Air Force groups that struck targets in what was referred to as the "soft underbelly of Europe."

"Soft underbelly of Europe?" Do not mention that to the men who flew against targets like Vienna, Linz, Blechhammer, and Ploesti. These were some of the most feared targets that the Army Air Force would fly against during the war.

As you read of their daily lives in Italy, remember that their valor and sacrifice was the price that they paid for us, not only to win the war, but to preserve our countries' democratic way of life. Their service is the legacy they leave to us and future generations.

It makes no difference whether these men faced flak and fighters in the cold skies, sweated out repairs to the planes, or served as clerks and cooks; they all heard the call and are to be treated with respect and honor.

During the research and writing of this history of the 464th, I have had the honor of talking with many of these American heroes. I call them heroes because I have come to learn that a hero is someone who does what has to be done without regard of the outcome or consequences.

One of these men remarked "I had friends at home, in high school, and even college fraternity brothers. But I never put them above the men I went through combat with. They gave everything. What they gave to this country is beyond what mere words can describe...."

I have referred to these men as "they" or "them." As you read on you will be introduced to the names and faces of the 464th Bomb Group. Men like Phillip Turner, tower operator; Robert Wingfield, pilot; Lonnie McMichaels, crew chief; and William Hedge, nose gunner. They are but a few who served with the 464th, but they are all heroes of America.

Memorial Day is upon us as I write this introduction to the 464th History. It is a day set aside to remember and honor those who have given their lives for our country. But it is more then a day of remembering; it is also a day to reaffirm our faith in our country. It is our duty as Americans to ensure that everyone who breathes the fresh air of freedom remembers what these men did for us. Memorial Day is about remembering and protecting the ideas that these men fought to protect so that their service and sacrifice will not have been in vain.

As the historian of the 464th Bomb Group, Betty Karle has a very deep knowledge of the group and the men who served in it during the war. Her interest and love of the group is much more than a passing interest—it is of a very personal nature. Lt. John

James, her brother, served with the group during the war. He and most of his crew gave their lives while flying a mission on August 24, 1944. It is only natural and fitting that Betty should help preserve the history of her brothers' group so that other generations can read of their service and sacrifice.

I have been asked many times about my interest in the men who fought in World War II. One obvious reason is that my dad served in the war and then made the military his life.

As a boy, I remember those special times when dad would dig into his trunk and get the photo albums out. Those marvelous photos of B-24s were aged to perfection in the eyes of a small boy. My interest grew with the fascination of a young boy's belief in the glory of armed conflict.

As I grew older, my boyhood belief in the glory of war was replaced by the stark reality of the horror of combat and what it does to those who have tasted it. I soon learned that these men who served our country paid a price for our freedom. There is no way that we can ever repay the debt that we owe this generation. The only thing we can do is to honor them in our daily lives and utter a special "Thank you!"

Writing about their valor and sacrifice so that it can be preserved as part of our American history is my meager way of saying my thanks to these men. It is with our thanks that Betty and I dedicate this history of the 464th to those who served with the group in World War II.

Michael Hill

1

Stateside Training

Across the desert near Benghazi, Libya, the morning of August 1, 1943, was shattered by the sound of 712 Pratt & Whitney engines belching to life. That morning, B-24s from the 9th Bomber Command took to the air to strike the oil refineries at Ploesti, Romania. The men flying the mission had planned and practiced it until they could see the target in their sleep. They had been told that if they knocked out the vital oil refineries, the war could be shortened by six months. Operation TIDAL WAVE was underway, and before the end of the day those who survived would know that they had made it through one of the most horrific missions they would ever fly.

On that fateful day, back in the states a new bomb group was activated. Under the provisions of General Order #78 the 464th Bomb Group came to life at Wendover Field, Utah. The four squadrons making up the group were assigned the numbers 776, 777, 778, and 779. It takes a great deal of planning, equipment, and men to get a group off the ground. For the next several weeks the 464th would exist on paper only, while orders were being cut to bring together everything that was needed to get the show on the road.

The 464th was transferred without men or equipment to Gowen Field, Boise, Idaho, on August 22, 1943. When a group was activated it had no personnel; it was standard procedure to transfer it to a base that was already established with personnel to begin a nucleus for the new group. The group had a number and a base to train at. All the group needed now was a lot of well trained people.

The original cadre of personnel were assigned to the group on August 26. Many of these men came from the parent group, the 29th Bomb Group then stationed at Gowen Field. Under provisions of a Special Order the following key personnel were assigned:

The Original Cadre Personnel, 778th Bomb Squadron. August 27, 1943.

Original Cadre 779th Engineering and Ground Sections. L-R Rear: Issac Saacs, Supply Sgt; Bill Davis, Tech Supply. L-R-Middle: Phil Singer, Armament; Wallace Pauley, Ordnance; Gene Hallock, Electrician; Harry Bruneau, Crew Chief; Carl Springenr, Radio; John Whitmeyer, Flt Chief; Michael Moyna, Instruments; E.F. Norman, 1st Sgt; Joe Hardin, Tech Supply Sgt. L-R Front: Jack Booth, Motor Pool; Clayton Morud, Welder; Frankie Mcglire, Supply; Paul Hutchinson, AM Mech; Art Chaney, Electrician.

Lt Col. Henry K. Seal	Executive Officer
1st Lt. Weldon K. Burton	Operations Officer
1st Lt. John W. Nance	Asst. Operations Officer
1st Lt. Floyd Beasley	Communications Officer
Capt. Royal F. Cato	Bombardier
1st Lt. Kyle Spiller Jr.	Navigator
Capt. Francis F. Elder	Intelligence Officer
Capt. Harold E. Blehm	Commander 776th Sqd
Capt. Thomas J. Carter	Commander 777th Sqd
Capt. Clarence G. Poff	Commander 778th Sqd
Capt. Arthur Hampson	Commander 779th Sqd

On 28 August, 33 officers and 67 enlisted men assigned to the 464th received orders to proceed to Orlando, Florida, to attend the Army Air Force School of Applied Tactics. The officers were told to pack four sheets, two pillow cases, a gas mask, bathing suit, and high top shoes. Enlisted men were allowed two sheets, a pillow case, and a swim suit. Everyone was supposed to bring 15 copies of their orders!

They arrived at Orlando on 2 October and met the newly assigned Commanding Officer, Lt /Col. Marshall Bonner. During the next three weeks the men were given accelerated courses in equipment and combat tactics, as well as how to operate a group under almost any conditions. The first three weeks were not bad, since there was a lot of classroom work. The next phase was pure hell, living and operating under the conditions at nearby Pinecastle Field. There were snakes, mosquitos, flies, bad chow, heat and humidity, and those were the good points. During this time at Pinecastle the group was assigned four aging B-24s for training. These ships already had a lot of air across the wings, and just getting them off the ground was an accomplishment. One of the planes was named FERTILE MYRTLE. Most of the men agreed that she must have been fertile, since it was evident that a lot of men had undergone flight training in her already. In spite of the horrible conditions of living in the field and trying to fly under next to impossible conditions, the men accomplished what they had been sent to Florida to do.

When these key personnel returned West, they found that the group had been transferred to Pocatello Army Air Base, arriving there on 1 October. For the moment, the group had the four ancient B-24s that they had used in Florida. Shortly after arriving in Idaho three were taken away and assigned to other groups. In spite of having only one aircraft to train with, the group did the best they could. By the end of October the B-24s had been replaced, and the group was back up to four flyable aircraft.

During October, the ground echelon of the 799th was dealt a cruel blow. 1/Sgt. E.F. Norman had not been feeling very well. Fi-

464th Operations tent at Pinecastle Army Field, Florida.

Some of the 464th personnel at Pinecastle during AFSAT.

nally, he became so sick that he was forced to go to the Hospital and have it checked out. He died in the hospital of a ruptured appendix.

Almost every day another group of men would arrive from training units with orders to report to the 464th Bomb Group. The 464th was taking on everything from cooks to clerks. It was a monumental task trying to get these men assigned to squadrons, quarters, and getting them used to the idea that they were now a member of a real outfit, the 464th Bomb Group (H).

Col. Bonner was a stickler for administrative detail. Those who worked with him in Group Headquarters soon learned that they had better have every word correct and all the periods in the right place before they sent a document to his desk. If they did not they knew they would first get a good chewing out and then have to do the whole thing over again. Some of the staff thought the 'old man" was ok, while others thought there was something about him that just was not right.

Ten crews from the 15th Operational Training Wing, based at Gowen Field, arrived on 7 November. They were followed by ten more crews on 11 November. This second group came from the 15th Anti-Submarine Patrol Squadron then based at Wendover Field, Utah. Now, just what in the heck was a sub patrol unit doing in the Utah desert? The answer is very simple, Not Much! These crews had spent many hours flying up and down the Atlantic coastline looking for German U-Boats. One of the patrol planes had even flown through a Hurricane while on patrol. Perhaps the fact that they had accomplished such a feat was the basis for the Air Force Hurricane Hunters. Another of the patrol planes was reported to have depth charged a whale. Either the crew thought it was a U-Boat, or just wanted to have some fun to break up the boredom of the long patrol flight. The anti-sub patrol crews were transferred to Texas and patrolled the Gulf of Mexico for the same dreaded U-boat. When the Navy said that they were no longer needed they were sent to Wendover for assignment to other groups as replacements. In many cases, entire trained and seasoned crews were broken up. The luckier ones remained together and were assigned to newly formed groups, such as the 464th. The sub patrol crews brought much needed experience in flying four engine bombers, even if they had flown their patrols at altitudes far below 10,000 feet.

With the arrival of these crews Phase Two training began, and there would be all kinds of classroom work. Every aspect of flying the B-24 in combat had to be covered in great detail. After all, in a short time the lives of every crewman on the plane would depend on how well each member of the crew performed his specific assignment. By the end of November these crews had completed about 60% of the required Phase 2 training.

On 16 November fifteen more crews arrived from the training base at Casper, Wyoming. Several of these crews had completed all of the Phase Three requirements and were quickly assigned as instructors or assistants to key areas within the different squadrons. For the rest of the men, Phase Two training continued with more and more detailed work to be done. Gunners spent hours going over how and why they were important to the crew. They learned how to do emergency repairs of their guns and the importance of keeping them clean. On top of that they also spent time using the weapons on the range. Flight Engineers worked out on the flightline alongside the ground crews so that they would have intimate knowledge of just what made the B-24 tick.

George Carney at Pinecastle.

One of the old Liberators used for training at Pinecastle.

Taking time out from training to relax and have a photo taken for the folks back home.

The 464th celebrated Thanksgiving by having the usual turkey dinner with all the trimmings. It wasn't bad, even if it was done up in the usual Army style of hurry up and wait in line. The sad part of the whole affair was that the chow was good for a change and they could not take any home as leftovers.

With crews arriving every day friendships developed that would last throughout the rest of the war. There always seemed to be somebody trying to get a bunch of the guys together to go to town and see the sights, such as they were. Those that didn't get a pass spent time at the various clubs. On many nights a loud chorus of "Pistol Packin Mama" could be heard coming from the Officers Club. This song was the unofficial theme song of the ex-anti sub crews, and naturally they brought it with them when they were assigned to the 464th.

The base at Pocatello, or Pokey as it became known, had only been open since December 1942. As with all new bases it was alive with construction, and improvements were constantly being made. The base had a fine Officers Club, as many would later remember. There was also a recreation center and a nice P.X. As with all Army Bases, there was a Chapel so that the men could worship. Several members of the 464th recalled exchanging nuptial vows at the Chapel. One of the nicer aspects of the base was the "Consolidated Mess." It was centrally located and served three meals a day. They also served meals at off time periods for those who were pulling special duty, such as late line duty, guards, and returning training flights.

The base also had its own newspaper, called *The Bombardier*. It was full of news from the base and sported a joke section called "Bombardier Cocktails." One of the more frequently read parts of the paper was the sports section, which had all the latest scores from around the country, no matter what sports were being played at the time.

For those that could get some time off and wrangle a pass to go into town there was the local USO Club located at 325 West Lander St. The folks who ran the club always tried to have a lot of interesting things planned. It was just nice to get away from the base and enjoy the off time by sitting around and talking with some of the local girls that worked at the club.

By 4 December thirty-six more crews had arrived. These crews came from Mountain Home Army Air Base and had completed their Phase One training at that location. Their Second Phase work began at once. The original crews had already completed their Phase Two by 18 December and were granted leave until the end of the month. As of 19 December the group had grown to an effective flying force of 37 B-24s.

When another crew or plane arrived they were assigned to a Squadron. Each airplane had to have a ground crew to service and maintain it. "Red" Moldenhauer recalled:

Training flight over Mobile, Alabama, enroute to Fort Worth.

The flight crews were on their last phase of training, so there was lots of work for all to do. Soon we were assigned to our flight crews. I got 1st/Lt. John H. Jones and crew; S/Sgt. Noble Shires was the Engineer, and how lucky can you get, they were the best! Our Squadron took over a night club in Pocatello. John and his wife, "Bunny," really made us a tight crew. This was when we had a chance to get really acquainted with our fellow members of the ground crews. There was Jack Shipman, Harry Bruneau, Lester Hacker, Mike Moyna, Chaney, Smokey Halonen, Robertson, Vernon, LeBlanc, Perlow, Fred Staton, Norman Jones, "Crash" Parrish, Lt. Leroy Marsh, Earl Gaston, our First Sergeant Richard Shores, Freddie Riggs, Art Hush, Rod Binger, Steve Stephenson, Lonnie McMichaels, Barrett, Caldwell, White, Bill Spivey, Wade, and Merino.

A lot can be said about the weather in Idaho during December. Ask any of those who trained there, and most of their comments will be that the weather was bad. Not only was it bad to fly in, with snowstorms and icing conditions, but working on the B-24s sitting on the ramp after they had become cold soaked was beyond belief. Because of the weather training slowed to a crawl. Another problem was the lack of spare parts for the old ships. Planes would be off flying status when the weather was good enough to fly. Thus, crews lost good flying time.

On 19 December the group lost its first B-24 in an accident. The plane was flown by 2nd Lt. Robert Gitt's crew. The probable cause of the accident was carburetor icing. The B-24 crashed, taking eight of her crew with her. Sgt. Fred Schilling, Jr., was able to bail out. Sgt. William Galasso had been grounded for medical reasons and was not on the flight. It was a sobering incident, and everyone in the 464th knew that training was getting to be serious business.

The Christmas holiday came and went. Those that were on leave returned with fond memories of spending the season with loved ones. They all knew that it would be the last holiday spent at home for a long time. Some wondered if they would ever spend another Christmas with their families. Those that could not get home for the holiday spent it either at the base or on a pass in Pocatello.

Weather continued to play an important part in the 464th's training. It had been so bad that word came down from higher command that only those training flights that were deemed a "must" would be flown. On top of bad weather and the training that had to be done there were still new personnel arriving that had to be processed.

The New Year began as the old one had gone out. Bad weather was still a problem. It seemed that if it wasn't snowing it was to darned cold to get any work done. The Phase Three requirements were being met, but it seemed the group was moving at a snail's pace.

By the end of the first week in January the weather broke a little, and activity quickened in hopes they could get some of the important missions flown. Thus began a series of full scale practice sorties. There were missions where the entire group would fly a full scale mission against a specific target city, like Salt Lake or Las Vegas. These missions included everything but dropping real bombs on the target. Then there were missions to the bombing range and dropping real practice bombs on the isolated targets. Gunnery missions helped the gunners sharpen their aim. Most of these missions were over South Dakota, and more then one B-24 landed at Pierre, South Dakota, for one reason or another. If they had to remain over-

776th Bomb Squadron Armament Section, Pocatello, Idaho, January 1944.

Gear down and locked, a B-24 heads for the runway after a training sortie.

night some of the crews would venture into town, and most of them found the Sod Buster bar downtown.

Tragedy hit the group a second time on 9 January when B-24E (42-7365), assigned to the 778th Sqd, crashed, killing seven of the crew. Three members of the crew survived the incident. On the 17th, another 778th Sqd B-24 crashed, taking the lives of two of the crew. The 777th Sqd suffered the loss of 41-29349 on 20 January. This aircraft crashed about 11 miles southwest of the base, taking seven crewmen's lives. After these incidents, flying a training mission appeared as dangerous as combat.

Scuttlebutt had it that the group was going to be getting orders to ship out any day now. Most of the crews had finished enough training so they were almost combat ready. To increase the rumors floating around the base the group flew a full scale simulated combat mission on 13 January. This mission was part of a Preparations For Overseas Movement inspection.

As the pace continued to move from fast to almost breakneck, several of the crews noticed something about Col. Bonner's behavior. Now, maybe it was just the fact that he had a lot on his mind trying to get the group in shape, or was it something deeper then that? Many of the crews that flew with him on training sorties noticed that he was fine as long as everything went according to the flight manual. If something happened in the air that was out of the ordinary he seemed to have trouble coping with the situation. At least one crew noticed that his approach to landing was under recommended airspeed and he wanted to flare out about ten feet higher than he should. Some of the crews dreaded the thought of flying with the boss.

Towards the end of January rumors really started to fly around the base. These rumors were backed up by some heavy last minute flying to get the final must items checked off the training schedule. On top of everything, everybody started a series of physical examinations carried out by the medical department. Everyone had to get the required poking and prodding so that their records were complete. The medical department went over the records with a fine tooth comb. If the men had not gotten their overseas shots, so they lined up and were vaccinated for typhoid, tetanus, smallpox, thyphus, yellow fever, and cholera. At least a few of the men had reactions to the shots and spent some time as patients in the hospital. Almost everyone that had to undergo the series of shots had sore arms, and perhaps were sore somewhere else.

In just a few short months the 464th had grown from a paper outfit to a well trained unit of men with one common goal. They wanted to get overseas and do their part to put an end to the war. They were eager and confident that they would be able to accomplish whatever they were assigned to do no matter where they were sent.

On 1 February the pace around Pocatello Army Air Base was nonstop. The ground echelon had been told to start packing for the trip overseas. Everything from tools to typewriters had to be packed, marked with the correct group stencil, and moved to the area for final packing aboard trains. Personnel were told just how much baggage they would be allowed for the trip overseas. Flightcrews were also told how much and what they would be allowed to take with them on the long flight to...? In all the hub-ub, it seemed that no one had told the 464th exactly where they were headed. But that was "ok" at the moment, since it was supposed to be a military secret.

On 5 February Special Order #36 from Headquarters was handed down, stating that the ground echelon would leave Pocatello by train and travel to Hampton Roads Port of Embarkation, Camp Patrick Henry, Virginia. The order also specified that they should be at that point by the 13 February. Well, at least the group now knew that they were headed for Europe instead of the Pacific.

On the morning of 9 February, four trains were backed onto sidings at the base. It was time to leave Pocatello. It seemed that "Mother Nature" was giving the group a special treat, as she had provided a driving snowstorm for the send off. Each of the four Squadrons had its own train to ride on for the trip to sunny Virginia. Group Headquarters had been assigned to travel with the 777th Sq. for the trip overseas.

In typical Army fashion there was a lot of hurry up and wait, while clerks and section chiefs sorted out just who was going to ride in what car and where in that car. As the men filed into the cars they noticed that this was not a regular civilian train, but a real Army troop train, complete with bunks that were stacked six high.

There were a lot of tearful last minute goodbyes for those who were married and had been able to get their families to Pocatello.

B-24s on the ramp at Pocatello.

Disaster strikes the 464th on January 20, 1944, when 41-29349 from the 779th crashes about 11 miles southwest of the base.

Who knew when they would see each other again. For the rest of the men there were the usual good natured bantering and cat calls from those that were staying behind with the air echelon. After what seemed to be a lifetime the trains got up a head of steam and started down the tracks. Again, in typical Army fashion each train would proceed towards Virginia by a different route.

The trip to Virginia can best be summed up in one word, miserable. The weather was cold, and in some cases sub-zero. So called heating pipes on the train froze, cutting off heat to most of the cars. Along with that water lines also froze, leaving the men with little water to drink or bathe in. Yeah right, have you ever tried to get a bath on a troop train? Next to impossible. The men made the best of the situation. There were a lot of card games, with poker being one of the favorites. Others read everything they could get their hands on, while many slept as well as they could under the circumstances.

The trains arrived at Camp Patrick Henry on 13 February, and the men gladly left the trains for their temporary home. As the ground echelon settled in they found that they had to be processed for their trip overseas. So it was stand in line, hurry and wait while baggage and medical records were double checked, and everything else was double checked. After the men had gone through the staging process many were issued passes so they could leave camp and see the local sights or spend a night on the town.

The movement of the air echelon began in earnest on 21 February, when 48 B-24s took off, circled the field at Pokey, and then climbed through a solid overcast. As each one broke out of the clouds they took up a heading towards Lincoln Army Air Base, Nebraska. Lincoln was one of the final modification centers for planes headed into combat. While the planes were there, any modifications that had been sent down from Consolidated were to be carried out before heading to the final point of departure for overseas duty. In

Tail section of #349. Seven crewmen were lost in the accident.

most cases these mods were small in nature and did not take very long. It was also here at Lincoln that the aircraft were readied for their flight overseas. Long range fuel tanks were installed in the bomb bays so that the planes would have the extra range needed to get across the Atlantic. While this was being done the rest of the plane was checked from tail turret to pitot tube to make sure that the B-24 was as ready as humanly possible to make the trip that lay ahead. This was known as a one hundred hour inspection, which seemed strange, since most of the group's B-24s had well under a hundred hours of flight time on the airframe. Several crews did not have an airplane assigned to them yet. They rode to Lincoln on several of the group's planes. At Lincoln they picked up a brand new B-24, fresh from the factory.

Ah, there was something about a factory fresh B-24. It not only looked brand new, but smelled brand new. They had not acquired the smell of a well used airplane yet. They didn't reek of fuel, hydraulic fluid, and body odor. No sir, they smelled good inside. Remember the smell of your first new car? That was kind of the same smell, only with wings instead of tires.

This inspection process took a few days, so the crews were sort of stuck in the heart of the corn belt. There were some sights to see in Lincoln. They could always visit the capitol building, take a ride to the top of the tower and gaze out across the prairie. Some of the men found a nice little cafe on "O" Street where you could get a fine homecooked meal and plenty of coffee for next to nothing. And who would ever forget the accommodations at the Cornhusker Hotel in downtown Lincoln? It was one of the finest in the midwest.

Some of the flight crews were dispatched to Topeka, Kansas, to pick up their "fly-away" aircraft. In most cases the B-24s that they picked up in Kansas were B-24Gs. Some of these crews then flew back to Lincoln, while others departed to Florida for overseas staging.

When the planes were ready to go the crews were given orders to fly to Morrison Field, Florida, for final staging. Since the planes were ready at different times they took off from Lincoln at different times. The flight from Lincoln to Florida was for the most part an easy one, and everyone made the trip without a major problem. So good, so far!

2

Crossing the Atlantic

At this juncture, the 464th Bomb Group was divided into two parts. The ground echelon was getting ready to board their ships for the crossing, while the aircrews were staging from Lincoln to Morrison Field, Florida. It would be almost a month before the group would be together again.

As with the troop train movement from Idaho, the Army had broken the 464th into several groups traveling on different ships and different routes across the Atlantic. Some felt this was a measure of security so that if one ship was sunk by a U-Boat there would still be at least three of the group's squadrons intact to carry on with the war.

The 778th Bomb Squadron was the first to actually leave the shores of the United States. On 22 February they, along with the Headquarters personnel, boarded the Liberty ship *FRANCIS AMASA WALKER* and set sail. To some of the men the ship was "ugly and slow looking." The 464th was on its way to Europe.

It took over another week for the next part of the group to leave. On 1 March the 779th was loaded onto a Liberty ship called the *JONATHAN GROUT*. The Squadron spent the night on board and left on the morning tide.

The 777th left port 3 March aboard the *WALTER REED*. The 776th left the same day on the *HENRY W. LONGFELLOW*. The 776th did not get too far out to sea when their ship started having problems with the engines and could not keep up with the rest of the convoy. They returned to port on 6 March and processed back into their former barracks. While the engines were being worked on many of the men got passes and went into town for one last fling. The good old *LONGFELLOW* had its engines fixed, and the 776th came aboard again on 12 March. They left the safety of harbor and joined a convoy for the trip across the Atlantic, but they were now almost two weeks behind the rest of the group.

No matter what ship the men were on they all seemed to have several things in common. First they were crowded; after all, they were troop ships, and were filled to the top with exactly that, troops. Space on board was a scarce commodity, and privacy was a rarity. About the only place that could be called your own was the bunk that had been assigned to you. If you had been one of the lucky ones you had a lower berth, and if luck played a cruel trick then you had one of the bunks on the top of the stack, about eight bunks up.

Ground Echelon arriving in Italy aboard the troop ships.

Naples Harbor, April 1944. The 779th ground echelon is more than ready to get on solid ground again.

The lighting in the holds was pretty bad. Some of the guys joked about using their zippos to get a little extra candle power. Then there were the meals. Two a day of whatever the ship's cooks could come up with, and in most cases it was C-Ration soup. It wasn't the best, but at least it sort of filled the stomach, that is, if you were first in the chow line. One of the most remembered items was the awful latrines, with seawater sloshing around in them and the smell beyond description. At times there was even a line to get to the latrines, or head, as it was known in the Navy.

Most people believe that everything in the military is done by the numbers or according to the manual. Not so! It is a fact of military life that almost everything is done in a hurry up and wait in line fashion. From the moment a soldier raises his right hand until the day he is discharged, he stands in line for something. These lines are in hot sun, driving rain, or cold snow. A soldier gets his pay, clothes, food, mail, beer, passes, entertainment, shots, and everything else—including his flat feet—by standing in one line or another.

Now then, exactly how did the men spend their time on the trip? There was a lot of poker and other types of card games being played. Several of the guys won a lot of money at these games. Others read every paperback book they could find. As much time as possible was spent on the outer decks. Those that could get there actually started to obtain a suntan if the weather was good.

A lot of the men were just not cut out to be sailors. They never got their "sea legs" under them. Or maybe it was a combination of the food, boredom, and pitching of the ship. At any rate, many of the men got seasick and made most of the trip "by rail."

The 778th aboard the *F.A. WALKER* passed the Rock of Gibraltar on the 17th day of the voyage and went on to the Island of Sicily. The convoy spent a night at Augusta, then went on towards Italy the next day. On March 19, 1944, they landed at Brindisi, Italy. The 778th loaded their gear and waited for the trucks to arrive to take them to the next stop. That next stop happened to be a place called Gioia del Colle. The men were hungry after the long truck ride. John Curtis, Jr. (778th) recalled:

D.I. Stanard in front of one of the "luxurious" rail cars that will transport the ground echelon across Italy.

A few scattered tents in the orchard, March 21, 1944.

Future area of the 776th Sq. on Pantanella Hill.

Our first meal in Italy was prepared out in the open. The cooks prepared a good meal under the conditions; the main dish was a large pot of pinto beans, which were very tasty. After most of us were through eating, they found the remains of a field mouse in the bottom of the pot.

That night the men spent their first night in Italy sleeping on the cold concrete floor of a former German barracks. On 20 March the convoy of trucks headed out in the early morning hours. After a long bumpy ride the men arrived at Pantanella Air Base around 4 o'clock that afternoon. One thing seemed really strange to the new arrivals—it was called an Air Base. The problem was that the base was nothing but a high hill: no tents; buildings; a few trees; piles of what looked like soft concrete blocks, whatever they were for; and not a B-24 in sight. There was a contingent from the Quartermaster Corps there to issue tents. They also had some food, if that's what it was supposed to be. Some of the guys found what appeared to be hay and stuffed it into their mattress covers. Coffee was brewed, but it was bad.

There was not enough time to pitch all the tents, and a lot of the men spent the night sleeping under the stars atop Pantanella Hill, in the cold Italian night. To make matters worse it snowed that night. Snow is supposed to be white, but some of this stuff was black. It seemed that Mt. Vesuvius had erupted several days before, and there was still plenty of ash in the air to greet the new arrivals. The spearhead of the 464th had arrived in Italy.

The 779th had left about the same time as the 776th aboard the *Jonathan Gout*. Their trip across the Atlantic was marred by bad weather all the way across the Atlantic. It was a rough trip, to say the least. The ship was battered by what was described as one of the worst maritime storms ever encountered. Even the ship's crew said

A field of wheat in the valley, and future airfield of the 464th.

Officers' row in the very early days at Pantanella.

Tent row for the 464th at Oudna.

A B-24 landing at Oudna with the nose gear up.

The end result of the emergency landing.

it was bad. The men were literally locked below decks so none would venture topside and be swept overboard. Everyone was sick as a dog. Only those that were there can truly envision what it was like. The ship would roll and heave from side to side. It was not long before the floor was covered with what can nicely be described as "moisture." It would slide from one side to the other and splash around as the ship rolled about. In the midst of all this the ship actually began to crack under the weight of the storm. Damage control parties worked through the night with torches to weld the cracks together, then hope that the ship would not break apart. The welds held and the *Johnny Gout* sailed on.

After passing the Strait of Gibralter on 20 March the convoy turned south and landed at Oran, Africa, the next day. The 779th could hardly wait to get off their old tub after the stormy crossing. The men were loaded onto trucks, and after an 18 mile ride were quartered at a place called Staging area #2. The 779th lived in tents at this location until 5 April, when they again boarded a troopship and set sail for Naples, arriving there on the 10th. From Naples they went by freight train to Canosa, Italy. From there it was a truck ride to Pantanella.

The 777th's trip across the Atlantic was uneventful. They arrived at Bari, Italy, with few problems, other than they were tired of being on the ship. From Bari they were trucked to Pantanella and arrived there in the wee morning hours of 30 March.

We left the 776th aboard the *HENRY W. LONGFELLOW*, repaired and back at sea. Their trip was already one to remember. On 31 March the convoy they were a part of came under attack by several U-Boats. The naval escort ships buzzed around the convoy, dropping several depth charges, and finally drove the subs away. The convoy passed through the Straits of Gibraltar around dawn on 1 April Shortly after that, the convoy was attacked by the Luftwaffe. Several ships in the convoy were hit, but the 776th's old *LONGFELLOW* came through the scrap without a scrape. The 776th dropped anchor at Augusta, Sicily, on 5 April for a brief stay to unload some cargo from the ship. They finally arrived at Naples on 8 April. After spending the night at the University of Naples, the 776th moved across Italy by train, then from Bari to Pantanella by truck on 10 April.

We left the members of the air echelon in Florida getting ready for their part of the overseas movement. Since the group was going to be stationed in Italy they would take what was known as the southern ferry route. This consisted of flying from Florida to Borinquen, Puerto Rico, then to Atkinson Field, British Guiana, then to Belem, Brazil, and finally to Natal, Brazil, before jumping off for the long trip across the Atlantic. If the planes got across the Atlantic they would first land at Dakar, Africa, then fly to Marrakech, and finally on to Oudna Field, Africa. Now, this looks fairly easy on a map. It was just a couple of inches on paper, but just think about the actual distances from place to place and you will come to the conclusion that these crews were in for a heck of a long trip.

On 29 February B-24 42-78126, with the crew of 2ndLt. Joseph Cummings (778th), ran into trouble. They were getting close to Georgetown, British Guiana, but the fuel gauges were getting low. The crew kept looking for the field, hoping with any luck they would make it. Their luck did not hold, as the big Pratt and Whitney engines began to cough and sputter. There was only one thing to do, and that was to try and get the plane down. They managed a crash landing about 22 miles southeast of Georgetown. The crash landing caused the death of five of the crew. Three of the survivors received major injuries, and two of the crew sustained minor injuries.

On 4 March B-24 42-78130, with Maj. Elvin Goodyear at the controls, also ran low on fuel. Maj. Goodyear did not take any chances and rang the bail out bell. Everyone, except Maj. Goodyear and Capt. Robert Chesser, jumped from the plane. They stayed with the plane and made a good belly landing about 30 miles southwest of Belem, Brazil. The crew was all right, but the plane was a washout. The 464th had not even gotten close to Europe and had already lost two airplanes and a crew trying to get there.

In the B-24 flown by Robert Wingfield there was a "mechanical problem"; actually there wasn't, but Wingfield decided that they were too close to Puerto Rico to let the opportunity slip by. Bob was one of the anti-sub patrollers who had found his way to the 464th. He was all too familiar with Puerto Rico and its treasures. With that in mind, his ship made an "emergency" stop at Borinquen Field (now Ramey AFB). Stopping in Puerto Rico was actually on the flight plan for the group, but since their ship had a mechanical problem they would remain for a little longer than scheduled. The crew remained at Borinquen while the "problem" was fixed. While the ship was being looked over Bob proceeded to fill every nook and cranny with cases of rum. After all, it was just 88 cents for a fifth. They flew onward crammed with 18 cases of the good stuff.

When the 464th's B-24s arrived at Natal, Brazil, it was "first things first." No one was allowed out of the airplane before the local mosquito patrol sprayed the entire inside of the plane and the crew with a good dose of DDT. The crewmen had to remain inside the sweltering fuselage for about ten minutes choking on the heat and DDT until all the little buzzing critters were dead.

Ready to leave Africa. L-R: Dick Niles; Stillman Harding; and Robert Hornbaker.

If the weather over the Atlantic was bad—and it always seemed that it was—the crews would have a few days layover at Natal. It was quite a place. There were a lot of sights to see and lots of fresh fruit from the local markets. A good number of the boys went to the beach, and what a beach it was. There, against the blue Atlantic, was mile after mile of white sand to gaze out across. It was as good a time as ever to work on a good suntan. Some of the men went into town and visited the local shops. At least one pair of the famous Mosquito Boots were purchased. These boots were an orange color and about nine inches tall. The trousers were supposed to be tucked into the top of the boots to keep the pesky critters from getting to the ankles. Those that had them swore by them, even if they were not regulation issue.

The time at Natal gave the crews a chance to check anything on the planes that had gone wrong during the first part of the movement. Everything had to be double checked, because the next part of the trip was going to be the long flight across the Atlantic. There would not be any land for almost two thousand miles.

At least several of the crews put the time at Natal to good use. It seems that while B-24 41-29458 was sitting on the ramp someone found a can of paint and a paintbrush. From that day on she would be known as SHOO SHOO BABY in honor of her pilot, Capt. William Shoemaker, and the fact that his wife was going to have a baby. Capt. Wingfield's crew also took time to christen their ship with a paintbrush. When 42-29453 left Brazil, she was known as BIG FAT MAMA.

When everything was ready on the plane and the weather was good over the Atlantic the crews would climb aboard and fly out over the water towards their next stop at Dakar. It would be a flight of about 10 or 12 hours, depending on the winds and weather.

The individual flights across the ocean varied from crew to crew. It was always drafty in the back of the plane, even though the waist windows were closed for travel. Up in the cockpit the pilot and copilot were busy "chasing shadows." That was the procedure for getting the props in synch. It was a simple procedure. They would look at the shadow between the two props, and if it was going one way they would increase the rpm, if it was going the other way they would decrease. Simple, yet it took a little time to get rid of the beating and get the props tuned to a drone. About the busiest guy on the crew was the navigator, since he was the one who was supposed to make sure that the plane was headed in the right direction. It seemed that someone was always hitting the intercom to ask if everything was ok, and that they were on time.

The rest of the men on the plane had little to do, so they passed the hours by trying to sleep, read, or talk with somebody else about home, how the war was going, or what combat might be like. After a few hours of listening to the drone of the engines everyone could hardly wait to get back on the ground again.

Unless someone on the crew had taken the time to stock the food larder with some of the fresh fruit and goodies at Natal, the only thing to eat on the plane was good old Army rations. These K-Rations came in three flavors (breakfast, lunch, dinner), but they all tasted about the same. The best things inside were the ever present smokes and chewing gum. Almost anyone who ever opened one of these made sure that the toilet paper issue was safely secured for future use. Robert Holcomb, copilot on BIG FAT MAMA, recalled:

The entry in my Form 5 for March 3, 1944, showed 12:30 hours total flying time, 9 hours of nighttime. That was our flight from Brazil to Dakar on a heading of 64 degrees. Our navigator, Waclaw Chilmonczyk, told us that if we changed the heading one degree he

STRICKLY FROM HUNGER about to leave Africa for sunny Italy.

would quit and we were on our own. He was a very dedicated navigator, spent many extra hours plotting our course to Dakar. As it turned out, after a bout with St. Elmo's fire he split the city of Dakar right down the middle—good old Chilmonczyk.

Several of the planes had "extra" crew members in the form of small monkeys that the crews had picked up in Brazil. One became the mascot of the photo section, while another would make the Atlantic crossing on BIG FAT MAMA with Bob Wingfield's crew.

When the planes reached the coast of Africa they followed the shoreline until they reached Dakar. Here there was a brief layover to refuel and stretch their legs before flying on to Marrakech, where there was another brief layover. Their final destination on the African Continent was Oudna, Tunisia. The first B-24 from the 464th landed there on March 9, 1944. Somewhere towards the front of the bomber stream across the Atlantic was 42-78092, flown by the crew of Capt. Erwin Elrod. Aboard this ship was Col. Bonner, who appeared to be in a hurry to get across and get the unit whipped into shape.

Robert Holcomb recalled that as BIG FAT MAMA flew towards Oudna they had to climb to high altitude to get over the mountains. They were up there a little longer than their little lice ridden pet monkey could stand, tucked away in the ball turret. When the crew realized what had happened they were of course very sad over the incident. The little traveler from Brazil was removed from the turret and buried at sea.

While the 464th was at Oudna they began a series of training missions to get the crews acquainted with combat tactics in the 15th Air Force. These missions were designed to sharpen navigational skills and hone the crews to a razor edge. For several of the crews it was actually the final portion of their Phase 3 training that they had missed back in the states, due to the frantic pace to get the 464th ready and on its way overseas.

Oudna was a place right out of Grimm's Fairy Tales. It was hot in the summer and cold and wet in the winter season. The 464th happened to arrive during the wet and cold season. The skies opened up and the rain fell, believe it or not in this desert place. The field became a sea of mud, and moving around from tent to tent was an exercise in futility. Many a shoe was lost in the mud as the hapless victim tried to make it to the latrine.

Le Roy Marsh (Capt., 779th Engineering Officer) had made the trip across the Atlantic as part of the air echelon. He recalled:

I had a mental picture of Africa as sun, heat, jungles, and some scattered desert—what I found was cold, wet, and lots of mud—adobe type mud. As you walked, the mud would stick to your shoes until it was 3-4 inches thick, then it would break off, and if you were lucky, you stayed upright. We lived in tents, and the Mess Hall was also a tent. It was used for cooking only and had a tarp extending over the serving area on one side. Food was served by Italian POWs. It was very democratic, only one single line in the rain for all ranks, first come first served, then carry it back to your tent to eat.

In addition to the POWs on the mess detail we had French Senegalese Army troops as guards for the aircraft. The Arabs could not be trusted, since they would steal anything they could get their hands on and were on the side of the Germans in sympathy and actions. There were no lights on the field at night, and if you had to go out to a plane after dark it was a scary trip. The sentries made no sound, and with their dark gray uniforms as well as coal-black skin they were virtually invisible. Your first indication that they were near was a soft "Halt," and you were looking at a long French bayo-

OLD GRANDAD leaving Africa—destination, Gioia del Colle, Italy.

net on the end of a rifle. They spoke no English, but after you were satisfactorily identified they disappeared again.

Shortly after his arrival at Oudna, Col. Bonner called for a formal inspection in Class A uniform. This seemed sort of odd, since all of the good uniforms were packed in the bottom of the crews' flight bags. Nevertheless, the Col. was not to be denied the inspection. The men rummaged through their bags and dug out their "pinks" to satisfy the head honcho. To say the least, it was a rather sloppy bunch of men who stood in front of the Colonel. Their uniforms were full of wrinkles and perhaps caked with a little mud for good measure. It was the last formal inspection the Colonel would call for in Africa.

On 27 March a 464th B-24 MONIN LISA (42-52492) crashed on takeoff at Oudna during a training flight. There were three fatalities and six injured in the mishap. On top of this one of the special GI built stoves blew up in the tent area, causing serious burns to several of the occupants of the tent.

The flight crews of the 464th observed Easter Sunday 1944 at Oudna. Lt. Charles Gibbs, Jr., wrote of the experience in a letter home:

I have spent 27 Easters so far in my life, and with few exceptions I have attended church services. But never before have I spent so memorable or more saddening an Easter, and witnessed a more impressive Easter service than the one I attended this morning.

I awakened this morning to a cold, rainy day—one as glum and depressing as any mortal can imagine. Every aspect was bleak and drab. We were scheduled for another formation flight, but it was canceled due to weather.

After breakfast I came into my tent, cleaned the mud from my shoes as well as possible, bathed in my little tin can, put on clean clothing and a fresh uniform, and with Rector started to church—the field tent which houses our mess kitchens. It was raining in torrents, and the mud was nearly ankle deep.

Our chapel tent, small and inadequate at best, was rapidly filling to capacity, and still the fellows kept coming. We rolled up the tent flaps so those outside could hear and then settled ourselves to wait for the Chaplain. His jeep got stuck in the mud and he was 45 minutes late. But not a whimper, not a complaint came from those cold, rain soaked men. They stood there in the rain and mud, cheerfully talking, patiently waiting for their "rations" of the word of God.

Finally the Chaplain arrived, and willing hands assisted him in carrying his equipment into the tent, as well as helping him set up his tiny portable altar and portable organ.

A hush settled over that crowd of men so that not a sound was heard, save the drumming of the rain on the tent top. Every face was alight and intent, waiting for the opening words. The Chaplain gazed over the motley assembly—officers and men side by side; many dirty and greasy from all night work, others sleepy and hungry from an all night guard job, and all of them cold, wet and muddy. He gazed at them for a moment, then in a kindly, benevolent voice called for prayer.

Instantly every head piece came off, and every head was bowed low. You could actually feel that prayer; feel it in the heavy breathing of the men next to you, feel it in that deep, all enveloping silence that was our tribute to Him who died and lived again to con-

The crew of STRICKLY FROM HUNGER waiting for transportation to their quarters at Gioia.

quer death for us. I was so impressed that I wept openly and unashamedly. Nor was mine the only moist eye there. Many were the furtive, self conscious attempts to dry eyes and clear throats.

And then they sang! "Christ Arose" was the song, and they sang like men inspired; sang with their clear deep masculine voices with a fervor and gusto that would shame any great choir. It was beautiful. Nor would they be stopped. Three songs they sang before they could be controlled.

At last the Chaplain began to preach. His text was from St. Luke 24:13-36, and his message was on "The Evening of the Resurrection Day." It was a simple, stirring sermon, and those men standing there in that downpour strained forward to catch his every word, avidly drinking in those words as a dying man might gasp for water. Not a sound, not a movement disturbed the flow of the Chaplain's voice as he preached. It was the most completely responsive, attentive congregation I have ever seen.

Finally the sermon ended, and Rock of Ages was sung—and I do mean sung—and the Lord's Prayer was intoned. Every man there joined in on the reciting of that grand old prayer, joined in with voices full and strong. It was not a recitation or incantation, it was a solemn, individual prayer from the heart of every man present.

At last the Benediction, and the service was over. The men broke up, scattered into groups, and began walking back to their tents to change into dry clothing and get warm. But not once did I hear a word of complaint or grumbling about the rain or the cold. It was truly a fighting man's response and indication of worship to his Lord, a response, I am convinced, of fighting men the world over. I was proud of them, and proud to be one of them.

On April 12, 1944, the 464th was up in the air for another training flight. For unknown reasons WISE WABBITT (42-78094) suddenly went out of control and spun into the water off the coast of Africa near Oudna, and the entire crew was lost in the accident. The 464th was getting off to a very bad start. They had not flown a combat mission and had already lost four aircraft in the trip from the United States. Some of the men were starting to get the notion that the 464th was a "hard luck" outfit.

On 20 April the B-24s of the 464th started engines and taxied out onto the runway at Oudna, and one by one they took to the air, heading for Italy. After their flight across the water they landed at a base called Gioia del Colle that afternoon. The group landed here due to the fact that their permanent base at Pantanella was not ready to take on the full weight of the air echelon. For the time being the

STRICKLY FROM HUNGER at Gioia del Colle.

group would fly out of Gioia, which meant that some of the ground echelon was moved down to Gioia in order to service the planes and get the group settled into Italy.

M.E. "Steve" Stephensen recalled the arrival of the Liberators at Gioia del Colle.:

They came in one at a time for the next few days. We sat on the edge of the runway waiting for our ship to arrive. When our plane arrived there was hand shaking all around. We were short of water, and I asked if I could have a drink and was promptly handed a canteen. I took a large swallow and started to replace the cap. I darned near strangled, as it was filled with rum. They had stopped somewhere on the trip where rum was cheap. It would be noon before I could get any water to get rid of the taste.

Col. Bonner stayed with the group at Gioia while some of the HQ staff moved back and forth on a daily basis from Gioia to Pantanella. It was a busy time for the men, as they tried to get the home field ready for the group and also get ready to enter the combat arena.

It was the policy of the 15th Air Force to have a new group fly what was called a "freshman" mission for its first combat mission. These freshman missions were against targets that were considered "easy." The whole idea was to get the new group into combat with the least amount of problems. In view of the problems the 464th had in getting to Italy, it seemed like a good idea to get the new boys on the block into combat with a "milk run."

On the morning of April 30, 1944, the 464th left Gioia and flew towards a place called Castel Maggiore in the northern part of Italy. Unlike all the practice missions they had flown in the past this one was for real. They carried live 500 lb bombs and live ammo in the guns. Their assigned task that morning was to hit the marshalling yards and derail the trains that passed through the Italian town. As with almost every new group that arrived in Italy the mission was a complete foul up. Charles Skinner recalled the first mission:

The group formed up perfectly and impressed the Wing Commander with great formation flying. We were to follow the 460th Bomb Group, I believe, but failed to make the right landfall. I was flying with a crew that I had never seen before. Needless to say, I was scared to death since it was my first mission and I did not know the crew. However, the navigator realized that we were going by our landfall immediately. When we finally made landfall, that's when the problems started. The group leaders did not know where to go and we began circling. The air speed was too low and the planes on the inside of the circles began to stall out. Because of the altitude the pilots were able to pull the planes out of the stall before crashing. When this happened to our plane, the pilot immediately asked the navigator for a heading for home. Right then and there I knew I was in good hands as far as the pilot was concerned.

After about 30 minutes into our flight home the pilot asked the tail gunner if he could see any other planes around. The tail gunner responded, "Yes Sir, the whole group has formed up right behind us and is following us back to base." The pilot made his decision to pull out and return to base because he did not see any reason to risk the lives of the crew after the mission had already been botched.

Nothing went right, and many of the planes never got over the target. Many of the planes never even dropped a bomb on the target. In the language of the times the mission was FUBAR. On top of everything that went wrong, the group wasn't given credit for the mission.

The 464th had finally made its way across the Atlantic and had taken up double residence in Italy. They had lost four planes during the trip, and after all of that they had made one trip against the Huns and had not even gotten credit for doing it. Many of the men believed that the group's luck had to change in the near future. Little did they know that the near future was closer than they thought, and their luck would change, from bad to worse.

3

Into the Fight

May 1944

On May 2, 1944, the 464th was briefed for their second combat mission. Again it was classified as a "freshman" mission with an easy target. They had been assigned to bomb the marshaling yards at Parma, Italy. Intelligence reports said that there were only a few flak guns in the area and that fighter attacks could be expected. Weather in the target area was supposed to be good, although there was a possible front moving that way later on in the afternoon. In all, it looked like the group would have a chance to prove that they could do the job that they had trained for.

The Liberators took off and assembled according to the battle plan. There seemed to be some trouble getting to altitude, but the mission was going along as planned.

As the planes arrived near the IP they began to turn towards the bomb run heading. Off in the distance there loomed the weather front that was not supposed to be there until later that day. As they droned onward several bursts of flak were seen in the area.

Capt. William Shoemaker was flying the lead position in SHOO SHOO BABY with Col. Bonner in the right seat as mission commander. At the sight of the flak, Col. Bonner took over the controls and started to turn to right. In the #2 position Lt. Sampson, flying SOUTHERN GAL, turned with the lead aircraft. What happened next is best told by Robert Wingfield, who was flying BIG FAT MAMA:

"At 22,000 feet on the bomb run while following the 465th Bomb Group, Col. Bonner, as I later found out, panicked at the sight of "flak," jerked the controls away from Shoemaker, and turned sharply to the right, almost running into me. At that instant I determined that Shoemaker was abandoning the lead and I moved to assume the lead position in order to proceed to the target. However Lt. Sampson, flying on the left of Shoemaker, followed him into the turn, and his right rudder slammed into the nose of my airplane. The collision flipped us over on our back, and we proceeded straight down to about 5,000 feet before I was able to recover and get the airplane flying straight and level again.

While most of the 464th was getting ready to fly, work was being done on their permanent home at Pantanella.

Postcard from Gioia del Colle, main town square. Card is from the time period of Mussolinni, as noted by the Italian planes flying over.

On the way down I rang the alarm bell for the crew to bail out, because at the time I did not know the total extent of the damage. I also looked at Lt/Col. Sylvan Hand (Deputy Group Commander) and motioned for him to get out, which he did. While trying to control the airplane I was looking for my chest pack, all at the same time. It had been placed just in back of my seat in case I should ever need it, but it had apparently fallen out of the airplane through the open bomb bay doors. I must say that I do not know if I would have stayed with the airplane if I had found my chute. The bombardier and navigator went out the nose wheel door. The bombardier and Lt/Col. Hand were captured by the Germans. The navigator and top turret gunner were not captured, but remained behind enemy lines until the Germans retreated through Northern Italy.

The remaining crewmembers came to the cockpit after we had leveled out. Bordak, the nose gunner, was in the damaged turret all the way down. It was cold, and with all the glass knocked out he had a cool and exciting ride.

Nose gunner Sgt. Mike Bordak (Borodajkiewicz) recalled for STAR AND STRIPES:

I am in the nose turret, all eyes and trigger fingers, when something slams into the left side of the turret. Something bigger than the whole world is spiked to my nose guns and slamming my left side where the glass is gone. It's the tail section of another B-24. The bail out bell is ringing, and I'm trying to get out of the turret to my chute pack, which is on the floor in the bombardier's compartment. I turn and there's the bombardier out by the nose wheel. Out he went, then the navigator."

Bordak finally managed to get out of the turret and made his way to the flight deck.

Capt. Wingfield determined that BIG FAT MAMA was flyable and turned towards the coast. When they arrived over the water they dropped the bombload into the water. Since they were at low altitude the blast from the bombs was enough to get their attention. Wingfield brought BIG FAT MAMA over the Island of Corsica, hoping that it was in Allied hands. He knew they would not make it back to Gioia.

After what seemed like an eternity, BIG FAT MAMA managed to land at a fighter base on Corsica with the rudder from Lt. Sampson's B-24 still impaled on the nose of BIG FAT MAMA. The landing was considered quite a feat of airmanship, since there was extra weight on the nose from the 9' x 12' rudder and the pitot tubes had been knocked out, which meant that there was no airspeed indicator to judge the landing speed.

Bob Wingfield remembers:

The rudder obstructed my view.... The collision had damaged the nose wheel, and we were having great difficulty getting it down. We circled the field with only the main gear down and the rudder still on our nose. We had forgotten to transfer fuel, and #1 and #2 engines stopped for lack of fuel. Fuel was transferred, and we were able to recover power on the left side and landed without further difficulty.

It just so happened that as FIG FAT MAMA was landing there was an Air Force film crew filming the action of the fighters at the base. They got the whole landing on film. When the crew emerged from the B-24 they had a quick look at the nose of BIG FAT MAMA. Then the rudder was taken off and placed into a truck.

The following morning the crew inspected their damaged B-24 and flew it back to Gioia, where they learned that they had been listed as missing from the mission. 2nd.Lt Robert Holcomb, the regular copilot on BIG FAT MAMA, recalled that he was the only occupant of the tent that night and figured that he had just inherited the remains of the booze that they had brought overseas with them.

While the crew of BIG FAT MAMA had been lucky to escape from the Germans or get back from the mission, luck was not with the crew of SOUTHERN GAL. Only the navigator, Lt. John Henderson, and T/Sgt. Robert Harvey were able to bail out in time. The rest of the crew perished in the crash.

While all of this was taking place, the rest of the 464th was trying to bomb a target—any target—in the area. The formation

A side street in Gioia del Colle, May 1944.

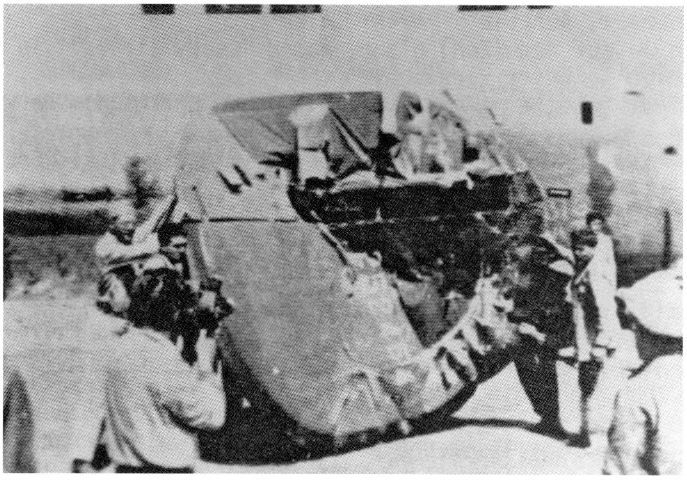

SOUTHERN GAL's right rudder being removed from BIG FAT MAMA after the mid-air collision. May 2, 1944.

Robert Wingfield points to the rudder and tells how lucky they were to get back on the ground.

had literally fallen apart after the accident. Small groups of B-24s found targets of opportunity and dropped their bombs.

Charles Skinner wrote:

I was flying with Maj. Blehm, and we were leading part of the formation. After the collision of the two planes, Blehm successfully escaped all of the confusion by diving towards the harbor. As we came out of the clouds, Blehm said, "Bombardier, we will bomb the harbor, air speed 160, and we will level out at 18,000 feet."

I knew I had very little time to do the things that I had to do. I flipped switches on my way down to the bombsight. I picked up my little computer to reconfigure the bombsight data as I looked for the target. To my amazement we were dead on course and almost right over the target. All I could do was toggle out the bombs and hope for the best. Some distance behind us were the planes we had been leading. They had seen me open the bomb bay doors and they did likewise, dropping their bombs when I dropped mine.

The rudder scarred nose of BIG FAT MAMA after she returned to Gioia on May 3, 1944.

Left: Nose gunner Mike Bordak explains what it was like in the nose turret of BIG FAT MAMA.

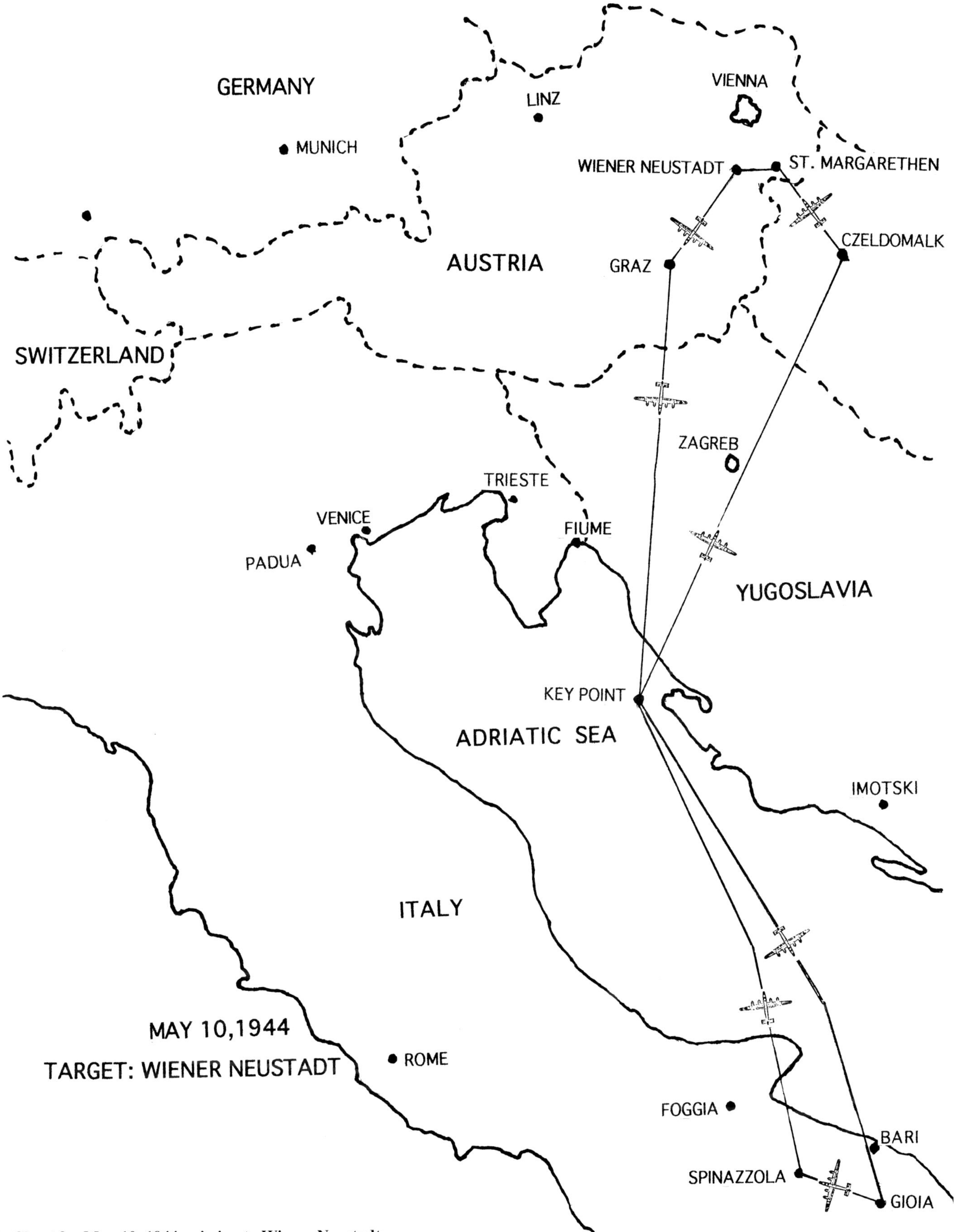

Route Chart for May 10, 1944, mission to Wiener Neustadt.

THE GREEN HORNET returned with over 600 holes in her hide from the mission on May 10, 1944. T/Sgt. Jaskalski peers from the right waist of the plane after repairs were made.

To say the least, the entire mission had been fouled up from the start. The score after two missions was nine killed, two POWs, two missing in action, and a bent up nose on BIG FAT MAMA.

Bob Wingfield recalled that after they got back to Gioia and he found out what had happened in the cockpit of SHOO SHOO BABY he marched up to Col. Bonner's tent and proceeded to have a "very private talk" with Col. Bonner. Wingfield also vowed never to fly with the Col. again. Many of the pilots felt the same way. There was even talk of maybe trying to shoot his aircraft down on the next mission, but that was thrown out because they would be hurting anyone else on the plane, and that would never accomplish a thing. Col. Bonner was summoned to 15th Air Force Headquarters for an investigation, but nothing ever came of it. For the present the 464th would have to suffer under the ineffective leadership that had already cost the group dearly.

When LtCol. Hand bailed out of BIG FAT MAMA it created another leadership hole in the group. Lt/Col. Charles F. McKenna III was relieved of his duties in the 465th Bomb Group and assumed the Deputy Group Commander's position for the 464th.

All of the danger was not in the formations on a combat mission. When the planes returned from the mission on the 2nd, John Graham was busy working on his PISTOL PAKIN MAMA. He recalled:

On May 2, I was shot in the hand while working on plane equipment. The bullet came from the belly turret of the ship on the hard stand next to mine. The gunner had forgotten to clear his guns in flight and accidentally discharged a burst when disarming the weapon. I was fortunate to only get one bullet and not in a vulnerable spot. After some time in the Army Hospital at Bari I was sent to the replacement depot and returned to the 464th Bomb Group, 776th Bomb Squadron at Pantanella Hill. It was a joy to return to my old outfit. I could still perform my job, even though I was missing two fingers on my left hand.

The group stood down on 4 May while the investigation at 15th Air Force was underway. On 5 May the 464th flew a mission to Podgorcia, Yugoslavia. The mission took off at 1030 hrs and was considered a "milk run." No flak or enemy fighters were reported on the mission, and all of the group's aircraft returned to Gioia.

The 464th had flown several missions and lost planes and crews doing it. Most of the missions were considered easy up to this point. They may have been considered easy, but the group was already taking it in the teeth. At the morning briefings the group Chaplain, John Eastwood, was always ready to give comfort to those that wanted it. He recalled:

Officers from Wing Headquarters paid a visit to our briefing one morning and heard me pray for our men, and advised that this time of prayer should be discontinued. I was informed of the matter and accepted the decision with great regret, but the men for whom I was praying made such a strong protest the decision was reversed. I think there were one or two mornings our men were sent off on a mission when prayer was not offered to God for their safety.

OFF LIMITS after her accident on 22 May.

Another view of OFF LIMITS. She was declared Class 26.

OUR PRAYER

Lord guard and guide the men who fly,
Through the great spaces of the sky;

Be with them as they take to the air;
In morning light and sunshine fair.

Eternal Father, strong to save,
Give them courage and make them brave;

Protect them whereso'er they go,
From shell and flak and fire and foe

Most loved Member of their crew,
Ride with them up in the blue.

Direct their bombs upon the foe,
But shelter those whom Thou dost know.

Keep them together upon their way,
Grant their work success today.

Deliver them from hate and sin,
And bring them back safely down again.

O God bless the men who fly,
Through lonely ways across the sky.

The group flew another mission on Saturday, 6 May. The target this time was Craiova, Romania, to bomb the marshalling yards. After refusing to fly with Col. Bonner, Capt. Wingfield was surprised to see that he was scheduled to fly the mission with the Colonel. Wingfield protested but lost the argument. Wingfield recalled:

The mission to Craiova was uneventful, except for a leak in the induction system of the #2 engine, which reduced manifold pressure to about 12 inches. In order to maintain group lead it was necessary to apply additional power to the remaining three engines. Because of the increased fuel flow I had to lean the mixtures so as to conserve fuel for the trip back to base.

Scattered bursts of flak near Valmontone, Italy, May 22, 1944.

The 464th rallies for home after dropping their bombs, May 22, 1944.

The marshaling yards at Givors, France, after a visit from the 464th on May 25, 1944.

Damage to the railyards at Givors,France was extensive.

The cylinder head temperatures soon became the topic of conversation between Col. Bonner and myself. He insisted that we return the mixture control to "auto rich," and I refused. As time went on Col. Bonner continued to protest the "lean" mixtures with me still refusing to comply. Shortly thereafter Col. Bonner moved the mixture controls to "auto rich" himself, and it was at this point that I physically knocked his hands off the controls pedestal.

That move by Wingfield apparently taught Col. Bonner that when sitting in the right hand seat of Wingfield's plane you had better keep your hands to yourself unless asked to help out. For the rest of the mission there was silence from Col. Bonner.

It is noted that there was some flak, and several German fighters were spotted by the formation. In spite of this the mission was classified as a "milk run." Several of the planes did return to Gioia with extra holes in them, but nothing of a serious nature.

On Sunday, 7 May the 464th was headed back to Romania, this time to hit the railroad repair shops at Bucharest. Take off proceeded according to the battle plan. During form up something went wrong inside of RAT RACE (42-78128). The aircraft went into a cloud bank, and the next thing anyone knew the pilot had lost control. RAT RACE crashed about 25 miles east of Gioia del Colle, taking the entire crew of Lt.Charles Gibbs with her. The formation proceeded without the fallen Liberator. The mission was recalled before reaching the target, so the group flew all that way, lost a plane, and did not get credit for another mission.

Due to bad weather over the prime targets the 464th stood down from flying missions on 8 May and again on the 9th.

On 10 May the 464th was briefed for a trip to Wiener-Neustadt to finish the job they had tried to start the day before. The mission was led by Maj. Clarence Poff, Commander of the 778th Squadron. The 464th would be leading the entire 55th Bomb Wing on this mission. Capt. Robert Hornbaker would be flying Deputy Lead in STRICKLY FROM HUNGER. Due to a mechanical problem, Capt. Hornbaker and his crew had to change planes at the last minute and fly a different B-24. Take off and the flight towards the target were uneventful.

Shortly after turning at the IP and beginning the bomb run, the German flak batteries opened up and started hurling shell after shell at the approaching Liberators. Since they were on the bomb run there could be no evasive action. The group had to fly straight and level and take what the Germans had to dish out for the next twenty minutes.

What the Germans were dishing out was perhaps the most dreaded defense that American crews had to face, FLAK. In order to understand why it was so terrible one has to consider just what it was. Flak is short for FLieger Abwehr Kanone. Most of the heavy guns used by the Germans were 88 mm. They did use other types of larger caliber, but the 88 was the most common. This weapon could hurl a projectile with a 10 kg explosive warhead to altitudes of over 40,000 feet at a speed of almost 2,900 feet/second. When the shell exploded it would hurl over 1,500 fragments into an area about 600 feet in radius. To increase the chances of knocking down a bomber the guns were usually placed in groups of four. When all four fired

Another view of damage to the Givor, France, railyards, May 25, 1944.

Black-Z from the 779th was lost to fighter attacks on May 29, 1944.

a salvo they could blast a sphere of shrapnel almost a quarter of a mile in diameter. At this juncture of the war there was little that the bomber crews could do to defend against flak. All they could do was fly through it and hope that the next shell didn't have their number on it.

It did not take long for the deadly black puffs to find the range of the oncoming 464th. The intercoms were full of calls of "Flak at ten o'clock, Flak at one o'clock, hell it's all over the place. Yea! Walkin stuff! Can the chatter you guys. Keep an eye out for fighters. What fighters, they aren't going to fly into this mess!"

Capt. Hornbaker's B-24 was in the Deputy Lead position, and that was the wrong place to be at the moment. A large chunk of burning hot flak came through the side of the plane and hit waist gunner Cyril Bolash above the eye. The impact knocked him back

A landing gear from Black-Z.

One of the engines that powered Black-Z

against the other gunner, Dick Viereck. Sgt. Bolash was dead before he hit the floor of the airplane. The tail turret had also been hit, knocking the motor to drive the turret out. The gunner, (Sgt) Graham Stafford, managed to get a leg out of the turret, and with leg power kept turning the turret from side to side, even though the guns were useless. The top turret had been punctured and the guns were knocked out of commission. At almost the same time the nose turret was put out of action by another hit. Only the ball turret was still capable of defending the aircraft.

Seconds later another burst wounded the copilot, Stillman Harding, Jr. (Lt). He recalled:

Draney, the radio operator, was standing right behind me when I got hit. It must have been a little unnerving to him as I turned around in the seat, held up my thumbless left hand, and motioned for him to give me a shot of morphine in the exposed area. Then he put a compress on it to stop the bleeding. He performed very well. He tried to help me out of the seat, but I didn't have the strength to help myself so I had him hook me back up to oxygen so I could help with the plane until bombs away.

The flak damage to the plane was evident by now to all the crew. The number four engine started to smoke, and fire was eminent. In spite of his wounds the copilot cut the throttles to the smoking engine. Next, number two engine started to run away. Again, Harding pulled the power off of that engine while Hornbaker was busy trying to keep the B-24 with the formation.

It was not until after they had dropped the bombs that the true nature of Harding's injuries became apparent. He recalled:

Dick Nilles (Lt.), the navigator, looked up from his charts and saw blood running out of my seat. He turned and poked Carl Gien (Lt), the bombardier, who crawled up to the flight deck. I did not know how badly I had been hit in the left leg. I knew of one hit, but I could not understand why I was so weak. The bad one was caused by a chunk of flak coming right through the top of the cabin in front of my face and into my left thigh, taking a plate and about an eight inch square of the flak suit right into the bone high up on my left thigh.

With one dead, the copilot wounded, two engines out, and a sieve for an airplane, Hornbaker had to leave the formation. It would take some fancy flying and a miracle for them to get back to base.

As the group turned away from the target and headed south for home, flak scored a direct hit on the left wing of CHERRY (42-64441), flown by Lt. Lawrence Wygal's crew. Fragments of flak had also hit the cockpit, killing Wygal. The left wing became a blowtorch as the plane fell from the formation. Several of the crew bailed out. Sgt. Donald Penrod's parachute was observed to be on fire as he left the plane. He was later found in a field. A few seconds later CHERRY erased herself in a ball of fire and debris.

Flak also found Capt. James Latimer's RED HOT RIDING HOOD (42-52468). It went out of control after several of the crew bailed out. Capt. Latimer rode the stricken Liberator all the way in. Those that had bailed out were taken prisoner by the Germans shortly after getting to the ground. Robert Garlock, in LITTLE GISMO, recalled:

We got shot up real bad. Over 250 holes in the plane. Nose turret just about shot off. #3 engine shot out and caught fire. Windshield shot out, and the flak tore my gloves and flight jacket, but I didn't get a scratch. Up to this time I thought war was fun, but after this I almost threw up every time I got in the plane.

Flak had turned THE GREEN HORNET into a series of holes that still resembled a B-24. The #4 engine was shot out, control cables cut, large holes in the underside, and the right wing was just jagged aluminum held together by thin stips of more jagged aluminum. Capt. John Fernsler and his crew were in a lot of trouble. For a few moments it looked like the better part of valor was to bail out. The problem was that John Jaskulski (Sgt) did not have a parachute, as it had been ripped to shreds by flak. On top of everything the control cables had been shot away, causing the plane to buck around like a rodeo stallion. Then, the final burst of flak exploded the signal flares in the waist. Until the crew was able to put them out, THE GREEN HORNET looked like a 4th of July fireworks display. The crew was able to splice enough control cables together for the plane to continue to fly.

When the formation returned to Gioia everyone on the ground watched as plane after plane fired flares to indicate wounded or battle damage. Everyone knew that this had been a rough mission in terms of wounded, flak damaged B-24s, and losses. As the crews climbed out of their planes a sense of numbness fell over many of them. They all believed, in a sense, that they had just returned from the jaws of hell.

For the crew of THE GREEN HORNET it was good to be back on mother earth. They had cheated the grim reaper on this mission and they knew it. They all took a few moments to try and count the holes in the HORNET's hide. They gave up after about 650, although there were still many more. The powers that be were going to scrap the HORNET since she had taken so much damage, but the crew fought to save their ship. After a lot of coaxing and

After having the rudder shot off, Lt. John Jones and crew managed to bail out of Black-Z

pleading, they did in fact save the damaged Liberator. The mechanics covered a lot of holes and managed to graft a new wing to the wounded HORNET. She would fly again, but she would never be the same as she had been.

Capt. Hornbaker had made it through with his badly damaged aircraft. They had been shadowed by several German fighters, but they peeled off without firing a shot. The limping Liberator managed to thread its way through the mountains and land at Foggia so that the wounded copilot would get fast medical attention.

At interrogation all of the men agreed this had been the worst mission the group had flown to date. Three planes had been lost, and one (Hornbaker's) was listed as missing. There were wounded men needing treatment. Almost no one who had flown that day refused the combat ration of whiskey to tone down the nerves. Out at the hardstands the ground crews could only shake their heads in disbelief at the number of holes and battle damage that they would have to repair before the 464th could take to the air again.

The 464th stood down on 11 May in order to repair the flak damaged planes and collect their nerve after the horrible mission they had just flown. The crew chiefs put the time to good use out on the revetments. There were a lot of holes to patch in the skins of the 464th planes. There were also a lot of routine things to accomplish in order for the planes to be ready for the next mission. As always, it seemed that the work of the ground crews was never done, even if the group was not flying that day.

The stand down gave the ground crews a chance to make their B-24s unique to the 464th Bomb Group. Each wing in the 15th Air Force had adopted special markings to be applied to the tails of the planes. These markings were supposed to make it easier to find the group during form up. The 55th Wing had adopted yellow and black as its colors. The top half of the tail was painted yellow, while the lower half was painted black. A black square was then painted on the upper half within the yellow. Each group in the wing was assigned a geometric symbol to designate the group. The 464th would have a vertical yellow rectangle centered on the lower tail. To identify each aircraft, they were assigned letters of the alphabet in the Squadron color. The 776th was red, 777th yellow, 778th white, and the 779th was black. Thus, a B-24 with a large red I on the rear fuselage could be identified as Red-I (Item) and was from the 776th.

Black-Z crash site near Loipersbach, Austria.

Now, it took a lot of paint to cover the nine foot by twelve foot twin tail of a B-24. It not only took a lot of paint, but it took time to haul out the paint, get a compressor and gun, and then paint the tail. With the time element in mind, it took more than one day to get all of the tails painted.

The group flew back to back missions on the 12th, 13th, and 14th. These missions were to marshaling yards in Northern Italy in an attempt to cut the railroad supply routes that the Germans were using to get men and supplies into the Italian campaign. All of these missions were considered "milk runs."

On the 17th the group flew to Piombino, Italy. to hit the railways again. Each B-24 carried 8 500 pound bombs. Even though it was a mission to Northern Italy, it still ended up taking over six hours to get to the target and back to Gioia. Some of the crews joked that in view of the time element the group callsign "Longnose" was appropriate.

The group flew missions again on 18 and 19 May. The mission on the 18th was to Concordia Vega Oil refinery at Ploesti. This was a dreaded target for everyone in the 15th Air Force. As always, there was concentrated flak and numerous fighters to defend the oil target. The 464th encountered lots of flak, and a few fighters made passes at the group. Gunners were busy for what seemed an enternity as they fought to drive off the attackers. The planes returned to Gioia with flak damage and feathered props, but at least they returned.

On Monday, 22 May the group was briefed for a mission to Valmontone, Italy, to bomb the railway yards and troop concentrations. It seemed like it should be another "milk run." The crews were briefed, and everything was proceeding according to plan.

As the planes began their takeoff rolls everyone watched each airplane struggle to get into the air with their full bombload and fuel onboard. As OFF LIMITS (42-78115) lifted off the men on the ground noticed that the wheels had begun to retract. Several commented that it was way too early to call for the wheels to come up. Due to a combination of prop wash and its heavy load, OFF LIMITS could not stay in the air and settled back onto the runway with a resounding scream of crunching metal as the props dug into the steel mat. OFF LIMITS slid down the runway, shedding parts, props, and sparks. Everyone was waiting for the inevitable explosion and deadly fireball. To the amazement of everyone the B-24 came to a stop in a cloud of dust. Her back was broken and there was debris all over the place. Fire trucks headed towards the crumpled plane to fight the fire when it came. The crew emerged shaken and battered, and several had injuries. For some unknown reason the plane never blew up like it should have. The 464th had escaped a major takeoff crash with no one killed. The mission for the day was delayed for about an hour.

The 464th flew again on 23 and 24 May. The mission on the 23rd was to Valmontone, Italy, to bottle up troop supplies. Their callsign was again appropriate, "Yardbird." The mission on the 24th was to Wiener-Neustadt, Austria, to bomb the Machine Shops and Airdrome. As with any of the missions to Austria, several of the planes came back well ventilated from flak.

On the morning of 25 May the combat crews of the 464th were awakened very early. They had the usual breakfast of fried Spam and powdered eggs. When they went to the briefing they expected the mission to be a long one; rumor in the Army Air Force always preceeded the mission. The red line of the route string stretched over towards France. The mission called for the 464th to follow the 465th on a mission to hit the marshaling yards at Givors, France. This would indeed be a long mission, almost 950 miles. The callsign for the group was "Longstick." Again, in view of the distance to the target the callsign was appropriate.

Take off and form up went without a hitch, then the armada turned and headed towards the target. The flight towards France was marred only by several of the B-24s aborting due to mechanical problems, however, the gaps in the formation were filled with spare ships. By 1145 hours the formation was close to bombing altitude of 21,000 feet, axis of attack 263 degrees, and so far so good.

At about 1300 hours the 464th had completed their bomb run, and the lethal load of 500 pound bombs was headed towards the target. There had been a little flak in the area, but so far there was not much damage to the group. A few Me-109s were prowling the outer limits of the formation, but they seemed more interested in looking for stragglers than coming in for the attack.

The 464th rallied left according to plan and headed down the Rhone valley. This route would take them just north of Marseilles, France. It was here that the Me-109s were waiting for the formation. Their attack was sudden and devastating, diving through the formation and reforming for another attack. The gunners on the B-24s were ready, and they threw out a curtain of half inch lead and tracers at the attacking fighters. Several bombers were hit, but they continued on straight and level. The fighters came in again from the rear of the formation. Gunners aboard the B-24s were dishing out a steady staccato of gunfire, and two of the Me-109s were seen to fall away smoking. On the third attack two more Me-109s went down.

The formation was nearly over the French coastline near Cap Roux. They would soon be over the water and headed towards Corsica. The problem was that the coastline bristled with flak guns, and the formation was headed right for them. On top of this the Me-109s had been joined by FW-190s, and these fighters were pressing home the attack, even in this deadly area of their friendly flak.

In STRICKLY FOR HUNGER (42-29412), flown by Capt. Robert Hornbaker's crew, there had already been some minor hits from flak and fighters. They were still with the formation as it passed near the coast. Alfred Karow (Sgt.) was busy in his top turret helping to fight off the fighters. He recalled:

At that time four German fighters approached dangerously close to us. A Me-109 disappeared from view, only to reappear almost at once at our left. Its gun spat bullets, devastating the left side of our plane. The #1 engine caught fire and we began to lose altitude. At almost the same time we were hit by flak.

STRICKLY FROM HUNGER was in mortal danger. The flak hit had caused the #2 engine to become a blowtorch. The plane was now on fire from both engines on the left side. The gunfire from the fighter had devastated the cockpit. Capt. Hornbaker had been hit in the chest and head, killing him instantly. The copilot, (Lt) Ray Burkland, was trying to fly the airplane from what was left of the blood soaked cockpit. Al Karow had unbuckled his harness and left the top turret, moving towards the flightdeck. The bombardier, Lt. Gein, had come to the flightdeck and was trying to help the copilot. STRICKLY FROM HUNGER had now dropped below the formation and was out over the water. Al Karow recalled:

The fire bottles had been activated in the two burning engines, but only the fire in #2 had gone out. The #1 engine had been shut down and the prop feathered. The fire was out in #2, but the prop would not feather; it kept spinning and making a grinding sound while emitting a lot of black smoke. The other engine was still on fire.

At about the same time 41-29382, flown by Lt. William Trotter's crew, took a devestating blast in the nose, killing the nose gunner and bombardier. The stricken Liberator fell from the formation, and the fighters attacked like a school of hungry sharks. The #2 engine was on fire, and the other engine on the left side was spewing a vaporous cloud of 100 octane fuel. The fuel ignited, and the Liberator became a torch. Lt. Trotter was able to keep the plane under control long enough to bail out with three others. One of the chutes was observed to be on fire as it fell to earth. Only Trotter made it to the ground alive, but he was horribly burned and would die on 25 August from complications caused by his burns.

ANGEL IN DE SKYS (42-52463) from the 779th had also been hit by flak, but was still with the formation. Lt. Donald Garniss was in the left seat, and it did not seem that his ship had been hurt that badly. They were able to stay with the group until they were about 20 miles from the coast. Then, the B-24 was observed to rock her wings to signal they were leaving the formation. Shortly after leaving the formation two chutes were seen coming from the plane. That was the last observation that was made. The aircraft never returned to base, taking her entire crew with her to a watery grave.

As the formation continued towards Corsica, STRICKLY FROM HUNGER's luck was running out. At this point the crew lost control of the B-24, and it started to turn almost 180 degrees towards the coast. The men in the back thought the plane was going down and bailed out. Just as STRICKLY FROM HUNGER crossed the coast the rest of the crew hit the silk. Al Karow landed in the driveway of a house. He got out of his chute and began to run but was captured, along with the other two men who had bailed out of the front part of the plane. Al watched the plane crash near the top of the hill of Croix des Gardes on the outskirts of Cannes. Karow, Raymond Burklund, and Roland Barenbruch were the only survivors.

Another of the 464th B-24s that was in trouble from the flak and fighters was BIG ED (41-29394), flown by Lt. Stachowski's crew. Altough they were badly battered they were able to crash land on the island of Corsica. They would spend about a week on the island listed as missing due to the fact that no one at the fighter base where they landed remembered to notify the 464th that one of their missing airplanes had landed in friendly territory. In the words of one of the returning crewmen it was "A bitch of a mission."

After nine hours and forty-five minutes the badly mauled formation returned to their base at Gioia. The disaster over the coast had cost the 464th three airplanes. There were several wounded onboard the planes that returned and a lot of holes to patch. Marshall E. "Steve" Stephenson (Sgt.), crew chief of ANGEL IN DE SKYS, recalled the wait for his plane to come home from the mission:

Ray (Raymond Perlow) and I were on the line with field glasses waiting for the return of the plane and crew from the mission to Southern France. We could pick our individual planes by the nose art the most planes sported. Plane after plane landed, and we still had not spotted ours. After all the planes had landed, Ray and I headed to the debriefing tent. As each crew came out of the tent we tried to find out what happened to our airplane and crew. They had been seen leaving the coast of Southern France with an engine smoking. Another crew had seen them turn back to France. That was the last we heard of the crew and plane we had trained with in Pocatello, Idaho. Ray and I went to work helping other crews and watched the landing strip every time a plane landed.

The 464th was back in the air the next day. This was another long mission to France. This time they were going to bomb the marshaling yards at Lyons. Since it was a long mission the planes began taking to the air at 0530.

While the mission was over nine and a half hours long, the group managed to hit the target and get home without losing a plane. There were several that had been hit by flak and several came back with wounded aboard. After the fiasco of the previous day this one was a lot easier.

On 27 May the group headed for Nimes, France, to hit the marshaling yards. The mission got off to a rather strange start for the crew of BELZEBUB (41-29444). Nose gunner Glen Gunn remembers:

After we took off and were about ready to rendezvous with the formation, the Navigator noticed that my parachute was missing. Apparently it had fallen out of the nose gear opening on take off. The pilot, unwilling to let me fly the mission without a parachute, radioed the base and had a chute carried to the runway. We landed, the parachute was handed to me, and we took right off again to join the group.

Glenn had no way of knowing that a parachute had been found on the runway after the the planes had taken off. BELZEBUB was able to catch the formation, but had lost their assigned place in the squadron box.

As with all trips to the targets in France, the 464th was met again this day with intense, accurate flak as they neared the target. On the bomb run just before the group dropped the bombs, OLD GRANDAD/OLD GRANDAD'S DREAM (42-78092) took a direct hit from flak, and the hapless Liberator exploded in a blinding flash. There was no time for anyone to bail out; one moment they were there, the next they were gone. Lt. Rodes Parish and his crew had given everything they had to try and get to the target.

From his position in the nose turret of BELZEBUB, Glenn Gunn saw the entire thing. Since they had lost their assigned position they were directly behind the exploding B-24 and had to fly through the remains of the explosion. Flames and burning fuel had scorched the plexiglass on BELZEBUB, making it hard for the pilot, Lt. Lester Raphel, to see what was going on in the rest of the formation. Several pieces of debris had imbedded themselves in the dome of the nose turret.

Ernie Latham in the left seat of MISMYSAKTIME.

The group rallied according to plan and headed back for Italy. Aboard BELZEBUB there was deep concern over the return flight. Gunn recalled:

Because of the length of the mission and our use of extra fuel in obtaining my replacement parachute, we did not have enough fuel to make it back to Gioia. We therefore decided to land at a Medium Bomber base on Corsica and refuel before returning.

It seems improbable that we could miss the Island of Corsica, but miss it we did. We were flying over and between huge cumulus clouds and were forced to rely on instruments. Our best explanation is that our compass was off, having been hit by flak or debris from the exploding plane in front of us.

As fuel ran low they made it over Italy but were lost. The crew bailed out and became POWs. It was fortunate that they had returned to get a parachute for Gunn.

On the 28th the group stood down from flying a mission. The time was needed to repair the flak damaged planes that had returned from the mission the day before. On top of this, orders had come down from group Headquarters to prepare to move to the group's permanent base at Pantanella, which was almost ready to receive the entire group. The men at Gioia started packing for the move and trying to get ready for a mission that was supposed to be flown on the 29th. To say the least, Gioia del Colle looked like a beehive with all the activity.

On 29 May the crews were awakened very early, had their usual meal, and headed for the briefing tent. Today the group had been given the task of bombing the Amme-Luther-Seek Aircraft Component Factory at Atzgersdorf, Austria. The briefing called for a long mission, at least eight hours up and back to the target. The route was supposed to keep the group as far away from flak as possible. Fighters in the area would have to be delt with if they attacked the formation. Take off was scheduled for 0600 hrs.

Col. Bonner was flying in the lead ship on this mission. For those who had flown missions with the Col, there was an uneasy feeling within the formation. Everything seemed to be going well until the formation turned at the IP. From now on it was fly straight and level and let the German flak batteries take a crack at the 464th.

It did not take long for the flak to open up on the approching B-24s. Flak was intense, accurate, and heavy. In terms of the crews it was "walkin stuff." Planes started to take hits. So far the damage to the planes was not serious, and all planes continued on the bomb run.

"Bombs Away," was called at about 1020, hrs and the formation began to rally according to the battle plans. As the planes left the ring of flak one of the last bursts hit DOLLAR RIDE (42-78257), being flown by the crew of 2/Lt. Erwin Elrod. The flak cut the control cables, and the plane lurched and wobbled about the sky. In the nose, John Baker (Navigator) recalled:

Immediately Buddy, the best darn pilot in the Air Corps, gave us the signal, "Prepare to Bail Out." It so happened that Lou, the bombardier, and I were prepared even before we reached the target, however, minutes passed and nothing happened so our tension was slightly eased. Bud was flying the boxcar in formation with only elevator and ailerons, which is a mighty neat trick if you can do it; however, the slightest wrong move might throw us into a spin that would be impossible to pull out of!

Shortly after leaving the flak it seemed that the entire Luftwaffe appeared from nowhere. Their attacks came from all around the clock as they dove on any B-24 that looked crippled. One B-24 had a feathered prop and became the target for the Me-109s. AINT MISBEHAVIN MINNIE throttled back and moved into position to cover the other B-24. Robert Jares (2nd/Lt) and his crew tried to keep the fighters at bay. At almost the same time RED-V (41-28969) joined the cripple. The Me-109s attacked with a vengence, hitting both of the good samaritans and shooting them down. The cripple was left to fight it out with the fighters. The crippled Liberator continued it's battle and was credited with three confirmed fighters shot down. They would make it back to Gioia, but the plane would be out of commission for almost a month.

Fighter attacks also claimed BLACK -Z (42-95336), flown by Lt. John Jones' crew. They all managed to bail out of their flaming B-24. TARGET FOR TONIGHT (41-28748) was also hit, and all but two of the crew bailed out before the plane hit the ground.

DOLLAR RIDE was still with the formation as they headed for home base. John Baker remembered:

Well, everything seemed all right on the way home. We warned the wing ships to stay clear in case she did act up, and that proved

The 464th formation as seen through the windshield of MISMYSAKTIME.

to be a fatal mistake. Little by little we fell behind our group formation; however, our little group of five planes was still more or less intact. At Graz the lead navigator led us over another flak area, and when the group turned sharply to the left to avoid it, we lost out completely. As we struggled along trying to keep up, I suddenly saw tracers going by outside the left window. They moved in towards me rapidly, and then the left half of the nose was filled with red streaks. Lou had climbed into the nose turret to replace Sgt. Freeman, who was attempting to help Sgt. Mezzatesta repair the severed cables in the bomb bay. The last of the tracers seemed to be about waist high and about six inches from me. Luckily I was looking out the right window at the city of Zagreb. Under normal conditions with Freeman in the nose turret and Lou and I in the navigator's compartment, one of us would have literally been cut in half. I looked out and saw the sleek fuselage of an Me-109 peel off about a hundred feet from our left wing, then turned, closed the turret doors, and yelled to Valente, "Get Him!" At that instant Buddy pressed his intercom and said in a very calm voice, "Pilot to crew, bail out."

I turned and opened the doors for Lou, then pulled the release on the nose wheel doors. No result! I crawled back and released the catch with my hands. Still no result, so I crawled on back to the bomb bay.

I opened the bomb bays and looked up to see Freeman and Mezzatesta standing on the catwalk. Mezz yelled, "Why did Styer bail out?" Without answering, I said, "Bail Out." Freeman, in a half panicky voice replied, "I ain't got a chute!" I reached behind me, grabbed a chute, and snapped it on him as he sat on the catwalk. "Go ahead and jump!" I yelled. He replied, "I ain't got no right arm!" "Ok, you jump and I'll pull your ripcord." As he slid out I jerked the cord and the chute opened."

All but one of the crew were able to bail out and land safely on the ground. Baker and several of the crew were hidden by friendly

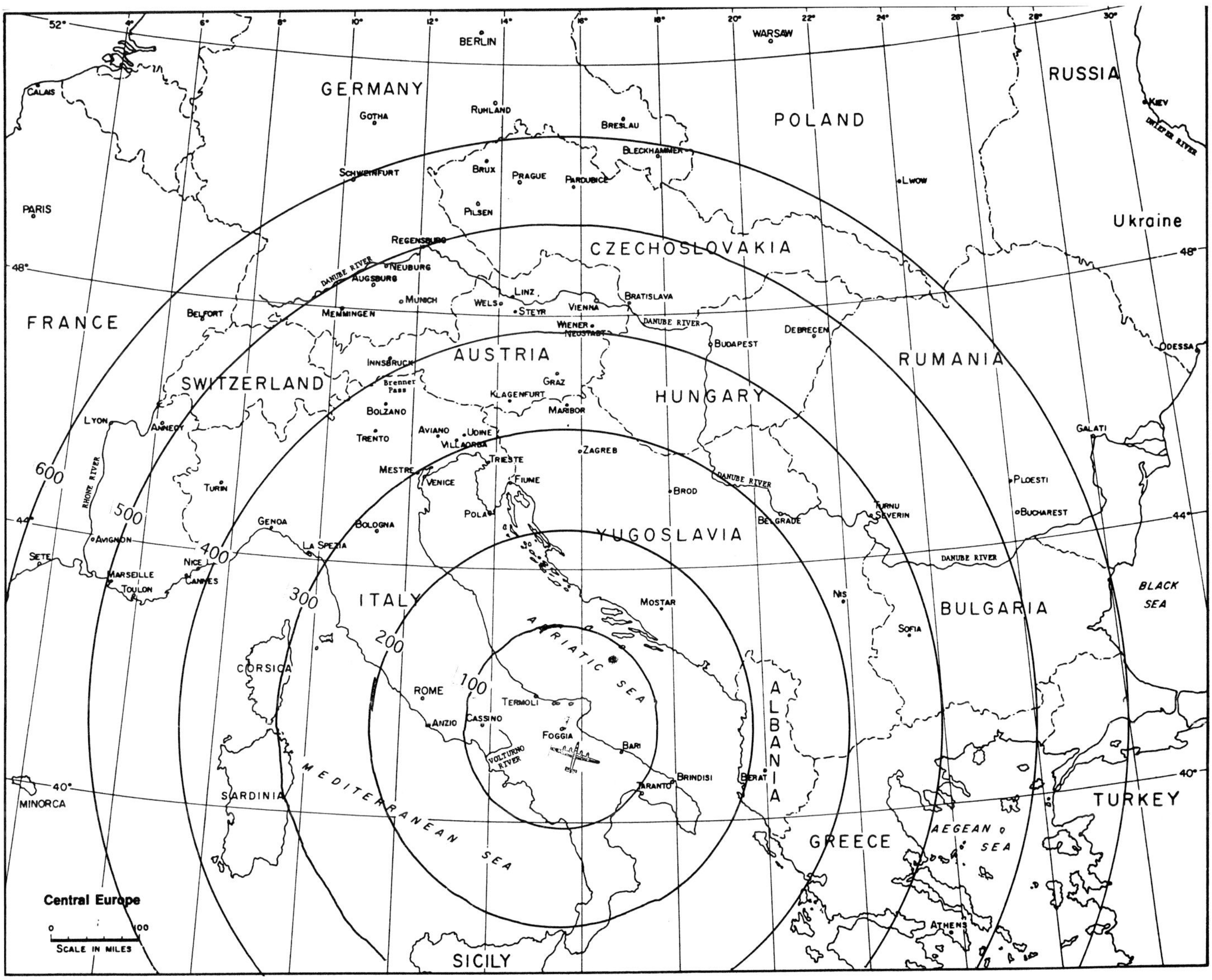

Map of central Europe showing approximate distance from Foggia to 15th Air Force targets.

partisans and made it back to base after a harrowing tale of escape and evasion. Sgt. John Rodgers was killed in the crash of DOLLAR RIDE, while the rest of the crew were taken POW.

The rest of the 464th managed to make it back to Gioia. Again there were wounded to take care of. The ground crews surveyed the damaged ships that made it back and knew they were going to be up all night trying to get them ready by morning. Five hardstands were empty, and the crew chiefs could only shake their heads. Sgt. Herman "Red" Moldenhauer still had his plane (117), but the usual crew of Lt. Jones and his men were missing. It was a hard night for "Red."

The group was able to put together enough planes to fly to Vienna the next day. Despite it being one of the worst flak beds on the continent, all the planes returned. There were some that had been hit, but at least all of them made it back to base.

The group had been in combat for only a month. They had flown 18 missions and had lost 16 planes and crews during the month's operations. Two of the planes were lost through accidents, while the rest were combat losses. It did not take a math wizard to figure out the 464th was bucking the odds. Maybe there was something in the rumors that the group was "snake bit," or maybe it was group leadership.

On 31 May word came that the base at Pantanella was ready for the 464th; the rumors had been correct for a change. There began a flurry of activity as the men of the 464th packed everything and began the move to their new home in Italy.

One of the first things to be done at Pantanella was to set up tents and dig slit trenches and latrines.

And just where was their new home? Look on a map of Italy, and one will search in vain for a spot marked Pantanella. The base was just a wheat field when the advanced elements of the 464th arrived, and the engineers had to carve out a bomber base for the 464th. There was no town, just a wheat field. The wheat field was located about 11 miles southwest of Canosa. Rumor had it that the land had belonged to a family of nobility named Pantanella. Research by several members of the 465th revealed that there was no such family in the area. Their research also shows that the name Pantanella is a derivation of "Pantano," or "field almost surrounded

The 464th's sister group (465th) ran short of tents. This cartoon shows "The great tent robbery of June '44."

by stream of water." Their research points out that Pantanella would be the diminutive, or "small field." With that in mind, Pantanella could be translated as "a small field almost surrounded by streams of water." The word Pantanella probably was on a map used by the Engineers when they surveyed the area for prospective bases. The name stuck, and so was born the permanent home of the 464th and 465th Bomb Groups.

June 1944

The first of June found the 464th on the move to their base at Pantanella. It had been a long wait, but the base was finally finished. The move was accomplished by the usual Army method of "hurry up and wait," along with bumpy Army trucks and good old B-24s. The lucky ones got to fly, while those that were not quite so lucky got to take a road trip. By B-24 the distance covered was about fifty miles. By road, it was closer to a hundred. Col. Bonner flew to Pantanella on KENTUCKY COLONEL so he could be there to make sure the tent stakes were lined up correctly.

The new base had started out as a wheat field in the Ofanto River valley. The wheat field was overlooked by two rounded hills that had been an olive grove. The 464th would occupy one hill, while their sister group, the 465th, would call the other home. From the top of the hill the view was rather nice, that is, if you liked looking at the runway and hardstands.

The runway had been graded, and a lot of crushed limestone had been put down for a base. This had been covered with Marsden Mat, also known as PSP (pierced steel planking). Since the 464th was sharing the base with the 465th there were two parallel runways. Close to the runways were the hardstands. There was one for each B-24 in the group. Like the runways, the hardstands were covered with PSP.

For the members of the ground echelon, who had spent a few days at "the hill" after they first arrived in Italy back in March and April, the base had undergone a lot of changes, though there were still a few tents dotting the hill. These had been used by the engineers while the runway and hardstand were being built.

When the first elements of the 464th arrived on 31 May they found few, if any, tents pitched for their quarters. There was a large pile of poles, stakes, and tents for them to use. It was a mad rush to grab a canvas castle, find a suitable location, and figure out how in the heck to get the tent to stand up straight. As more and more men arrived there was an increase in activity on the hill. Everything had to be set up and ready for the group to fly on 2 June.

Many of the ground crews grabbed a tent and pitched it down in the valley near their hardstand. They would live near their planes so they did not have to waste a lot of time traveling from the hill to the hardstands.

The men of the 464th did not know that during one of the first nights at Pantanella they were the victims of a robbery. The 465th Bomb Group had also moved to the new base and would share the facilities. The 465th would pitch camp on the other hill, just to the east of the 464th. During the mad dash to secure tents in the 465th area they came up a few short. In the dark of the Italian night, several members of the 465th visited the 464th and "found" a tent that

White-R as seen through the windshield of a sister ship.

Left: The 464th climbing out for a mission.

The 464th over a target, June 1944.

was unattended. They grabbed the canvas casa and made their way back to the other hill.

With all the activity going on there were several comments that the base looked more like "Bonner's anthill" than an Army base getting ready to do battle with Hitler's Third Reich.

Rod Binger worked as a welder, and he recalled some of the early activity:

My job required repairing plane parts, but also building components for the base (mess kits, washers, tanks for photography, you name it), and we had nothing to work with or make it all out of except 50 gal. barrels that held 100 octane gas for the planes. I needed metal to build with, and the barrels were it! I had transportation bring me a load of drums filled with water to kill the gas fumes. On my first attempt to cut an end out, I lost my eyebrows and the front of my hair. There *had* to be a better way. So, with a big chisel, I put slots in the barrel bottoms, laid them on their sides 6 to 10 at a time, and poured 100 octane around them with a trail of gas approximately 50 feet away and touched a match to it. Some blew 8 to 10 feet high, but this cleared the gas fumes so I could immediately cut the ends out. Now I had metal to make stuff out of.

By sundown on 1 June the photo lab was set up and ready to process film. A large "circus tent" had been erected for mission briefings. The mess tents were up, but the food tasted about the same as always. Some of the more fortunate occupants of the hill were able to tune in their radios. Sure enough, Axis Sally welcomed the 464th to their new base. She was sure to mention that just because they had moved from Gioia to Pantanella they still could not hide from the Luftwaffe and would continue to get special treatment any time they ventured over Europe.

The 464th was back in the air on 2 June. They were going to take a crack at the marshalling yards at Cluj, Rumania. The group managed to put 68 tons of bombs onto the target with good results. The Luftwaffe seemed to be somewhere else, as no fighters were seen. All of the planes returned to the field except Lt. Ernie Latham's crew in MISMYSAKTIME (41-29361). They were forced to ditch in the Adriatic due to fuel starvation. Four of the crew went to the bottom of the Adriatic with MISMYSAKTIME.

Due to bad weather over the target the mission to Craiova was canceled on 3 June. This gave the group some time to continue setting up tents and trying to get a few more creature comforts around the base. With a full schedule of missions coming up, it would take some time before everyone would get settled onto the hill.

On the 4th, the 464th put 32 planes in the air for a mission to the Turin Central marshaling yards. The lead ship carried Maj. Elvin Goodyear, CO of the779th Sq. The mission was flown according to the briefed plan of attack.

Over the target the group was greeted by the usual flak, which was described as moderate but accurate. Four ships were hit by flak fragments, and one was damaged enough to cause it to limp to an alternate base. The results of the mission were classified as poor due to cloud cover over the target, and for some reason the lead plane did not drop their bombs. In spite of the results it was a good mission, since there were no planes or crews lost.

Col. Bonner led the group to the Ferrara marshaling yards on 5 June. Some of the crews commented that form up went a little better than usual, despite the fact that the Col. was leading.

At the IP the flak began to blossom. It was moderate, accurate, and heavy. Four planes were ventilated by flying shards of flak. So far everyone was still in formation. As the formation got closer to the target the flak increased until it was intense, accurate, and heavy.

At the release point the bombardiers toggled 63 tons of high explosives onto the target. The results were classified as good, with lots of hits noted in the railyards. Several bombs hit the roundhouse, and several more impacted near the choke point. Rest assured, the trains would be a little late for the next few days.

As the group rallied for home, enemy fighters were seen lurking in the distance. Everyone kept an eye on them as they turned

The 464th on the way to Ploesti, June 6, 1944.

towards the 464th. The gunners were ready, and held their fire until the Me-109s closed to within range. Suddenly the sky seemed filled with tracers arching towards the oncoming fighters as the Me-109s fired back with bursting 20mm shells.

The fighters managed to break through the defensive fire and hit LITTLE GISMO (42-78133), flown by Lt. Paul Leonard's crew. The plane was raked by exploding 20mm gunfire and caught fire. Seven parachutes were seen to come out of the strickened ship before she erased herself in a blinding explosion. Lt. George Ely and Sgt. Francis O'Neal went down with the remains of LITTLE GISMO.

The gunners of the 464th racked up a good score, as they were credited with four Me-109s destroyed, two probables, and one damaged.

When the group returned to Pantanella they found that there were several wounded aboard the planes. While it appeared that the mission had gone rather well, several men noted in their diaries that due to leadership problems the group had flown over a known flak concentration on the way home. Thankfully, the gunners on the ground had not fired a shot as the "furniture vans" flew over.

June 6 dawned clear and bright. The flight crews were awakened and shuffled off to breakfast, and then to the briefing. A low moan went out as the curtain was pulled from the briefing board. The target was the Dacia Romano Oil Refinery at Ploesti. Ploesti meant two things: flak and fighters! After all, Ploesti was the third most heavily defended target under control of the Third Reich. To make things worse, the sun would be in the pilots' faces going to and coming from the target.

Form up went as planned, and the group found its place in the 55th Wing bomber stream. It seemed that the entire 15th Air Force was headed to Ploesti that day. As far as the eye could see there were bombers headed in the general direction of Ploesti.

Nerves climbed to the edge, and the "pucker factor" tightened as the planes neared the target. If the 15th Air Force could mount a maximum effort to hit Ploesti, then the Luftwaffe would reciprocate in their defensive effort. The first fighters were spotted heading for the formation before the group had even turned at the IP. The escort fighters bounced the oncoming Me-109s, and the fight was on.

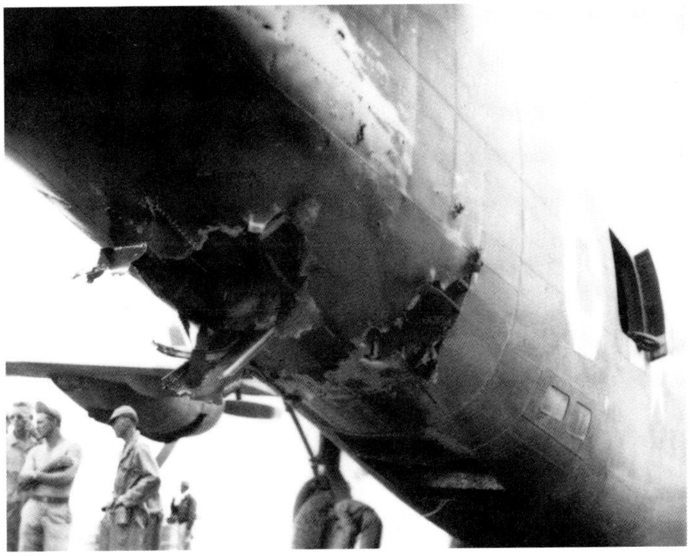

THATS US after returning from Ploesti with damage from fighter attacks.

Firemen spray foam on the hot engine of Yellow-D, June 6, 1944.

About twenty of the German fighters managed to break through the escorts and headed directly for the nearest group, the 464th. They came in with guns winking and yellow-red tracers flying towards the B-24s. The first attack hit 42-50411 from the 776th Sq, flown by Lt Eugene Stout and crew. The plane was last seen heading down under apparent control. The next victim of the Luftwaffe was 41-29379 from the 777th Sq. This plane was crewed by Lt. Grady Stapp and his flightcrew. As the plane fell from the formation six chutes blossomed from the stricken Liberator.

PAPPYS PUSS/PAPPY'S PRIDE (41-29410) was also hit by the fighters. Co Pilot Duane Buckmaster recalled:

As we approached the IP we were attacked by fighters. It was a frontal attack, with the fighters diving through the formation from above and ahead of us. We received numerous hits, including some in the flight deck area that resulted in fire and dense smoke. Lt. Ullman directed me to take the controls while he checked the damage. He left his seat and looked back, quickly concluding that we were too badly damaged to continue. He returned to his seat, took the controls, and told me to give the bail out signal, which I did. We salvoed the bombs and the crew began to bail out.

Everyone on the crew bailed out. The bombardier, Lt. Robert McCaslin, apparently hit the tail of the plane. He was killed on impact or knocked out, and his chute never opened as he fell to the ground. The rest of the crew used the nylon let down and landed just north of Ploesti, where they were taken captive.

The Luftwaffe tactics were daring and aggressive. They were making head on attacks, closing to within 75 to 100 yards before diving under the first unit, then pulling up through the second unit.

As the formation approached the target the fighters broke off the attack and the flak began to blossom.

The 464th flew on towards Ploesti. The planes were now gathering flak damage and hoping that the lead ship would call "BOMBS AWAY" shortly. As the formation got closer to the target, the bomb bay doors rolled up the sides of the Liberators like the top of a roll top desk. With the doors open the planes were ready to drop their lethal load. Even on a short bomb run seconds passed like hours. This run to the target lasted several minutes, which seemed like an eternity.

Finally the group reached the release point and sent 52 tons of bombs raining down on the oil fields. The target was covered by smoke and haze from the defensive smoke pots. All the men could hope for was that they hit the target, since there could be no accurate accounting from the strike photos.

The group rallied for home, and the fighters were there to greet them as they came off the target. Again the fighters were aggressive and came at the bombers from 12 o'clock. 20 mm shells blasted into the nose turret on REPULSIVE RAIDER (42-78088), killing Sgt. Claude Orrell. The RAIDER was riddled with gunfire and in deep trouble.

42-78223 had been badly damaged by flak over the target. Coming off the target they were hit by fighters looking for cripples and started down. Lt. Thomas Mills rang the bail out bell, and the crew started to bail out before the plane exploded.

The fighters kept coming, and the 464th gunners kept hammering back at them with their big .50s. With the fighters using 20mm it was a mismatch of firepower, and at the moment the fighters were winning the battle. HARD HEARTED HANNAH (41-28755) from the 778th was hit by fighters and fell from the formation, leaving six chutes floating through the air. The fighters also got HEAVEN'S ABOVE (42-50405) from the 779th. Lt. Bert Hays, Jr., held the plane level so the crew could get out. As he tried to leave the plane it went out of control, pinning him in the stricken Liberator. He was finally able to bail out, but was killed by ground fire as he drifted towards the ground in his chute.

The 464th rallies for home, June 19, 1944.

The target on June 19th was the oil storage depot at Sette, France.

Lt. Robert Hughes was at the controls of one of the ships. As fighters made a pass he was hit in the neck and arms by exploding shell fragments. He stayed at the controls of his plane and flew on until the formation was out of danger from fighter attack.

The 109s attacked THAT'S US (778th). Waist gunner John McGovern recalled:

A Me-109 made a pass at us from downstairs, and he caught us in the bottom of the waist section. The other gunner was wounded by exploding framents. It wasn't a serious wound, just small shrapnel fragments in the arm. The damage to the plane was not very serious, just a lot of sheet metal work for the ground crews when the Liberator got home.

The 464th gunners were credited with eight Me-109s and two Fw-190s destroyed. They were also given one probable and five damaged. They had made the Luftwaffe pay a heavy price, but the 464th had paid an even heavier price that day over Ploesti.

After what seemed like an eternity in hell the fighters turned away with low fuel warnings. Aboard the B-24s of the 464th the crews now fought to stay in the air long enough to reach the safety of Pantanella. Their biggest worry now was how much fuel they had left, and how to make the wounded as comfortable as possible for the long trip home.

As the planes approached the field the ground crews strained their eyes to see the formation. Those that had binoculars focused on the arriving B-24s and counted out loud. There were sighs of relief and several silent prayers.

One by one the planes pulled into the pattern. Those with wounded aboard were cleared to land first by the men in RACECARD TOWER. The other planes had to circle and try to figure out who could stay in the air and who had enough damage to give them higher priority in the pattern.

Imagine the stress in the control tower, listening to the pleas from the pilots to let them come in next and then having to tell the pilots that there was another plane that was in worse shape and had to come in now.

REPULSIVE RAIDER and her crew had made a valiant effort to get the ship all the way home. Sadly, about sixty miles from the base the plane would go no farther, and the crew had no choice but to leave the plane by parachute. Lt. Kline and his crew hit the silk, leaving their dead nose gunner to bear the pall of REPULSIVE RAIDER.

At the debriefing the crews relived the mission in detail, so it could be documented and then sent on to 55th Wing. For many, the 2 ounces of mission whiskey provided little relief from the tension of the day. Chaplain Eastwood was on hand in case anyone wanted to say a prayer for those that had not returned, or to just get something off their chest.

The ground crews surveyed the damage to the planes and started thinking about just how in the hell they were going to get enough spare parts to fix them. Of course there was always the chance that one of the hulks down in the boneyard might just have the part that was needed to fix the problem on their ship. They knew it was going to be another long night of work. One of the first things that had to be done was clean away the blood from the planes that had brought back wounded. It was a grim chore, but it had to be done. None of the crew chiefs wanted the next crew to see a sight like that.

Word filtered down that the Allies had landed on the beaches of Normandy early that morning. For the crews of the 464th it had been a horrible day. They had lost six planes, and a seventh had crashed on the way home. For many it had been one of their "Longest Days." For the ground crews it would be another "Longest Night."

The bombers left the target burning.

That night the men that felt like eating trudged to the mess areas to find an infamous meal. John McGovern recalled:

They had what we called "Billy Goat stew." Actually, it was mutton. I remember we had to dip our mess kits through a layer of orange fat to get to the stew.

Despite the losses on the previous day the 464th was back in the air on the 7th. Twenty-one planes headed for the La Spezia Harbor installations led by Maj. Thomas Carter. Weather over the target was 10/10 cloud cover, so the group headed for the alternate target at Leghorn Port.

There were no fighters to greet them this time, much to the relief of the crews. Flak was said to be slight and inaccurate. It may have been classified as inaccurate, but seven planes collected hits. The results of the mission were reported as good. Several ships in the harbor received direct hits and were burning as the group rallied for home. The mission was classified as a "milk run." All of the planes returned to base, and no one was injured.

That night word came down from 15th Air Force that the 464th would stand down until further notice. The group would fly daily practice missions. Those crews not flying would attend classes on various subjects associated with combat flying. The exact reason for this stand down is lost in history. The rumor mongers had a field day with it. From the top of the hill to the hardstands below, rumors spread like wildfire. "The 464th is being taken out of combat because of the heavy losses." "The group is going to the Pacific." "Col. Bonner is going to be relieved!" And the ultimate rumor, "The war is over!"

While the rumors flew, so did the 464th. They practiced flying tight formations, group assembly, aerial gunnery, and bombing. These practice flights were usually a late morning take off, since their sister group, the 465th, was still active flying combat and needed the runways.

The stand down allowed some time to work on projects, like better quarters, the briefing building, and other structures around the field. Many of the men were busy building actual houses out of the native Tufa stone that was abundant in the area. Some of the houses were complete with a basement or a second story. Others were just Tufa stone walls with a G.I. tent pitched over the top. No matter what kind of dwelling it was, they all seemed to come with hot and cold running mice.

Down in the 779th Sq area, Sgt. Herman "Red" Moldenhauer used the time to try and figure out the latest problem with his B-24. He was never able to prove it, but he was positive that B-24G Serial Number 42-78117 (Black-P) was infested with gremlins. This was a new plane that had been flown overseas by Lt. John Jones and crew, and they had problems with the plane from the start. It would not trim, and the auto pilot was erratic. Then there were the strange things that would just happen. One night, Red and his crew were working on the plane when a life raft blew out of the compartment over the wing. No reason, it just blew out. No one on the ground crew was even near the darn thing. Another time, one of the main gear tires developed a large bulge that kept growing until it burst. Lt. Jones even reported falling out of formation and having an "out of body" experience. It always seemed something unexplained was going on. It may have been that 117 was just a "dog," or maybe she really was infested with those little creatures called gremlins.

Getting planes off the ground and into formation is not an easy thing to do. The procedure sounds simple, but it takes a lot of good flying and good timing to get everyone in the right spot at the right moment. When the lead plane was airborne, they would fly the runway heading for a predetermined amount of time. The actual time depended on how many planes would be in each box and how many planes were going on the mission. After flying the determined time the lead plane would turn and start back. In the meantime, the next plane would take off and fly straight for a shorter time period. Then they would turn, and if everything was on schedule they would be in fairly close proximity to the first plane. It was all in the timing. Each plane taking off, flying for x amount of time, turning, and climbing into the ever growing box. When Able Box had all of their aircraft in position they would almost be back over the field at about 5,000 feet. They would then head for the group form up area and fly in a general racetrack circuit until the rest of the boxes had taken off, formed, and arrived at the form up area. The group would continue to fly the racetrack until all of the boxes were in the right place. When the planes of the 464th were formed up they would rendezvous with the 465th and then head for the Wing rendezvous area.

The practice missions were marred by an accident on the 9th. B-24 42-52194 crashed on landing when she returned from that day's flight. The crew emerged with minor cuts and bruises. Nevertheless, it seemed that bad luck was still with the group even when they stood down.

The stand down was lifted on 14 June. The group got 36 planes into the air for a strike on the Petfurdo Oil Refinery at Petfurdo, Hungary. Maj. Poff led the group, while Col. Bonner led the second attack unit. Group assembly was carried out in record time. After all, they had just spent the last five days practicing how to do it.

The formations were a little tighter than before the stand down, and everything seemed to go a little better. The group released 69 tons of bombs onto the target, which was covered by smoke from previous strikes. Flak was accurate enough to put holes in seven of the ships.

When the group rallied for home the smoke from the burning target billowed up to about 15,000 feet and could be seen from over a hundred miles away.

All of the planes returned to Pantanella. On landing approach COFFIN CORNER CUTIE (42-78317) from the 776th could not get the nosewheel down. There was only one thing to do, and that was to bring the ship in and hold the nose off as long as possible. The resulting crash landing injured several of the crew, but at least they made it home.

The combat crews were rousted out of bed early on the morning of 16 June. They had the usual breakfast fare of powdered eggs, burnt toast, and coffee, then trudged to the briefing. Many of them were still half asleep, that is, until they found out where they were headed that day.

The red string on the map ran from their base up to the Oil Blending Plant at Lobau, Austria. Since the target was in Austria, the crews figured it would be another long haul and most likely a rough mission.

Lt. Edmund Leet's crew had been put on the flight schedule at the last minute. They were not supposed to fly that day. Actually, they all had been looking forward to the day off. At the hardstand they went through the usual preflight checks on their new B-24 42-95382, which they had dubbed REPULSIVE RAIDER II. This was going to be the crew's 22nd mission, but it was the first mission for the plane. Several of the crew got "a funny feeling that it wasn't their day" as the engines started. Navigator William Hollmann was not wearing his lucky hat on the mission. Shortly after forming up, one of the crew lost his lucky baseball cap. It seemed that the cards were being stacked against the crew.

The 32 planes were led by B/Gen. George Acheson, Commander of the 55th Bomb Wing. He came down from HQ, apparently to observe if the stand down had improved the 464th. And perhaps to see if there were any changes that should be made in leadership. At least that is what the rumor was. At any rate, the Wing boss was in the lead ship.

About twenty minutes from the target the prop governor on the #3 engine of REPULSIVE RAIDER II went out. The pilot feathered the prop, and the rest of the crew really felt their luck was running thin.

The photo department stated that this is Col. Bonner's ship (center) on fire and going down. The ship at the left was labeled as Maj. Carter's plane heading down.

Flak opened up just after the turn at the IP. As always over Vienna it was intense, accurate, and heavy—another round of "walkin stuff." On top of that, over fifty German fighters were in the area. All kinds—Me-410s, Me-110s, and even Ju-88s were spotted.

Over the target, the oil line on the #1 engine of REPULSIVE RAIDER II was either hit by flak or broke. The engine was shut down, and the #3 was started in spite of the bad prop governor. RAIDER II limped off the target and began to fall behind the formation. She was fighter bait! Lt. Tudberry and Lt. Judy were flying on the left and right of the crippled B-24. They throttled back and stayed with REPULSIVE RAIDER II.

German fighters pounced on the trio. The crew of RAIDER II had been ordered from their turrets in case the bail out bell rang. The two protective B-24s fought the fighters to a standstill. Their selfless act of compassion had saved the crew on the crippled B-24.

The fighter attacks had riddled the tail turret on RAIDER II and had knocked out the #3 engine for good. They were now limping toward the Island of Vis on two engines and a lot of prayers.

Flak had taken its toll on several other planes in the formation. BLACK-T (41-29417) managed to land at Bari. COM-BAT (42-78091) limped to Vis and made a good landing. Both of these planes would return with their crews. Seven other planes made it back to base with battle damage.

REPULSIVE RAIDER II was still trying to make it home. The crew had thrown out everything they could to try and lighten the plane and get to Vis. Near the Yugoslav coast their luck ran out. The #4 engine failed, and they were down to a single engine. The crew had no choice but to bail out and send their brand new plane crashing to the ground. They all managed to find a group of partisans and evaded capture.

On the 17th the mission scheduled to Subotica marshaling yards was canceled due to bad weather over the target. Col. Bonner received a visit from his father-in-law, Maj/Gen. James Fechet. He just happened to be head of the Promotions Board back in Washington. Again the rumors began to fly about the true nature of the General's visit.

The missions for 18 through 21 June were scheduled, then canceled because of weather, either over the targets or enroute. Another small vacation from combat gave the men time to work on housing or fine tune the planes for the next mission, whenever it came along.

On 22 June the weather cleared, and Col. Bonner led the group to Bologna Main marshaling yards. Thirty-five planes headed for the target, along with a special guest observer, Lt/Col. John Tomhave from 55th Wing. Again, rumor had it that Col. Bonner was under the gun because of all the rumors about his ability to command.

Flak was encountered at the target, and seven planes took hits. They were minor, as everyone was able to stay in formation. About 18 Me-109s attacked the 465th BG, but none of the fighters turned towards the 464th. Almost 70 tons of RDX were delivered to the rail yards, with good results showing up on the strike photos.

On the way home the group flew through an intense barrage of flak about 12 miles south of Fano, Italy. FAST NUMBER (42-95337) from the 779th was hit by a burst. The shrapnel cut the lines that went to the fuel sight gauges, causing fuel to pour out at an alarming rate. Lts Stoll and Ravaschieni, along with Sgts Parker and Chucte went to the bomb bay to try and stem the flow of fuel. The bomb bay doors were open to allow the fuel to drain out. Working on the narrow catwalk, the four men took turns working on the damage. Several times they almost passed out because of lack of oxygen. Flak was still bursting, and Lt. Stoll suffered a small wound from another hit. After what seemed like hours the damage was under control. The four men climbed out of the bomb bay soaked with 100 octane fuel and ill from the fumes. FAST NUMBER made it back to base, but would not fly again for several days.

A mission to the oil installations at Giurgiu, Rumania, was flown on the 23rd. The second attack unit became separated from the first unit because of overcast near the Yugoslav coast. They tacked onto the 465th for the rest of the mission.

The first attack unit, led by Maj. Carter, arrived over the target with 24 planes and dropped 45 tons of explosives onto the target.

Flak over Romanian targets was noted for its intensity. On this day the German gunners must have been low on ammunition. There were just enough bursts to cause some minor damage to three planes. Several enemy fighters were reported, but most of the fliers felt this mission had been a "milk run."

On 24 June the group stood down, but they were back in the air on the 25th. The mission profile called for them to hit the oil refinery at Balaruc, France. Thirty-four planes led by Maj. Poff dropped 68 tons of bombs just to the left of the aim point. Results were still judged as good. A few bursts of flak were seen over the target area. There were also several fighters, but they did not attack. All planes returned to Pantanella to chalk up another "milk run."

That night the 464th and 465th were treated to a USO show. The makeshift stage was filled with a band, dancers, and singers,

Crash site of Col. Bonner's aircraft.

and even some pretty good looking American women. It was a welcome relief to the usual humdrum evenings in Italy for those who could attend.

For the ground crews it was just another night of working on the planes. M.E. "Steve" Stephenson wrote:

My crew and I replaced the tail on my plane after it was damaged by flak on a mission. The job was completed about 11:30 PM, and a pilot and copilot arrived at my hardstand about an hour later. They informed me that I was going as their flight engineer, and that I should go check out a parachute. I informed them that I had never flown as a crew member, much less as a flight engineer. With a laugh the pilot said, "You put the tail on this bird, and if you did a good job fine, if not we would like to have you along with us." You can't argue with that kind of logic. That was my first flight as a flight engineer. It was a beautiful moonlit night until the pilot tried some stress maneuvers to see if he could pull the tail off. I was a little unsettled, but soon the test was over. I was not ready for the unexpected noise of the landing, and I came completely unglued and left a few claw marks on the interior of the plane. To tell the truth I was sure the tail had fallen off and was dragging down the runway. When I looked to see what had gone wrong I saw the landing mat bubbling up in front of the wheels. It was like a wave in front of the wheel. This was exaggerated by the landing lights.

The crews of the 464th headed for the Florisdorf Oil Refinery and marshaling yards on 26 June. This complex was in the Vienna area, so everyone knew this mission could be a rough one; the ones to Vienna always were. The first attack unit was led by Maj. Harold Blehm, while Col. Bonner would lead the second attack unit. After briefing there were several comments overheard about the "blind leading the blind."

"Good old Vienna" lived up to her deadly reputation as one of the flak capitals of Europe. The 464th came under attack as they turned at the IP. At first it was just scattered, but as the group moved closer to Vienna the intensity and accuracy increased. By the time the group reached the target, bursts of flak covered the sky with angry black clouds of destruction.

THREE CORNERED KID after mishap on June 26, 1944.

Over the target the group toggled their 72 tons of bombs into the smoking target and continued their flight through the heavy, deadly flak.

Just after "Bombs Away" the group came within range of Flak-Gruppe North and Flak-Gruppe West. These batteries were composed of 88mm, 105mm, and a few 128mm guns. These batteries fired 288 rounds of 88mm, 122 rounds of 105mm, and 76 rounds of 128mm shells at the formation as it flew over. With all those shells flying towards the group, it was a sure bet that they would hit something.

About two minutes after dropping their bombs, YELLOW-Z (42-50401) took a devastating direct hit in the nose. The blast blew the nosewheel away and killed the bombardier and navigator. Fire erupted in the nose and rear bombay, and the plane slid away to the right of the formation. Two of the crew bailed out when it became apparent that the ship was doomed. On the flight deck, Col. Bonner was flying in the right seat. The regular copilot, Lt. Henry Dangler, was standing between the pilots. The pilot, Lt. Lamar Dunn, rang the bail out bell for the rest of the crew to abandon ship. Col. Bonner started for the bombay when the plane took another burst of flak in the forward bombay area. The plane was racked by an explosion that blew Lts Dunn and Dangler clear. Luckily they were wearing backpack chutes and were able to pull the rip cord. It is unclear if Col. Bonner was hit by the flak burst in the bomb bay. He and the rest of the crew perished as the plane hit the ground.

A few moments later 42-95451 was hit in the #2 engine, which caught fire. Maj. Thomas Carter tried to control the fire with the fire bottles in the engine nacelle, but the fire continued to burn like a blowtorch. He rang the bail out bell and the entire crew jumped from the stricken Liberator.

By the time the 464th cleared the outer ring of flak to the west, 23 more planes had been hit by flak. So far everyone was still able to stay with the formation.

On Red-C (42-95355) Maj. Blehm was really sweating it out. Flak had cut the aileron controls on the left wing. The #1 engine had been hit and was throwing oil. #2 supercharger went out after the target, and both inverters were shot out, causing all the engine instruments to fall to zero. On landing approach the #1 prop governor ran away, but Maj. Blehm was still able to get the plane on the ground without further problems.

The ground crews surveyed the damaged planes and knew it was going to be another long night trying to patch enough planes together for another mission if one was called. Thankfully, word came down later that night that the mission scheduled for the next day was scrubbed.

On 28 June the 464th left Pantanella with 33 planes to hit the Prahova Oil Refinery at Bucharest, Romania. The mission was under command of Capt. William Moore, newly appointed commander of the 777th Squadron.

Flak was encountered at the target, and several fighters were seen. The fighters seemed more interested in doing aerobatics than attacking the bombers.

At the bomb release point the only major problem occurred. Each of the planes carried a load of 100 pound bombs. The drop intervalometers were set at 25 feet. On several of the planes the lower bombs did not clear the racks before the upper bombs released, and they began to pile up in the bomb bay. This caused a very poor bomb trajectory and flapping bomb doors on five planes.

On SKIRT PATROL (42-95371), flown by Capt. John Kibler, sixteen of the bombs were hung up on the racks or piled up in the bomb bay. Sgt. Richmond Davis (Engineer) and Sgt. Leo Tygart (Ball Turret) went into the bomb bay and started to work. At 23,000 feet they worked without oxygen masks to clear the bombs. The hydraulic lines had been ruptured by the pile up of bombs and fluid was spraying in the slipstream. Despite freezing cold, no oxygen or gloves, and the fact that the bomb fuzes were spinning in the wind, the two managed to throw the bombs overboard. Sgt. Davis stayed in the bomb bay, balancing on the slippery catwalk, and made temporary repairs to the hydraulic lines. He returned to the flight deck blinded by hydraulic fluid, almost frozen, and suffering from anoxia.

The bombing results were reported as good in spite of 115 bombs being dropped "by hand." The best part of the mission was that all of the planes returned to the base.

The group finished the month of June by starting a mission to Blechhammer North Oil Refinery. Due to bad weather over the target the group was recalled. One plane managed to bomb a target of last resort. Although the group had recorded one effective sortie, they were not given credit for the mission.

When the group returned to Pantanella they learned that Col. Arnold Schroeder had assumed command of the group to replace Col. Bonner. He announced his arrival with a pretty good buzz job down the center of the runway.

June had been another costly month for the 464th. They had lost fifteen planes due to combat or accidents. On top of this, several crewmen had been killed in action on planes that had returned to the base. Maybe with a change in command the group would have a change of luck, but only time would tell.

July 1944

The 464th started their third month of flying combat by standing down on the first of the month. This gave the ground crews a little extra time to fine tune some of the planes that needed it, and perhaps patch just one more flak hole. It also gave the men time to work on their housing and start construction on several other projects around the base.

During the afternoon of 1 July, the Operations Order came down from Wing for the next mission. The order called for the 464th to schedule 39 planes to attack and destroy the rail yards at Budapest, Hungary. The order outlined all of the nuts and bolts of how the mission was to be flown. The teletype printed out the mission schedule for take off, rendezvous, altitude, bomb load, and when and from what direction the group was to drop. While the order outlined all of the nuts and bolts, it was up to the men of the 464th to assemble parts into the whole.

Looking towards the runway from Pantanella Hill, June 1944.

The 464th taxiing out for a mission.

Each of the planes was to carry a bomb load of 6 500 pound bombs. That meant the Ordnance crews had to drive to the bomb dump and load 234 bombs, drive back, and then hoist them into the bomb bays of the Liberators. Since each plane had to have ammo for the guns, the crews loaded over 151,000 rounds of .50 cal ammo.

Fuel trucks made the rounds of the 39 scheduled hardstands. At each stop they pumped 100 octane fuel into the cavernous fuel tanks of the planes. By the time the trucks had completed their appointed rounds they had accounted for nearly 91,000 gallons of fuel.

The crew chiefs crawled over, around, and through their planes. They made sure that each of the oil reservoirs had 32 gallons per engine as called for in the manual. They checked the hydraulic fluid—yep, 18 gallons in the system. Wise crew chiefs may have placed a container with an extra couple of gallons near the flight engineer's station, just in case.

While this was going on the clerks were attacking the mountain of paperwork that went with every mission. There was the flight crew schedule that had to be posted so the lucky men who would fly knew they were going to fly. Then there were the briefing flimsies, route charts, maps, weather maps, and charts. The Engineering section had to complete the fuel reports, armament reports, Form 1As and all forms from B to X, Y, and Z.

The mission would require 390 K-Ration flight lunches, escape kits, oxygen masks, parachutes, and other personal equipment. Add to this as many flak vests as the crew dared to haul aboard the already overloaded Liberators.

The mess halls came to life getting things ready for the morning meal. The cooks started opening bags of powdered eggs and pancake flour. Lots of cans of Spam had to be opened so that the men would have some "mystery meat" to eat. Then there were the hundreds of gallons of good old "G.I. Joe" (coffee).

Getting all of the logistics together, typed, loaded, and ready took a lot of time and physical labor. Now, multiply this by every group in the 15th Air Force that was scheduled to fly the mission and you will see why the unsung heroes of the ground echelon had to work through the night to have everything ready for the flight crews in the morning.

The group was back at the briefing room on 2 July. The attack plan called for them to hit the marshaling yards at Budapest, Hungary. The 464th managed to get 39 B-24s into the air, formed up, and rendezvoused with their fighter escort in record time. Five aircraft aborted the mission because of mechanical problems.

Over the target the 464th was greeted by the usual flak, though most of it was below the main formation. Dog Box was flying at about 19,000 feet because the lead ship had two superchargers out and could not struggle any higher. This element bore the brunt of the flak.

The group dropped their bombs and rallied for home. At 1031 hours four Me-109s were spotted as they deployed for attack. The escort fighters bounced the 109s, but one got through, attacking Dog Box head on. Sgt. Walter Stutts, nose gunner on LIBBY RAIDER (42-52549), fired a burst when the Messerschmitt closed to about 200 yards. It pulled up and flew past smoking. The fighter was last seen going into a dive and crashing. Stutts was given a confirmed kill.

All of the planes returned to base. Seven ships had taken minor hits from flak. Three of the planes had enough holes in them to be out of commission for several days. Four crewmen had also been injured by shrapnel from the flak.

The fliers were back in the air again on the 3rd. This mission was against the Belgrade Shell Oil Depot. Thirty-four B-24s got airborne starting at 0744 hours. There were three ground aborts, and during form up six more ships returned with mechanical problems.

The remaining 28 planes reached the target and dropped 70 tons of 500 pound bombs at 1245 hours. Results were good, with a good bomb pattern within 2,000 feet of the aiming point. Ten bombs were plotted at the aiming point, taking out several storage tanks and setting large fires in the area.

Moving out to take off position.

As always, the group encountered flak over the target. It was classified as moderate, and no planes took significant damage. It appeared that the Luftwaffe was either sleeping or somewhere else, as no fighters greeted the 464th on the mission.

July 4th was celebrated by standing down from flying a combat mission. While the flight crews had the day off, it was just another 14 hour work day for the ground crews. They put the time to good use by working on the planes for the next trip to the Third Reich.

That night several crew chiefs saw fireworks coming from Pantanella Hill. Someone had taken a flare gun from one of the planes and was celebrating by shooting red and green flares into the night sky. While it was good natured American celebrating it did cause a bit of commotion; several of the residents on the hill thought that the base was under attack and headed for the slit trenches.

The group was back in the air on 5 July. This mission was to the U-boat base at Toulon, France. Each plane carried 10 500 pounders to drop on the subs. The weather enroute was playing against the group. Cumulus clouds billowed up to and over 21,000 feet, so the group climbed to 22,000 feet.

The formation hit the IP and turned for what was to be a long bomb run, as the flak opened up shortly after the turn. The planes were on the bomb run and had to fly straight and level. The flak increased as the group approached the target .

Several bursts of flak bracketed FREE DELIVERY (42-52484) from the 776th Sq. The flak had hit the plane hard. On the flight deck, copilot Lt. William Newborg had been killed. The flak had also killed the top turret gunner, T/Sgt. Ory Creswall. Lt. Ed Grunewald rang the bail out bell for the crew to abandon ship. The plane was on fire and quickly became a flying torch. Back in the waist, S/Sgt. Joseph Higgins, Jr., was trying to fight through the flames and reach the ball turret to raise it and get S/Sgt. Foy Holcombe out. Navigator John Porter wrote:

Of those who survived, Grunewald, myself, and Allen suffered severe burns, primarily about the face, plus a variety of other injuries. Wooding (Bombardier Charles Wooding) was wounded in the area of the knee. Higgins had some trouble with his hands after a very courageous attempt to get Holcombe. The fire burned his leather gloves so badly that his fingers were immobilized due to the stiffened leather.

A small explosion wracked the plane, blowing several of the men clear. Grunewald had stayed with the ship. At about 16,000 feet FREE DELIVERY erased herself in a flash of exploding fuel. Grunewald was blown clear and managed to open his chute. The survivors of the plane were captured.

The flight home had to be flown above the clouds again. This meant that on this eight hour mission the men were on oxygen for almost five hours. It sure would be good to have a cold beer when they got back to cut through that dry oxygen throat. That is, if you could find a cold beer!

Throughout the formation flight engineers kept a worried eye on the sight gauges; the climb over the weather had sure used a lot of fuel. By the time the planes were over base several were technically out of fuel. All of the planes made it, but most did not have enough fuel to fly much farther.

Planes of the 464th heading for the target.

On the 6th the 464th was up and flying at 0650 hours. Thirty-three planes were headed towards the Porto Marghera oil storage facilities. The two attack elements were led by Maj. Poff and Maj. Blehm. This time the weather was not a problem. There were scattered clouds, but nothing serious. Over the target it was severe clear.

The bomb run was another long one, which gave the flak gunners more time to find the range. They managed to fill a good part of the sky with deadly bursting shells.

Just before bombs away, F/O Willard Layne, the bombardier on BIG WHEEL-N-DEALER (42-78374), was struck by a piece of shrapnel. Although he was bleeding "like a stuck pig," he stayed at his bomb sight until release.

All of the planes returned to Pantanella. BIG WHEEL-N-DEALER landed at Foggia Main so that their wounded bombardier could get fast medical attention. Later that afternoon they flew the plane back to base.

July 7th found the 464th awake and ready for takeoff at 0600 hrs. The mission was scheduled to hit the Synthetic Oil Plant at Blechhammer North. Blechhammer was just over 600 miles from Pantanella as the crow flies, but crows are not Liberators that have to try and doge flak concentrations on the way. With that in mind, the actual distance to the target was a lot farther. Blechhammer was never one of the favorite places to fly against.

The mission appeared to be "snake bit" almost before it started. One ship suffered a ground abort when two generators malfunctioned. By the time the group was actually headed for the target, nine more planes had turned back with various mechanical problems.

As the formation flew over Hungary there were several encounters with flak as they passed near known flak concentrations. No planes reported any damage. Several enemy fighters were reported, but the escorting P-38s drove them away before they could get close enough to attack.

The group turned at the IP, and the flak started to blossom. As the flak intensified the planes began to take hits from the flying steel. The group could only fly straight ahead and take what the flak batteries dished out. It was going to be a long six minutes to the target.

LIBBY RAIDER after a mission. She would be lost on July 8, 1944.

Just before bomb release 42-50408 took a heavy burst in the fuselage. The auto pilot was knocked out and the rudder cables were cut. The bombardier salvoed the bombs so they could try and stay with the formation.

The 25 remaining planes released over 62 tons of bombs at 1120 hrs. They were almost an hour late getting to the target, according to the attack plan.

As the group rallied off the target, BROWN NOSE (42-95228) was hit by flak. Copilot Charles Yoast recalled:

A burst of flak was very near, which caused us to lose #3 engine and prop—they came completely off the aircraft. The tail gunner called and said we were on fire, and the flames were coming back as far as the tail. It was then we decided to bail out.

As BROWN NOSE fell towards the earth the crew started to leave their ship. Seven managed to clear the burning Liberator before the fire and fuel combined to tear BROWN NOSE into a spinning cauldron of debris. Navigator James Mydland and Gunners Elwin Majors and Francis Holley were lost in the spiraling wreckage.

Flak had hit the #2 engine on DEATH OF ME YET (42-78241), flown by Lt Clyde Judy's crew. They were last seen headed down under control with the prop on the ailing engine feathered.

PRINCESS PAT (42-78350) was last observed at 1124 hrs trailing smoke from the #3 engine. Six chutes were observed in the general area, but there was no way of telling if they where the crew of PRINCESS PAT. Records reveal that six of the crew managed to bail out and became POWs.

SULTAN (42-52489) took several near misses, and the ship shuddered from the impact of exploding flak shells. Almost everyone on the crew was hit by flying shrapnel. The #3 engine was hit badly and began to burn. The pilot, Earcel Green, feathered the engine and pulled the fire bottle. Neal Cobb (bombardier) recalled:

John Schianca was wounded seriously, and since I was also a qualified gunner, I went back and took over his tail turret. As soon as we pulled out of formation the fighters jumped us and knocked out #1 and #4 engines. We were falling rapidly and were given the bail out signal. We threw Johnnie out of the escape hatch in the waist of the plane. Others went out, and I told Parker (Andrew) to go ahead and jump. He refused, so I did not hesitate. I took three steps and went out feet first. If I had counted to ten I would not be alive. People who saw this happening said that I bailed out at 500 feet and that my chute opened about 50 feet above the ground.

Six of the crew managed to get of the falling Liberator before it hit the ground. Earcel Green (pilot), Roy Gulledge (copilot), Jack Elliot (radio operator), and Andrew Parker rode SULTAN all the way to the ground.

42-50408 tried to stay with the formation, but found it almost impossible with the damage to the rudder cables. The plane slowly descended to about 18,000 feet. T/Sgt Alvin Peterson and S/Sgt

Results of dropping 500 pound bombs on closed bomb bay doors. LITTLE ONE's crew chief will have a lot of work to do.

Francis Ramsey cut part of the radio trailing antenna and spliced the rudder cable well enough to continue the trip home.

The crew of DEATH OF ME YET had managed to get their crippled ship to the Yugoslav coast, hoping to make it to the island of Vis. Just off the coast the plane and crew ran out of luck. As the plane started down the crew bailed out. Sgt. Joe Dominetto's chute came out of the pack but never opened. He and Sgt. Robert Hughes were never seen again. The rest of the crew were picked up by friendly partisans and would return to the 464th.

The planes started arriving back at Pantanella around 1440 hrs. White-A landed at Bari. Sgt. Walter Walden had been hit by flak while manning his tail turret. The wound was a serious one to his thigh that also broke the bone. He was sent to the 26th Hospital at Bari.

Eight planes came back with serious flak damage. They would be out of commission for a few days while the ground crews cleaned them up and repaired the damaged systems. The sheet metal crews would have a lot of holes to patch before the next mission.

In spite of the losses and battle damage to the planes from the last several missions, the ground crews were able to have 27 planes ready for the 0630 hr take off on 8 July.

Group form up and rendezvous with the 55th wing went without a hitch. The 464th would lead the wing to the Florisdorf Oil Refinery and marshaling yards at Vienna, Austria. Vienna was always a long haul and never considered even close to a "milk run."

Three planes returned early. One plane returned because a waist gunner lost his helmet and oxygen mask when he leaned out the waist window to check the #1 engine on his plane, while others returned for mechanical problems.

Since the target was at "good 'ol Vienna," the crews figured the German flak batteries would serve the usual intense and accurate walkin stuff. The crews were right, as moderate flak began as the group turned at the IP. By the time the group was over the target it was the usual Vienna style: intense, accurate, and heavy.

On the way in it seemed that the entire Luftwaffe was in the air trying to stop the bombers from reaching the target. Me-109s, Fw-190s, and even several Ju-88s were lurking as the bombers approached. The fighter escort moved in to protect the bombers, and a large "fur ball' of dog fights broke out. The gunners in the bombers watched as the escorts sent several Me-109s spiraling down in flames.

Bombs away was called at 1038 as 24 planes released almost 60 tons of bombs onto the target. Observed results were good. The northwest choke point in the railway yard was plastered. Rolling stock and buildings within the rail yards also took direct hits. Several of the main buildings were also hit by bombs. In all, it looked like it would be a while before oil would be flowing through this particular rail yard.

Several of the planes had taken flak hits, but so far no one was in serious trouble. As the bombers left the target area about 30 fighters broke through the protective cover. Across the formation came the call "Fighters, 6' o'clock!" The fighters came at the bombers wingtip to wingtip, and with all guns blazing. After the initial pass the fighters would climb and attack in pairs or as single attackers.

The attacks were some of the most aggressive that the men of the 464th had seen. Many of the fighters closed to within 100 yards before they would roll inverted, show their armored bellies, and dive away. For the next twenty-five minutes the German fighters would continue to attack the 464th.

LIBBY RAIDER (42-52549) was hit by flak on the way to the target. She was damaged in the elevator and rudders, and fighters pounced on the cripple to finish her off. Lt. Ben Varner and his crew fought back for their lives. The first attack did more damage to the tail section. The second attack hit the #3 engine, causing it to erupt in flames. As the fire spread, Varner rang the bail out bell. Several witnesses reported that two men jumped from the waist area, then the left stabilizer snapped and the burning plane started

Solid undercast greets the formation on the way to the taget.

to fall "tall end first." The two men from the waist area were the waist gunners. Charles Simonelli recalled:

I was at the right waist, Ted Filicsky was on the left. As a result of the fire in the plane we were both on fire when we left the plane. He must have lost his chute pack as a result of the fire on himself and fell to the ground with no chute.

The rest of the crew managed to bail out and became POWs.

Fighters also attacked THE SKIRT PATROL (42-95371), flown by Capt. John Kibler's crew. She had been raked by cannon fire as the 109s came in from behind with their guns ablaze. One engine was one fire, and the plane was last seen spinning down. Everyone managed to bail out except Capt. Kibler and Sgt. Ferinando Arigone. They rode the plane all the way to the ground and were killed on impact.

THE BLONDE BOMBER (42-78333) was last seen leaving the formation after the target, and several fighters were attacking the cripple. At debriefing the plane and crew were listed as missing in action. Several hours later THE BLONDE BOMBER came limping back to base. They had managed to fight off the attacks and fly back to Italy alone, stopping at another base to take on enough fuel to get back to Pantanella.

BLACK-D (42-95319) had also taken heavy flak damage. Three Ju-88s jumped the wounded B-24 after the target, and the crew fought for their lives in a running aerial gun battle. The gunners managed to win the aerial duel, and the Germans finally turned away. The badly damaged Liberator limped to Foggia so that three wounded crewmen could get quick medical attention. The plane was declared Class 26 and salvaged.

A survey of battle damage on the returning planes showed 23 planes were damaged, and 15 of them would be non-operational for at least 24 hours. The ground crews could only stare at the damage, shake their heads, and start working. They all knew what had to be done, so they rolled up their sleeves and got crackin.

When the flight crews arrived at interrogation they relived the last several hours in as much detail as their combat fogged memories could muster. They reported on how bad the flak was, how many fighters attacked, and from where. What kind of markings did the fighters have? Who was lost, how, and when. It all had to be written down to send on to 55th Wing. The gunners of the 464th claimed that they had shot down eleven German fighters, six probables, and at least one damaged during their aerial battle with the Luftwaffe.

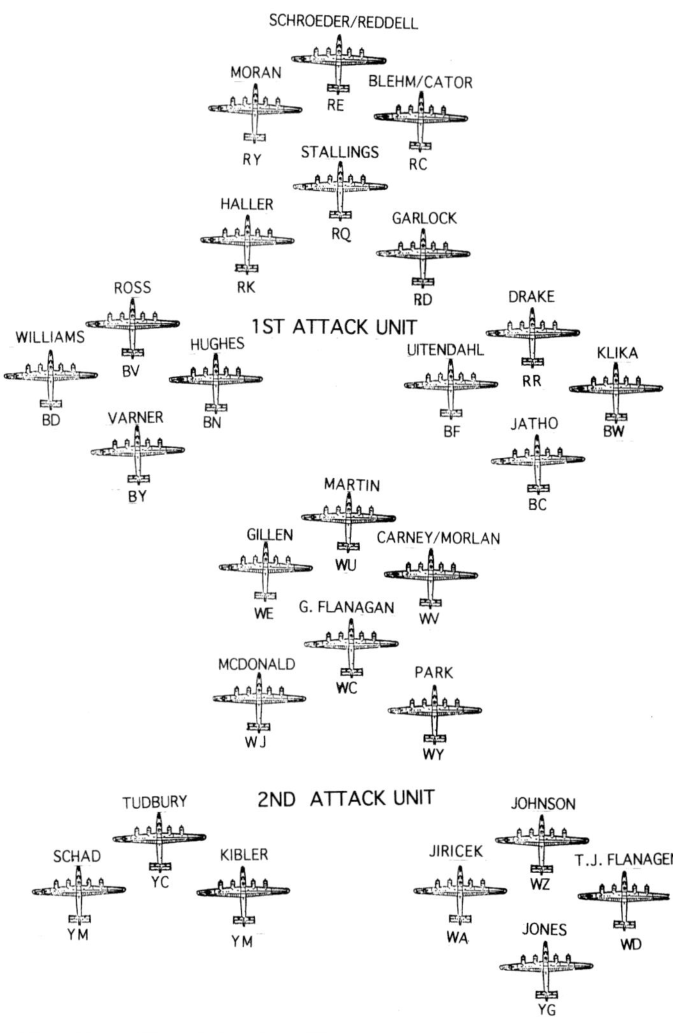

Route chart for the July 8, 1944, mission.

Left: Formation Chart for the mission on July 8, 1944.

Black-Z (779th) sustained this damage on July 15, 1944.

When the daily reports from the 464th reached 15th Air Force Headquarters it was realized that because of losses and battle damage sustained during the last several days the 464th could not continue flying missions until replacement aircraft were assigned and the battle damage repaired. The survivors of the mission and the men on the ground had no way of knowing it at the time, but the 464th had just earned its first Distinguished Unit Citation.

The two day stand down gave everyone—except the ground crews, of course—a chance to relax and catch their breath. For those on the hardstands it was the usual 14 to 16 hour day, though this time it was during the day instead of at night under the lights. Damaged engines were changed, and systems checked and repaired as needed. Sheet metal crews patched the major flak holes. Smaller holes were simply covered with masking tape and painted for the time being. It was a quick fix, but at least the crews could not see any daylight through the skin of the plane. There was not much time to take a break and go to the mess tent. If the crew chiefs were lucky someone would bring them a cold Spam sandwich and maybe a cup of good old Army java.

On the 11th the target was the oil storage facility at Porto Marghera, Italy. The group got off the ground, formed up, and headed for the target. The mission was recalled after the group had made it out over the Adriatic—another "no credit" day for the 464th.

The group was back up to regular strength on 12 July. At 0615 hrs the first plane left the ground and climbed into the sky. The mission for the day was to the marshaling yards at Mimes, France. By 0725 there were 37 planes in the air, formed up and rendezvoused with the 465th.

Just short of the IP the mission started to fall apart. The 465th was in the lead position for the wing. For some reason they made a correction to the left and then turned sharply back to the right, and the 464th made a sharp turn to avoid collision. This put the 464th

White-T of the 465th joins the 464th for a mission.

A refueling truck arrives to top off the fuel tanks on LITTLE ONE prior to a mission.

out of position for the bomb run. Several planes bombed what they believed to be the target. The rest of the group dropped 40 tons of bombs on the briefed target, then rallied left for the coast.

The FLYIN PHARTSAC (42-28999), flown by Lt. Harry Stroud Jr.'s crew, was last seen off the coast with the #1 prop feathered and turning away from the group to a heading that would take them to Spain. The crew managed to land and were interned. Several managed to "escape" and return to the group in October.

The group returned to the base at about 1450 hrs. that afternoon. Three planes landed at other bases due to being short on fuel. CRACK UP (42-52357) lived up to her name. She had been badly damaged on the mission, and the ship just could not make it home. The crew abandoned her between Bari and Pantanella.

Thursday the 13th found 37 planes in the air and formed up in two attack units as usual. Three planes aborted the mission due to mechanical problems.

When the group arrived at the IP the target was totally covered by clouds, so the mission leader turned the group towards the Mantua Marshaling Yards. There were clouds at this target, also. There was no flak in the area, so the lead ship maneuvered the group to make a second run after making a 180 degree turn and coming back over the target. Believe it or not, the trick worked. The group was able to drop their bombs and rallied for home without a single burst of flak. Everyone made it back from a rather strange type of "milk run."

On 14 July the planes lifted into the air, starting at 0600 hrs. The 464th put 37 B-24s up for the mission. Porto Marghers was the primary target for the day. One plane suffered a ground abort, and three others aborted after getting into the air.

Everything went well until the formation reached the IP. Complete cloud cover obscured the target. The group turned and headed for the secondary target, which was also covered by clouds. The target of last resort was the marshaling yards at Mantua, Italy. Since they had been there yesterday they figured they would take another crack at it.

The remaining 34 planes dropped another load of high explosives on the rail yards and headed for home at 0948 hrs. No flak, no fighters, so it was another milk run.

The 15th found the group scheduled for another crack at the oil fields of Ploesti. Next to Vienna, Ploesti was one of the most dreaded targets a group could draw from the target folder. Oil was the lifeblood of the German war machine, and they defended it as if the Reich depended on it to stay alive, which it did.

The first of the 38 planes lumbered into the sky at 0630 hrs. Just getting airborne was half the battle. Each plane carried maximum fuel, ammo, and a lethal load of 5 1,000 pound bombs. Ploesti was always a long mission, and no one was ever happy to see it as a target.

Group form up and rendezvous were routine. The 55th was the next to last wing in the mission formation going to Ploesti. The 464th was the last group in the 55th Wing. That meant that the 464th would be a long way back in the bomber stream. The German flak gunners would have plenty of time to find the range and fill the sky with flak.

Between take off and reaching the Adriatic, seven planes aborted with mechanical problems. The remaining planes were in the usual two attack elements. The first was led by Lt./Col. McKenna, Deputy Group Commander. The second unit was led by the 464th Commanding Officer, Col. Schroeder.

Before the group arrived at the IP they could see the results of the previous strikes on the target. From over a hundred miles away they could see thick clouds of smoke boiling up to about 20,000 feet. The group was now flying at about 22,000 feet, so they would not have to fly through the thick oil smoke.

The flak opened up on the group at the IP. As usual it was the Ploesti variety of flak, intense and accurate. At the IP, 42-50408 (776th) left the formation with the #4 engine smoking from a flak hit. They skirted the target and rejoined the formation as they came off the target.

White-Z (778th), THE GREEN HORNET, headed for the target.

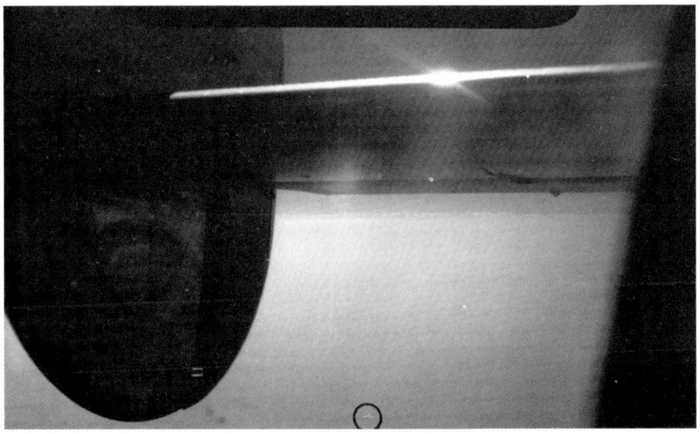

A B-24 from another group headed down under control on July 20, 1944.

The stricken Liberator falls toward the ground.

As the crew bails out the plane erupts into a ball of flame.

Finally, the plane breaks apart in flaming chunks of debris.

The group arrived over the target at 1059 hrs. and dropped 75 tons of bombs by Pathfinder (radar). The target was covered by smoke and flames from the other attacks and a visual bomb run was impossible. Accurate results of the bomb run were also impossible.

Flak over the target was very accurate. White-B (42-78261) took a direct hit just behind the waist guns, and the blast literally cut the plane in half. The front lurched forward and fell into a steep dive, while the tail tumbled away trailing debris. A gunner in the plane directly behind remarked that the plane "fell like a dead duck." Lt. Benjamin Folsom and his crew never had a chance to escape. They were pinned in the dying Liberator and rode it to the ground.

As the formation flew back towards Italy, 42-50408 started having problems with the #3 engine. Copilot Richard Ferris reached up to hit the feathering button on the #3 engine, then pulled the throttle back to idle-cutoff and cut the ignition switch. With only two good engines the plane left the formation and started down at about 100 feet per minute. They continued down until they faced the Yusterbutz mountain range. Bruce Cator knew they would never get over the top of the peaks, so he turned the limping Liberator to a parallel course with the range. Shortly after getting the plane turned Cator gave the bail out signal, and all of the crew managed to bail out. Most of the crew landed in the mountains. It took several days for them to get together after being found by local partisans. They would be listed as missing, although they would be returned to Allied hands.

Twenty-eight planes returned to Pantanella at about 1417 hrs. Another arrived late after setting down at Bari for gas. Twelve planes had suffered battle damage from flak. For the 464th it was one of the easiest missions they had ever flown to Ploesti. That is, if you could call it an easy mission!

At 0630 hrs on 16 July, B-24s from the 464th started heading down the steel mat runway again. The heavily laden planes made a lot of noise. One pilot remarked that the sound of a plane on take off reminded him of dumping a load of tin cans onto the ground. He always knew when the plane was airborne because the racket stopped.

Thirty planes managed to get off the ground, formed up, and headed for Wiener Nuesdorf. The aircraft engine factory there was the primary target for the day. Maj. Moore (777th CO) led the first attack unit, while Capt. Fowler (779th) would lead the second unit.

Near Lake Balaton the group was joined by P-38s from the 306th Fighter Wing, which would provide cover for the penetration. It was always a comforting feeling to have fighter escort just in case the Luftwaffe showed up.

At the IP the Luftwaffe did show up. About 40 enemy fighters headed for the group. The P-38s were on the ball and bounced the oncoming Me-109s, and the fight was on. About 25 of the "black crossed" fighters broke through the escort and attacked the formation.

"Fighters coming in, six o'clock!" The attack was very aggressive, closing to within 150 feet of the bombers before breaking to the left and right, then diving away to reform for another attack on the Liberators.

The first attack damaged several of the planes. THE KENTUCKY COLONEL (42-52487) was hit hard in the tail. 20mm shells had riddled the tail turret, wounding the gunner's head. Although badly damaged, THE KENTUCKY COLONEL stayed with the formation.

Fighter attacks had dealt a death blow to THE BLACK FOX (41-29398), flown by Lt. James Jatho and crew from the 779th. The plane had been hit in the #3 engine and bomb bay. The engine was steaming fire and smoke past the tail turret. Two men were seen leaving the plane from the waist area. The ship was last seen heading down under control. Everyone managed to escape from the falling Liberator except T/Sgt. William Magill.

BOOZIN SUSAN (42-52502) was hit in the #2 engine and fell from the formation with her wing on fire. Pilot Lt. Richard Williams and four other crew members were able to hit the silk before the fire ravished wing folded and broke away, taking the rest of the crew to their deaths.

THE MIDDLE DIGIT (42-95372) was last seen headed down with the #3 engine on fire. Three chutes were seen to open before the plane was lost from sight. Three other crewmen were able to jump before the plane hit the ground.

The fighters broke off and the flak opened up. Two minutes before the target Maj. Moore's lead ship was hit by flak, causing a bad fuel leak from the #3 engine and the bomb bay area. Maj. Moore stayed in the lead and got the formation over the target.

Bombs away was at 1030 hrs. as 52 tons of bombs fell towards the cloud covered target. As the bombs fell Maj. Moore pulled out of the lead position and let the Deputy Lead take over the formation.

As the group rallied for home the flak continued to blossom about the sky. Several planes took more hits before the formation could fly beyond the range of the flak guns. They were now relatively safe from the flak, but what about enemy fighters? Thankfully, the fighters had reached their fuel limits and left the area. All the 464th had to do now was fly back to Italy.

Coming back, three damaged planes landed at the island of Vis. The planes and crews returned after refueling and repairs. THE KENTUCKY COLONEL managed to make it back to Foggia for a crash landing. The wounded tail gunner was sent to the hospital. THE KENTUCKY COLONEL was declared Class-26.

As the planes came over the base the men on the ground took the usual count to see if everybody had made it back. Sadly there were gaps in the formation. One by one the planes landed and taxied to their hardstands. At BOOZIN SUSAN's hardstand crew chief Lonnie McMichaels waited for his plane to land and taxi back. Even after all the planes were down he waited with growing concern. Maybe she was one of the planes that was at Vis? Maybe she had landed at another friendly field? Finally, the gut wrenching reality caught up to "Mac"; his plane and crew had been lost over the target. For the moment he did not have a plane to worry about. He moved over to another hardstand and started helping. He tried to hide it, but everyone knew how "Mac" was feeling. The other ground crewmen did not say too much when they saw "Mac" wipe a tear from his eye.

The B-24 was close to a million different parts flying in very close formation through the air. The crew chief and his ground crew had to have intimate knowledge of just how those parts fitted and functioned. After all, the lives of the flight crew would depend on just how well the ground crew maintained the plane. The men who serviced the Liberators took their work very seriously. They worked hard to "keep 'em flying" no matter what the operations orders called for. They put in long sleepless nights to make sure that their ship was ready for "stations" in the morning. The bill of their fatigue cap was turned up from peering into the dark cramped spaces that they had to work in. Their hands were stained with oil and hydraulic fluid, and their fatigues were almost always covered with at least two shades of grime. Only another crew chief could understand how McMichaels felt when a ship did not return to the hardstand.

The 464th stood down on 17 July. On the 18th they got off the ground, but the mission was recalled before reaching the target.

On 19 July the flight crews were awakened before "O light hundred." Breakfast was the usual bill of fare. Still half asleep, the crews shuffled to the briefing tent to find out why they had been rousted out of the sack so early.

The mission was going to be a long one. The target for the day was the Aircraft Engine Factory at Allach, Germany. Since it was a strike into Germany the mission had all the aspects of being a rough one for the group.

When the crews arrived at their ships the hardstands were already a beehive of activity. The ground crews had the planes ready and were busy "pulling the props" to get the oil out of the bottom of the cylinders. When the crew was ready, the crew chief would stand fire guard on the #3 as the pilots primed the engine when the fuel pressure reached 4 lbs. The big Hamilton Standard prop began to turn, and the engine would catch and belch blue-gray smoke as she came to life. The throttle was moved to auto-rich and the eyes of the flight crew danced to the oil pressure gauge to make sure the pressure was coming up. When everything was ready, a small nudge of the throttle would get the big Liberator moving and headed towards the taxi strip.

At 0655 hrs the planes began taking off. Each one was loaded to the maximum with fuel, ammo, and bombs. All 34 B-24s made it into the air. The first attack unit was led by Maj. Clarence Poff (778th CO), while the second unit would be led by Capt. Robert Wingfield.

Fighter cover was provided by P-51s and P-38s for the entire trip to and from the target. Since they were headed for Germany the fighters just might come in very handy if the Luftwaffe's Focke Wulfes came sniffing around.

Lt. Raymond Drake was in the left seat of ROUGH AND READY (42-52402) when the #2 engine started running rough and belching a little smoke. He had little choice but to shut the engine down and feather the prop. He was a little upset, to say the least; he had just aborted on what would have been his 50th mission.

As the gunners fired a short burst to check and clear their guns an empty casing struck the top turret on SHOO SHOO BABY (42-52563). The empty casing smashed through the Plexiglas and hit the gunner in the head. He was knocked out for a moment. SHOO SHOO BABY also aborted the mission.

The planes reached 20,000 feet and hurdled the Alps. The formation tightened up for protection. Across the formation many of the crewmen realized that this was a "big one." As far as the eye could see there were formations of B-24s headed in the same direction. Just before reaching the IP, a small fire broke out in the electrical equipment on LITTLE ONE (42-78339), flown by Lt. Tom McDonald's crew. They managed to control the fire. Then the #1 prop ran away. Quick action by McDonald and copilot Lt. John Rucigay got the engine shut down and the prop feathered. With only three good engines the plane descended to about 16,000 feet. The bombardier, Lt. Joseph Lidiak, salvoed the bombs on a target of opportunity near the outskirts of Munich.

Twenty-eight planes reached the target at about 1145 hrs and dropped 70 tons of bombs onto the target. A large workshop took two direct hits. Another workshop on a railway siding also took a direct hit. A large secondary explosion was recorded in a fuel dump just to the north of the factory. The results were very good for this mission. The German fighter resistance should dwindle in the near future. A fighter needs an engine, and a lot of manufacturing capability had gone up in smoke.

After bombs away the group made a sharp rally to the left. This took the formation out of the flak after being under fire for about five minutes. Five minutes was all it took for SLEEPY TIME GAL (42-99813). The plane had taken a hit in an engine and slowly descended to about 10,000 feet. About 30 minutes after the target the wounded plane was seen on a heading that should take SLEEPY TIME GAL and her crew to Switzerland.

Just before the formation left the flak area it had scored a hit on HOME FOR CHRISTMAS (42-52437), flown by Lt. Roy Anderson's crew. They had already taken a few hits over the target. The bombardier, Lt. Bruce Callender, had taken some scratches on the face when the Plexiglas in front of the bombsight had been hit.

HOME FOR CHRISTMAS shuddered from the impact of an 88mm shell. The shell went through the wing between the #1 and #2 engine. For some unexplained reason the shell did not go off on impact. The hole and jagged aluminum killed the smooth airflow over the wing, causing the B-24 to act more like a bucking bronco than an airplane. The crew was called from their stations and told to prepare for bail out.

The pilots were finally able to get the plane under better control, that is, if holding the plane in a 20 degree bank can be called control. The pilot gave the crew the option of bailing out or staying with the ship. The entire crew stayed with their airplane for the ride home.

It was a long ride home for several other B-24s. BIG FAT MAMA landed at San Severo to refuel, then returned to Pantanella. LITTLE ONE (42-78339) was trying to get home alone. The #2 engine failed after the target, and the electrical system went out. There was no power to any of the gun turrets or radio, and most of the instruments were out. LITTLE ONE limped over the Alps with the #2 propeller windmilling and causing even more drag. A few German fighters started after LITTLE ONE, but were driven off by a flight of American fighters that just happened across the lone B-24. LITTLE ONE limped on until they were near Pola, Italy, where they lost the #3 engine. They had no choice but to bail out, as LITTLE ONE was losing altitude at about 500 feet per minute. It seemed that everyone got out before LITTLE ONE erased herself in a ball of fire. Nine of the crew survived and spent over a month with Yugoslav partisans. The bombardier, Lt. Robert Denison, was missing and presumed to have perished. He was later returned to Allied control.

As HOME FOR CHRISTMAS neared Pantanella the pilot again gave the crew the chance to get out and walk. They figured that riding beats walking, so they stayed with the plane again.

The landing gear came down without a problem. Pilot Anderson and copilot Ernest Astroff held the 20 degree bank until just before the plane settled onto the PSP. At the last second they brought the wings level, pulled the power off, and flared the B-24 onto the runway. It was a nifty piece of flying.

Back at the hardstand the crew looked at the hole in the wing. It had just clipped the wing spar, but had missed the landing gear, fuel lines, and control cables. Bombardier Callender admitted to feeling a little queasy after seeing the hole in the wing.

Bruce Callender remembered that usually after a mission he would trade his ration of combat booze for a coke if anyone had one. After this mission he took the whiskey and thought it had been a long day.

On the 20th the 464th put 35 planes into the air to hit the Zeppelin Works at Friedrichaffen, Germany. Six planes aborted the mission due to mechanical problems.

The 464th seemed to be in the right place at the right moment on this mission. Groups all around the 464th lost planes to both flak and fighters. The 464th came through without any of the planes being damaged or anyone injured by enemy action.

When the planes returned to base Lt. Raymond Drake pulled his MAIDEN USA (42-78392) out of the formation and proceeded to lay down a fantastic buzz job for the boys on the ground. He had just completed his 50 missions over Europe and was headed home just as soon as the paperwork could be filled out. He was the first member of the group to finish his tour of duty and had done it in record time.

The flight crews did not know it at the time, but at almost the same time their bombs were hitting the target, another bomb went off. This one was at Hitler's headquarters, known as the "Wulfes Lair." It was an attempt by several high ranking officers to kill Hitler and end the war.

The group took Friday, 21 July off from flying any combat missions. While the flight crews rested, the ground crews used the extra time as usual. Inspections were completed as outlined in the tech manuals. Repairs to any flak damage that had not been done was done in record time so the planes would be ready again when the call came down from 55th Wing.

Contrary to popular belief, the planes did not belong to the flight crews. In a lot of cases they were privileged to paint the name on the side of the ship. No, the plane did not belong to the Army Air Force, either. Despite what the crews and Uncle Sam thought, the planes actually belonged to the crew chief and his ground crew. They were the men who sweated blood over the planes. They spent countless hours fixing the damage and worn systems on the ships until they were as perfect as humanly possible. If it had not been for these heroes the planes would have never gotten of the ground. Yep, the plane belonged to the crew chief; he was just loaning it to the flight crews.

At the briefing on the morning of 22 July an audible moan was heard coming from the briefing tent when the target was revealed. It was Ploesti again! This would be the fourth mission the group had flown to that dreaded target, and no one was looking forward to the trip.

The planes began taking off at 0730 hrs. Thirty-four overloaded planes struggled into the air. When the last plane was airborne the rattling of the PSP went silent until their return, and the group formed into the usual two attack elements. Col. Schroeder led the group on this mission.

Because of low clouds in the area, rendezvous with the rest of the 55th Wing was delayed for about five minutes. Visual contact could not be made, and Col. Schroeder was not about to lead the formation into clouds with all of those other groups milling about in the general area. At last visual contact was made and the 464th slid into position.

All the way to the target area there was trouble keeping the bomber stream together. One group then another would wander out of place for a few miles, then another would slide out of place. As a result, the bomber stream was strung out for miles across the Romanian sky. A bad situation, as it would give the flak batteries a chance to reorient their fire to each group as it passed over.

As the group neared the IP, Col. Schroeder passed the lead to the Deputy Lead when the Pathfinder radar equipment in his ship went on the fritz. Since the target would be covered with smoke from previous attacks, the bomb run would most likely have to be done by radar.

The flak batteries served up the usual Ploesti greeting of intense, accurate, and heavy flak. Some of it seemed to explode into two parts, shaped like a dumbbell. Flak scored a hit on MAIDEN USA (42-78392), flown by Lt. Dale Gutherie's crew from the 777th. The pilots shut down the flak torn engine and managed to stay in the formation.

Just before bombs away, a burst of flak hit the lead plane of the second attack element in the bomb bay area. 42-51136 was a new "Mickey" ship and on its first mission. The flak burst started a fire in the bomb bay. The rudder cables had also been hit. T/Sgt. Richard Straw left his tail turret and moved to the bomb bay to fight the fire with a small extinguisher. The #3 and #4 engines lost power, then the #4 caught fire. Copilot Lt. Guy Hudson recalled:

Our aircraft commander, Major Blehm, although he had not ordered abandonment of the aircraft, did at this point proceed to bail out through the bomb bay.

A combination of power on the left side and no rudder control caused the plane to fall into a flat spin towards the ground. Hudson wrote:

I have always had great respect for Frank (Lt. Frank Hayes, radar operator, on his first mission). As the ship augured on down that day, Frank could only see one chest pack on the flight deck lying between his position and my seat. Thinking it was mine he was scrambling around the flight deck on all fours, flat spin and all, trying to find his chute. It was not until he saw me get my pack from in front of the seat that he grabbed his and bailed out. A lesser man would have been long gone. As I bailed out of the ship through the open bomb bay, I saw Sgt. Straw's body wedged near the rear of the bomb bay, engulfed in flames.

The bombardier, Lt. Ray Williams, went out through the nose-wheel. He saw Sgt. Newhaus and Lt. Kahn leave the plane and their chutes billow. They were both killed, either in the air or on the ground. The rest of the crew from the back of the plane rode the stricken Liberator to the ground. Lt. Hudson landed near a burning refinery complex and hid in a bomb crater. He and the rest of the survivors were captured. Sgt. Straw was awarded the Silver Star posthumously for his efforts to save the plane and crew.

Bombs Away was called at 1145 hrs as the remaining 28 planes released over 70 tons of bombs towards the smoke covered target. As the bombs fell the group began to rally to the right and head for home. Up to this point the crews had been flying for Uncle Sam. Now with their bombs delivered, they were flying for themselves and their crewmates.

After the target several Me-109s were spotted near the formation. It looked like they were getting ready to attack the 464th. A quick call to the fighter escort brought the P-38s screaming in for the rescue. The Me-109s spotted the P-38s and dove for the ground before they arrived.

MAIDEN USA was still with the formation, but just barely. Navigator William Schneider recalled:

We passed over Vis, but felt we could make it back to Pantanella. When we were about half way over the Adriatic Sea, at about 1600 hrs, we lost one more engine. Then, almost immediately, the other two engines quit. I figure that we must have been hit in the fuel transfer system, because we had enough gas to reach our base. The pilot tried to ditch the plane. There were 4 to 5 foot waves in the sea, and we hit nose down at about 120 mph. The section in front of the wings broke off, as did the tail section back of the ball turret. I was sitting in the waist section with my back to the bomb bay bulkhead. The ball gunner, Toledo (Louis Toledo), sat opposite me. After we hit the water, I was upside down beneath the surface and my leg was caught in the ammo belts. When I untangled myself I was able to reach the ball gunner, whose life jacket was punctured and of no use. The life rafts were broken and would not inflate. William Weber, the engineer, was alive in the water, but we could not reach him and he died before the PBY Dumbo picked us up."

The survivors would spend over two hours in the water before being rescued.

When the planes arrived at Pantanella, they found it was one of the few bases that had not been closed by weather. There were B-24s all over the place, with about every tail marking in the 15th Air Force represented. By the time the last plane landed, Racecard tower was calling for marginal landing conditions due to the blowing dust and threatening thunderstorms.

The 464th newspaper *Bomb Blast* for 22 July showed the headline "Herky Heads Home." The story outlined the highlights of "Herky" Drake's 50 missions. He was headed home. MAIDEN USA, which he had flown overseas and that had seen him through many of his missions lay broken at the bottom of the Adriatic.

The group stood down on the 23rd and 24th due to bad weather in Italy and over targets in Europe. Locally, a strong frontal system had invaded the Italian boot and was causing high winds and blowing dust. The wind was almost strong enough to cause the movie for the night to be canceled. Nonetheless, a few brave souls treked to the outdoor movie area to see "The Bridge at San Luis Rey."

On the 25th the 464th put 39 B-24s into the air for a mission to the Herman Göring Tank Works at Linz, Austria. The mission was under the command of Capt. Bill Reddell, commander of the 776th BS. The second element would be led by Capt. John Nance.

Take off, form up, and wing rendezvous were delayed because of hazy conditions. At times visibility was only three to five miles. The 464th and 465th finally got things sorted out and found the rest of the 55th Wing.

Over the Italian spur the gunners cleared their guns with several short bursts. Everyone was ready in case the German fighters showed up. Fighter escort appeared, and the fliers breathed a little easier. If the Germans did show up the P-51s and P-38s would take care of them.

At the IP the German fighters did not show up, but the flak sure did. It seemed that the batteries were firing in salvoes, and the flak was scattered all over the sky. Some was high, while some of it was low and off to one side of the group. Several of the escort fighters were carrying chaff canisters. These were designed to open and spread a cloud of aluminum foil streamers to confuse the radar controlled guns on the ground. Today, it seemed to be working.

At 1128 hrs 82 tons of bombs were toggled towards the smoke obscured target. Results were still excellent, with hits on a transformer station, railways, and the southwest section of the steel works.

The group rallied for home. One plane was hit by flak and was last seen with the #2 engine smoking and the prop feathered. Flak had also wounded nose gunner Robert Lamb. It was not a serious wound, just a scratch on the cheek. It was just enough for a Purple Heart.

The flight home was according to the briefing, though there was a slight detour near Klagenfurt to avoid a nasty flak area. One plane landed at Foggia to refuel and then flew on to Pantanella. The rest of the formation came home, landed, and taxied to their hardstands.

During the summer it can get very warm and dusty on the hardstands in Italy. Nothing could cut the dust and heat better then a cold can of beer. The problem was how to get it cold! Sgt. M.E. "Steve" Stephenson of the 779th used good old Yankee know how to solve the problem. He and his ground crew would put their weekly ration of beer on their plane before it took off for a mission. Since the missions were flown at high altitude, the beer was chilled by the time the plane landed. The ground crew would meet the plane, get their beer, and have an ice cold brew. This generally went well, except on one occasion, the flight crew found the beer stash and drank it. After that it became a contest for the ground crew to hide the beer and the flight crew to try and find it. "Steve" and his ground crew knew when the fliers had found the beer. He recalled that several times the plane would fly over before landing and bomb the hardstand with the empty cans. One night, as the ground crew worked on the plane for the next day's mission they came up with an idea to keep their beer safe from the marauding fly boys. They pulled a crew chief stand up under the wing, removed an access panel, and put their beer in the wing. To keep it from moving around they used masking tape to secure it to the spars and ribs. Just let the flight crew try and get their beer now! It is a well documented fact that many ground crews used the same basic method to chill their beer. Countless cans of the amber liquid flew combat missions throughout the war. Many groundcrews went thirsty if their plane did not return.

The 26th found 38 planes of the 464th headed towards the Zwolfaxing Air Drome near Vienna, Austria. It was another early morning take off for the long haul to the flak infested area of Vienna. One plane suffered a ground abort, and another aborted after form up.

Flak dotted the sky as the group turned at the IP. For the next 15 minutes the group would be within range of the guns on the ground. On top of the flak, the first and second attack units got separated. The first unit arrived over the target and dropped their bombs at 1131. The second unit missed the primary target and dropped their bombs on an airdrome near Bad Voslau.

The group rallied for home, but they happened to rally right over a heavy concentration of guns. The group was bracketed by the first angry puffs. One Liberator was hit in the #2 engine, then took another hit in the #4 engine. The first hit caused the engine to catch fire, while the #4 engine was throwing a little oil but still turning. The plane could not keep up with the formation. The crew began throwing out everything that was not needed to fly the plane. After what seemed the longest flight in history, the plane managed to limp home to Pantanella. All of the other planes on the mission had made it back. Thirteen planes had taken battle damage. Four of the Liberators would be sitting on the hardstands for several days before they were fit enough to fly again.

Eight crewmen had been injured by flak, and several were taken to the hospital. The most serious was S/Sgt. Peter Doelder from the 776th. He had been hit several times while manning his nose turret. In spite of good medical attention, the nose gunner would die in October from his injuries.

When Col. Schroeder talked with the debriefing officers and read the mission reports he was furious. As a result, he wrote an addendum to the mission report. He stated that the mission "was a failure due to poor discipline in flight and faulty navigation." He blamed the navigator of the second unit for the separation between the two elements. Those who knew Col. Schroeder knew that there would be a certain navigator being called on the carpet.

The 464th stood down for the next two days. In view of the fouled up mission on the 26th, Col. Schroeder had the crews up in the air flying practice missions. The group concentrated on maintaining formation integrity and navigation. Now according to the book, the best formation for defense had to have the planes close together. That meant about 55 feet from wingtip to wingtip and 55 feet from nose to tail in the combat boxes.

On the 28th the briefing was subdued when the target curtain was pulled back. Ploesti again! It looked like another trip to hell. The first plane took off at 0600 hrs. The mission would be led by Maj. Weldon Burton, Group Operations Officer. The group got into the air, formed up, and headed out over the Adriatic in record time.

Six planes aborted the mission. SOUTHERN COMFORT (42-52514) aborted when an empty .50 cal. shell casing came through the windshield, making a six inch hole.

The formation flew across the Adriatic to Yugoslavia and into Bulgaria. They crossed the Danube River and noted that it was a muddy brown, not blue like the song. The flight to the target was long and full of thoughts of the unknown laying ahead of the formation. Crews delt with the tension in many ways. William Hedge was the nose gunner on Donald Nance's crew. He recalled how their crew broke some of the ice:

Jack Harr's mind was not bound to his field of vision from the seat in the tail turret. It needed more activity than searching the skies for the specks that could turn into fighters. We had no more then four or five missions under our belts until Jack comes on the intercom "Hey, Nick! There's a Gremlin on the wing behind number four!" Glad of some of the relief from the endless waiting and watching, the idea appeals to the crew and there's some response. Jack's Gremlin had to have a name, so he dubbed him George F. Ploesti. I don't remember hearing what the F was for. I assumed it was for Flak. Later a female counterpart appeared on the elevator. This was Josephine.

That we profited from it was just a side benefit. Jack and Nick were the main participants in the George and Josephine drama. To the rest of us, it was akin to turning on a radio comedy program. "Hey, Nick! George is cutting the safety wire on the number one gas cap!" One instantly visualizes one hundred octane gasoline

BUTCH M LOVE on the way to Ploesti, July 28, 1944.

streaming back over the wing, and the strong possibility of fire. At best, running out of fuel long before reaching home. "Hey, Harr! George is swapping tubes in your radio!" From any kind of start it could go on for five to fifteen minutes. Tensions relaxed, and drowsiness was replaced by new alertness.

You say childish foolishness! What possible place can this child's play have on a quarter million dollar machine bound to or from its mission of death and destruction, in which the machine and its occupants might reap the same fate? Well, weren't we kids? Hardly dry behind the ears. Yes, we were just kids, but situation sometimes demanded and made us mature far beyond our years. I don't think Jack went into deep Greek philosophical thought over this. It was just his fun loving way of getting life into an otherwise very somber situation. It worked very well.

Flak greeted the formation as they turned at the IP. About thirty German fighters were also waiting for the group near the IP. The German fighters were bounced by the escort and the dog fight was on. At least the bombers would not have to worry about the Luftwaffe.

Seconds before bombs away Yellow-I (41-29275) took a tremedous blast from flak. The stricken B-24 drifted out of position. What happened next is unclear. Several witnesses say that bombs from a higher plane hit the stricken Liberator, while others dispute the bomb theory. Either from falling bombs or flak, Yellow-I was erased in a sickeningly blinding explosion. Sgt. Robert Stein and T/Sgt. Robert Tong were blown clear and managed to pull the rip cord on their chutes. The rest of the crew was killed.

Directly behind the exploding Liberator was Red-B (44-40497), flown by Lt. Lewis Perkins. He had no time to avoid the fireball. Perkins held course 350 degrees and entered the ball of flames and debris. They emerged, but the plane was damaged. The #1 engine had to be shut down. The fireball had damaged the left aileron and burned most of the control surfaces away from the rudder. The plane shuddered and momentarily went out of control.

Fire from the exploding B-24 had been sucked into Red-B's bomb bay. Copilot Lloyd Aclin began to unbuckle his seat belt to bail out, but he stayed in his seat when he saw Perkins fighting to save the bucking Liberator. While the pilots fought for control, Bombardier Lt. Francis Marley and Sgt. Bronislaus Pizion figured that the plane was going down and bailed out over the target area. The pilots managed to regain control and told the rest of the crew to "sit tight."

During any one given mission that was flown by the crews of the 464th Liberators, there were always fleeting items that stuck in the minds of those who were there. Sometimes it was a very small thing that would be remembered. William Loughlin recalled:

On my first trip to Ploesti on July 28, 1944, over the target the flak was heavy, black puffs all around. Something happened up ahead and I saw, out of the corner of my eye, something go by my window. I realized later that it was a crewman from a B-24 up ahead that had been hit by flak and the crew was abandoning ship. His chute was not open at the time. I still don't know how or if he missed all the other aircraft in the formation.

Bombs away was called at 1021 hrs as 76 tons of bombs rained down on the target. The group rallied left and ran into several Me-109s that were prowling for cripples, but the escorting P-51s drove them away before they could attack the formation. The formation flew back to Italy along the briefed route.

When the formation approached the base the ground crews grabbed their glasses and made a quick count of the returning planes. They came up two planes short of what they had sent out that morning.

Red-B was one of the missing planes. She was still in the air fighting for her life and the lives of her crew. With an engine out and burned control surfaces, Pilot Lewis Perkins and crew were having a hard time staying in the air. They had thrown out most of their ammo belts and everything else that was not nailed down. Cameras, flak vests, and other gear went into the slipstream, and they tried to get the plane light enough to stay in the air.

To add to their woes, there was a problem with the fuel transfer system. They could not crossfeed from the left to the right wing tanks. Within sight of the Adriatic the engines started to cough and sputter. The crew had no choice but to hit the silk. The remaining eight crewmen bailed out and became the guests of the Chetnicks. Several of the crew would spend the rest of the war with the Chetnicks.

The Adventures of George F. Ploesti.

Sgt. John "Jake" Schuffert was flying as a replacement on Red-B that day. He had been an original member of "Herky" Drake's crew. Now he was trying to get his "magic 50th" in and go home. He made it out and would later return to Allied Control. "Jake" always had a good sense of humor and liked to draw cartoons. He had painted a lot of the nose art on the planes of the group. After the war, many members of the Air Force would get a chuckle from his cartoon segment "No Sweat," which appeared in many military publications.

On 30 July the crews were briefed for a mission to the Duna Aircraft Factory at Budapest, Hungary. It was going to be another long mission into German held territory. Some of the crewmen tried to figure out if this mission would count as a double credit. Even if the mission did not count as a "double," it was still a milestone for the 464th. If they completed the mission, it would be the 50th mission that the group had made against the Third Reich.

The first of the 39 planes lifted into the air at 0730 hrs. One plane aborted on the ground, and three others aborted after take off due to mechanical problems. That reduced the bomber formation by four planes, or forty defensive guns in case the Luftwaffe showed up.

The fighter escort showed up out over the Adriatic. The bomber stream was headed towards the target, and finally the gunners were cleared to test fire and clear their guns.

Just after turning at the IP, 10 Me-109s came out of nowhere and attacked the group from 3 o'clock high. The Me-109s suddenly broke off the attack and headed for the group directly behind the 464th. They attacked that group head on, then dove through it and started to reform for another attack. The escort fighters were on the ball and drove the enemy fighters away.

Just as the group reached the target area the first bursts of flak appeared. It was intense, accurate, and heavy. Before the group reached the release point the flak was getting very heavy, no matter how much chaff was thrown out of the planes. It would take the group about three minutes to clear the flak. That was more than enough time for the flak gunners to score.

ROUGH AND READY (42-52402) from the 776th was being flown by Lt. Paul Kirkland and crew. Within seconds of the first burst of flak their plane took a devastating burst between the #3 engine and the fuselage. The burst opened a huge hole near the cockpit. Immediately, the #3 engine emitted smoke. At almost the same moment a bomb from an overhead plane struck the left wing, tearing the #2 engine from its mounts. The engine twisted off the wing, came through the fuselage, and ended up on the flight deck, near the forward part of the bomb bay. Kirkland and copilot Michael Voytish fought the dying Liberator for enough time so the crew could bail out.

In the nose, bombardier Leslie Schwien helped the nose gunner climb out of the turret, then both of them went through the nose wheel hatch. Apparently the navigator, Lt. Earl McDonald, hit the tail of the aircraft as he bailed out. His chute never opened.

Back in the tail section the tail gunner had vacated his turret and bailed out of the camera hatch. The waist gunners managed to get the ball turret back up into the plane and the gunner out before they also hit the silk. On the flight deck the crew appeared trapped. They could not get to the bomb bay because of the embedded engine. In desperation these men escaped through the large flak hole in the side of the fuselage. Sgt. Fred Cook delayed his jump too long before pulling the D-Ring on his chute. It never fully opened before he hit the ground, and he was killed. Eight of the crew made it to the ground alive to become guests of the Germans.

At 1115 hrs the 464th dropped over 85 tons of RDX towards the target and rallied for home. More German fighters showed up near Lake Balaton on the way home. The P-51s escorting the group drove them off before they could attack the homeward bound bombers. One of the Me-109s did manage to break through and get close

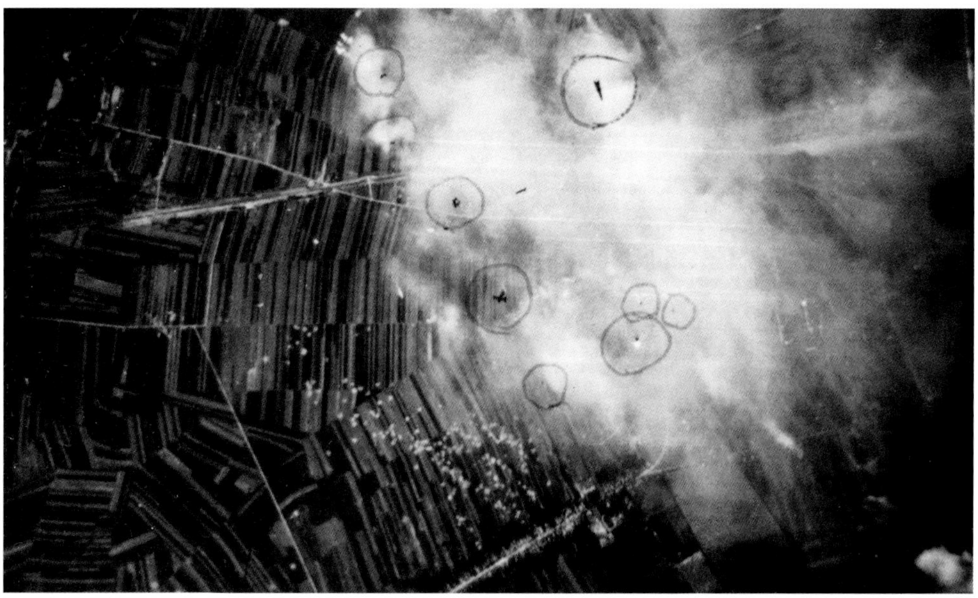

Cameras caught this Liberator heading down with sections falling away on July 28, 1944.

enough for one of the 464th gunners to give him a short burst of defensive fire as the 109 flashed by on the way to another group.

When the planes landed, the flight crews went to debriefing to relive the past few hours for the daily reports. There were conflicting reports as to just where the bombs that hit ROUGH AND READY had come from. Some reported that a group of B-17s had slid over the group and dropped their bombs. Others believed that the planes were B-24s with 460th Bomb Group markings. This was the second mission in as many days where bombs had done as much or more damage to the group as had the flak and fighters.

The third full month of combat operations had been costly to the 464th Bomb Group. The group flew a total of 19 missions that were counted as actual missions. On those missions the group had lost 18 planes to enemy fighters and flak. That was almost one plane per mission. The loss rate was sustainable according to the 15th Air Force, when you figure in all the other statistics like sortie rate and crews available. The bottom line was that it had been another rough month for the boys on Pantanella Hill.

On the brighter side of the operations coin was the fact that the first men had completed their 50 mission tour of duty. Lt. Ray "Herky" Drake was the first, and by the end of the month several others had completed their tours and were ready to go back to the Zone of Interior.

The base chapel had been started on 26 July. The plans for the building looked very impressive. It was going to be made of the native tufa block. If everything worked out as planned it would have a bell tower and a real brass bell hanging there to call the men to worship services.

By the end of July, many of the men were buidling tufa block houses.

There were rumors circulating that the 464th was going to have a gunnery school opened soon. The idea was to give some of the ground crewmen a chance to take the course and qualify as gunners. Then they could fly an unspecified number of missions and be able to complete their tour of duty in Italy and go home.

The best thing about the end of the month was the fact that it was supposed to be pay day. The men lined up, then stood there in line for what seemed an eternity to get their pay. There always seemed to be the Squadron "loan shark" at the end of the line, notebook in one hand and the other hand out. "Now let's see, according to my notes, I loaned you five for ten on payday."

4

Fall 1944

August

It had been a full year since the 464th had been activated back in the good old USA. A lot of air had passed over the wings of the group's Liberators since that date. There had been a great deal of hard luck so far, but the group had fought hard and was determined to finish the task that they had been sent to "sunny Italy" to perform. There were a lot of new faces around Pantanella, and a lot of the original faces were missing.

On August 1, 1944, the group celebrated their first year since activation by standing down from combat. The reason for the stand down was not to celebrate, but because of bad weather over potential targets.

The men of the 464th were back in the air on 2 August. The briefing map showed the crews that the target for the day was the harbor installations at Genoa, Italy. Since this was a short hop the planes did not start taking to the air until almost 0900.

SHOO SHOO BABY aborted on the ground when a cylinder on #3 engine blew during run up. Her crew chief, Lester "Smokey" Halonan, could not believe it. His plane had not aborted a mission in a long time. There was nothing to do but start pulling the cowling so that he and his assistant, Sterling Lawrence, could start working on BABY. LIVELY LADY aborted after take off when the right main gear would not retract. Lt. Norbert Kustka and his crew landed, grabbed another plane, and were airborne by 1010. They managed to make up the time and distance and caught the formation.

At 1306 the formation dropped their bombs from about 20,000 feet. At almost the same moment the first burst of flak was seen. The planes rallied left and the flak followed, no matter how many bundles of chaff were thrown out. After about four minutes the flak tapered off to just a few scattered bursts.

Results were reported as good. The photos showed hits from the pier area all the way back to a rail yard. Several small ships had either taken hits, or near enough misses to cause a lot of damage. It was also noted that a lot of the bombs hit the water.

All of the planes returned to Pantanella. One was damaged by flak, but it would be back in the air in a couple of days. Another

LITTLE ROCKET on the right headed for Genoa, Italy, on August 2, 1944.

B-24 from the 464th leaves the harbor facilities at Genoa on August 2, 1944.

MICKEY after losing oil pressure on #1 engine. She was photographed from a Liberator of the 451st BG after she aborted the mission. Ploesti is below, burning from a strike on August 10, 1944.

bright spot was that no one was injured. In all, the mission for that day had been judged a milk run.

Thirty-nine planes headed for Friedrichschafen, Germany, to bomb the aircraft factory there on 3 August. Col. Schroeder led the mission, and Capt. Robert Wingfield was in the lead ship of the second attack unit.

Over the target the group was subjected to about three minutes of flak. Most of the bursts were below the formation, and no planes were hit by the hot shrapnel. It appeared for once that the chaff they kicked out was effective against the German radar.

The bomb release point was reached at 1110 hr, and the formation dropped over 95 tons of high explosives towards the target. COFFIN CORNER CUTIE (42-78317) had three bombs hang up in the bomb bay due to a rack malfunction. The crew could not get the bombs out, in spite of a gallant effort. They had no choice but to bring the bombs back to Pantanella.

Just after the target the B-24 flown by Lt. John Klika and crew started to have problems. Ever since getting to altitude the number 2 turbo had fluctuated badly. They were able to stay with the formation, however. Shortly, another problem came up. John Klika later wrote in his diary:

I feathered #3 engine 10 minutes after leaving the target. Blew the pushrod and lost all the oil in a minute. It vibrated severely before I could feather it. If I would have lost it over the target I'd be in Switzerland right now.

From his lead spot in the second attack unit, Robert Wingfield was informed that one of the planes was in trouble. He pulled the throttles back on his plane, and the rest of the unit throttled back to stay with the leader. With the reduced speed Klika's plane was able to maintain their position. Klika recalled in his diary:

If Capt. Wingfield hadn't slowed up the flight to help me keep position, I might have been a straggle and no doubt attacked by the fighters.

Flying the lead position for the group or an attack unit was one of the most difficult things a pilot could undertake. Those that never had the responsibility of flying lead thought that it was just a matter of driving a B-24 through the air and letting the rest of the formation follow. Those that knew the ins and outs of formation flying knew that if the leader flew a bad formation lead, then the rest of the formation was bad. A good leader would fly at a constant speed, altitude, and heading. If the leader was having a bad mission then everyone would have a bad one. Those in back of the leader would have to constantly jockey throttles and elevators to stay in the proper position. It was no secret that it was important to have the best pilots in the formation and element lead ships.

All of the planes made it back to Pantanella that afternoon. Even though the mission had been to Germany, most of the men regarded it as a milk run. That is, everyone except John Klika, since he felt that "it was too close for comfort."

The group stood down for the next two days. As always, the ground crews put the time to good use to get the planes fine tuned for the next mission. Some of the flak holes that had been covered over with tape were repaired with real aluminum patches. Some of the men busied themselves by helping with the base chapel. Over in the 779th area, Rod Binder was putting the finishing touches on his "patented" bomb fin and oxygen tank heating stoves. Since they burned 100 octane aviation fuel there was no guarantee they would not explode. If they did, well, just bring it back and Rod would try and make another to replace it. In a bit of irony, the movie that played those nights was called never a dull moment.

After two days of rest the planes were back in the air again on 6 August. The planes scheduled for the mission started taking off at 0655 hrs. The operations order called for the group to hit the Oil Storage facility at LePontet, France. Forty-four planes from the

The 464th heads home after hitting gun positions in Southern France, August 14, 1944.

Bombs and fuel explode after 42-51082 crashed on take off, August 15, 1944.

This pile of junk was once B-24 #42-51082.

group formed into two attack units, rendezvoused with the rest of the 55th Wing, and headed for France.

Near the target several Me-109s were seen headed in the opposite direction from the formation. They either did not see the bombers or were headed somewhere else at the moment. Either way, the fliers were glad to see the fighters headed away from them instead of queuing for the attack.

At the target intense flak greeted the 464th. The group was in the stuff for about five minutes. The German gunners on the ground did not seem to know just where the planes were headed. Although the flak was intense, it was not accurate, and no planes took any hits.

The bombardiers "killed the drift" and dropped over 105 tons of bombs onto the target. Results were classified as good. A lot of the oil stored in the tank farms would never reach the German war machine.

The flight back was almost routine. Everyone was in formation, and so far no one was reporting any major problems. Then mother nature stepped in to play a little joke on the returning planes. She had brewed up a line of fairly intense thunderstorms across the Italian boot. Because of the weather at Pantanella four planes landed at Naples, one at Rome, and one sat down at Corsica.

While the mission was not a milk run, everyone was safe. The group had flown three missions without a loss—maybe their luck was changing. That night the men that could break away from duty trudged up to the outdoor movie area. They plunked themselves down on the bomb fin case seats and waited for the flick to start. Again , the movie was appropriate for the day. The movie was "Is Everybody Happy."

August 7th found the 464th headed towards Blechhammer, Germany, with 28 planes. Their target for the day was the synthetic oil refinery. For a change of tactics the group formed into one attack unit made up of four combat boxes. Col. Schroeder was flying the lead B-24.

Assembly went off without a hitch. The 464th was on time and right where they should be, along with the other groups from the 55th Wing. Two ships aborted the mission before getting out over the Adriatic due to mechanical problems.

The formation arrived at the IP and turned towards the target. So far no Luftwaffe and no flak could be seen in the area. The weather ahead looked clear enough to make a visual bomb run. Maybe the lucky streak was going to hold for another mission.

The formation was over the target and hit the release point at 1130 hrs. The 464th dropped over 65 tons of bombs towards the target. At almost the same moment the formation was bracketed by a deadly barrage of heavy, accurate flak. The lucky streak had been broken.

ALL MEAT-NO POTATOES (42-78318), flown by Capt. James Tudor's crew, took a direct hit in the #1 engine. The engine was blown completely off the wing. The #2 engine caught fire as a result of the same hit. On the flight deck the pilots fought to control the wounded Liberator. The B-24 rolled over on its back like a dying fish and went into a death dive. Those in nearby ships figured

Men on Pantanella Hill pause to look at the firey end of #082.

that the ship and crew were doomed. On the flight deck, James Tudor and copilot James Ryan fought the controls with superhuman strength that only the fear of death can muster. After falling from the formation upside down, they finally managed to get the plane under control and pull out of the dive. Alone in unfriendly skies, they turned and headed for Pantanella.

COFFIN CORNER CUTIE was also damaged by flak. Lt. Richard Roode's crew kept her in the air, but were out of position in the formation. As a straggler, they were fair game if the Luftwaffe showed up.

The ship flown by Lt. Bob Holcomb had taken a hit in the #1 engine. The flight crew feathered the prop on the flak torn engine and adjusted the power and trim so they could stay in formation. Several other planes had been hit. Altogether the 464th had been in the flak for about six minutes. That had been enough to stamp out the group's streak of luck.

The group rallied for home and was greeted by several Me-109s making a half hearted attack from the rear. They came in and closed to about six hundred yards, then peeled away looking for some easier prey.

Lt. Roode had managed to keep his ship close enough to the formation so that the fighters did not attack. Near Bratislava, he could no longer stay close and left the group with all engines running. Inside the plane, the crew was busy throwing everything out that wasn't nailed, bolted, or essential to flight. Their fight to lighten the load was lost; they would not make it back to Pantanella and were reported missing. Thankfully, they were able to bail out over friendly territory and would return on 19 August.

ALL MEAT-NO POTATOES had managed to evade any German fighters that were looking for easy prey. Shortly after they started their journey homeward they sustained a flak burst near the bomb bay. Then the #3 and #4 engines were hit by flak and started to burn. The jig was up; they did not have any engines left. James Tudor had been wounded in the upper thigh by flak. Copilot Ryan tried to lock the controls in a right hand gentile spin. He and Tudor managed to bail out. Three other crewmen were able to leap from the falling plane before it hit the ground. Those that bailed out were taken prisoner by the Germans.

As the formation passed near Zagreb, several bursts of flak dotted the sky. One of the black mushrooms was close enough to Bob Holcomb's plane to cause damage to the #3 engine. Now he had two engines out on the same side. The plane dropped from formation, and Holcomb called for the crew to check in when they were ready to bail out. Everyone except the ball turret gunner checked in. After what seemed an eternity, Sgt. Royal Saylor reported that he could not retract the turret. In a case like this one procedure was to jettison the turret, so the gunner could then open the door and bail out. Holcomb recalled:

"I asked him if he knew the emergency procedure, and his response was 'But I'm not wearing a parachute.'" Holcomb polled the crew and told them they could get out and walk if they wanted to. No one elected to take the long step, and everyone stayed aboard. The wounded Liberator plodded on across Yugoslavia towards the Adriatic. The crew sweated it out all across the steel blue water of the Adriatic.

When they got close to the coast of Italy they called Big Fence, the direction finder station, and asked for a straight approach to the nearest runway. Big Fence told them that Foggia was where aircraft requesting DF information would land. At this point Holcomb told Big Fence just what the situation was; they had two engines out and could not make large turns in either direction. On top of this they had to set their crate down as soon as possible. Big Fence told them to change heading 10 degrees and they would be headed straight for Bari. Holcomb recalled:

Big Fence had us lined up perfectly; gear cranked down by hand; Number 3 engine provided hydraulic power for the landing gear and flaps. The runway at Bari had a steel matting at each end and dirt in between; we landed on the first few hundred feet of the steel matting, then onto the dirt. I pulled the lever for emergency brakes and nothing happened. We ran out of dirt and were back on the steel matting. A burst of power on #1 and #2 engines changed the heading enough that we departed the end of the runway at about a 45 degree angle and into a ditch. The front of the plane was touch-

Left: Lt/Col. Elvin Goodyear and Col. Schroeder after a mission to support Allied landings in Southern France.

ing the bottom of the ditch. The ball turret was now about 20 feet in the air, and Sgt. Saylor was ok. It took about 30 minutes to get him out of the turret. His feet hit the ground running, and he gave me a big hug!

Holcomb and his lucky crew would spend the night at Bari. They went to town and got something to eat and a lot of vino to drink. The next day Holcomb and his crew went back to Pantanella by truck. After reporting in and explaining what had happened to the plane, he was handed a stack of paperwork to "hand carry through Wing Hq." It was his promotion to 1st Lt. and DFC citation for bringing his ship back. They were both dated August 7, 1944.

After the planes had landed and taxied back to the revetments a lone P-38 made a pass down the runway. At the end of the PSP the twin boomed fighter pulled up and started to turn around for another pass. As the P-38 came back over the field it got lower and lower. A lot of the men turned to watch the Lightning's pass. Some of the men wondered who it was. It was none other then Ernie Latham coming back to say hello to the boys. Ernie was one of several pilots who had transferred to fighter outfits and was flying a sleek fighter, escorting his old friends over the targets.

Some of the men who watched the buzz job had just returned to Pantanella from rest and recreation at the island of Capri. All combat and no play make a soldier flak happy. At one time or another, almost everyone from the 464th was granted a period of rest from the everyday grind of flying combat or fixing a B-24.

One of the popular spots for R&R was Capri. This small island was near Naples harbor. It had been used as a holiday spot since the time of the Roman Empire. The trip to Naples was a short ride in a "hackship," usually a B-24 that had been retired from combat. Then it was about a two hour boat ride from Naples to the island.

When the men arrived they would either walk up the hill or take the Funiclare. This was a small cable car that ran up the steep incline to the hotels where the men would stay. Since the hills were very steep, most of the men would ride the cable car. A lot of them would pick grapes that grew along the way.

Compared to their casas at Pantanella, the hotels on Capri were "the ritz." Officers stayed at the Qusiana, while the enlisted men checked into the Bella Sojorno. Both had beds with real mattresses and sheets, tile floors, running water, and even toilets that actually flushed.

The food was a heck of a lot better than the fare the men ate at base. If you happened to be real lucky, ice cream was even served at several of the meals.

Since the idea of going to Capri was to rest and relax, that is exactly what most of the men did. There were all kinds of things to do on the island.

There were several beaches where the men could lay in the sun or take a swim. Granted, the officers had a beach and the enlisted men had a different one. Some of the enlisted men recalled that they would "crash" the officers' beach and swim with their pilot. It worked as long as the enlisted men acted as though they were supposed to be there.

The ruin of the Villa of Tiberius was located high on the hill near Anacapri. Legend recalled that Tiberius would throw unwanted slaves or other undesirables off the cliff for sport.

Almost everyone took the boat ride around the island, stopping at the famous Blue Grotto. The Grotto was a cave at sea level with a small entrance. Depending on the tide, you either had to duck to get in or just rode in with the next ocean swell. Once inside the cave, it lived up to its reputation. Reflecting sunlight on the bottom cast an almost fluorescent blue color to the water and the surrounding walls of the cave. Although the water about 15-20 feet deep, it looked like you could wade in it.

As with all tourist traps, there were a lot of shops where the men could spend their lire. A lot of the guys bought a pair of the Lucky Little Belles of St. Michel. Some of them later found out that after the Americans arrived the price of the bells was inflated to over triple the price that the German soldiers had paid. Oh well, it was still a souvenir of their trip.

All too fast the time at Capri had passed, and it was time to go back to Pantanella and the war. The boat ride back to Naples and the flight back seemed too fast, as well. Back in the real world, the men could only hope that the war would be won so they could go home.

The men of the 464th stood down from flying combat on the 8th. The weather over Europe was not good for bombing. Those that could tried to wrangle a pass so they could get away from the base. Some just went down to the river for either a swim or to try their luck at catching a fish with their homemade equipment. A lot of the guys tried to catch up on some sack time.

Ground crewmen working hard to change two engines on a 464th Liberator.

The otherwise nice day was marred by a truck accident on one of the roads near the base. Sgt. Richard Wuller, an armorer from the 778th, was killed in the crash. Corp. George Colabella of the 766th had taken the day off from working on the planes. He received massive head injuries and would die on 11 August.

When the curtain was pulled back on the briefing board there was a low audible moan from the crews that were going to fly that morning. On 9 August the red string stretched from their base in Italy to Budapest, Hungary. The target was the airdrome facilities there. After getting all the particulars on how the mission was to be flown, Chaplain Eastwood gave his usual pre-mission prayer and the boys boarded the trucks for the bumpy ride down the hill to the waiting planes.

Lt. George Flannagan and crew had been assigned to 42-78374, better known as BIG WHEELER DEALER from the 778th. Sgt. Patrick Carr (Waist gunner) recalled:

After checking out the ship, we were all sitting around on the hardstand by the plane waiting for time to start engines for taxi and take off. I particularly remember that our bombardier, McCowen (2nd/Lt. Walter McCowen, Jr), seemed to be rather depressed that morning. I asked him what was wrong, and his answer was something to the effect that we could not retain our luck indefinitely. I replied to this by repeating one of his favorite phrases, "They'll never nip us." He said that may be true, but he was getting awfully tired.

That morning 28 planes took to the air, formed into two attack groups, and headed for Hungary under the leadership of Maj. William Reddell. There were no mechanical aborts on this mission, so the entire formation was at full strength.

The mission progressed better then expected. Adverse weather had been predicted by the base weather wizards for the route to the target. It seemed that weather front had stalled out just enough for the bombers to pass it.

As the group approached the turn at the IP they expected the usual flak to greet them. It seemed that the German gunners were

Dramatic photo of Black-O as she explodes on the night of August 21, 1944.

Twisted aluminum, a propeller, and junk are all that is left of Black-O.

Daylight reveals the devastation of Black-O's explosion.

Remains of the top turret from Black-0.

Bombs away! Pardubice, Czechoslovakia, August 24, 1944.

trying out a new tactic. Instead of blasting away at the bombers from the IP to the target, they would hurl up an intense barrage in the immediate area of the target, hoping to throw off the bombardier's aim.

At 1113 hrs 67 tons of RDX cascaded towards the ground. Strike cameras recorded that the airfield was plastered. It also showed that about twenty bombs strayed into a row of houses near the airfield.

Aboard BIG WHEELER DEALER, Sgt. Carr was manning the right waist gun. He recalled:

I saw a string of flak coming from our left toward the front of the formation. A shell burst very near our left wing and jarred the ship terrifically, sending pieces of shrapnel through the bomb bay. I raised up and looked out of the left waist window at the engine to see whether or not flak had caused any fire, of which I was deathly afraid. I heard the Bombardier say "bombs away," and then I remember only a blinding flash. I was blown into the tail section and knocked unconscious.

The plane had taken a direct hit near the ball turret, killing Sgt. William Floyd, Jr. The blast literally cut the Liberator in half. T/Sgt. William Brown was blown through the left waist window, breaking his arm. He managed to pull his rip chord and open his chute. The tail gunner, Sgt. Gerald Ford, managed to climb out of his turret and hit the silk. Patrick Carr:

When I regained consciousness I was alone in the tail section and jumped out of the end where the plane separated. The tail was not spinning, but was in a gentle glide. I pulled the rip chord and the chute opened. I landed at the edge of a cornfield and was captured almost as I hit the ground.

Results of the Pardubice mission as seen from the ground.

Pardubice, August 24, 1944.

On the flight deck there was utter chaos. Copilot Harris Frausel recalled:

The front of the airplane snapped down, throwing everything and everyone forward and upward. At this point I believe I was thrown through the plexiglass over the cockpit. Then I was thrown back into the cockpit again. I remember being thrown about like a marble in a tin can that was being shaken. There were oxygen bottles and debris slamming all through the cockpit from other parts of the plane behind us. I remember seeing Anderson (Theodore Anderson, 2nd/Lt., Navigator) slammed against the instrument panel and windshield, his back against it, arms outstretched, completely pinned and unable to move. First I was on top of Flanagan, and then he was on top of me. I found myself close to an opening with air rushing in, and I grabbed either side of this opening. I struggled to pull myself out and got as far as my waist, then something happened that knocked me out. I came to falling head over heels in the air. I pulled the rip cord and blacked out again.

Just how Flanagan and Frausel managed to escape is a matter of debate. Years later Flanagan believed that he had been thrown through the side window of the cockpit. Frausel believed that he went through a hole in the plexiglass that he had made with his head. It is possible that they both were thrown out through the top escape hatch.

Frausel landed in the target area between two burning hangars. He crawled into a bomb crater as the bombs from the next group arrived:

For the next few minutes all hell broke loose. Bombs dropped all around me, and the ground shook and heaved. Dirt flew into the hole from all directions, and I had to continually come up for air, as I was buried under several inches of dirt sometimes.

Five members of the crew were trapped in the spinning wreckage of BIG WHEELER DEALER. The bombardier, Walter McGowen, Jr., who had been depressed and was tired of flying, found eternal rest in the wreckage of the plane.

When the planes landed at Pantanella another B-24 was missing. HOME FOR CHRISTMAS (42-42437) had been flown by Lt. Emmett Drake. They had taken several flak hits but had managed to stay in the air long enough to make a landing at Vis. Both plane and crew would return after repairs. Three other planes had been damaged by flak and would be back in the air within a few days.

August 10th found the group headed for their sixth crack at the dreaded oil fields at Ploesti. At 0710 in the morning the first of 28 B-24s struggled into the air with a full load of fuel and RDX. The formation was led by the Deputy Group Commander, Lt/Col. Charles McKenna III.

After form up and wing rendezvous the group headed out over the Adriatic and towards the rising sun. Weather was some of the best the fliers had seen going towards Ploesti. It always seemed that there were more clouds to contend with whenever they started towards Ploesti .

As the group got closer to the target it was evident that the entire 15th Air Force was going in the same direction. Bombers could be seen ahead and behind. From over a hundred miles away, pillars of billowing smoke could be seen rising from the Ploesti area.

Two planes ran into trouble at the IP. MICKEY (42-52526) began to lose oil pressure on the #1 engine. The pilots shut it down and feathered the prop. WILLIE (42-78473) lost manifold pressure on #3 and #4 engines. They both fell behind the formation.

It just so happened that both planes spotted a formation of B-24s coming off the target and heading for Italy. Both planes abandoned the mission and banked to the left to try and intercept the homeward bound B-24s.

As they approached the formation they could see the red tail markings of the 451st Bomb Group. Little did they know that they had their picture taken by one of the photographers on one of the red tailed B-24s. They also had no way of knowing that a lot of 451st gunners had drawn a bead on them in case they were a captured B-24 trying to sneak into the formation and raise havoc.

Smoke from the target billows into the air, August 24, 1944

The Pardubice Oil Rfinery is reduced to rubble after the attacks by Liberators of the 464th.

The rest of the group turned at the IP and started for the target. No flak was seen until just before bomb release. Then it was the usual Ploesti stuff, intense and accurate as the German flak gunners filled the sky with bursting death. There was nothing to do but grind ahead and hope the flak gunners would not have your number on the next shell they slammed into the breach of the gun.

Flak hit JOLLY ROGER (42-29429). Tail gunner Pete Stults would later write:

Our #2 engine was hit and feathered. #3 engine was also hit, but was partially usable. We dropped to about 10,000 feet and went off oxygen. Don Knotts' (Pilot) first thought was to head for the Adriatic, go as far as we could, then ditch and hope to get picked up. Then a gas leak was discovered, and the engineer said we would never make the Adriatic. Navigator said the best thing to do was go over Bulgaria and head for Turkey. Knotts came back and told us he was going to fly as long as he could. When no longer flyable, he would waggle the wings and we would have 20 seconds to get out... then he and Biddle were leaving. We gathered around the open escape hatch, said the "Lord's Prayer," and that was it.

Sometimes we could use the #3 engine for a little while, but it would get too hot and he would feather it. We were getting very low on gas. Knotts came back, told us he was not sure where we were, but anyone wanting to get out should do so now. We all decided to stick. Later Biddle spotted a short runway on the ground, long enough for a Piper Cub. The ground beyond the runway was fairly smooth. It was decided to do a wheels up landing beyond the end of the runway and pop the chutes out the waist windows to help slow us down. It was a rough landing, but we were all in crash positions. Nobody was hurt badly, just cuts and scratches.

The crew would be detained by Turkish officials and taken to Istanbul, where they were interned. After about thirty days they were able to "escape" and made their way back to Allied control via Cairo.

At bomb release, 57 tons of RDX headed towards the smoke obscured Astro Romano Oil Refinery. It seemed the group's aim was a little off. Strike photos showed bombs impacting in a field over a quarter of a mile away from the MPI.

Rally was to the left to get out of the flak as quickly as possible. As it turned out the planes and crews would spend over seven minutes within the black blossoms of flak. Seven minutes in what seemed like hell.

When the planes arrived back at Pantanella, the ground crews found a lot of battle damage that would have to be repaired. Eleven planes were damaged to the point where they would not be flying for several days.

FUN HOUSE(42-78248) had made it back to home base, but the crew could not get the nosewheel down. They tried all of the standard and emergency procedures in the book and still the gear would not come down. There was only one thing to do, and that was to make an emergency landing. As the plane touched down on the main gear the pilot held the nose off until airspeed started to drop. As the speed bled off the men in the waist area moved further back to try and hold the nose in the air. It would have worked if the main tire on the left side had not ruptured, causing the nose to slam down and the B-24 to slide around to a quick stop. Oh well, any landing you walk away from can be called a good one. A quick survey of the damage to FUN HOUSE showed that it should be declared Class 26. However, it would be repaired, even if it did take more than a couple days to do it.

The flight crews stood down on 11 August. On the 12th and 13th the group flew back-to-back milk runs against enemy gun emplacements at Sete, France. These missions were long hauls, but at least everyone made it home.

On the 14th, 28 planes were scheduled to take off at 0700 hrs to hit more gun positions in the St. Tropez area of Southern France. As 42-51082 reached flying speed and lifted off the runway, something went wrong. The B-24 slammed down onto the ground and slid like a bar of soap into the field, about 700 feet beyond the west end of the runway. The shaken crew managed to climb out of the broken Liberator before it caught fire. The flames spread over the entire airplane, and in a short time the bombs reached the critical point and began to explode. There was one crewman who sustained some serious injuries, while the rest were cut and shaken up.

The mission was delayed while the 464th and 465th regrouped and turned around to take off to the East. This was no easy maneuver, since everyone had to turn 180 degrees and make a downwind take off with a full load. Almost all of the bombers used every bit of runway just to get off the ground.

As the bombers got into the air they would gain some altitude and head for the group form up area. As each one entered the racetrack in the sky, they scanned the area looking for other B-24s from the group so that they could move into position as quickly as possible. When the group was formed up they flew to the Wing rendezvous area, met the rest of the 55th Bomb Wing, and turned for their trip to southern France.

As the formation got closer to their target area they could see a great panorama unfolding below. On the water there were hundreds of Allied ships preparing for the invasion of Southern France. Irl Mitchell (777th, ball turret gunner) recalled:

As we approached the target, I noticed that we were maybe 300 yards to the left of the targeted gun emplacements. I called the bombardier on the intercom and so advised. He, of course, advised me that we could not pull out of formation and that we would drop our bombs when the lead plane did so.

It was disappointing to me to see our 500 pounders fall so short of the target and landing in the sea. Disappointing, because we had so many other missions much more important to the war effort. It was our crew's 50th mission, too. What a conclusion to a fine record. It was our 50th mission, and we had killed fish!

The rest of the mission was flown as it had been briefed. All of the planes returned home. YELLOW L-LOVE pulled into the pattern, and Capt. John Luque advised Racecard tower that he was going around. Luque pulled the gear up and pushed the throttles forward. He then proceeded to lay down a special 50 mission finale buzz job complete with red flares fired from the waist area.

Fire trucks, ambulances, and jeeps followed the plane to the hardstand. "How many wounded! What the hell is the problem!" came the rapid inquires from those on the ground. Capt. Luque simply informed them that they had just finished their 50th mission and just felt like celebrating a little.

On the 15th, 30 Liberators from the 464th took to the air to hit a Highway Bridge at Donzere, France. All of the 15th Air Force would be heading towards France to support the Allied landings there. As far as the eye could see were B-24s and B-17s in the air under the code name OPERATION DRAGOON.

As predicted at the morning briefing, the flak was light and the Luftwaffe was busy somewhere else. The group was over the target at 1254 and released over 70 tons of 500 pounders towards the bridge. Direct hits were scored on the western span, blowing part of the wooden roadway to smithereens. There were several hits near the eastern end, too. A lot of bombs hit the river about a thousand feet from the structure, but at least the bridge was hit.

The flight home was uneventful for all of the planes except one. The crew of HOME FOR CHRISTMAS from the 778th had started to relax. They had broken out their usual homeward flight lunch of K-Rations and were listening to some music over the intercom. Bruce Callender (bombardier) recalled:

Then it happened. With no warning, all four engines quit. In seconds HOME FOR CHRISTMAS dropped 1,000 feet and showed no inclination to stop. With no land in sight, our best hope seemed to be to ditch and hope we were picked up.

Roy Anderson, our pilot, struggled to bring the plane under control, but with no power the B-24 confirmed its reputation for gliding like a streamlined brick. Unless Andy could put her into a dive and pull up in time to skim the water and bleed some speed, the chances of our surviving seemed minimal.

The flight engineer, Al Ness, shot up from his jump seat on the floor of the flight deck, turned around, and flipped a switch on the bulkhead. Three engines returned to life; Andy feathered the prop on the fourth and leveled off well above the water. We were back in business.

Ness checked the fuel gauges and found there was barely enough in the three tanks to register and none in the fourth. We weren't home free yet!

Pilot Anderson called the navigator, Dave Kellogg, and asked for a bearing to the nearest Allied airfield. Kellogg came back with a heading, and the Liberator continued to limp on. Bruce Callender continues:

After what seemed like hours Kellogg reported he saw land, and a few moments later said he had the field in sight. Anderson declared an emergency and asked for a straight in approach. The tower approved, but told him to touch down as close to the near end of the runway as he could. What we were headed for, he said, was a fighter strip.

Anderson killed as much power as he dared, dropped the bomber onto the numbers at the start of the runway, and when he thought it was safe, hit the brakes as hard as he could. We rolled the full length of the short strip and stopped with our props just feet from a clump of small trees. Andy taxied off the runway and switched off the engines. It was a little more than a formality. One prop feathered, another engine had quit during landing, and the other two were coughing. Ness scrambled onto the wing, pulled the fuel caps, and looked into the tanks with a flashlight. We asked what he saw. "Just wet metal," he said.

It appeared that the fuel system had been set at "crossfeed" instead of "engine to engine." In "crossfeed," if one tank ran dry it could cause air to be sucked into the system and cause all of the engines to stop. According to Callende:

Ness had done the right thing at the right time to save the bomber and nine other men. But what made him think of it was a mystery.

Ness himself had no explanation. He could not remember anything like this being covered during his 27 weeks of training. It seemed that it had been an instinctive move.

HOME FOR CHRISTMAS was refueled, and the lucky crew got back to Pantanella. Anderson laid down a buzz job just to let everyone know they were home. It just so happened that the 55th Wing commander was at the base for a visit when HOME FOR CHRISTMAS buzzed the field. After getting chewed out by Col. Schroeder the crew was confined to base for a week, except for flying combat missions.

On the 16th, the flight crews were briefed for a mission to the Ober Raderach Chemical Works at Friedrichshafen, Germany. Since it was a mission to "der Fatherland" it would be a long one. A total of 28 planes and three spares started taking off at 0655 that morning. There were four aborts due to mechanical problems. Out over the Adriatic the gunners cleared their guns. An empty shell casing hit the top turret of 42-95374. The casing smashed through the

SULTAN II (42-95348) after crashing on take off August 27, 1944.

plexiglass and hit Sgt. Marvin Miller in the face. The injury was enough to cause him to abandon his turret. The pilot decided it was best to abort the mission and get Miller medical attention as soon as possible.

Twenty-six Liberators reached the target at 1130 hrs. As usual, flak opened up just before bomb release. The flak was intense. Twenty-five planes dropped their load of 500 pound RDX bombs. 42-51644 had a rack malfunction and could not release with the group. They were able to salvo their bombs about a minute after the rest of the group had bombed.

It appeared to be a good drop. Strike photos showed lots of hits in the target area. The aiming point was covered with smoke, so real damage assessment was impossible. Several near misses were scored on a hydrogen plant.

The flight back was almost uneventful. Four Me-109s were spotted near Bolzano. They were several thousand feet below the formation and flying at a right angle to the formation, and they made no move to intercept the bombers.

Another interesting thing happened on the way back. Out of nowhere a lone silver B-24 appeared about 2,000 yards behind Charlie Box. The lone wolf had orange cowlings and wing leading edges. There was a white star, but it did not have the blue background on the left wing. It also had a large orange R on the fuselage, but no group markings on the tail. The tail turret was olive drab. The gunners of the 464th drew a bead on the intruding Liberator just in case she tried something. After dogging the formation for a few minutes the lone Liberator pulled away and was lost from sight.

Twenty-six planes landed at home base. THE GREEN HORNET (42-52504) landed at Fermo to refuel. White-E (42-78472) landed at Pescara, refueled, and then came back to Pantanella. One plane was damaged by flak and bellied in at the base. After some sheet metal work she would be back in the air within a week.

On the 18th, the flight crews got the usual "still-o-dark hundred" wake up call. Breakfast, the usual powdered eggs, and coffee. Then they were off to the briefing to find out where the heck the group was headed for—Ploesti again!.

As the crews left for their planes, Chaplain Eastwood was on hand to say a prayer and give last minute communion to those who wanted it. It always gave the crews a little comfort knowing that they had "the padre" in there pitching for their safe return.

Take off was scheduled for 0630, One plane aborted at the hardstand because the pilot was throwing up. Twenty-seven planes took off, and three spares followed them into the form up area. Before the formation was over the Adriatic, eight B-24s had aborted because of various mechanical problems.

One of the Liberators that aborted that day was THE GREEN HORNET. Her pilot that day, Nelson Ashwill, Jr., later wrote:

I remember flying old White-Zebra (THE GREEN HORNET) on a mission to Ploesti, 18 August. The old worn out plane just would not keep up with the formation, and we were using gas at an outrageous rate! Over Bulgaria we knew we would not make it to Ploesti and back, so I made the decision to drop the bombs on a railroad and abort the mission. We were about 5 miles behind the rest of the formation and about three thousand feet below them. Well, I caught the devil back at the base—especially when I wrote up the Form 1, filling in the complete sheet on the faults of this old worn out plane, and at the bottom in quite large letters I wrote THIS PLANE IS NOT FIT FOR COMBAT DUTY.

The 460th BG was leading the 55th Wing. For some reason the leader of that group was not maintaining the briefed airspeed. As a result, the 485th started to bunch up behind the lead group. The 464th was forced to fly even slower and soon found itself in almost echelon right formation with the 485th. The planes of the 464th were hanging on their props trying to stay behind the 485th. The 485th started moving to the right to avoid trailing elements of the 460th. As a result, the 464th was pushed farther off the briefed route to avoid collision. At one point the 464th was almost 14 miles to the right of where they should have been.

At this point the group was passing over Surdulica, Yugoslavia. For the next three minutes they would come under intense and accurate flak. The group broke to the right about 45 degrees to get away from the exploding shells. On Red-H (42-50533) it was too late for evasive action. A shard of flak had entered the nose area and instantly killed Lt. John Sevey, the navigator. Lewis Price would later write:

I was flying as co-navigator with John Sevey when he was killed. As a matter of fact, he and I were talking on the intercom when he was hit. We could see the fire from the barrels of the flak guns and were pin-pointing it on the charts when the first bursts of flak opened in the formation.

Other damage had been done to the aircraft. When the group managed to clear the flak, the wounded B-24 turned back towards Italy bearing its sad cargo.

As the planes turned at the IP, one of the planes jettisoned some of their bombs because they were having trouble staying with the formation. About a minute later, another ship dropped its load accidentally. If bombs continued to drop like that, there wouldn't be any left to drop on the target.

At 1036 hrs the group was over the Romana Americana refinery, and 16 of the 28 planes sent 30 tons of bombs towards the refinery. The rest either had already dropped or suffered problems that made it impossible to release their loads.

Just before bomb release the flak appeared. For about four minutes the group was surrounded by the usual Ploesti variety of flak. The four minutes was enough to damage eight planes. Several had taken some severe damage but were able to stay in formation.

The trip back to Italy was flown as they had been briefed. When the fliers landed they were off to interrogation to refly the mission while all the gory details were still etched in their minds. A lot of the crews were very upset at the way the 460th had led the wing. It had put the rest of the wing in great danger, and had cost the 464th the life of one of their navigators. Several of the men wanted to be sure that the true details of the mission reached 55th Wing.

This mission to Ploesti had been a bittersweet pill for the group. It had been their seventh trip to the oil fields since they had started operations. The thirty tons of bombs that they had dropped that day would be the last that the group would drop on that godforsaken target.

Since April, the 15th Air Force had Ploesti near the top of the target list. After mounting a virtual aerial siege the refineries had been reduced to rubble. The Russian army was advancing on that front, and the Germans were beginning to pull back towards the fatherland. After the mission of 18 August, Ploesti was removed from the list of targets.

The group took a day off due to bad weather over Central Europe on 19 August. After eight mechanical aborts on the previous mission, it was evident that some of the planes needed to be worked on. The crew chiefs rolled up their sleeves and started working to chase the gremlins out of the planes.

On the 20th, the 464th went prospecting for oil again. This time the target was the refinery at Czechowice, Poland. Twenty-eight planes took to the air in the early calm of the Italian morning. In spite of the hard work on the planes by the ground crews, two aborted for mechanical problems. Their positions were filled by two spare aircraft that had taken off with the formation.

The flight to the target was quiet and flown as they had been briefed. At the IP, the bombers turned towards the target and began the bomb run. Flak was expected at any second.

The group was at 20,000 feet about two minutes from release. At 1105 a dark colored B-17 approached from about the 2 o'clock position and closed to within 600 yards of the group. After repeated radio calls to the B-17 and no answer, several of the 464th gunners sent a stream of tracers towards the rogue ship. It banked and wheeled away to the left of the formation.

The crews were greeted by a real treat over the target, no flak! Several bursts were seen coming from the general area of Oswiecim, but they were low and to the right, just out of range.

At about 1108 the planes hit the release line, and 60 tons of bombs began their ballistic flight to the ground. Bomb strike photos showed that the 464th would be given a big goose egg for score. Bombs started hitting almost 7,000 feet to the southeast of the refinery and walked through open fields for a mile and a half. All that way just to plow fields with high explosive RDX.

About five minutes after bomb release the same B-17 showed up from 2 o'clock again. It overran the formation, then seemed to throttle back. It just wanted to dog the formation, maybe reporting altitude and heading to the ground below. Finally, it turned away and headed back towards the target area.

The flight home was uneventful, that is, if you can call sweating out fuel supply uneventful. Fuel was so critical on 44-41084 (White-L) that she made a pit stop at Foggia to refuel. She made it back to Pantanella at about 1605 hrs. that afternoon.

On the morning of 21 August, the 464th had 28 planes ready to take a trip to Nis, Yugoslavia, to bomb the airfields. One spare ship had taken to the air in case of any early returns. Form up and rendezvous went according to the briefing. There were no aborts, so the spare ship came home and the crew took the rest of the day off.

The 28 planes arrived over the target, and 26 planes dropped their bombs. The formation sent 54 tons of fragmentation clusters towards the ground from about 19,000 feet and rallied for home. Two of the planes did not drop because of a malfunction with the racks, so they brought their bombs back to base.

Very little flak was seen. Most of it was either off to one side or lower than the formation. That was just fine with the crews in the planes. That meant they did not have to worry about taking hits or injuries on the mission.

The 464th made up for their goose egg on their bombing score card from the day before. The bomb pattern started short of the target, but walked right through the target. Hits were observed on parked aircraft and the runway. A bonus was a line of freight cars parked on a siding near the field.

Everyone got back to base, although one plane had to stop at Bari and take on enough fuel to reach Pantanella. The two planes that brought back their bombs had to be downloaded before the next load could be hung on the racks. Taking the frag bombs off the racks was even more hairy than putting them in. It took a while, but the ordnance men got the job done.

Some of the men remembered that when a plane brought bombs back from a mission they would just toggle them out onto the hardstand beneath the plane. Not exactly by the book, but an easy way to "clear the bay."

Word came down from 15th Air Force that the 464th was alerted for a mission in the morning. Orders called for 28 planes to be ready to fly. Each was to carry a full load of 500 pound General Purpose (GP) bombs.

The men on the ground started working almost before the engines had cooled from the last mission. While the armorers were loading bombs and ammo, the crew chiefs were busy checking everything else to make sure the planes were ready to go. It would be another all night shift for a lot of the ground crews.

That night, over in the 779th hardstand area, Sgt. Ted Moldenhauer and his crew were working on their ship Black O-Oboe (42-51129). On the next hardstand, Ted's brother "Red" was trying to figure out the latest gremlin attack on his "old dog," 117.

Ted was working on the V-2 APU on Black-O. He had installed a new one and was in the process of making some final adjustments. Just before midnight Lt. LeRoy Marsh, Engineering Officer, had checked on the progress. Ted assured the Lt. that he was just about done, so Lt. Marsh went back to his quarters.

Without warning, the APU started to run rough and very erratic. Ted tried to shut it off, but before he could, the fuel line broke and 100 octane fuel poured onto the hot engine. The fuel sizzled on the hot putt-putt and flashed into a ball of flame. Ted grabbed one of the plane's fire bottles and fought the growing blaze.

The fire was out of control in the blink of an eye. Ted abandoned the burning plane and started yelling to the other ground crews in the immediate area. Red Moldenhauer and Lester Hacker were able to get a couple of engines started on FLAKMAN and taxied the B-24 out of harm's way.

Lt. Marsh arrived on the scene and started directing traffic away from the burning B-24. He climbed into Black-P, which was directly across the taxi strip from the growing inferno. He recalled:

I had a premonition that Black-O was going to explode. I shut off the one engine that had finally been started and began exiting the plane. The explosion came, and suddenly I was laying on the hardstand under the bomb bay. I don't remember taking any steps after getting out of the pilot seat, but except for scrapes and bruises I was unhurt."

When the heat of the fire reached the fuel tanks full of 100 octane fuel and the 500 pound bombs it did not take long to reach the critical point. Black-O was erased in a blinding mushroom shaped flash. Parts of the disintegrating Liberator became missiles as they flew through the Italian night.

The fire crews arrived and started to battle the fire in hopes of keeping it from spreading. The ground crews managed to get several of the planes out of danger, but several others had been damaged by flying debris. Fred Stranton (779) recalled:

I was awakened by a loud cracking and snapping sound. My first thought was that the wheat and grass surrounding us was on fire. Jumping up, I raised the tarp window to see utter mayhem. One plane was totally in flames, spouting .50 cal rounds and tracers in all directions. Before I could react she blew up, exploding in a fireball that mushroomed into the night sky. The concussion threw me to the floor without any harm. The other two men did not know what had happened; one ran into the wall trying to find his way out, not yet fully awake. Rushing out, I ran into a complete landing gear lying about 30 feet from our shack.

When the sun finally came up the scene was one of absolute destruction. Black-O and her hardstand had been replaced by a five foot deep crater. Twisted and mangled remains of the B-24 littered the area. A prop here, a tire over there, just pieces of a once proud B-24.

A quick survey showed that along with Black-O, "Red" Moldenhauer's Gremlin infested Black-P was damaged beyond repair. The ailerons and other control surfaces were burned away, all of the plexiglass had been blown out by the concussion, and there were way too many holes in her hide from flying debris. She was declared class 26. Two other planes had been damaged by flying chunks of Black-O and would require a lot of work before they would take to the air again. On top of this, the Moldenhauer Mansion had caught fire: Ted, Red, and their housemates lost almost everything in the fire. They vowed to rebuild it even better than it had been before. For their bravery that night in saving aircraft and fighting fires, LeRoy Marsh, William Spivey, Clarence Avonius, Ted and Herman Moldenhauer, Dole Caldwell, Harry Bruner, Lester Hacker, and Wayne Merino were awarded the Soldiers Medal.

Despite the mayhem during the night, the 464th was ready to fly a mission on the morning of 22 August. Twenty-eight B-24s were scheduled for the mission. The target for the day was the oil storage area at Koreneuberg, near good old Vienna. This would be a long haul, so the planes started getting airborne at 0550. It would also count as a double credit mission for the men who flew that day.

As the group winged its way out over the Adriatic, each of the crewmen on the planes had specific things to take care of. Radios were tuned to the appropriate channel, and oxygen systems were checked and then double checked. When at the right point on the map, the safety pins were pulled from the bomb fuzes. As the formation got closer to the danger zone, the gunners manned their guns in case the Luftwaffe showed up.

At the IP the group turned and started for the target. Several Me-109s were spotted, but they were busy trying to stay away from the escort fighters. None of the enemy planes managed to break through to the bombers.

Near the release point the flak opened up on the incoming B-24s. Angry black bursts were coming up from the guns at Vienna. These guns were firing from near maximum range. The flak would last for almost seven minutes.

At 1115 KEE WEE BIRD (42-50920) was hit on the left side by flak, and both engines were knocked out. Lt. Albert Feldt and copilot Lt. Richard Wellbrock fought the controls to hold the Liberator level. The bombs were salvoed and the plane went into a steep controlled glide. Six of the crew bailed out before KEE WEE BIRD hit the ground.

Bombs away was called at 1116 hrs. The group dropped 56 tons of bombs onto the target with excellent results. Strike photos showed that the target had been plastered. After hitting the rally point the planes turned for home.

A trail of debris leads to the crash sight of SULTAN II, August 27, 1944.

The flight back was filled with almost as much tension as the flight to the target, because now fuel was the main concern. Each of the flight engineers kept a close eye on the sight gauges and kept checking the transfer system.

All of the planes except for KEE WEE BIRD made it back to Pantanella. As they pulled into the pattern, they could see the mangled hardstand and smoldering wreckage from the night before. In all, it had been an interesting 24 hour period. After debriefing and later that night, John Klika wrote in his diary about the mission:

Rough mission, and we came home with several flak holes. TOO ROUGH FOR MY LAST ONE, DON'T HAVE TO WORRY ANYMORE—I'M FINITO." He had just finished his 50th mission.

On 23 August the group headed for Markersdorf, Austria, to hit the airfields there. The 49th and 55th Wing were acting as a diversion, while the rest of the 15th Air Force would hit targets at Vienna.

The 464th put 26 planes into the air under command of Maj. Poff. The second unit was led by Lt. Emmett Drake from the 778th. Form up and line rendezvous went according to plan. The 55th wing climbed out over the Adriatic and headed north towards the Yugoslavian coast.

When the 49th Wing reached the IP, the lead group aborted the mission due to heavy clouds. One group from the 49th (451st) found the IP and turned for the target. As they approached the target they found it covered by scattered clouds and began their run. Their red tailed Liberators were hit by "the whole damned Luftwaffe."

The 465th was leading the 55th Wing on this mission. They missed the IP and signaled for the 464th to assume the lead while they did a 180 degree turn to take a second run. Shortly after the 464th took the lead, Lt. Drake lost an engine. He signaled for the Deputy lead of the second attack unit to take over.

The group arrived over the target and released their bombs on time. The results of the mission were classified as very good. All of the planes in the 464th rallied according to plan and flew home without seeing a German fighter.

A historical note shows that the reason no fighters attacked the 464th was because they were busy mauling the 451st. After hitting the 451st, the fighters had reached their fuel limits and had to land to refuel. By that time, the 464th had hit the target and were on their way home. The 451st was awarded a DUC for their part in the mission. The 464th was treated to a milk run, complements of the Castelluccia kids.

On 24 August the flight crews of the 464th were after oil again. The mission for the day was to the Pardubice Oil Refinery in Czechoslovakia. Twenty-eight B-24s were scheduled to take off at 0730 that morning. Three spares also climbed into the air to fill any gaps that might form.

Lt. John James was at the helm of LITTLE LULU. In one of his letters to the folks back home he wrote, "I love flying the B-24. It's like sitting on the front porch and flying the house." He and his crew were anxious to fly the rest of their missions and get back home to the states. LITTLE LULU climbed into the Italian sky and headed for the form up area.

Form up went without any problems. As the 464th and 465th turned for wing rendezvous, the 460th flew through the formation at a right angle. There were a few hairy moments as planes scrambled to avoid unwanted mid-air get togethers. Because of this, the 464th had problems getting inline with the rest of the wing. They finally managed to catch up and find their slot with the wing over the Adriatic.

The 464th reached the target and dropped their lethal load without any sign of enemy opposition. So far it looked like the group would be treated to another milk run.

The 8th and 15th Air Forces had flown hundreds of sorties against strategic targets that provided the Luftwaffe with planes, fuel, oil, and ammo. Because of this campaign the threat of fighter attacks had diminished from the hectic air battles of 1943 and early 1944. The Luftwaffe would fly and fight when they had enough reserves to mount an effective force. On 23 August the Luftwaffe had showed up at Markersdorf and mauled the 451st. On 24 August it was the 464th's turn to face the Luftwaffe.

At 1235 the call. "Fighters, 6 o'clock!" flashed through the formation. Almost 40 Me-109s and Fw-190s were coming in from behind the B-24s. They were not in a hurry to attack. They seemed to be sitting back there, sizing up their prey like a pack of hungry sharks. "Where the hell is our escort?"

"I don't know, they were with us at the IP!"

"Get off the intercom, Gunners, call out the fighters as they come in!"

"Steady guys, this is it. Don't waste your ammo, short bursts!"

" Make 'em count!"

Over the German radios came the call, "Victor, victor!" as the fighters closed for their attack on the oncoming Liberators.

The first attack was a pair of Me-109s from 6 o'clock. Their pass was a hit and run tactic to draw the gunners' defensive fire. Another pair of 109s made the next attack, also from the rear of the formation. These Me-109s were from 1/JG 302. Their attack was well planned and was supposed to try and draw the fighter escort away from the bombers. The trick worked better than the Germans had hoped. There wasn't a P-38 to be seen. The initial German attack left the sky wide open. It was now time for a line plunge through the center by the Wulfes.

On WILLIE (Black K-779th) tail gunner Sgt. Frank Dansereau had a 109 in his sights about a hundred yards out and closing. The gunner got off a burst at the 109. Then a 20 mm shell hit the right side of his turret, shattering the safety glass and blowing the gunner out of his turret. The dazed gunner looked around and saw T/Sgt. Bill Wrinn snapping his chute to his harness. "Bail out!" he yelled. The waist area was full of holes, and fire had started from the exploding shells. Some of the .50 cal shells were cooking off in the fire. Thinking that the ship was doomed, Wrinn bailed out of the camera hatch.

The main fighter attack came from Fw-190s from IV Strumgruppe/JG3. Their attack was well planned and even better executed. They attacked from behind the 464th formation, coming in very close and pumping 20 mm shells into the bombers with deadly effect.

Black-H (42-51083) from the 779th took several 20 mm shells in the fuel tank and #3 engine. The explosive shells turned the wing into a blow torch of burning vaporized fuel. Moments later 20 mm shells stitched the left wing, causing more damage. Lt. Kermit Dannehl put the plane into a shallow dive and rang the bail out bell. He and seven others were able to hit the silk before the plane disintegrated in a boiling mass of flame and debris. Sgts. Kermit Hardy and Frank Sheppard were killed.

LITTLE LULU (42-52479) from the 776th was sitting in the gunsight of an attacking Fw-190. Sgt. John D'Amore wrote:

I was firing the left waist gun when six 20 mm shells entered the waist section. Three went through the waist gunner, Sgt. Edward Ivan, and the other three went between my legs. Then our ship went into a flat spin. I believe another group of shells exploded in the front section of the plane, instantly killing the pilot, Lt. John James, and copilot, Lt. Maloney, because there was no effort to bring the ship out of the spin.

Sgt. Ivan and myself were the only ones with our chutes on at the time of the attack, and he appeared to be dead. I was pinned down to the fuselage beside him due to the centrifugal force.

After spinning down about 20,000 feet, the ball turret fell out of the ship with the gunner still in his position. The ball turret gunner was Sgt. Ralph Robinson. Then the plane broke just about where the ball turret fell off. The force was off my body, and I immediately rolled out of the plane and pulled the rip cord. My chute opened about 75 feet above the ground. The front section had already hit the ground, and the four engines were a mass of fire. I pulled the side lines of my chute and avoided the fire. Being unable to walk, I crawled until two farmers picked me up and carried me into a farm house. Several hours later I was turned over to a German officer and taken prisoner. After I left the plane, I never saw any of my crew members again.

Sgt. D'Amore was the only survivor of LITTLE LULU. Lt. James and the rest of the crew perished in their plane when it crashed about two hundred yards north of the village of Vlcice, Czechoslovakia.

On Red-J, navigator Lewis Price recalled:

I couldn't believe how much punishment it (LITTLE LULU) had taken and continued to take. It was flying to our left and just to the rear.

Then an Me-109 flashed by Red-J and was nailed by defensive fire from the nose turret. Price wrote:

The German pilot bailed out on our level and just to the right front of me. I felt I could have reached out and swatted him as he bailed out, he was that close. My legs and feet got very cold, and it took awhile to see that the B-24 in front of us had shot out our bombsight window. I don't know how long the fighters were attacking, all I know is that I was scared spitless!

Aboard COMBATTY (42-52520) from the 776th, the crew was fighting the approaching Focke-Wulfes. In the tail turret, Sgt. Ed Gaspari was laying down a stream of tracers at the oncoming fighters. The wings and nose of the Fw-190s began to blink like flash bulbs going off. Twenty mm shells hit the Liberator in the tail section, exploding in white blasts of smoke and flying shrapnel. The plane took several 20mm hits on the right side near the camera hatch. The right waist gunner was badly wounded in the leg and fell to the floor. Another shell hit the ball turret, mortally wounding the gunner.

COMBATTY was in deep trouble, but still able to fly. Lt. Thomas Vague could not hold formation because of the damage to the plane. COMBATTY descended to about 10,000 feet and headed home alone.

LITTLE GISMO II (42-78376) had also been badly mauled by the aggressive attacks. Pilot Virgil Leverett recalled:

I could hear 20 mm shells exploding behind me in the airplane. They must have hit the fuel transfer system, because we caught fire from the bomb bay back. The fighters were very aggressive. They came up our tail firing their guns. I got a look at them as they flashed by about 15 feet from our plane. We were on fire, and I rang the bail out bell.

In the nose, navigator Robert Weinberg looked through the tunnel toward the back and saw a mass of flames. He pulled the nosewheel door release and bailed out. He was followed by the nose gunner and bombardier.

In the back of the plane the flames were unbearable. Gunners Richard Hinckley and Raymond Bloxson had apparently been killed by gunfire. Peter Suchor was able to jump, but his chute was on fire. He was killed in the fall to earth. Tail gunner Thomas Monacelli was able to clear the plane and pulled his rip chord.

On the flight deck copilot Clifton Selby was trying to go out through the bomb bay. He was burned about his face and hands as he struggled through the blowtorch that had been the bomb bay.

Pilot Leverett left his seat to go through the bomb bay. LITTLE GISMO II was now down to about 16,000 feet and falling fast. Leverett could see flames blowing back up onto the flightdeck. He was trapped:

I tried to go out of the top hatch, but the plane was in a spin and I could not move. The plane exploded and I was blown clear. I pulled the rip chord and nothing happened. I frantically looked over my shoulder and saw silk hanging out of the pack. I grabbed it and started pulling it out. Finally the back of the chute opened and the chute came out. The force of the explosion had ripped my coveralls off from my waist down. My legs were bleeding, and you might say I had everything hanging out, while hanging out there in my chute. I landed on a small barn and crashed through a tile roof. I finally managed to climb out and slide down the tile roof on my rather bare butt.

Now here's a strange thing. That morning, before take off, I went to the equipment shack and got a new flak helmet. They also had new flying coveralls, and I got a new pair of coveralls. I put them in a duffel bag and put the bag on the flight deck behind my seat. After getting down from the roof, I spotted something laying by a tree. I managed to hobble over, and there lay a brand new pair of flying coveralls. I managed to put them on, so I was fully clothed when the German soldiers arrived.

When LITTLE GISMO II exploded, flaming debris showered down in all directions. Part of the burning wing landed on a house in Cimers, Czechoslovakia, and a woman perished in the fire. Another woman was killed by a falling engine as she worked in a nearby field. Leverett recalled:

When I was captured they took me and several of my crew to the town of Cimers. People were fighting the fires that the plane had caused. When they saw us, they stopped and were going to hang us right then and there. The German soldiers saved our skins that day.

The fighter attacks had lasted for about six minutes. That was all it had taken for the Luftwaffe to spread havoc in the formation. Finally, a flight of P-51s responded to the frantic calls for help and arrived like the old west cavalry to the rescue. The Me-109s and Fw-190s saw the Mustangs coming and dove for the safety of the ground.

Without enemy planes to worry about the homeward bound Liberators could now fight to save their wounded crewmates. Aboard many of the planes there was battle damage to contend with. The crews would try to repair as much as they could while still in the air. It would be a long flight back home, that is, if they made it.

COMBATTY had last been seen going down. She was far from the formation but still in the air. With the fighters gone, Ed Gaspari climbed from his tail turret and into the shattered remains of the fuselage. The left waist gunner and Gaspari managed to get the ball turret gunner out of the turret and laid him near the waist guns. They broke out the first aid kit and gave him a shot of morphine to ease the pain. The intercom was out, as were most of the other systems in the plane.

Gaspari recalled that the plane was riddled with holes from the gunfire. As they neared Klagenfurt, Austria, Gaspari started to move to the front of the plane to see what was going on and to report on the way things were in the back. As he got to the bomb bay he met Lt. Merle Riley, the bombardier, face to face on the catwalk. At that moment COMBATTY was hit by flak and bounced around. Gaspari recalled, "The last thing I heard was Lt. Riley yelling 'Get out, get out!'" Gaspari could not remember whether he jumped or was thrown out of the plane. Lt. Riley had tried to get to the back of the plane to help. Riley and Sgts. John Renz and Stanley Grzesik would ride COMBATTY to the ground.

WILLIE limped back without their gunner, who had abandoned ship near the target. The crew had managed to put out the fire. There were four wounded on board, and the plane was a mass of holes held together by jagged aluminum. They landed at Bari so the wounded could get quick medical attention. WILLIE was so badly damaged that she would go to Depot 52. She would be repaired and fly again with the 450th BG.

When the planes came within sight of the field, all eyes were trained to the oncoming formation. Those that were near a radio heard the frantic calls to Racecard Tower. Crew chiefs grabbed the nearest pair of field glasses and were scanning the formation for their plane. Red flares arched from several of the Liberators indi-

White-L (44-1084) and BIG ED from the 778th head for the target. Note that White-L still does not have her call letter painted on her side.

cating that they had wounded aboard. Racecard tower cleared them to land first.

One by one the planes came in to roost at Pantanella. Twenty-five planes had made it to the target, but only twenty planes made it home. Of these, three planes were badly damaged and six had minor damage. The ambulances met the ships that had fired the red flares. Aboard these planes the medical teams removed two crewmen that had been killed. There were another four that had major injuries. Two others had minor wounds.

The flight crews surveyed the damaged planes, then headed for interrogation to report on how the mission had gone. It was a long rough ride up the hill. The mission had been a lot rougher.

On top of all the damage caused by the Germans, there was a final irony at the conclusion of the mission. As MICKEY (42-52526) taxied to her hardstand a truck ran into her, causing major damage. She would be repaired to fly again.

At debriefing the men had to relive the horror of the mission in as great a detail as their combat fogged memories would allow.

"Ship No 520 was hit by enemy aircraft. A large hole was near the camera hatch. Ship No 520 dropped out of formation. No chutes were seen."

On it went, until all the returning crews had been debriefed. As they left, they lined up for their shot of combat whiskey to help settle their frayed nerves. Even those who did not usually take their medicine took it this day.

Chaplain Eastwood was on hand as always for those who needed some spiritual reinforcement. After this particular mission, Chaplain Eastwood would have more letters to write to the families of those who did not return.

By the time the flight crews were able to get back to their quarters, they were bone tired and numb from combat. Yes, the ration of post mission whiskey helped to take the edge off their nerves, but they were still tired of everything. They were tired of the food, the living conditions, and most of all, they were tired of flying combat. Most of them could have cared less about the latest news from the western front. Few of them took time to talk about the fact that the German commander of Paris had called it quits and declared the "City of Lights" an open city. Although the men did not know it at the time, nor would they receive the credit until June 1945, the 464th had just flown its second DUC mission.

Turn about was fair play. The 451st had treated the 464th to a milk run on 23 August by taking on the whole Luftwaffe. On the 24th the 464th bore the brunt of the German defenses while the 451st was treated to a milk run. It was not a matter of just how good you were, but where and when you happened to be in the bomber stream headed to the target.

The ground crews worked through the night as usual, and the group was able to have 34 planes ready for take off at 0645 on the morning of the 25th. One plane aborted on the ground because a prop governor failed. 42-78514 did not take off because the bombload had not arrived in time to be hung on the racks.

The group Commander, Col. Schroeder, led the mission. The second attack unit was under command of Lt. Frank Price (779th). Group form up and rendezvous came off without any problems. The 55th wing headed out over the Adriatic and then on towards the target.

The 464th was over Prostejov Airdrome, Czechoslovakia, at 1128 hrs and released over 55 tons of bombs onto the target. Strike photos showed that the target was plastered. The 464th had taken revenge on the Luftwaffe. They would not have to worry about enemy fighters using that particular airfield for a long time.

At the rally point, Lt. Lawrence Kalgreen from the 779th radioed the lead ship to tell the leader of a serious problem. PAPER DOLL (41-29351) had 300 gallons of fuel left. Kalgreen said he would fly as long as he could before ringing the bail out bell. At about 1220 hrs. the fuel gauges showed zero and the engines started to cough. Ten chutes blossomed, then PAPER DOLL rolled over and spiraled to the ground.

The rest of the formation continued towards home base and started landing at 1436. Except for the loss of PAPER DOLL the mission had been a milk run. No one had been hurt aboard the returning planes. On top of that the 464th had extracted their pound of flesh from the Luftwaffe.

That night some of the men took a few minutes to write a few lines to the folks back home. These letters reflected a lot of different thoughts. William Laughlin was one of those who wrote home that day:

It is very quite here. A few voices off in the distance, with the faint drone of a far off B-24. The sun has just gone down and is showing up the shape of the blue hills off in the distance. A nearby mountain stands out dark blue against the lightish gray sky. A few small stratus clouds show black against the reddish orange sky. Some smoke drifts lazily out of the valley, and a few lights of trucks shine in the distance. In the valley, pools of water reflect the last light of the sun. Another day is almost ended. Up above the moon is shining brighter by the minute. One lone star appears low on the horizon. Another B-24, its red passing light burning brightly, flies past. Italy prepares for another day.

Due to bad weather over Europe, the mission for 26 August was canceled and the group took the day off from flying. This gave the ground crews some welcomed extra time to work on the planes. If they did not have any routine things to do, it was a good time to change spark plugs, or maybe an entire engine if the total time was getting close to the top end. The ground crews could always use extra time. The problem was that the weather was not bad just over the targets, it was bad in Italy, as well. The entire day was overcast, and the rain would come and go. Since there were no hangars at Pantanella, the ground crews would have to work on the planes in the rain. Some of the crews tried to rig tarps over the engines so that they could work out of the rain. No matter what they tried it was still damp out on the hardstands.

When the planes returned from a mission the flight crews would leave the hardstand and head up the hill to interrogation. In most cases, they were gone before the engines had even started to cool down. It was now time for the groundcrews to work their special kind of magic and get the planes ready for the next mission. If the plane had battle damage, it would have to be repaired. Most of the flight crews had little idea of what went on during their time away from the hardstand. All they knew was that the plane would be ready for the next mission when they returned from the hill.

One of the most time consuming duties of getting a plane ready was changing an engine if it had failed or had taken damage from flak or fighters. "Red" Mouldenhauer, Jack Shipman, Steve Stephenson, Mike Moyna, and Harry Bruneau recalled just what went into changing an engine.

The first step was to order a replacement engine and put in a work order for the prop specialist to bring a prop sling, tools, and a dolly:

We got an A-Frame to remove the prop and put the prop on the dolly. We did this if the prop men were not available. We would then get three crew chief stands and put one on each side of the engine and one in the front. The cowling was removed and laid on the ground. Then it was back up on the stands to get started again.

We removed all of the fuel, oil, hydraulic, and electrical lines from the old engine. Depending on what engine it was, we also removed air pressure and vacuum lines. In some cases we would cover the lines with tape or something else to keep blowing dirt from getting inside.

The A-Frame was moved into place and the sling was attached to the engine. At this point we put just enough tension on to remove all the slack on the sling. We then removed the four bolts on the mount at the firewall. We would then move the A-Frame forward very slowly to be sure that everything was detached from the firewall. We then moved the engine and A-Frame to the edge of the hardstand and lowered it onto blocks, or whatever was handy.

By now, hopefully, the new engine had arrived, and we took it out of the shipping crate. When we were ready, we would unhook the old engine from the sling and put the new engine into the sling. With the new engine in the sling we would remove the accessories, such as the carburetor and fuel pump, and then put them on the new engine. We used the old equipment only if it was serviceable.

If the engine change was the result of internal engine failure, we had to drain and flush all of the oil lines and oil tank and replace the oil cooler.

At this point we would remove the portex plugs from the cylinders on the new engine. These plugs removed any moisture that may have collected in the cylinders. We put the spark plugs into the holes, except for the ones below the horizontal line.

Now the new engine was ready to hoist into position, so we would crank the engine up while moving the A-Frame into position in front of the nacelle. We installed the four mounting bolts and torqued them to specifications. The sling and A-Frame were then removed. All of the electrical, fuel,oil, hydraulic, and air pressure lines were hooked back up and torqued to specifications.

At this point the prop specialist would use the A-Frame and sling to remove the prop from the dolly, wheel it into position, and then hoist it upward and secure it to the propeller shaft. They would then check to make sure that all of the blades were aligned with the index marks and install the prop dome and torque it.

It was now time to check for liquid lock, pickling fluid in the lower cylinders or intake pipes. We made sure all of the magneto

A Big Friend protecting a Little Friend. Close examination shows that the P-38's (center) right engine is shut down.

switches were, "off." We then pulled the prop blades through eight or more times. Any oil in the cylinders or pipes would run out of the open spark plug holes. We would pull the blades through another eight or more turns, and if no oil ran out we would install the spark plugs in the lower cylinders.

We would then fill the oil tank and check for leaks under pressure. We would also check the other lines under pressure to make sure of no leaks in the system.

If everything checked out, we would climb into the cockpit and start the number three engine so we had hydraulic pressure for the brakes. We then started the new engine and checked to make sure that the oil pressure came up to normal. We would then idle the engine at 1,000 RPM, mixture at auto lean for five minutes, noting oil pressure, which should be 65-80 psi, and fuel pressure at about 15 psi. There was a groundcrewman outside watching for leaks. If anything was not right we would adjust it until everything was according to the book.

Finally, we put the cowling on the engine. We would run the engine about 45 minutes, checking different settings and RPMs. If everything went well we would shut it down and pull the oil screen to check for any metal fillings.

It was time to call OPS and let them know that we were ready for a crew to test hop the plane and "slow time " the engine. The crew chief usually went along with the crew on this one.

After getting airborne the engine would be run at about 2,200 RPM and 25 inches of manifold pressure. At about 6,000 feet the pilot would feather and unfeather the prop on the new engine. After about an hour, we would land and taxi back to the hardstand.

At the hardstand we would again check for leaks. Then we would pull the oil screen and check for metal. If everything was ok, the plane was ready for another mission over enemy territory, taking the war to Adolph.

Now remember, this all had to be done outside. There were no hangars at Pantanella. Engines were changed in all types of weather, and by flashlight or the headlights from a cletrac. If an engine had to be changed, it was done in the rain, snow, blowing wind, or the dead of night.

On the morning of the 27th low clouds covered Pantanella. The crews had been awakened early and briefed for a mission to the Synthetic Oil Plant at Blechhammer South. Another long haul; maybe weather would cause the mission to be scrubbed again.

No such luck; the green flare arched into the Italian morning, and the ground crews were ready to stand fire guard. Across the field, came the familiar call, " Clear on number three !" Propellers began to turn, and the engines coughed to life and belched blue gray smoke as the RPMs came up. Soon the aerial armada was taxiing into position. Those who would stay on the ground watched as the planes began to take off. When the planes were airborne they would knock off and get some well deserved sack time.

SULTAN II (42-95348) and her crew from the 778th started to roll down the steel matt runway. Frank Kinberger (bombardier) was starting his 46th mission. He recalled that he really did not feel like flying that day. He had been the last man to climb into the plane. During the take off roll he was standing near the top turret. For some reason he moved forward and stood behind the pilot on the flight deck.

As SULTAN II lifted off, Lt. Gillen called for the gear. The wheels were just in the wells when the #3 engine coughed and the rpms fell to zero. Kinberger recalled hearing the flight engineer yell, "We're going to crash!"

Gillen chopped the throttles and killed the switches. SULTAN II came down like a ton of bricks and slammed into Italian real estate. She slid along the ground like a slippery fish, shedding parts along the way. Frank Kinberger was thrown to the flight deck floor, breaking his left arm.

As the plane came to a stop the top turret came loose from the mounts and telescoped towards the flight deck, killing the radio operator, Joseph Bailey, and nose gunner Harold Harer. They were riding on the deck directly below the turret.

It was a miracle that SULTAN II had not exploded on contact. She was full of fuel and over 2 tons of bombs for the mission. Despite the loss of two crewmen, the pilots had pulled off a miracle. Kinberger remarked, "Gillen was either a damn good pilot, or we were awfully lucky—maybe a lot of both!"

The rest of the planes took off and groped about in the low cumulus clouds trying to get the group formed up. Wing rendezvous seemed to be SNAFU. The 460th BG kept getting in everybody's way at the wrong time. It took a long time to get all the planes sorted out and in the right position for the formation to continue on to the target.

The fighter escort showed up right on time. The 332nd FG (red tailed P-51s) were to provide cover to the target, while the 52nd FG and the 31st FG were to cover the withdrawal for the mission. If the Luftwaffe came sniffing around there would be escort fighters to hold the Wulfes at bay.

A few minutes before reaching the IP Black-Q, also known as EASY MAID (42-50796) from the 779th, reported a bad fuel leak on the #4 tank. Pilot George Drew had little choice but to leave the formation and head for home alone.

The rest of the formation continued from the IP and arrived over the target at 1216. They released 57 tons of RDX onto the target. One B-24 had dropped its load near the IP after they had lost the #4 engine. They were able to stay with the formation.

Flak had started just before arriving at the release point, and it was intense and accurate. The group was within range of the heavy guns for about five minutes. Several of the planes had taken hits, but none were bad enough to cause the planes to leave the safety of the formation.

The planes rallied and headed home. The fighter escort for the withdrawal finally showed up, then faded away in the scattered clouds. Many felt that the 52nd and 31st FGs had not done as good a job as the red tailed Mustangs flown by the Tuskegee Airmen.

George Drew and the crew aboard #796 were still in the air. They had dropped their bombs on a line of barges as they crossed the Danube. They almost made it to the Yugoslav coast and possible safety at Vis. The #4 engine suddenly blew up and caught fire. With a bad fuel leak nearby the fire spread along the wing, and Drew ordered the crew to bail out. He finally left the plane about 300 feet above a mountain. He and seven others on his crew were captured. Two men were able to link up with the local underground and evade capture.

When the rest of the group landed at Pantanella, a survey of the planes showed that four planes had taken hits from flak. While it had not been a milk run, it still was not like the mission several days prior.

That afternoon Chaplain Eastwood held the first service in the new base chapel. Granted, it did not have a roof yet, but that would soon be added. Then the "Padre" would have a complete church to work from.

On the 28th the fliers headed for Szony, Hungary, to hit the oil refinery. The first of 28 planes was airborne at 0715 that morning. The mission was under command of Capt. Myron Mershon. The planes formed into two attack units and headed out over the blue water of the Adriatic.

The formation reached the IP at 1030 and turned towards the target. Within a few moments the lead element started to see flak blossoming out in front. It appeared that their sister group, the 465th, was catching the brunt of the gunfire.

The Liberators reached the release point at 1138. They were seven minutes early according to the mission briefing flimsy. Maybe it was better to be early than late. At least they would get it over with a little sooner then called for. Bombs away was called, and the formation rallied for home .

The group flew through a few bursts of flak, but it was not the usual flak that the men expected. There were several bursts close enough to one plane to cause some damage, but it wasn't serious enough to cause the plane to go down.

Bomb strike photos showed that the target was covered very well. There were several direct hits in the shop areas. Several bombs had walked into the storage tank farm, and it was blazing as the formation left the area. On top of that an underground pipeline had been cut and was belching streams of fire.

All of the planes returned to the base. No crewmen had been injured on the mission. The plane that had been hit by flak also returned, and it would be back in commission within a few days. In all, this mission could almost be considered a milk run.

B-24s started taking off at 0710 on the morning of the 29th. A total of 30 aircraft were in the air under the command of Lt/Col. Charles McKenna. The second attack unit was led by Capt. Art Robertson. The planes were headed to Meravska, Hungary, to bomb industrial targets in that area.

Fighter escort was provided by about 20 P-51s from the 332nd FG. Several Mustangs from the 52nd FG were seen during the flight to the target. It would be good to have the Mustangs close by in case the German fighters showed up.

The weather was still clear until about 40 miles from the target. At that point, the group started running into cloud cover. As the formation reached the IP it looked like the group would have to bomb by radar. Aboard the lead ship the radar had already been turned on, and the operator could see right away that there was a problem. At the IP it was evident that nothing could be done to get the radar working, so the formation leader turned the group over to the Deputy Lead, Maj. Weldon Burton.

As the planes lumbered towards the target the first burst of angry looking flak appeared in the distance. Shortly it was all over the sky. Higher than the group, then it was lower than the group. Within a matter of moments the flak was bursting at the same altitude as the group.

At the last moment the undercast opened just enough to see the target. There wasn't enough time to switch to a visual run, so the 67 tons of bombs were dropped by radar and disappeared as the clouds closed in again.

The planes rallied for home. Shortly after leaving the target area, FUN HOUSE (42-78248) was seen falling behind and losing altitude. The pilot, Lt. John Kellogg, had feathered the #4 prop. At about 1315 hours a radio call was heard from what was believed to be FUN HOUSE . It sounded like Kellogg, saying he was going to bail out the crew. The entire crew did manage to bail out of FUN HOUSE. They would return to Pantanella on 6 September.

The 464th was treated to another milk run to the Railway Bridge at Trieste, Italy, to finish the month. No flak, no fighters, and best of all, no injuries. Strike photos showed that several spans of the bridge had been dropped.

August had been another hard month for the 464th. They had flown 22 missions in 30 days. A total of 595 sorties were flown on those missions. The cost to the group was 109 crewmen listed as missing.

Living conditions continued to improve, as many men had traded their canvas casas for a more sturdy tufa block house. Plans were in the works for more club facilities, and word had it that a touch football league was in the works. The group already had two basketball courts, 10 volleyball courts, and two softball and one baseball diamond. Along with this there were eleven horseshoe pits.

Another new item that had started around the first of the month was a gunnery school. The school was under the leadership of Capt. J.S. Edwards. He had been a newspaper reporter in civilian life. He knew how to get things done, and it did not take him long to get things set up and running. One of the instructors, Marvin Nelson, recalled one of Capt. Edwards "supply trips":

An example of his brass was that he needed a lot of cement. He got a six by six truck and driver and then drove over to a British materials storage facility that was not far away. The facility was guarded by Italian guards. Getting out of his truck in a very authoritarian manner, he pulled a small book out of his pocket, looked at it for a moment, then, pointing to the stockpiles of cement bags he could see from the gate, he ordered the driver forward. The guards opened the gates and even helped him in loading the cement. He then proceeded back to the base with his loot.

September 1944

The 464th started the new month on 1 September by flying a mission to hit the rail yards at Szajol, Hungary. The first of 31 planes took off at 0715 that morning. Form up of the 464th went without a hitch. When it came time to meet up with the 465th, their sister group was nowhere to be seen. The 464th made a quick 360 degree turn and saw the 465th still trying to get together as a group. The 464th turned again and headed for Spinazzola, assuming the lead position for the wing. The 465th finally caught up with the wing and took the lead as the entire wing turned at the IP.

The attack force reached the target at about 1100 hours without any sign of German opposition. They dropped 65 tons of bombs on the railyards and started to rally for home. Several of the planes could not release their bomb loads at the target because of malfunctions. These planes returned with their bombs in the racks.

The target was plastered. Direct hits were made on rolling stock in the yards. The station house and several other buildings also took direct hits. The majority of the bombs landed on the tracks and walked about a quarter of a mile, right down the middle of the tracks. It was safe to say that the trains would be running late for quite a few days after this mission.

All of the planes returned to the base. It had been a milk run. No planes had taken any damage, and no one was hurt. It had been a nice change of pace and a great way to start September.

On the 2nd, the fliers were treated to a second milk run to the railway bridge at Supovac, Yugoslavia. The bombardiers were getting pretty good at this railway work.

The bombs hit the tracks on the east side of the bridge and walked for about 2,500 feet, right up to the bridge. Four direct hits were scored on the eastern span, dropping it into the valley.

No fighters were seen at any time during the mission. A few bursts of flak were seen, but they were so far off that it did not come close to hitting a plane. Another milk run under their belts, the planes returned with no damage and no injuries.

There was no mission on the 3rd. The men of the 464th spent the day either trying to catch up on sack time or working on the planes. For the men in Headquarters it was the usual day of paperwork. Just because there was no mission did not mean that the daily report did not have to be made. The 4th saw the 464th back in the air to take a crack at the rail yards at Bronzolo, Italy.

That morning, 28 planes took off in what could be described as marginal weather. SOUTHERN COMFORT (42-52514) had to abort the mission because of mechanical problems. When they got back to Pantanella, the base was "socked in," so they had to land at the 460th BG base near Spinazzola.

No flak or fighters met the group over the target. The bombs were released onto the target from about 22,000 feet and hit the railyards smack in the middle of the aiming point. Bombs also hit about 1,800 feet to the north near the workshops.

The planes returned to Pantanella to find scattered clouds over the base. Racecard tower advised the returning planes that there was a strong crosswind. Getting the planes safely down would be the hairiest part of the mission.

The planes broke formation and slipped into the pattern. The pilots cranked in a little more trim, held the downwind wing a little low with aileron, and shuffled the rudders to keep the ships lined up until the wheels kissed the PSP of the runway.

On the morning of 5 September, Col. Schroeder announced that he would be leading the group during the mission briefing. According to the operations order, the group was to attack and destroy the railway bridge at Szob, Hungary. Maj. James Gilson would lead the second attack element.

Col. Schroeder left the runway in the lead plane at 0700, followed by 30 more planes. The two elements formed into two units, met up with the rest of the 55th Wing, and headed out over the

BUTCH M LOVE taxies out for a mission in September 1944.

White-J over the Adriatic.

Adriatic. Near the north end of the Adriatic the fighter escort arrived to take the formation to the target. For this mission, P-51s from the 52nd and 332nd Fighter Groups were assigned. No planes from the 464th aborted on this mission. The ground crews had done a very good job of getting the planes ready for the mission.

The formation arrived at the IP and turned onto the bomb run heading. Just after the turn, LUCKY STRIKE (42-78431) accidentally dropped their two and a half tons of bombs. It seemed that the release handle had slid past the safety stud and into the salvo position.

Five other planes did not release because of problems with either the bomb release or bomb doors that would not open all the way. The remaining 25 planes dropped their 1,000 pounders on the target with good results.

Very little flak was encountered. Several German fighters were lurking in the distance. They took one look at the Mustangs guarding the bombers and made no effort to attack. Several of the "Red Tailed" Mustangs from the 332nd FG started to go after the Me-109s, while the rest of the Mustangs stayed with the bombers. The 109s saw the Mustangs coming and dove for the ground. The P-51s returned to the formation to guard against any other German fighters that may have been in the area.

It had been a good mission for the 464th. No planes had been hit by flak, and no members of the attacking planes had been injured by flak. So far, the month of September was proving to be a good month. The boys were getting some missions in towards their magic fifty. In view of the fact that all of the missions for the month had been directed against railway targets, there was talk of making "I've Been Working on the Railroad" the unofficial song of the 464th.

On the 6th, the 464th was treated to yet another milk run. The target was the rail yards at Nyiregyhaze, Hungary. The fighter escort was provided by the 52nd and 332nd Fighter Groups again. It is noted that the flight crews heaped a lot of praise on the 332nd Red Tails and how they stayed so close to the bombers. It is a historical fact that the 332nd Fighter Group never lost a bomber to enemy fighters while they were on escort duty.

The most interesting thing about the mission was the reports of all the barge traffic that was spotted on the Danube River. The work the group had done on the German railway systems was making an impact on how the Germans were trying to move equipment and war materials.

The weather over Europe closed in and prevented flying missions on 7 and 8 September. Again, this break in the action gave the men a chance to work on the base to get it ready for the upcoming winter months. The base chapel almost had the roof completed. Work had also started on a group Headquarters building.

On the morning of the 8th, the group almost got off the ground before the mission was canceled. As 41-28701 was taxiing back to the hardstand, the left main gear collapsed. The whirling props dug into the taxi strip and the B-24 danced around, coming to a halt facing in the other direction. There were no injuries, but the plane was bent up pretty good. That particular ship had been loaned to the 464th from her sister group, the 465th.

The morning of the 10th dawned bright and clear at Pantanella. Thirty-two crews were awakened, and when dressed they shuffled to the chow line. After eating they were off to the briefing to find out where they were headed.

When the curtain was pulled from the target map there were a lot of moans and groans. "Oh God, Vienna!" The route string went to the Diesel Works. Robert Wingfield had been to Vienna several times before, like a lot of the other pilots. He, like all the rest, knew this mission would not be a cake walk or milk run.

The first B-24 left the ground at 0650 with Maj. William Reddell leading the group. Bob Wingfield would lead the second attack unit. The planes kept the PSP shrieking until the entire force was off the ground and headed for the form up area.

Coming back from a mission.

As the formation headed out over the Adriatic the mechanical Gremlins started working overtime on the formation. Here and there, a B-24 would be seen to feather a prop and pull out of the formation. They would turn and head back towards Italy. In all, four planes aborted. Spare ships moved into the open spots of the boxes as the formation droned on towards the target.

The weather started getting a little worse, and clouds were moving in as the group penetrated hostile airspace. Near Graz, the clouds were nearly 8/10s at 20,000 feet. If this continued, it would end up as a "Mickey" ship mission.

The formation had not arrived at the IP when the flak started to blossom. At first it was light and off to the side. As the formation began the turn at the IP the flak increased and got much closer. For the next 12 minutes the 464th would be in the thick of it. There was flak all over the place; black, white, and even red bursts. The white bursts were exceptionally large. Maybe they were the 128mm guns that the crews had heard about?

At what seemed the last moment, the target broke through the undercast, and the clear view gave the lead bombardier a chance to make a visual run. At 1043, he hit the release point and toggled the bombs. The rest of the group followed, as 67 tons of RDX explosives poured from the bellies of the B-24s. With the weight of the bombs gone the planes had a momentary surge upwards, as if relieved that the weight was finally gone.

Strike photos were disappointing. They showed that the bombs had landed over a mile from the target in a wooded area. All that way, from Italy to Austria, just to chop a lot of wood for the folks on the ground.

The group rallied to the right and the flak followed. It was still intense, accurate, and heavy. Several planes had taken hits from the flying steel. So far everyone was still in formation, although it was not as tight as it had been before the target.

Shortly after the rally point the formation was bracketed by a deadly barrage. Black-M (44-41053) from the 779th took a direct hit in the forward bomb bay, and a blow torch of flame billowed from the stricken Liberator. She held course for about ten seconds, then wheeled out of formation to the left and went into a flat spin. Several figures were seen falling away as the plane spiraled towards the ground. The pilot, Lt. Norman Overholt, and three of his crew never made it out of the plane before it was erased in a flash of exploding 100 octane fuel.

The 464th heading for a target, September 1944.

Red-C (42-78430) after her crash on September 8, 1944.

Lt. Thomas McGovern from Norbert Kustka's crew was hit in the head by a flying piece of shrapnel. He was killed by the missile. Sadly, he had just removed his flak helmet, thinking that the group was out of danger.

As the formation arrived back at Pantanella, Racecard tower was busy as usual. The ships carrying wounded were cleared to land first. The Medical crews lifted four crewmen from the flak damaged ships. Two of the men were sent directly to the hospital because of their injuries.

Fourteen planes had come home with battle damage. Two of the planes would be out of commission for a couple of days. The ground crews faced another long night of work to get their planes ready for the next mission. Few of the crew chiefs had time that night to break away and see the movie that was playing. Ironically, the movie that night was "This is the Life."

Weather over prospective targets gave the 464th two extra days to repair and service the planes. It also gave the flight crews a breather from harm's way. The group had received some replacement crews, and the stand down time was a good opportunity for them to get into the swing of things with the group. When a new crew arrived they were given a three day crash course on how things were done with the 464th. Pilots were given practice flights, while navigators learned just where in the heck things were located in Italy. The gunners had to go down to the gunnery school area and go through sessions about gunnery. Now, a lot of the gunners thought this was a bunch of baloney. They proudly pointed to their gunner's

White-Y in heavy flak over Vienna, September 1944.

wings and proclaimed that they were qualified. The instructors would then ask how long it had been since they had actually fired a .50 cal gun. Most of the new gunners would answer that they had qualified back in the states. There was no sense in arguing the point; besides, it might be kind of fun to go to the skeet range and bust a few clay pigeons. That is, if enough unbroken ones could be found.

On the morning of the 13th, the briefing officer pulled the curtain back to reveal that the group was headed to Ozwiecim, Poland. The primary target was the Synthetic Oil and Rubber plant. Lt/Col. Poff would lead the group, and took off at 0620 that morning. He was followed by 32 more planes, which formed into the usual two attack units. During assembly, the 460th strayed into the areas used by the 464th and 465th. There were a few tense moments as the formation merged in a criss-cross pattern.

The formation finally got together, and the 55th Wing headed towards the target. Weather along the way was cloudy, but it looked like the formation could skirt it enough to get to the target.

The 464th turned at the IP and made a long run towards the target. Flak opened up at the approaching planes as they neared the target. At the release point the B-24s dumped their load and rallied for home. The group had been in the flak for almost six minutes. At this point it was noticed that the 465th had not hit the target and appeared to be heading for a secondary target. The 464th turned back to the right to stay in position with their sister group from Pantanella.

Now the mission became FUBAR (Fouled Up Beyond All Recognition). Groups were trying to take over the lead, then figure out where everyone else was headed and who had actually dropped their bombs and who hadn't. The 464th tried to radio the 465th on VHF Channel "B," and the 465th was trying to talk to the 464th on a different VHF channel. The 464th assumed the wing lead near the IP for the secondary target, while the 465th dropped their bombs. The 464th then rallied and finally headed the formation back towards Italy. At the Yugoslav coast the wing broke up and flew back to their own bases. What a mess it had been. Because of bad leadership in the 465th, the 464th had been forced to fly over two targets, one with bombs to drop and the other one with empty racks.

Seven planes from the 464th had taken hits from flak with all the extra traveling they had done. Luckily, no one had been hurt. With all of the extra flying the fuel tanks on the planes were just about dry when they landed. Several of the crews were overheard remarking that this should have been a triple credit sortie.

At debriefing there were a lot of comments about the role that the 465th had played in the mission. Col. Poff was irate at the fact that the 465th had exposed the group to a dangerous turn of events. He was ready to go over to the next hill and find out just "what the hell happened." There were several inquiries sent through channels about the events of the day.

Bedford "Daisey" May had flown PISTOL PACKIN MAMA on that mission. She was one of the original planes that had come across the pond when the 464th came to Italy. MAMA had flown a lot of missions and had brought her crews home every time. Crew chief John Graham and his ground crew had taken good care of the old war horse. They had patched a lot of flak holes and changed a few engines. Time and the stress of combat flying had taken its toll on the old gal. The powers that be had decided to turn the old horse out to pasture and retire her from combat. She would be stripped of her guns and would be used as a taxi ship. John Graham and his crew would be given a new plane, fresh from the states. It did not take long for them to paint a large Red-J on the fuselage near the waist windows.

Bad weather hamperd operations from the 14th through the 16th. With all the bad weather causing missions to be canceled, some of the crews began to wonder if they would ever manage to finish out their "fifty" and go home. For the older veteran crews, it was a welcome relief not to face the stress of flying through flak. Besides, they could always go up to the outdoor theater and catch the movie "Buffalo Bill."

PISTOL PACKIN MAMA was retired from combat on September 13, 1944, after a long career of flying combat.

After a mission it was off to interogation—"Time, Place, Altitude."

On the 17th, 31 planes took off at 0759 to bomb the Shell Oil Refinery at Budapest. Lt/Col. Goodyear flew the lead ship for the 464th. The second attack unit was led by Lt. Sharon Waggoner from the 776th.

As the group approached the target area they could see smoke billowing upward from the earlier attacks of other groups. Just short of the IP, Lt/Col. Goodyear turned the group and changed the axis of attack to 250 degrees. This offset was just enough to provide a corridor of good visibility to the target.

At about 1200 the lead plane hit the release point and dropped its 500 pound RDX bombs. The rest of the group followed until a total of over 69 tons of high explosives had been delivered to the target.

At the target the flak opened up on the group. It was very intense and accurate, filling the skies with black blobs of flying steel just after the target. The Liberators and crews of the 464th were in the thick of it for about five minutes, and that was long enough for three planes to take damage from the flying chunks of hot steel.

The flight back to Pantanella was actually rather calm. The planes started landing at home base at about 1415 that afternoon. The flight crews headed for debriefing with the feeling that the mission had been fairly easy, in spite of the flak.

The Medical crews treated three men for minor wounds caused by flak. They also treated something that they had not seen in a while; four crewmen had suffered frostbite while on the mission. Now that was something; there were more injuries to cold weather than there were to enemy action.

On the 18th, the 464th Liberators began taking off at 0630 in the morning. Col. Schroeder led the group, while Capt. Robert Fowler flew the lead ship for the second attack unit. A total of 31 planes took off and climbed into the low overcast that hung over Pantanella. Col. Schroeder made three passes over the field at about 2,500 feet.

As more and more planes broke through into the sunlight the group traveled to just south of Spinazzola, then climbed to about 5,000 feet. Finally, the 464th was formed up, and the other groups from the 55th Wing were spotted. After holding back on the throttles a little the wing got formed up, and Col. Schroeder assumed the lead position, not only for the group, but for the entire wing.

The mission plan called for the 55th Wing to bomb the railroad bridge at Szob, Hungary, The planes carried a full load of 1,000 pound RDX high explosive bombs. With that kind of a bomb load even a near miss would cause a lot of damage.

At the target the weather was clear, so the group made a visual bomb run from about 18,000 feet. At 1116 the group released their bombs and rallied for home. So far it was a milk run. Strike photos showed that there were two direct hits on the bridge and several near misses. Most of the bombs landed on the tracks leading up to the bridge on the west side. Several bombs hit a highway about 900 feet northeast of the bridge. In all, the results were classified as good.

The flight home was uneventful until the group approached the base. There were still some low clouds in the area, which made finding and landing at Pantanella one of the hardest parts of the mission.

The 464th was treated to another milk run on the 20th. It was an easy run to hit the railway yards at Hatvan, Hungary. No flak, no fighters, and for some cream to the milk run, no injuries.

Strike photos showed that the group's mixture of RDX and M-17 incendiaries walked along the length of the yards and through the choke point. Although the MPI (Maximum Point of Impact) was missed, the group still was given a good score for the mission.

The boys did not fly on the 21st because bad weather covered most of the targets that were within reach of the 15th Air Force. The men and planes were ready, but they never got the green flare to take off.

On the 22nd the planes were still ready to go from the day before. At 0755 the first plane rolled down the steel matt runway

Even flying a routine check flight could be dangerous. On 21 September Black-A (42-51856) blew a tire on landing. Note the black tracks on the PSP.

and lifted off into the cool Italian morning. Four planes aborted due to mechanical problems.

As the group flew deeper and deeper into occupied airspace, the weather went from good to bad. By the time the B-24s reached the IP, there was solid undercast below the formation. It looked like it was going to be a Mickey Run to the target.

Between the IP and the target, the crews saw something that they had not seen for a few missions—flak! Depending on where you were in the formation, it was either intense and accurate or just in the general area of the planes.

In view of the undercast the group had no choice but to let the "scope dopes" take a crack at the target and release by radar. As the formation crossed the release line over 62 tons of bombs cascaded towards the clouds, along with a silent prayer that they hit the target.

The flight home seemed longer than normal. That was because of the weather enroute back. It seemed that the closer the formation got to home base the worse the weather became. Red-C (42-95355) from the 776th landed at Pescare because one of their engines was out and they were getting low on fuel. The rest of the planes made it back to home plate. Eight planes had suffered minor damage from the flak over the target.

The morning of the 23rd dawned dreary and overcast. The briefing called for 28 planes to bomb the Railroad Bridge at Pinzano, Italy. The crews were trucked to the hardstands and made their usual preflight checks. Some of the men moved to the side of the hardstand to relax and smoke a final Camel before heading off on the mission. In view of the weather, it seemed that they had all gotten out of the sack early for nothing.

To almost everyone's surprise, the green flare was fired and the mission was on. Crew chiefs grabbed the fire bottles and stood fire guard. Starters whined, and the props began to turn. The planes readied for taxi as the ground crews said a silent prayer for the safe return of their ships. The first plane rolled down the runway and lifted off at about 0725. At the specified intervals the other planes would pull onto the runway and gangbar the throttles for take off.

Taking weather into account, the group was able to take off and get into position in record time. It was always dangerous to try and form up in bad weather. More than one plane and crew had been lost to the 15th Air Force by weather induced mid-air collisions.

At 1118 that morning, 30 planes from the 464th reached the target area. The lead element dropped their bombs on the primary target by radar. Lt/Col. Poff, flying the lead ship, signaled the second attack unit not to drop their bombs. The lead ship in the second unit was a Mickey ship, and their radar had gone on the fritz. The group proceeded to the 1st alternate. At 1140 the rest of the group was able to make a visual bomb run on the Piavel Ponte Di Piave railway bridge.

Strike photos at the alternate showed that the bridge had taken several direct hits, and the tracks on both ends had been cut. The Primary target was photographed several days later and showed no damage. There was a bomb strike pattern in an open field about 500 yards from the bridge.

All of the planes returned to Pantanella to find that bad weather had moved out and the base was clear as a bell. The flight crews were almost overjoyed to be able to make a normal approach to the field and not have to worry about another B-24 lurking in the mist, clouds, and whatever else happened to be hanging over the field at the moment.

On the morning of the 24th, the group was up and ready to go as usual. At the briefing, the "red string" seemed to go in the wrong direction. Instead of going towards the north into Germany, the red line headed towards Greece. Col. Schroeder was at the briefing and told the crews that he would be up front in the lead plane.

Two planes aborted on the ground. RUTHIE THE RAIDER could not get more than 2,500 rpms and 44 inches of manifold pressure on the #4 engine. SOUTHERN COMFORT suffered a complete failure of the electrical system.

Col. Schroeder led the other 26 planes into the air at 0935. The group formed into two attack units and passed over Spinazzola three minutes early, trying to avoid some clouds that were moving into the area.

At 1300 the formation was over the Scaramanga Harbor Installations, dropped over 57 tons of bombs onto the target, and rallied to the right for home. While several bursts of flak had greeted the 464th, everyone agreed that it was not the same kind of stuff they were accustomed to over targets up north.

The right main tire of Black-A. More work for the ground crew.

The flight back to Italy was uneventful, except for some cumulus clouds over the Adriatic and along the coast of Italy. Again, by the time the planes reached home field the weather was clear and the planes had no trouble landing.

When the strike photos were developed they showed that the group had flown a good mission. There were lots of direct hits on the main jetty, seaplane hangars, workshops, and buildings. An added bonus was several hits on a submarine near the jetty and several merchant ships. On the down side, the photos also showed 36 bombs landing well short and in the water.

Weather over targets turned bad, so the group resorted to flying practice missions. On the 28th BLACK-T (42-29417) had the left main gear collapse as she taxied out for the practice flight. The wing and props dug into the tarmac, and she wheeled around to face the direction that she had just come from. Three members of the crew were hurt in the accident. The plane was badly damaged and was declared Class-26. The crew chiefs would descend on the hulk of Black-T like a pack of wolves as they picked her clean of any usable spare parts. The practice flight was canceled.

On the 29th the 464th suffered another accident when BLACK-B (42-50963) had the right wing stall out during a simulated 2 engine landing. The wing and rudders were damaged, but none of the crew were hurt in the accident. Two accidents in two days had cost the group more injuries and damage than the last several combat missions. Maybe the group should go back to flying combat, it seemed almost safer.

September would go into the books as the most lackluster month for the 464th since beginning combat operations. The group had managed to fly 373 sorties and drop 840 tons of bombs. Only one plane had been lost to enemy action, and one plane was listed a missing.

Group morale was at the highest it had been since anyone could recall. The group's losses were very low, and some of the crews had finished out their tour. The base was getting to look a lot better, and the base HQ building was up and functioning just fine.

The base chapel was almost finished. A bronze bell had been installed, and real stain glass windows adorned the entrance. Above the door was the inscription:

Dedicated To The Glory Of God, In Loving Memory Of Those Men In The 464th Bombardment Group Who Gave Their Lives For Peace And Righteousness

October 1944

The 464th was alerted for a mission on October 1, 1944. Because of bad weather over the target area and enroute, the mission was canceled before the planes even started engines. It seemed that mother nature was starting the new month where she had left off in the old. During the day, the weather at Pantanella began to turn sour. By evening chow call the clouds looked downright angry. If the men from the midwest did not know that they were in Italy, they would swear that it was twister weather.

Later that night, Pantanella felt the full force of the storm. The wind picked up and the rain started coming down. Within a few minutes the wind seemed to be at gale force, and the driving rain was coming down, not only sideways, but in torrents. The S-2 map tent, message center, and the large briefing tent were the first to go flying. Men inside their tents grabbed the center pole and tried to keep their canvas casa from heading for parts unknown. For many, it seemed it was a losing battle with nature. Wlliam Laughlin wrote:

It was a hell of a storm, believe me. The wind and rain started about 1 or 2 in the morning. At 4, I was holding one corner of the tent up with my hand. The wind was blowing about 50 mph with sheets of cold rain. There I was with just underwear. I soon gave up and climbed back into bed. At 5:30 Captain McLaughlin said, "Boys, you'd better get some dry clothes put away. This tent is going to go." I was so cold that my foot was moving too fast, and I could not grab my shoelaces to tie my shoes. Well, since we were dressed we went over to breakfast and were soon joined by others who had lost their tents. When we returned from breakfast our tent was lying on the ground. Boy, was I disgusted. We managed to get some dry things out, and we carried them to one of the other tents. We spent the day at the club, where someone had started a huge fire in the fireplace.

The men in the tufa huts faired a little better, but not much. On several of the dwellings the rain ate away the mortar between the blocks and the walls came tumbling down. The men grabbed what they could to try and stay dry, but again, it was a losing battle as tent after tent and house after house suffered from the wind and torrential rain the storm produced.

As they surveyed the damage the next morning, most of the men from the midwest swore that the base had indeed been visited by a tornado during the night. The weather people insisted that a tornado was impossible. They said it had been a severe storm, not a tornado.

WHEEL N DEAL bringing them back from Vienna.

Tornado, supercell, or just a severe Italian thunderstorm, the group's living quarters had taken it in the teeth. Tents were all over the place. Personal belongings were scattered from hell to breakfast. And speaking of breakfast, where the hell were the mess tents? Breakfast would not only be late, but cold if served at all.

Down in the valley, the planes were just fine. The ground crews had tied them down real good and tight, and none were damaged from the storm. On several of the hardstands that were a little lower than the rest, the planes were sitting in what appeared to be a shallow lake. One end of the runway had also joined the submarine service.

Because of the damage across southern Italy, there would be no missions on 2 and 3 October. It was evident that a lot of the 15th Air Force bases had been hit by the same storm, and very few, if any, groups were ready to fly, or could fly a mission until things dried out a little.

The Italian countryside dried out just enough for the group to fly a mission on the 4th. The 15th Air Force was going to try something different. In an attempt to put more bombers into the air and hit more targets, the Able and Baker Force, or Red-Blue Force concept was being attempted. It was simple. Each of the groups would launch two different attack formations. and each would consist of the usual two attack elements. The Red Force would usually have four Pathfinder aircraft assinged to it along with fighter escort. They would usually attack the harder targets. The Blue Force was supposed to fly with no escort and hit targets closer to the Italian mainland. While this was the way it was supposed to be according to the operation profile, there were many modifications to the actual way it was carried out. In many cases, both the Red and Blue Force would hit the same target, however, they would bomb at different times and different altitudes. In some cases, both would be provided with fighter escort.

While the concept was simple, execution was a real pain in the keester. It meant that everything from paperwork to fuel load had to be done twice. The typists up in HQ were saying that they should get double sortie credit towards their mythical "Distinguished Typing Crosses." For everyone, it meant double the work, less time to do it, and still getting the planes into the air.

Operations Order #195 called for 48 planes to form Able and Baker forces and hit the marshaling yards at Munich, Germany. "Oh great! They not only want us to put up two forces, but on top of that, attack a target like Munich! Who in the sam heck thinks of these things at 15th HQ?"

The crews that were going to fly the mission had eaten and attended the briefing for the mission. Down at the planes they went through the usual preflight routine of checking the planes and stowing their gear. As William Hedge was stowing his gear in the nose of the plane he spotted an extra crewmember. There, near his nose turret was a large rat. Bill reached for his knife, but the rat was too quick for him and it disappeared somewhere in the nose.

Lt/Col. Goodyear left the ground at 0729 in the lead ship for Able Force. By 0820 the last of the planes was in the air and headed for the form up area. This first Able Baker mission was going to have both forces flying together to hit the same target. Lt/Col. Poff would lead the Baker force coming in behind the Able Force.

The formation headed out over the Adriatic and met the fighter escort near the Yugoslav coast. The 50 P-38s were a welcome sight to the men flying in the planes. At least if the Luftwaffe showed up they could call the escort and let them deal with the German fighters.

As the strike force droned along towards the target, Bill Hedge's rat showed up again. This time the navigator saw it and hit the intercom switch to let the rest of the crew know that the rat was still

Mission to Vienna. One ship with the #2 engine on fire.

aboard. Since they were going to be flying even higher, it is safe to assume that the rat died from cold or lack of oxygen. Now, conversation about the rat was not the only thing going on over the intercom. William Loughlin wrote:

The Alps were beautiful. A recent storm had given them a beautiful coating of clean white snow. As we were flying along with nothing interesting going on Harr, radio operator in the tail turret, said over the interphone, "Is that snow down there?" Yep, I replied. A few minutes later Harr said, "Hey Hedge (Nose turret), don't those look like rabbit tracks on that mountain over there?" Yea,sure do. Wonder where he is now. Again silence. A little later from the tail turret comes, "Hey, look at the snowman down there. I wonder where they got the pogo sticks to put in his hand." Things like that were always going on all the time. It at least relieved the tension.

Near the IP, the 465th turned to the left and forced the 464th's Able force out of position. Lt/Col. Goodyear reduced speed and managed to fall in behind the Baker force at the IP. Now Lt/Col. Poff and the Baker force were leading the 464th to the target.

Just before reaching the target the flak started to dot the sky ahead with black clouds of exploding shrapnel. The group was on the bomb run and had to plow ahead into the flak. The Baker force reached the target at 1201 and released their bombs. Able force followed a minute later. The combined formations sent over 111 tons of bombs towards the railyards 23,000 feet below.

While over the target, several rocket like projectiles were fired from the ground. They were well short of the group's altitude and burst into flame, then fell back to earth. The exact type of weapon was a mystery to the men in the planes. Perhaps it was an early form of surface to air missile.

Coming off the target, the lead ship was bracketed by flak. The plane banked to try and avoid the black puffs of exploding flak. As the rest of the formation followed, so did the flak. One burst exploded near the belly turret of one of the 779th Liberators. It was close enough to blow the turret door off the hinges. William Pratt was still in the turret when the burst hit. The only thing that saved him from falling out of the turret was his safety strap. He stayed inside the turret with the slipstream howling frigid air across his back until the formation was out of flak range. He was then hauled back into the belly of the Liberator, safe but cold!

As the group rallied for home the flak intensified to the point that it was getting quite thick and accurate. Several of the planes had taken hits from flying steel fragments. BROWN NOSE JR. (42-52485) had been hit by flak before the release point had been reached. Flight Engineer Joseph Krajewski recalled:

We were hit by four bursts. The bomb bay doors had just been opened when we were hit. I was sitting on the radio operator's stool behind copilot Lt. Frank Heck when he was knocked out of his seat. I was hit above my right eye by a piece of flak, and the blood ran down my face. Both hydraulic accumulators had been hit, and the fluid caught fire. The Navigator, Lt. Earl Thompson, pulled the emergency handle to the front wheel doors in order to jump if necessary. The gush of air could have blown out the fire, or the liquid burned itself out. The flak cut a hole in the right side of the ship from the front of the ship to the bomb bay under the right wing. The second shot was above the ship and knocked the front turret gunner, Sgt. Lewis Loftus, out of the turret. Fragments hit Lt. Abernathy in the right upper arm in the fleshy part near the biceps. Loftus was hit in the right front part of his head. At this time three engines cut out and stopped, and we started to dive. The copilot was on the floor unconscious, so I jumped into his seat to help the pilot, Lt. Sam Peskin, fight the controls. The plane dropped in a steep glide from 21,000 to 14,000 feet when two engines started up for a split second and pulled 60 inches of manifold pressure (30 is normal) until Peskin pulled the throttles back and regulated the controls.

Heavy flak over Vienna.

According to Krajewski the #3 engine never came back, because the fuel tank had been hit and fuel had drained into the bomb bay and was being blown around, causing a dangerous mist ready to catch fire and blow BROWN NOSE JR. out of the air. With wounded aboard and the plane under control, the pilot knew they would never get back to Pantanella. He asked the Navigator for a course to France. Krajewski recalled:

The navigator and bombardier bandaged the unconscious nose gunner's head, not knowing that he had also been hit in the right arm at the shoulder and was bleeding. The bombardier's arm was also bandaged. They (nav and bombardier) came up to the flight deck. We started throwing out all excess or unneeded equipment: guns; ammunition; extra clothing; bombsight; and anything we could get our hands on.

The top turret gunner, Sgt. Michael Mitchell, called down that two planes were heading towards us, and they looked like Me-109s. With that, I loaded the Very pistol and started to shoot up a distress signal. When the two planes were along side, they tipped their wings to show their markings, which were a white cross on a red background—Swiss, and boy were we overjoyed. We could not communicate because the radio was out. Sam gave them the thumbs up and followed them to Dupensdorf.

We could not land until we lowered the gear. We kicked out the nose gear and manually lowered the main gear. We couldn't tell if the gear was locked because the light on the panel did not come on, and could not talk to the guys in back to have them check to see if the white marks on the main gear were visible.

The pilot told me to bring Loftus up on the flight deck when I was going below to kick the nose wheel out and lock it. After taking care of the nosewheel I checked Loftus, but he was unconscious. He had a pulse, so I placed him in the corner of the bombardier's compartment and braced him up with three parachutes so he would not bleed from his head wound.

After circling the field three times the two pilots in the Me-109s were upset because we did not land. They did not know that we were getting ready to land and trying to get the gear down. We had everyone prepare for a crash landing by bracing against the bulkheads.

BROWN NOSE JR. came in for a landing at about 170 mph, with no flaps and no brakes. The ball turret was down because the men in the back of the plane could not get it up. Krajewski wrote, "I hollered to the copilot to cut the switches as soon as the wheels touched to prevent fire."

BROWN NOSE JR. came in hot. She rolled down the runway without much sign of stopping. At the far end of the runway was a deep drainage ditch. The Liberator was still rolling when the nose wheel went over the edge of the ditch, shearing off the nosewheel. She finally came to a stop about fifteen feet from some trees that were on the other side of the ditch.

The battered crew climbed from their broken Liberator. Swiss Guards had to cut a hole in the side of the nose to get to the wounded nose gunner. When they got him out they found that he was bleeding very badly. Krajewski later learned that if he had been able to move the gunner to the flight deck, the gunner may have lost his arm or bled to death. At the hospital the gunner was given four blood transfusions to save his life.

BUTCH-M-LOVE (42-78340) was hit by flak in the #1 and #4 engine. That ship was last seen going down with both engines feathered.

The flight back to base was fairly calm after the storm over the target. There were two brief encounters with flak near Trieste and Pola, though no planes were damaged by the scattered bursts of flak as the formation flew over.

The ships managed to get back to Pantanella, and the last plane was down and at its hardstand by 1520. One of the planes had landed at Bari so that three injured crewmen could get faster medical attention.

At nine hardstands the crew chiefs could only look at their flak damaged birds and wonder what the flight crew had done to their planes. That morning one of the crew chiefs had told his pilot to be sure and bring the plane back just like it was. Now it was full of holes. Oh well, at least the pilot and crew had managed to bring it back!

It had been quite a day for Donald Nann's crew. First, there was Hedge's rat, then rabbitt tracks in the snow followed by the snowman and the ball turret incident.

When the story of Bill Pratt's exploits reached the Public Affairs Office, it was a story just too good to be true. The story was written up and sent back to the States. Of course, it was embellished quite a bit. It had the young gunner hanging out of the turret, 20,000 feet over Germany with nothing holding him in the turret but the fact that he had a death grip on the turret controls. There was no mention of the fact that he was being held in the turret by the safety strap. The story appeared in Pratt's hometown paper. To say the least he was somewhat embarrassed about it when he finally got home and was proclaimed a hero.

White-J (42-78336) after her crash landing on October 13, 1944.

Weather reared its ugly head again, as the 464th was forced into a 48 hour vacation due to weather over Europe. The extra 48 hours gave the men a chance to clean up some of the storm damage. It also gave the ground crews a little more time to get the planes ready for whatever the future held in store for the group.

Operations Order #200 called for the 464th to hit the railway yards at Ersekujver, Hungary, on 7 October. It would be another Able Force Baker Force type of mission. The night before, the Ordnance section started hanging 500 pound RDX bombs from the racks. As day broke they were still working. A weather delay gave them a extra hour to finish the job.

At 1007 the lead ship started to roll down the runway. At about 30 second intervals the next plane in the lineup would turn onto the runway, make a last minute check, and gangbar the throttles. By 1050 the last of the 45 planes was in the air and forming up with the group.

BONNIE-ANNIE-LAURIE (42-51760) was one of the last planes to take to the air. She lost a prop governor just after getting into the air. The plane returned, and the ground crew changed the faulty governor in record time. The plane took off again and tried to catch the group. The pit stop was too long for the plane to make up the time, so they aborted the mission and came home.

Over the Adriatic, about ten minutes after passing the Italian Spur, the gunners cleared their guns with several short bursts. Then they settled into their usual routine of just waiting. There wasn't much else to do but wait and watch the skies for any signs of enemy fighters. Waiting and watching was hard on the nerves, but then so was just being on a B-24 headed out for a mission.

The IP was covered by clouds, and the group missed the turn. The momentary overflight caused the attack axis to change to 151 degrees instead of 104 degrees. A minor adjustment was made by the lead bombardier to offset for course and smoke in the target area.

Bombs away was called at 1353 as 105 tons of RDX fell toward the trains below. The lead bombardier had made a good run. Strike photos showed a heavy concentration of bombs on the northwest half of the railyard. Another group of bombs walked through the choke point and into several workshops. The station itself took several direct hits.

The 464th rallied for home and wondered where the flak and fighters were. There had not been one burst of flak! Perhaps they had caught the German gunners asleep or low on ammunition. The only fighters that were in the sky were the escort fighters.

Coming back the group had a little problem with weather. They made several turns back and forth and finally managed to get around the clouds and back to Pantanella. Everything considered, it had been a milk run.

October 10th found the group back in the air. According to Operations Order #206, the group was to fly 28 planes to the bridge at Piove S. Dona, Italy. The first plane left the ground around 0800.

Weather during form up was marginal, and all along the route there were clouds to contend with. At any moment, the crews expected to hear the recall code over the radio. All they heard was static, and occasional chatter as the radio operators turned the dial from channel to channel

At 1132 the formation reached the target. It was completely covered by clouds that reached up to about 10,000 feet. Now, for some strange reason, no one had remembered to schedule a "Mickey" ship for this mission. Since they didn't have a radar plane, they could not see the target. All of the planes turned for home with their bombs still hanging from the racks and the crews trying to find a target of opportunity to drop the bombs onto.

All of the planes came back to Pantanella with their bombs. Except for the few rounds that the gunners had fired to clear their guns the planes had a full load of ammo. The only thing that had been used was a lot of 100 octane fuel and a lot of jangled nerves.

The flight crews all wondered why the hell the recall hadn't been sent. It had been an awful risky sight seeing tour, especially since all of the sights were covered with clouds. The crews' anger was softened a little when they learned that since the group had made the target area, they would get credit for the mission even if they did not drop any bombs.

While no one was hurt on the mission, the grim reaper was still in the area. The medical log for that day noted that Cpl. Gordon Schlichting choked to death on a chicken bone.

On the morning of the 12th the group launched a total of 41 planes towards the Stores Depot at Bologna, Italy. The planes formed into three attack units for the mission. Lt/Col. Poff would be in the lead aircraft. Four B-24s aborted the mission for mechanical reasons and returned to base. The remaining planes formed up and rendezvoused with the 55th Wing. The mission was classified as a milk run, although seven of the returning planes had sustained battle damage from flak.

Friday, 13 October, 1944. The sun crept over the Italian countryside like it had done since the time of Caesar and the glory of the Roman Empire. The crews were rousted from their sacks and fed a

White-J's landing gear, October 13, 1944.

Map showing mission route for 17 October mission to Vienna.

hearty meal of powdered eggs and pancakes if they wanted them. Coffee in the mess cup was optional, but most of the men needed something to get the eyes opened up, and good old GI coffee was just the thing.

The men shuffled into the briefing hut and really got an eye opener when the curtain was pulled back. The target was Blechhammer, Germany. They were going to bomb the South Oil Refinery. Some of the men had been there before. They knew that a trip to Blechhammer was never a picnic.

The first of the 49 planes lumbered into the air. SOUTHERN COMFORT, THE GREEN HORNET, THAT'S US, and 42-51514 aborted on the ground for various mechanical problems. That reduced the strike force to 45 planes. So far, it had not been a good beginning for the day.

Over in the 778th hardstands the crews of Lt. William Price and Lt. Raymond Borg had misgivings about flying the mission. Not that they were superstitious or anything, but this was both crews' 13th mission since arriving in Italy. The crew of Lt. Borg looked at the name on the side of their plane, BE COMIN BACK, and hoped that it was true.

The group formed up and met the rest of the 55th Wing without any problems. As the formation headed out over the Adriatic, the mechanical Gremlins started spreading their mayhem. Six planes signaled that they were aborting and turned back for Pantanella.

A flight of P-38s showed up as escort, but they didn't stay very close to the bomber formation. The crews hoped that the Luftwaffe did not show up, since a lot of damage could be done before the Lightnings could come to the rescue.

The group turned at the briefed IP and started the run to the target. So far, so good! Moments before the group arrived over the target, the first black puffs of flak dotted the sky ahead. It was at about the same altitude as the oncoming 464th, and the group was now committed to the bomb run. Far below, the German flak gunners were committed to putting as much flak into the sky as possible.

At the release point flak nailed BE COMIN BACK. Top turret gunner Bert Landberg wrote, "We were hit by ground fire, three out of four in the pattern." One of the bursts killed both waist gunners, Sgts. Wilton Abbott and Robert Wegner. Flak also wounded Lt. Borg in the cockpit. The crew had no choice but to abandon the plane. Everyone except the two dead waist gunners and the tail gunner, John Anderson, were able to jump from the falling Liberator.

NO EXCUSE was also hit by flak, but continued on towards the target. If their luck held they just might back it back to Italy with NO EXCUSE.

The formation reached the release point, and the bombs fell towards the target at about 1120. The first attack unit had been able to make a visual bomb run, while the second unit had to resort to radar.

At the rally point the flak bracketed the planes. Across the formation planes were collecting flak like large aluminum magnets. It would be another five minutes before they cleared the black dumbbell shaped clouds. That five minutes would seem like five hours.

As the planes headed for home there were several gaps in the boxes. Several of the planes had smoke coming from engines, and feathered props were their cockade. In individual ships there were heroic efforts underway to stay in the air long enough to reach safety.

NO EXCUSE was trying to make it all the way. Gunner Nick Masselli wrote, "We were shot up over the target on our 13th mission on Friday the 13th. We turned towards Russia and got about 20 miles from Budapest before we jumped." The entire crew was able to jump from the plane and became "guests of the Germans."

42-78434 from the 777th was last seen over the target, and appeared to be wobbling due to control problems. Yellow-O (42-78418) had been hit in the #1 engine and was last seen losing altitude after the rally point.

Racecard tower was one of the first to hear that the group was over the Italian coast. They could hear the calls from damaged aircraft asking Big Fence for the fastest and best approach. When the formation appeared the boys on the ground made a quick count. It appeared there were about 32 planes coming towards the field. Even with the aborts that morning it did not take a math professor to quickly figure out that the 464th had taken a pounding.

As the planes landed and taxied in, the crew chiefs looked at their planes and could not believe their eyes. That morning they had sent out the planes in good condition; now they were coming back all shot to hell and full of wounded. In all, 14 of the returning planes had taken damage from flak. White-J (42-78336) came back with the hydraulic system shot out. The crew managed to belly the ship in. The damage was enough for her to be declared Class-26 and become a source of spare parts. Medical crews treated two men for minor wounds.

Later, word came in that LADY ESTHER (42-50500) had made it back to Vis and landed there. 44-41213, also known as BIG FAT MAMA, had been damaged and landed at Tesi. They had put down there not only because of their battle damage, but because gunner Roy Allen had been grievously wounded by flak over the target. By the time the props on BIG FAT MAMA had come to a stop, Sgt. Allen was dead.

Word was also received on the fate of Yellow-O (42-78418) and her crew. They had made it all the way from the target to Vis on three engines. As Lt. John Suber was trying to land the stricken plane something went wrong. The plane crashed, and the entire crew perished in the wreckage. It just didn't seem right. They had made it all the way from the target, only to die on an island that was there to try and save lives.

Chaplain Eastwood would have a lot of letters to write, and the mail room would have the grim duty of returning a lot of incoming mail. At headquarters the clerks would burn the midnight oil getting the mission report typed and ready to send on to Wing HQ.

Friday the 13th had dealt the 464th a cruel blow. Anyone who was not superstitious before that day sure had second feelings after it. The use of lucky talismans was bolstered after that fateful day.

The mission on the 14th was recalled because of bad weather over the target and along the briefed route. SOUTHERN COMFORT crash landed at Bari while returning from the mission due to mechanical problems. She would be back at Pantanella within 48 hours

The fliers of the 464th were back in the air on the 16th. They had been forced into a 48 hour stand down due to bad weather at Pantanella and over Europe. It seemed that the weather was becoming more of a factor in the war than the German defenses, thats is, if that was at all possible.

The mission briefing called for 36 B-24s from the 464th to launch at 0650 and hit the St. Valentin Tank Works at Linz, Austria. Oh goodie, another trip to scenic Austria! The bladder buster would be led by Maj. William Moore, while the second attack unit would be led by Lt. Dean Lovitt.

Four planes aborted the mission. The three spare aircraft that had taken off that morning moved into the vacant spots within the boxes as the formation headed out over the Adriatic. At the usual turn point, the group banked and headed for the Yugoslav coast.

As the planes flew over the mountains the flight crews were treated to a beautiful sight. There below was a vista of bright colors from the changing foliage. Hues of red, yellow, and blazing orange spotted by green passed below as the bombers flew over. For a fleeting moment it gave some of the men a thought of home back in the States. If they survived the mission, maybe they would write home about the sight they had seen.

According to the briefing flimsy, the fighter escort was supposed to show up at 1010. Sure enough, right on time about 40 P-38s crossed over the formation and took their position to cover the bomber stream.

At 1015 Maj. Moore signaled that he was losing oil pressure on his #1 engine. He pulled FLAKMAN (42-95332) out of formation and headed back towards Italy. Lt. Donald Nann, Deputy Lead, slid his B-24 into the vacant slot and assumed the lead.

The reshuffle of the bomber deck resulted in the formation drifting about twenty miles off course to the right of the main formation of the 55th Wing. By the time the Key Point was reached, the 464th was back where they should be and on course.

At the IP the group found the ground almost hidden by clouds. It looked like it was going to be a "Mickey" run. The group turned at the IP and started for the target. The radar had already been tuned up and was working just the way it was supposed to. The "Mickey" men started calling range and course corrections to the bombardiers.

Two minutes before the release point the flak opened up. Not bad at first, but as the group moved closer to the target, the flak moved closer to them. From the waists of many of the B-24s clouds of silver metallic chaff blossomed in the slipstream. For a few moments it seemed that the more chaff they threw, the more flak was thrown up at them.

At the release point, flak seemed to fill every corner of the sky, no matter how much chaff the gunners threw out. They had only been in the flak for a couple of minutes, and already that was too long.

The 464th formation heading for the target, October 17, 1944.

At 1136, the radar and bombardier agreed that it was time for Bombs away. Thirty-three of the 34 planes dropped their loads towards the undercast. One plane did not drop because the release lever had been broken.

As the group began to rally the flak caught up with 42-51389, flown by Lt. William Lee and crew from the 776th. The burst scored a direct hit on the #1 engine, which exploded and caught fire. The fire spread across the wing. Lt. Lee rang the bail out bell, and copilot Robert Keller and Sgt. Sidney Elder jumped from the burning plane. The B-24 fell from the formation. The fire eaten left wing folded, and the plane spiraled into the clouds, taking the rest of the crew with her.

Flak had also tagged 44-10573. The hydraulic system was hit, and the fluid was spraying all over the place. An oil line had also been hit. and the #2 engine was shut down. Several fuel tanks had also taken hits. Raw 100 octane fuel sprayed into the slipstream until the holes sealed just like they were supposed to. Hopefully they had enough fuel left in the tanks to make it home.

Several strike photos were taken through holes in the clouds. They showed that most of the bombs landed on the south side of the city of Linz. Other hits were observed in an open field about a mile southwest of the target. It looked like "Mickey" had muffed it!

The flight home was as briefed. The planes pulled into the pattern at 1407 that afternoon. Thirteen planes landed with battle damage. 44-10573 had made it back to base, but could not get the gear down because the hydraulics were shot out. The crew was trying to crank the gear down by hand when the fuel gauges hit zero. The crew bailed out about five miles southeast of Pantanella.

On the night of 16 October the teletypes buzzed, clattered, and started to print. At bases across Italy the wires were busy with what was headed as Operations Order No 217. The text began THIS IS PLAN ABLE. The directive outlined the entire upcoming mission from bomb load to call signs. It called for every B-24 group in the 15th Air Force to put up a "Normal Effort."

It would take a while to get everything typed up and ready for the briefing officer. The typists worked on into the night. Down in the briefing area, some of the men were putting up the maps and marking the route. They didn't have to fly the mission, yet they still did not like where the string ended. They knew that it could be a rough mission for the flight crews.

Early on the morning of 17 October, 31 flightcrews were jostled from their sleep. They went through the usual ritual and headed for the chow line. It was the usual bill of fare that morning. And as usual, there was the same grumbling going on in the line.

In defense of the cooks, one must point out several things. First, they were up and working a lot earlier than almost anyone on the base so they could have the meal ready when the men hit the line. Also, they could only cook what they had gotten from supply, unless they had found an outside supplier of goods. It wasn't easy to prepare a gourmet meal when all you had to work with was powdered eggs, spam, and powdered milk. It was all G.I. issue, but some thought it was either issued or left over from the Civil War. Finally, they had to eat the same stuff that they threw on the mess kit for everyone else.

At the briefing, the half asleep fliers were jolted back to reality when the curtain was pulled from the map. "Oh, s**t, Vienna again!"

The briefing began with the usual intelligence summary. It then moved on to a summary of the enemy defense.

"Flak, no change. Expect Intense Accurate and Heavy."

"Avoid the area of Bratislava"

"Enemy is capable of intercepting with over 50 single engine fighters in the Vienna area."

Next came the weather briefing for the route to the target and back to base. It looked like the weather was going to be a potential problem on the mission.

The 5th Bomb Wing would be in the lead for the entire 15th Air Force. The 55th Wing was next, and the 464th was going to lead the wing. In all, there were five wings headed for the same target.

Then it was down to the nuts and bolts of the mission. The IP was MICHELBACH. Axis of attack 79 degrees, target time 1200 Able. Bombing Altitude 23,000 feet. Rally left to Ganzerdorf.

On and on the briefing went. To a lot of the men it seemed that the briefing was longer than usual. Or maybe the briefing officers just wanted to talk or make sure everybody knew what was going on.

Col. Schroeder told the group that he would be in the lead plane. His callsign for the day was PUSSCAT 1. He also told the group that they would get to the target "Come Hell or high water."

The fliers filed out of the briefing, got their personal gear, and boarded the trucks for the trip to the hardstands. At the planes they noted that the ground crews were busy loading extra boxes of chaff. Last moment checks were done, and everything was stored onboard the planes. There was still some time for a last smoke before the props began to turn.

After what had happened to the group on the 13th, everyone made sure they had their "lucky talisman" with them. No sense taking any chances on this mission. At "Red" Moldernhauer's hardstand, "Junior" grabbed Red and rubbed his red hair just for luck. That simple act before take off had become a ritual for "Junior."

Col. Schroeder's plane left the ground at 0815, followed by a total of 30 more B-24s at approximately 30 second intervals. The second attack unit would be led by Lt. Bedford May. An interesting mission, as the "old man" would lead the group and one of the youngest pilots would lead the second unit.

Group form up and line rendezvous were on time. The 464th passed over Andria at 0901, exactly the briefed time. The wing was over Spinazzola at 0916. Everything was going according to the plan of attack.

Out over the Adriatic the weather started to go to pot in a hurry. Almost complete cloud cover, and it looked even worse farther up ahead. Five planes aborted the mission that day. All of them lost the formation in clouds as the group flew through the overcast. Rather than fly on and try to find the group, they turned for home to avoid blindly flying through the soup.

Over Yugoslavia, the clouds billowed to 25,000 feet. The formation flew in and out of clouds. There were several turns as Col. Schroeder led the formation between and around cloud vallies. Across the formation, many wondered when they would hear "DARKHORSE" over the radio. That was the recall signal for the 55th Wing.

At this point there is some controversy about the recall. Several men of the group are sure that they heard the recall to all Wings that were airborne that day. After searching through the microfilm of eight different groups and reviewing the mission summary from the 55th Wing, there is no evidence that a mission recall was ordered that day.

Due to adverse weather the 460th BG aborted the mission and bombed the third alternate target at Maribor. The 485th also left the bomber stream and hit a target of opportunity. The 464th and what was left of the 55th Wing continued towards the primary target.

Just before the IP the #4 engine on Yellow-Y (42-50843) started to run rough. The pilot shut the engine down and feathered the prop. The bombardier spotted a railroad through the clouds and dropped their bomb load. With over two tons of weight gone, the B-24 was able to stay with the formation.

At the briefed IP the formation encountered another weather obstacle. There in front of them were stratus clouds reaching up to 25,000 feet. These clouds bottomed out at about 22,000 feet. If the group stayed at the briefed altitude of 23,000, the clouds would swallow them during the bomb run.

At this point Col. Schroeder made a command decision to take the formation under the cloud layer. The group lowered to 21,000 and made several corrections on their heading.

Some of the fliers recalled Col. Schroerder's statement at the briefing that morning. He was going to get the group to the target "Come hell or high water." They were already in high water (clouds), and hell was about to come to the 464th.

Dropping the group to 21,000 feet had caused the 464th to overfly the IP. Flak started to darken the skies as the group had begun their descent. As a result, the first bursts were high. It did not take the Germans long to adjust for the change, however. As the Liberators droned towards Vienna, the flak came closer and closer until it was bursting in and around the formation. George Carney (778th Operations Officer) recalled:

We took a hit that got the hydraulic system. The aircraft filled with what I thought was smoke, but after pulling my oxygen mask aside, I realized what it was. Shells exploding at our altitude all around us, one not more than 50-75 feet directly in front of us, and in a tenth of a second we flew through the center of the dumbbell shaped flak. Perhaps it saved us, as we'd have taken a lot of shrapnel if we had been above or below. It was then that I decided that it was not a question of whether they'd get us, only when.

Warren MacDonald was flying his first orientation mission with another crew. Since it was his first trip, he suffered from rookie naiveté. He recalled looking ahead at the angry burst of flak. Shortly the shrapnel was bouncing off the plane, and he yelled, "What's that noise?" The pilot replied, "We call that hail on the roof!"

Flak bursts bracketed THE GREEN HORNET, flown by Lt. Ryland's crew. Ryland had been hit in the leg and had most of his calf shot away by flak, however, he stayed at the helm of the wounded Liberator. Tail gunner Cpl. Richard Ross was killed when flak riddled his turret. THE GREEN HORNET had a lot of extra holes in her but stayed in her slot for the moment. The next burst caught THE HORNET in one of the engines. With the loss of power the ship struggled to stay with the group, but started to lag behind.

At this point the group had been under flak attack for about four minutes. The bursting shells had damaged several planes. Ahead the sky was even darker, with bursting black clouds of flak as the formation approached the target area.

The missed turn at the IP caused the group to be out of place on the briefed axis of attack. They were now on a heading of 140 degrees instead of the briefed 79 degrees. Cloud cover obscured the Primary Target. At the last moment the target appeared through a gap in the clouds, but the group was too close to make any final corrections. What appeared to be a marshaling yard came into view and became a target of opportunity for the 464th.

Several quick adjustments were made, and bombs away was called by the lead plane. Of the twenty-three ships that reached the target area, all but one toggled their bombs. A total of 51 tons of RDX hurtled towards the ground.

Intense and accurate flak continued to pound away at the group. Some of the experienced crews thought it was the worst they had seen on any of their missions. As the group rallied for home the flak continued to follow them, despite the chaff that was being thrown into the slipstream.

Flak scored a direct hit on LIVELY LADY (44-41070), flown by Donald Waldron's crew. The #3 engine had been blown from its mounts. Fire erupted, licking across the wing as the plane started to fall from the formation. Eight figures were seen tumbling from the plane, but only two chutes were recorded. Just moments after the men jumped, LIVELY LADY erased herself in a sickening trail of yellow orange fire and debris. The eight who jumped would become POWs. The bombardier, Jack Abrams, and Radio Operator Russell Reimer would ride LIVELY LADY to their deaths.

White-A (42-51964) from the 778th took a direct flak hit near the bomb bay. Waist Gunner Lyndle Clark wrote:

The flak was brutal. We must have taken a direct hit in the bomb bay after dropping the bombs, since the doors were still open. Lonsdorf (John) and I were on the waist guns, and realized we were in trouble when we left formation in a glide spiral. The intercom was dead. I opened the door to the bomb bay to go forward, and it was like looking into a blast furnace. At that instant I saw Lt. Bob Cunningham jump from the bomb bay. As I turned around, Hadden

(Raymond, Tail Gunner) went out the hatch. Lonsdorf motioned me out, but I hesitated and pointed to the ball turret and Haigh—"Pinch Bottle," we called him. Lonsdorf just shook his head, and the next thing I knew I was outside. I can only assume that Haigh was dead and Lonsdorf pushed me out.

The plane crashed near the small town of Zohor, across the Danube from Vienna. Lt. Fassnacht (pilot) and Merton Haigh were killed. They were given a solemn funeral with music and masses of flowers in the village church.

The sky was filled with the debris of aerial combat. Pieces of aluminum from dying Liberators fluttered through the air. Smoke from flak and burning planes marked the aerial arena. Men, jumping for their lives from stricken ships, hurtled through the air, narrowly missing oncoming planes that were still in formation. The cries of the dying and wounded were muffled by the din of battle.

SOUTHERN COMFORT (41-29441) from the 777th had been hit by flak before the target, but had managed to stay with the group. Over the target the plane took three more bursts. Copilot John Miller took the brunt of one of the blasts. One of his legs was nearly severed by shrapnel. Flak had also knocked out the intercom, and the hydraulic system was a shambles. The plane had also taken a hit in the #3 engine. The pilot, Lt. Joe Karas, feathered the prop, and the plane started down in a slow spiral. It is unclear whether the pilot lowered the gear, or if it fell from the wells because of the lack of hydraulics. It was obvious that the plane would never make it back to Pantanella. It is believed that the pilot was going to try and make an emergency landing to try and get medical help for the wounded, even if it meant landing in German occupied country.

Near the town of Gotzendorf, Karas spotted what appeared to be an airfield and headed his cripple towards it. As they approached, they flew over Ebergassing, Austria. In that town, 13 year old Felix Rameder watched the Liberator fly past his upstairs window. He recalled that the plane was trying to land with an engine that was burning. It looked like the plane would make it when it was fired upon by a 20mm gun battery. Either the pilot pulled up to try and avoid the stream of tracers or the plane was hit in the control cables. The B-24 pulled up into a steep climb, then stalled and crashed in a field. Felix remembers seeing a figure fall from the nose of the plane. It was the lone survivor, Bombardier Horace Lund.

Lund was trying to pull the nose gunner, Mayo Price, from the turret, and the next thing he knew he was falling through space and pulled the rip cord on his chute. He landed in a field and hurt his knee. He was captured immediately by an anti-aircraft gun crew.

Karl Antosch was a member of 5/657th Flackbatterie Kuckucksberg and would later write in a history of his group:

We saw the plane get lower and lower. Suddenly, we heard the hollow rattling beats, and saw "cords" rise. The plane rose up to a great looping and crashed steeply down from the summit.... Personally, we felt that this downing was unfair."

After five to ten minutes in the worst flak that many had ever seen, the 464th cleared the outer ring of flak batteries. They now faced the long trip back to Italy with the prospect that there would be German fighters lurking in the clouds looking for easy prey.

BLACK-I (42-51683) was still in the air, but she was badly damaged. The crew threw everything out that they could to lighten her load. Over Yugoslavia the plane would go no farther. The pilot, Charles Salivar, rang the bail out bell, and the crew hit the silk. Two of the crew were captured, while the rest were able to return to Italy several weeks later.

The flight back to Pantanella was long and harrowing. Clouds still caused the group to deviate from the briefed route. Over the Adriatic the clouds thinned a little, and the homeward bound crews gave a little sigh of relief.

White-K approaching the Dalmation Coast.

In Racecard tower, Phil Turner listened to the planes calling "Big Fence" for help getting to the nearest friendly field. He knew it wouldn't be long before the planes would be nearing the field and his work would really start. He recalled, "the depressing sound of the voices calling for Medical personnel to meet the planes because of injured and dead crew members."

Two planes damaged by flak landed at Gioia del Colle. Another landed at Bari due to battle damage. All three would undergo repairs and later return to Pantanella.

One by one Racecard tower got the returning planes into order, and the Liberators started landing at about 1420 that afternoon. Some of the planes were met by ambulance so the wounded could be rushed off to receive care. Aboard the returning planes there were two men that had taken serious wounds from flak, and three others had taken minor wounds. One plane brought their bombardier back. He had taken mortal wounds from flak over Vienna.

The radio in the tower crackled to life with a call from Black-H (42-50736), flown by Lt. Leistekow's crew. He was reporting that he was inbound and they were having some trouble getting the gear down because the hydraulics had been shot out. He also wanted the base to know that they had bombed a R.R. bridge in Hungary as a target of opportunity. The crew had voted to stay with the plane instead of bailing out near the base. After all, several crewmen had injured themselves by bailing out.

The grim reaper smiled and pointed his finger of death one last time that afternoon. While circling the field trying to crank the gear down, something went wrong and Black-H fell from the sky, killing the entire crew.

Nearby, three men had witnessed the crash of Black-H. Cpl. John Fisher, PFC John Raleigh, and PFC Tony Tumminello raced to the burning Liberator to help if they could. When they arrived they climbed through the burning wreckage searching for the crew. Without regard for their personal safety, they pulled the remains of the crew from the pile of junk that had been an airplane. Time after time they went back into the raging inferno, trying in vain to save the crew. One of the fliers was pulled from the wreckage alive, but he died before medical help arrived. For their heroic efforts, the three Samaritans would receive a written Commendation from Col. Schroeder.

Stress and fatigue clouded the faces of the flight crews as they climbed from the planes. They did not have to say a word to the men who met them. The crew chiefs only had to look at the planes and the thousand yard stares to know that the 464th had flown through the fires of hell over Vienna.

The crews boarded the trucks for the trip up the hill to interrogation so they could relive the terror of the last several hours. Some took the Red Cross handout of donuts and coffee. After they had met with the debriefing people and told them what they had been

Black-O heading back to Italy after a mission.

through they were ready to try and relax. Most of them were ready for their shot of combat booze to take the edge off the tension. George Carney recalled, "I figured if I was still alive at noon, I'd make it through to another day."

Eleven planes had come back with battle damage. Eight of them were damaged to the point that it would be several days before they would be ready to fly again. There was talk about scrapping THE GREEN HORNET again. She had taken more than her share of flak on this mission, like she had on so many other missions. She would be repaired again and fly more missions with the 464th. This was the second time that THE GREEN HORNET had come back from a mission with a dead tail gunner.

The mission on 17 October had been a rough one. The group had flown other missions to Vienna. They had flown to other targets and lost more planes on other single missions. To those that were there, October 17, 1944, would be remembered as that "Bloody day over Vienna."

That night there was a visible tenseness across Pantanella Hill. Not only visible, it was more then that; it was thick enough to cut with a knife. There were a lot of missing faces in the chow line, and a lot of empty bunks in the tents that dotted the hill.

At SOUTHERN COMFORT's hardstand, crew chief Luther Boone and his crew waited for their ship to pull into the hardstand. They were waiting in vain. Even after all hope of the return of their beloved old war horse seemed lost, they waited until word came down from Headquarters that SOUTHERN COMFORT was not coming back this time. Boone and the rest of his crew didn't have a plane to get ready for the next mission. Slowly, they moved to another hardstand and pitched in to get that ship ready for the next flight to the Third Reich.

The men at Group Headquarters burned the midnight oil getting the reports ready. They did that after every mission, but this one seemed different for some reason. The typewriters were smoking as they typed the reports. There were Missing Air Crew Reports (MACRs), a narrative of the entire mission from start to finish, damage reports, and stacks of debriefing statements. It all had to be ready to send on to 55th Wing.

The weather section looked at the current maps and counted the isobars. It didn't look like the weather over Europe was going to be very good for the next several days. More low pressure moving in from the west could make for bad flying. Maybe the 464th would stand down and take a breather.

The weather wizards were correct. Possible targets for the 15th Air Force were covered with clouds and other weather murk. The 464th stood down on the 18th and 19th. This was not only because of the weather, but also the fact that the group did not have the planes to fly a mission. A review of the 55th Wing records for that time period reveal that on those days the 464th had only 28 planes that could be considered mission ready. The total strength of the group was listed at 57 B-24s.

During the stand down the ground crews worked overtime—if that was possible—to repair the damage from the last mission. Crew Chief Marshall Stephenson from the 779th recalled:

We did things in a matter of hours that would have taken days, if we had done it the way it was done back in the states.

Some of the men volunteered to work on the chapel. Others worked on the officers club for the Headquarters staff. With cooler weather on hand, many of the men worked on getting their quarters ready for the Italian winter. Several had time to think about a touch football league. More than a few of the men used the time to right letters back home.

The weather on the 19th was not just bad, it was downright miserable. Across Pantanella Hill the tents flapped in the wind. Then, it started to rain. The men on the hill scrambled to tighten the tent ropes to keep the tents from flapping apart, then hoped they didn't tighten them too much. There was a small margin of error. You either had a flopping tent or tent stakes pulling out of the ground as the wet canvas contracted.

The weather lifted just enough over Europe for the 55th Wing to transmit Operations Order #220 for a mission on the 20th. The primary target was listed as the marshaling yards at Innsbruck, Austria. The orders called for each plane to carry 500 pound RDX bombs, which meant that it would be a long night for the crews that hung the bombs on the racks.

At 0820 that morning the first of 34 planes lumbered into the air. The form up was a little "hairy." Low hanging clouds made it interesting. Added to the fact that the entire wing was trying to form up in the 464th designated area made it downright dangerous. There were B-24s all over the place. It was a major miracle that no one had a mid-air while trying to get in proper position. The group finally got formed up into three attack elements. The group was led by Lt/Col. Goodyear. The second unit was led by Lt. Richard Price, while the third was under the leadership of Lt. Bedford May.

The planes headed out over the Adriatic, then turned to the north. Because of weather and the fact that the 55th Wing was not completely formed up, the mission lead group (460th) held the airspeed down. The wing did not get formed up until the northern part of the Adriatic was reached. This would cause problems for the bombers.

Because of the slower airspeed and bomb load they were toting, 42-78452 stalled out at about 140 indicated. After recovering from the stall the plane could not get back into position and aborted the mission. One other plane from the 464th aborted when the induction system failed. Both planes returned to Pantanella.

Over the Alps the weather really started to go to pot. On the south side of the mountains the clouds were not too bad. On the north side the sky was almost completely covered by clouds reaching up to about 13,000 feet. Somewhere along the way the fighter escort had gotten misplaced or lost in the soup.

As the formation reached the IP the cloud cover had become complete and the ground was lost from view. The cumulus clouds topped out at about 10,000 feet. Lt/Col. Goodyear signaled for a right turn to the alternate target. The group followed and took up a heading for the new IP at Rosenheim. The new axis of attack was now 300 degrees.

At 1253 the B-24s reached the release point over the railway yards and began to drop their loads. Of the 31 planes that reached the target, 23 actually dropped their bombs. A total of 57 tons of RDX rained towards the ground.

Lt. May, flying LITTLE WILLIE (42-51178) had lost the #1 turbo and could not bomb with the formation. Several other planes had not released because their respective box leader hadn't released. HELL'S BELLS did not drop because the box leader didn't, and for another reason. It may seem strange, but someone had forgotten to put a bombsight into the aircraft.

The formation rallied for home. On the planes that still had bombs, the crews were looking for targets of last resort. The best thing about the mission was the fact that they had not seen a single burst of flak.

Near the Austrian-Italy border one crew saw something that sent a chill up their back. Off to the left of the formation they spotted two swept wing aircraft flying faster than they had ever seen an aircraft fly. The two planes came up abreast of the formation, then made a fast dive and came up on the right side of the formation. They peeled off and were out of sight within seconds. It seems that the 464th had one of their first close encounters with the Me-262 jet aircraft.

BIG FAT MAMA (41-29453) had not dropped its load because of problems with the #4 engine. As they passed over Latisana, Italy, the bombardier dropped the bombs on a target of last resort. We must note that at this time there were two BIG FAT MAMAs in the 464th. White-L (44-41084) dropped their bombs on a bridge on the way home.

The first returning plane was cleared to land at 1515. About half an hour later, the last of the planes were back on the ground and nestled in the hardstands. One plane was reported missing. Later that afternoon it was reported that Yellow-Q (42-51643) was safe at another base.

The strike photos showed that several hits had been scored on freight cars on one of the sidings. There were two direct hits on the choke point and a possible hit on a bridge near the yards. The rest of the bombs landed about 1,500 feet northeast of the station in a mixed industrial and residential area.

Weather caused the missions for 21 and 22 October to be called off before the green flare was fired. It looked like mother nature had defected to the Third Reich.

On the 23rd, the crews were briefed for a mission to Regensburg, Germany. The night before the planes had undergone the usual loading of 500 pound bombs, ammo, and fuel. Again, as the crews arrived they noticed that the ground crews were putting extra boxes of chaff aboard the mission bound planes.

Lt/Col. Poff led the group into the air at 0920. When his plane had climbed to 4,500 feet it was swallowed by the low hanging clouds. Thirty-four more planes followed at the usual interval. Because of the local weather conditions the group formed up over the Cerignola area instead of the regular form up area.

Bombs away as the 464th reaches the release point.

P-38 escorting the group during a mission.

Three planes aborted the mission. LITTLE WILLIE (42-51178) lost the #4 supercharger and #1 engine. WILLY (42-51903) had a fuel leak and could not keep the main gear in the well, and THE GREEN HORNET, now repaired, came back when the crew could not find the formation.

Over the southern Adriatic the formation found 6/10s swelling cumulus, 5/10s cirro stratus, and 3/10s cumulonimbus billowing up to 25,000 feet. As they turned north the weather got even worse. Soon they were in multi-layer 10/10 clouds ranging from 4,500 to 25,000 feet. At 1208, Lt/Col. Poff heard the words "SPOONFED" over the command radio. The recall had been given, and the mission was aborted for the day. All they had to do now was turn around and get back to base.

By the time the planes got back, the weather at Pantanella had gone from bad to "hope we can find the field." In spite of 10/10 clouds at 4,500 and rain, all of the planes managed to grope their way through the clouds, spot the end of the runway, and leave a rooster tail of spray as they settled onto the rain slicked PSP runway.

Mother nature closed the skies over Europe again. Missions were canceled before the group could even get off the ground 24-27 October. The men around Pantanella were getting rather put out with the fact that they were being rousted out of bed to go to a mission briefing, only to have the mission canceled.

During the month there had been some talk about trying to do something for the Italian kids that were in the area, if the group was still around when Christmas came along. On 27 October the first meeting of the "Christmas for Kids" committee met to start planning the event.

On the 27th the weather over the Italian boot had cleared enough so that a few test flights could be flown. These were for planes that had engines changed and needed to be slow timed, or for new planes to be taken up and checked out before flying a combat mission. One of the planes that had just arrived was a new "Mickey" ship. Her serial number was 42-50867, and now she wore Black-Z on her fuselage. Warren McDonald later wrote:

Col. Goodyear asked me to go with him to check it out. We recorded on the A-1 Form that the automatic pilot processed the plane into banking to the left.

On the morning of the 29th the crews of the 464th were awakened and briefed for a mission. The men went through the usual routine and headed for the planes. The weather at the base was marginal for takeoff. By that, it was meant that the pilot could see the end of the runway. The group just might be able to get a mission in before the next frontal system moved in.

Maj. Weldon Burton would lead the group in the new Mickey ship, Black-Z. He was the first plane off the ground, and the group followed him into the low clouds that covered the base. The group had trouble getting together because of the clouds. Out over the Adriatic the clouds got even thicker. It looked like the 464th would get the recall signal at any moment. Warren McDonald recalled:

Black Zebra was the group lead, and I was assigned as copilot in the plane on Black Zebra's right wing. Somewhere near the head of the Adriatic, we were in heavy clouds in a "Recall" situation. Couldn't see anything on the right side, but I could see Black Zebra's wing and not much more to the left. Sweeping the instrument panel I noted that we were in a 60 degree left bank. I looked past the pilot just in time to see Black-Z's wing over to the left and disappear nose down. I grabbed the controls, righted the plane, started a climb, and asked for a fix to the base.

Andy Caldwell wrote:

I was on a plane flying on the left wing of Black-Z. Suddenly, Black-Z pitched left, missed us by an inch, and plummeted upside down, falling like a rock.

Black-Z was gone in a matter of seconds, taking the crew to their deaths. There is no way of knowing exactly what happened. Could it have been spatial disorientation in the clouds? Was it the auto pilot that had been noted on the A-1 Form during the check flight, or had something else happened?

Several planes went down and scanned the water for possible survivors. They reported flying through a "haze of tiny aluminum particles, or some other debris." The search over the water produced nothing but an "oil slick" where the plane had hit the water.

The 464th had gotten the recall and returned to base with the bombs still hanging from the shackles. They hadn't even gotten close to the target and lost a plane and crew to a screwy situation in the clouds over the Adriatic. The crews went to interrogation and told the sad story. Many of the men did not even know what had happened. All they knew was that the mission had been called off.

Later that afternoon there was a steady stream of men moving up the hill towards the chapel. Construction had started on 26 July. It was now finished, and the dedication service was about to begin.

Before the service began there was standing room only, as officers and enlisted men came together and rubbed shoulders for the event. The 464th choir led the gathering in the Hymn "Faith of Our Fathers." Chaplain Eastwood then presented the chapel to the men of the 464th, and Col. Schroeder accepted on behalf of the group. The choir sang several Hymns and led the men in "Rock of Ages." It was a fitting service for all of the men who had worked hard to complete the project.

It may have been the emotion of the service, or the sad events of the last several days that had triggered the large attendance. As the men filed out of the church, more than one paused, focused, and then reflected on the last line of the inscription over the door ".....Who Gave Their Lives For Peace and Righteousness."

If September had been lackluster, then October would be remembered as the month nature went over to the Third Reich. The 464th had flown only eight missions during the month. That amounted to 282 sorties and 607 tons of bombs on the targets. Mother nature had caused targets in Europe to disappear under a heavy blanket of clouds, causing fifteen missions to either be canceled or recalled. Hopefully, November would be different and the group would get to fly more missions so that the men who were closing in on the magic number 50 could get their tour over and go home. The newer crews figured that at the present rate of eight missions per month they wouldn't be done until summer or maybe next fall.

5

Winter 1944/45

November 1944

The 464th started the seventh full month of combat operations by flying to the Graz marshaling yards on 1 November. A total of 31 planes left the base at 0850 that morning and formed into two attack units. The first unit was under command of Col. Schroeder, while the second unit was led by Capt. Charles Fowler from the 778th.

Just after take off, 42-52066 suffered a broken hydraulic line and aborted the mission. The plane circled the field until the rest of the planes had taken off and left the area. The crew flew the plane out over the Adriatic and dumped the bomb load into the water. The return landing was a little tense, but the plane and crew were back on the runway at 1120.

Four other planes aborted the mission because of mechanical problems after taking off. 42-51563's tail gunner suffered an attack of sinus problems. The plane returned, and the gunner was sent to the hospital.

The flight to the target was just about the way it had been briefed. Several small course changes were made to skirt some clouds and bad weather. The closer the group got to the target the worse the cloud cover became; this would be another radar run. About 70 miles from the target the ground was covered by the undercast. So far no one had heard the recall, so the formation flew on towards the IP.

At the IP, the clouds were thick and layered. The formation was sandwiched between a layer below and another over top. The Mickey operators had already fine tuned the units, and everything was set up for the run to the target. About halfway from the IP to the target the clouds broke just enough so that the bombardier in the lead plane could make a visual release.

Bombs away was at 1308 as the group dropped 54 tons of bombs onto the target. Three planes were unable to drop because of problems with the racks. These planes would either release later using the "hand release" method or carry the bombs all the way back to the base.

The German flak batteries could not let the group pass without sending up a greeting. Over the target the planes ran into a barrage of exploding 88s. For about five minutes the fliers were subjected to intense and accurate fire from the ground. Two planes were hit by flying steel, however, they were able to stay with the formation for the return flight to Italy.

While it had not been precisely a milk run, the mission was scored as successful. No planes had been lost, and no one was hurt. On top of that the strike photos showed that the group had hit the target pretty well. It was a relief to finally get back onto the bombing score card after all the radar runs with no results posted.

The mission for 2 November was canceled because weather had moved back over the prospective targets. The weather pattern over Europe was strange in 1944. There were frontal systems backed up and then moving across Europe at more than the usual pace. Weather like this was almost normal for the middle of January, but it was rather strange for that time year.

Since weather was putting a damper on bombing operations for the 15th Air Force, new tactics had to be tried. One of the new ideas developed into what would be known as "Lone Wolf" missions. The concept was simple. Individual radar equipped planes would take off alone, fly to the selected target, and bomb by radar. Several planes could be sent to the same target, but each aircraft would be on target at a different time and perhaps from a different heading. On some of the missions each plane was assigned a different target.

The use of radar to bomb targets had been introduced by the Royal Air Force. They had experimented with it and had developed the H2S system. MIT had improved the British unit in late 1942. At the time, it was considered top secret and was given the code name "Mickey." The official designation was AN/APS-15, although it was referred to as H2X. The unit transmitted a high frequency pulsed radio wave to the ground, and the reflections were converted to a map-like image on the cathode ray tube. Water appeared black, while land was a gray color. Cities, industrial areas, and other features on

Track Chart for 5 November mission to Vienna.

Thomas Potts ditched 42-78521 into a small lake in Yugoslavia.

the ground showed up as a bright yellow or green. Using radar, the Mickey ships could bomb at night or in all kinds of weather. The 8th Air Force had experimented with the use of H2S and H2X and found that they could hit targets in bad weather. The 15th Air Force introduced the use of radar equipped bombers in early 1944. By the end of 1944, the 15th was getting far better results with the pathfinder concept than the "Hollywood Air Force." Although the 15th was getting better results, it was still a hit and mostly miss situation for the duration of the war.

On 3 November the 464th flew its first lone wolf mission. Three Mickey ships left Pantanella to bomb the marshaling yards at Munich, Germany. The first plane, Yellow-A (42-52070), was flown by Lt. August Lechner, Jr., and crew, and took off at 0752, followed by White-W (42-95613) and RITZ (44-49073) at one minute intervals. The planes continued to the line of departure and maintained the one minute separation.

Over the northern Adriatic the planes were in the clouds. They broke out of the clouds just south of the Alps. At this point rime ice developed on the leading edges of the wings. The anti-icing system took care of this problem, and the planes continued towards the target.

The first plane reached the target and released a ton of bombs towards the undercast. The crew reported that there was some flak in the area, but it was at least a mile behind them. White-W, flown by Lt. Frank Lane's crew, was the next one over the target. They hit the release point and toggled another ton of bombs towards the target. This plane was greeted by intense and accurate flak over the target. The plane was under fire for about five minutes and took several hits. RITZ, flown by Lt. Forrest Robin's crew, was the last ship over the target. They ran into accurate flak on the bomb run, though it faded as they reached the release point. RITZ added another ton of RDX to the target.

Each of the planes flew back to Pantanella without problems, except for minor icing over the Alps. The three lone wolves were back at their hardstands by 1424 that afternoon.

Hopefully, the three planes had accomplished their mission. Due to cloud cover at the target, the strike photos showed only the bombs headed for the undercast and results could not be scored.

The ground crews of the 779th were saddened that afternoon by the news that their fellow crew chief, Sgt. Lonnie McMichaels, had died at the hospital. For his close friends it was a crushing blow. On 31 October while working on his plane, McMichaels had hit his head on a prop blade that was hanging down at just the wrong angle. At first he didn't think too much about it, except for the "goose egg," and kept working on his ship. M.E. "Steve" Stephenson recalled:

The group was standing down that day. "Mac" was working at his hardstand, and I was at mine. After a while I noticed that Mac wasn't around and went over and talked with his crew. They told me he had gone to our hut to lay down. It was not like him to do that unless something was up. I went over to our hut and Mac was indeed laying down. He told me what had happened, and that he was not feeling too good. I checked on him again before I went for some chow. He said that he was feeling bad and couldn't eat a thing. I told him I'd check on him after chow. When I came back, Mac was unconscious. We called for the medical staff, and they took him to the hospital. Lonnie was a fine crew chief and a good soldier. He would always give you a hand whenever you needed it.

A total of 37 crews were rousted from their bunks on the morning of the 4th. According to the briefing, their target was the Linz Benzol Plant at Linz, Austria. The group would attack the target in three elements. Lt/Col. Clarence Poff would be assigned as the mission leader.

It had taken most of the night to hang over 82 tons of bombs onto the racks of the scheduled B-24s. It seemed to take longer this time because over 16 tons of bombs were fitted with delayed action fuzes. These delay fuzed bombs would explode anywhere from four to seventy-two hours after they had been armed. The idea was to make it even more difficult for the Germans to repair the damage from the strike. It also made the job of loading the bombs more difficult. The delayed fuzes were touchy and had to be handled with utmost care. Another thing about the bombs with the delay fuzes was that they were booby trapped. Once they were loaded, they were not to be returned to the base.

The first plane took off at 0738, followed by the others. Form up and wing rendezvous went very smoothly despite some low hanging clouds in the area. By the time the bomber stream hit the Italian spur the clouds were billowing to about 10,000 feet.

Two planes aborted the mission. 42-51563 signaled her abort about 1015 hours when it was discovered that the fuel sight gauges indicated they were 350 gallons low on fuel. Since the plane seemed to be a gas guzzler the pilot returned early.

As the formation turned at the IP they were still in marginal weather conditions for good bombing. Below, the ground was covered by clouds. Above stretched another layer, so the Liberators were sandwiched between cloud layers. It was evident that bombing would have to be done by radar. The radar tubs had already been lowered and the sets tuned in. The Mickey operators began calling corrections as the group turned for the target.

Just before the target the crews saw the first puffs of flak appear. It was off to the right of the formation and a little low. In the waist areas the gunners busied themselves by throwing bundles of chaff into the slipstream. Clouds of shredded foil billowed and began to float to the ground. The trick seemed to work, as the flak became inaccurate, and after about three minutes the flak was bursting well behind the 464th. It was almost as if the flak guns were trying to shoot the chaff down.

According to the Mickey equipment, the bomb release line was reached at 1150. Thirty-five Liberators of the 464th released their lethal load of RDX from about 21,000 feet. Two planes failed to release over the target. Black-J (42-78671) had the bomb bay doors fail to open. The crew would jettison their delay fuzed bombs in the Adriatic on the way home.

The flight back to Italy seemed long. Bad weather always made the crews a little edgy when they had to sweat out the weather. At Pantanella, the planes ran into cumulus clouds ranging from 4-8,000 feet. Nothing real serious, just enough for Racecard tower to be very busy for a while, sorting out the planes and getting everyone down. It took over 40 minutes for all of the planes to land.

It had been a good mission since no one had been injured, though two planes had taken minor flak damage. They would be back in the air for another mission within a few days. One plane had landed at another field because they were low of fuel.

On the 5th the group flew a Red Force, Blue Force mission. Red force was made up of 28 planes and two spares under the command of Maj. William Reddell. Their target was the Vienna Florisdorf Oil Refinery. The seven planes of the Blue Force were to hit the rail yards and road junction near Mitrovica, Yugoslavia. This force was under the command of Lt. David McKeaver (778th).

Red Force took to the air at 0735. They formed into two attack units and headed for the wing rendezvous area. At this point the group ran into problems. The lead group for the 55th Wing could not seem to maintain a suitable airspeed. First, they were too fast, then they were too slow. It made staying in the proper line up almost impossible. By the time they reached the Italian spur everything had been ironed out, and the bombers turned north over the Adriatic.

Over the Dinaric Alps the clouds started to billow. By the time the bombers were near Lake Balaton the clouds almost covered the ground below and topped out at over 10,000 feet. By this time two planes from the 464th had aborted because of mechanical problems.

At the IP, the formation found solid clouds from the turnpoint to the target; it was going to be another radar run. Several of the planes were starting to have mechanical problems but were able to stay with the formation.

The release point was reached at 1219, and a mixed load of M-17 incendiaries and 500 pound RDX bombs rained down towards the clouds. Five and a half tons of RDX bombs had delayed fuzes that were set to detonate from 24 to 72 hours after the arming propellers spun off. Several planes were unable to drop because of rack problems. BREEZI WHEEZI (42-78613) could not release because the bomb bay doors had crept shut. Eleven minutes after the target the load was dumped into what appeared to be an open field that they spotted through the undercast.

Flak had greeted the formation over the target, but it was classified as light and inaccurate. It seemed that the leading groups had laid down a good blanket of chaff, and the flak was following the cloud of chaff instead of the bombers.

While the Red Force was hitting their target, Blue Force had taken off at 0905 for their trip to Yugoslavia. This part of the mission was snake bitten from the start, as only six of the seven planes managed to get off the ground. THE BLACK FOX (42-78618) aborted on the ground due to a bad gas leak. It later took off at 1015. 44-40503 aborted when a plug blew out the hydraulic system and the landing gear would not retract. That left five planes headed for the target.

When the five planes crossed the Dalmatian coast another plane ran into trouble. 42-78521, flown by Thomas Potts' crew, was having trouble with the props on three engines. Potts recalled:

#2, #3, and # 4 props ran away as we crossed the coast. We feathered and unfeathered them several times trying to control them. I turned back and had the crew throw everything they could out. We got to the Adriatic, and I figured we could not make it back to Italy. We turned back to Yugoslavia, and I had the crew bail out. Devine (John Devine, Jr.), the engineer, had been working with the engine problem and could not find his chute. It must have gotten kicked out of the bomb bay during the bail out. I told him to get in the right seat. As we came down I spotted a small shallow lake or pond, so I sat the plane down in the water. Devine hadn't buckled his seat belt and was injured real bad when we hit. I passed out, and

Potts had three props run away and aborted the mission on November 5, 1944. Here, several of the crew use a life raft to survey their plane.

when I came around just my head was out of the water. Boy, was that water cold! I tried to get out of the seat, but my seat belt held me in. I couldn't get it unfastened and finally had to cut it with my knife that I wore. I climbed out through the top hatch and tried to figure out how I was going to get Devine out of the plane. A man was rowing out to us in a little boat. I figured I would have a hard time telling him what we had to do since I didn't speak a word of Yugoslavian. As he got close he asked if he could help in the most perfect Brooklyn accent that I have ever heard. It seemed that he had gone to Yugoslavia before the war and had been trapped there at the start of the war.

Potts and the rest of the crew were united later. Devine, although badly injured, received medical attention, and the entire crew were helped by local citizens and the man from Brooklyn to get back to Allied control.

According to the operations orders a flight of P-38s was supposed to provide escort and act as flak suppression by going down and strafing the target area before the bombers arrived. The P-38s were never seen by any of the bomber crews. The force was now down to four planes. William Loughlin remembered the mission:

The bombardier and navigator of the lead plane missed finding the target the first time, so we swung around for another run. The fourth airplane wasn't with us, so the three aircraft in a "V" headed for the target. The German guns were not knocked out, and they were putting very accurate fire at our altitude, and in the area directly behind the lead aircraft and between the two wing men. It seems to me that we picked up speed on that run to stay ahead of the flak. We picked up lots of holes, and pieces of flak nicked the control cables in several places near the waist positions.

After two runs at the target the leader still could not find it, and the three ships did not release their bombs. The plane that was separated on the run, LUCKY STRIKE (42-78431), was able to live up to her name and make a single ship attack, dropping the bombs through a hole in the clouds.

The last plane to reach the target area was Black-F (42-78618), who had taken off late. They dropped their bombs at 1215 after

The remains of the plane in the small lake.

missing the IP and putting together a makeshift bomb run from a heading of 270 degrees. Since the target was still covered by clouds no results were recorded.

The planes that did not release returned to Pantanella with their bombs hanging from the racks. In all, the Blue Force mission would be classified as FUBAR.

The Red Force came back to Pantanella with three planes damaged by flak. The damage wasn't, serious and they would be back in the air by the next morning if they were needed.

Yellow-Q (42-51643) failed to return to its handstand. It was last seen about 1110 that morning when it left the formation with the #2 engine smoking. Lt. Robert Ray, Jr., and most of the crew would return to Pantanella on 26 November.

The 464th had used a lot of 100 octane fuel to fly that day, and a lot of manpower had been used to get the planes into the air. Two planes and crews were unaccounted for, and all the group could say for the experience was that a lot of fish had been killed by dumping some of the bombs into the Adriatic. It would be very interesting to know just how many tons of bombs were "jettisoned" into the blue waters of the Adriatic during the war. Imagine all of the unexploded weapons that are corroding away beneath the water.

On the 7th, the group took a crack at the Isares Albes Railway Bridge. The 464th put a total of 31 planes into the air for the mission. Maj. James Gilson lifted the lead plane into the air at 0830 that morning.

Except for clouds over the Adriatic, the flight to the target area was uneventful. The planes hit the IP and turned towards the bridge. It was something that the fliers hadn't seen in a while. Below them was the target, as clear as day and not a cloud in sight!

At 1308 the formation hit the release point, and over 75 tons of bombs rained toward the target. CHICK (42-95340) had the right bomb bay door jam and could not release with the rest of the group. WILLY (42-51903) had a couple of bombs hang up on the rack when the shackles failed to release.

Although the target was partially covered by smoke from the first group, the results for the 464th were still very good. There were several direct hits on the railway leading to the bridge. One cluster of about ten bombs appeared to be almost dead center in the middle of the bridge, dropping the center span.

After the last several missions, this one was a good one. At least they had gotten to the target and dropped their bombs. On top of that, they actually could see that they had hit the target. An added blessing was there was no flak seen at all on the mission.

While the flight crews were off flying, Pantanella looked like an anthill with all of the activity going on. Word had come down from 55th Wing that everyone that was not essential to work on the line or anywhere else was to report in "uniform" for drill!

The reason; the group was going to be presented with a Distinguished Unit Citation. In view of this, Col. Schroeder figured that the men needed a little practice at marching and drill so that when the 15th Air Force big wigs arrived they would not embarrass anybody, especially him. The men looked at each other and shrugged. Some of the men hadn't marched a step since they had arrived in Italy. The dress rehearsal was to get the men back in step, so to speak—hopefully.

November 8, 1944, would go into the daily reports as a "Red Letter" day for the 464th. Maj/Gen. Nathan Twinning, Commander of the 15th Air Force, arrived aboard his special C-47. Arriving with "the boss" was Brig/Gen. George Acheson, commander of the 55th Wing.

Every man that was not on essential duty, and perhaps some that got railroaded, were dressed in their best uniforms. Granted, some were a little wrinkled, and maybe the shoes were not as polished as they could have been, but the formation still looked pretty good.

Lt/Col. Poff, CO of the 778th, was the troop commander. Lt/Col. William Reddell, CO of the 776th, read the Citation for the group's first DUC. After reading the citation, Gen. Acheson made a few comments about the group. When he was finished, Gen. Twinning took a little time to give a "pep talk" to "his boys." When he was finished, he stepped to the unit flag and tied the DUC Streamer to the top of the mast.

With the pomp completed, the circumstance began as the entire group marched in review before the big wigs of the 15th Air Force. Col. Schroeder and the group staff watched with a certain gleam of pride in their eyes as the Squadrons passed by. After the review, Gen. Twinning took some time to tour the base and personally pin decorations on some of the men of the 464th.

On the 9th the group was scheduled to make another visit to the Third Reich. By the time the crews had eaten and gotten out of the briefing it looked doubtful that they would get off the ground. The wind was blowing hard from the wrong direction. As a matter of fact, it was almost a 90 degree cross wind from the north. The planes could not take off with the wind blowing across the runway. They had to wait and see if the wind would change direction enough to make a safe take off.

The wind did not change direction. Low scud clouds rolled in from the mountains to the west, and it started to rain. The mission for the day was canceled, and the crews made their way back up the hill.

November 10th was a repeat of the day before. Wind and rain beat down on Pantanella Hill. Like the day before, the crews could not fly. There wasn't much to do except stay in the sack and try and stay warm. For those who wanted to do something besides stay in the sack, this was a good time to drop a line to the folks back home. There was a war going on, and one had to be careful about just what he mentioned in the letter home. If you happened to be an officer there was no problem with censoring your letter. As an "officer and gentleman" you could censor your own letter. For the enlisted men it was a different story. They had to have their letters censored by an officer. This duty fell on the copilot a lot of times; after all, he was the jack of all trades. On days when the planes couldn't fly, a lot of mail hit the outgoing bag after it had the proper notation "CENSORED."

The 464th rallies from the target at Vienna.

Lead B-24 from the 465th was hit by flak over Bleachhammer on November 20, 1944.

On the morning of the 11th, 27 planes fought their way through the overcast and managed to get into the air starting at 0610. The mission was another Red Force-Blue Force mission. The Red Force was led by Lt/Col. Goodyear, while Blue Force was under command of Lt. Henry Heinemann (779th)

The group formed up and managed to find the Wing with some problems due to bad weather and clouds in the 464th form up area. After some rather tense moments of flying in heavy clouds the planes broke out into almost clear skies and headed over the Adriatic.

As the group approached the Dalmatian coast, Lt/Col. Goodyear could only see clouds ahead. They spanned the entire horizon and billowed beyond 27,000 feet. To fly into that soupy mess would be dangerous at best. The mission was in a recall situation, but so far, the radio was silent. Lt/Col. Goodyear was faced with a command decision. They could fly on and risk the chance of mid-air collisions, or they could turn away and return to base.

It seemed that Goodyear valued the men he was leading more then a mission credit. He signaled for the group to abandon the mission and return to Pantanella. After the formation was turned and headed home, some of the planes that were loaded with delayed action bombs released them into the water, causing more fish to bite the water.

Because of unprecedented bad weather over Italy and Europe, the 464th was forced into a three day stand down. Weather was

Another B-24 from the 465th going down on November 20th. The 464th came through with far less damage than her sister group.

Cameras on Yellow-Q record the final explosion of the ill fated B-24.

starting to chip away at the morale of not only the flight crews, but everybody on, around, and even near Pantanella Hill. It was cool, windy, rainy, and in another word, miserable!

Weather was still marginal on the 15th. In view of the situation the 15th Air Force called for another Lone Wolf mission to be flown. The pathfinders of the 464th drew the Linz Benzol Plant as their target.

Five "Mickey ships were scheduled for the mission. The first one left the runway at 0815 that morning, followed at 3-5 minute intervals by the remaining planes. Each of the planes climbed into the overcast and finally broke out into clear sky at about 10,000 feet.

Each of the planes took up a heading for the line of departure, which was an imaginary line running from the tip of the Italian spur to Bari that served as a check point. The five planes crossed the line and headed over the Adriatic.

Over the Dinaric Alps the planes ran into thunderstorms, and along with the storms came turbulence. Aboard Red-H (42-50533) the turbulence was more than bone rattling, it was downright dangerous. It seemed to be shaking the B-24 to pieces. Lt. Forrest Robbins finally had enough of the bucking and shaking. He turned the plane for smoother air and aborted the mission.

The clouds thickened even more, and the tops climbed up to over 26,000 feet. The crews had no choice but to fly into the gray

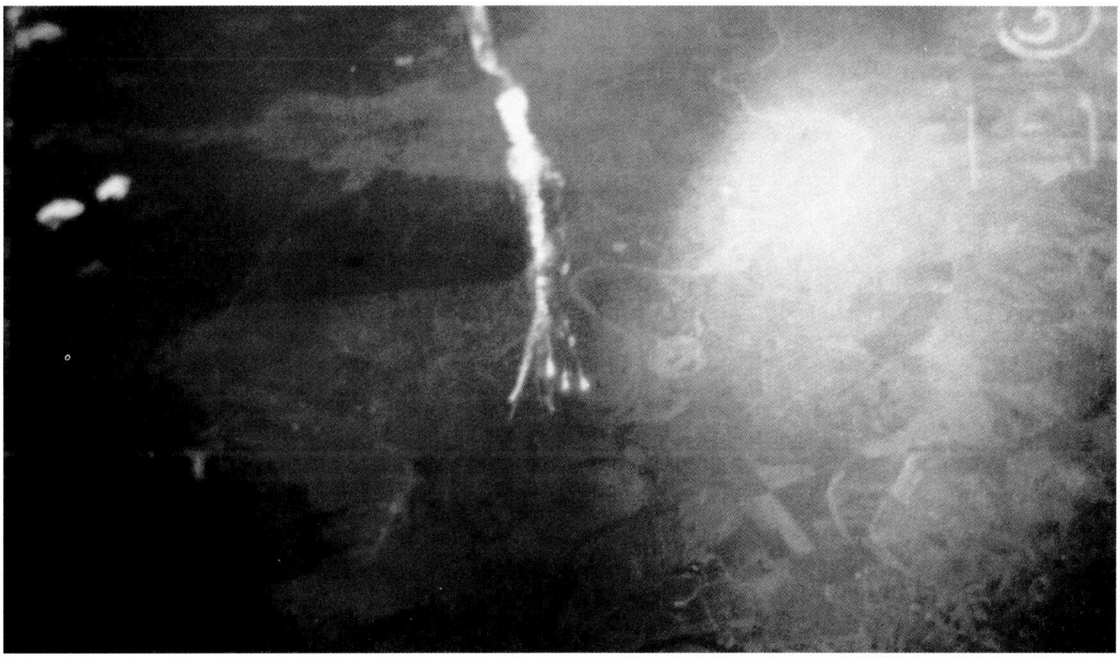

The final plunge of exploding debris.

soup and endure the roller coaster ride that mother nature was providing.

About 30 minutes from the target the planes started to break out of the heavy clouds and the ride got a little smoother. That was fine with the flight crews, as so far it had been a real bone-rattler of a ride. They still had to contend with the undercast. That was not a big problem, since they had been navigating by radar almost as soon as leaving the base. Now they could bomb by it, also. It should be pointed out that one of the criteria for the Lone Wolf mission was that they should only bomb if the target was covered with clouds. Their only defense against the flak guns was the clouds, the chaff that they could throw, and a device called "CARPET."

CARPET was a rather new item that had been added to some of the B-24s. It was one of the first electronic jamming devices that had been invented. The Carpet Blinker was a small antenna that was placed on the bottom of the plane. It was covered by a tear drop shaped plexiglass dome. The unit would send out an electronic "raspberry" that would confuse the German radar. This device was also known as "Panther Defenses."

On Yellow-A (42-52070) the PFF equipment went on the fritz about 45 minutes from Linz. Lt. August Lechner, Jr., turned the plane toward a target of opportunity. They managed to drop their two tons of bombs at Salzburg and headed for home.

White-B (44-49032) had lost their radar over the coast of Yugoslavia and flew through the weather by the old method of dead reckoning. The radar started working a little better by the time they reached the target area. By the time they were about 17 miles from the target the returns in the scope were very erratic, and Lt. Frank Lane turned away from Linz for an alternate. They dropped their bomb load at Hieflau with unknown results.

Red-Y (44-49048) reached the IP and turned to a heading of 120 degrees. Over Linz the target return was good. Several last minute corrections were made, and at the release point over 2 tons of RDX was toggled at about 1140.

The flight back was as bumpy as it had been on the way to the target. The planes finally started to clear the real bad weather as they approached the Italian spur. Over the base, the clouds had cleared enough for a routine let down and landing.

That morning, five planes had taken off from Pantanella. One plane had returned early because of the shaking it had taken in the clouds. Black-R (44-49028), flown by Lt. Homer Mower's crew, had taken off and vanished into the overcast. That was the last time that the plane or crew were ever seen. They may have fallen victim to the turbulence or storms, they might have had a mechanical problem, or a hundred other things may have happened. Both the plane and crew just vanished into the gray misty overcast.

That night there were the usual evening activities around the Hill. Some of the men sat out in the Italian night and watched the movie. Others ambled over to their respective clubs and traded war stories or played cards. Down on the hard stands the ground crews were getting the planes ready for the next mission. It was a night just like any other night that had come and gone since the group arrived in Italy. Yet, this night was different. There was a strange aura of anticipation drifting across the hill. If the group flew a mission in the morning and completed it, the 464th would chalk up the 100th mission since starting combat.

Operations Order #251 had come down from Wing, and the 464th was indeed scheduled for a mission on 16 November. As usual, there were the mission particulars to iron out. That meant a lot of late night scheduling and typing for the men up in Group HQ. Capt. Orton and the weather wizards checked the latest weather charts, and it looked like all of the isobars lined up for a possible radar run, unless things changed.

The target for the Red Force mission was the rail yards at Munich, Germany. The Blue Force would attack the rail bridge at Prejepolje, Yugoslavia. As with all of the Red-Blue Force missions, there was always twice the paperwork and twice the work load for the men who had to load the bombs into the planes, not to mention the fact that the crew chiefs had to make sure that there were more than enough planes to fly.

At 0755, Lt/Col. Goodyear pushed the throttles forward and started his take off roll, and after using most of the runway he lifted off the runway in the lead plane. One by one, another 28 heavily

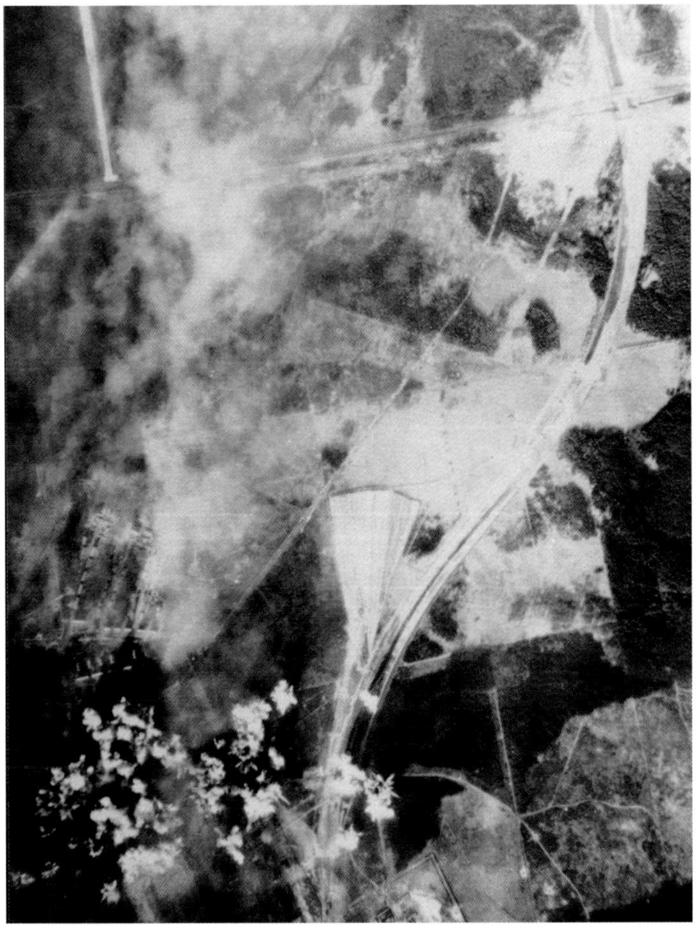

Vertical strike photo Blechhammer South Oil Refinery, November 20, 1944.

laden B-24s took to the air and headed for the form up area. The 465th had problems with their form up and did not join the rest of the Wing until the bombers were well beyond Spinazzola and headed out over the Adriatic.

Over the water the weather was marginal. Soon it cleared a little, then turned back to marginal. By the time the formation neared the target area it was obvious that the bomb run would have to be done by radar.

In the lead plane the Mickey operator picked up the target area from about 50 miles out. The Deputy Lead aircraft picked up the target at about 40 miles. From the IP to the target the Mickey operators were busy checking their scopes and calling corrections to the bombardiers. At five miles from the target the last reading was taken to confirm the range to the target.

Bombs away came at 1301 as over 37 tons of explosive RDX were released towards the undercast with hope that the target was down there somewhere.

At almost the same time, the first angry bursts of flak began to dot the sky. It was intense and inaccurate. The group was under fire for about six minutes, and that was enough to cause damage to several of the planes.

The flight home was rather nerve racking because of the weather. The formation was in and out of clouds and thunderstorms most of the way to Pantanella. Some of the planes were low on fuel. Then, there were the planes that had taken battle damage. They had delivered Uncle Sam's bombs, and now they were flying for themselves; boy oh boy, were they ever flying for themselves!

When the last propeller stopped on the hardstands a quick talley showed that four planes were missing. Later, word came in that BIG ED (41-29394) had landed at the 97th BG's base with the electrical system shot out. Red-D (42-51761) was last reported leaving the formation under control with an engine out. Over the target, flak had scored on the #3 engine of Red-D. The pilot, Merle Hoffman, had the engine shut down, and the plane remained with the formation for a while. Bill Weisberger, the bombardier, recalled:

We could see Switzerland to the west, and we took a vote. Should we go to Switzerland, or should we try to make it home? Everybody voted unanimously to go home. We were nuts. We know, but we were gung ho! As if it made a difference if we went to Switzerland or went home.

As they approached the Yugoslavian coast Hoffman took a battle damage survey with the rest of the crew. The navigator, William Mahota, told Hoffman that he didn't think they would make it across the Adriatic. At that point Hoffman had to figure out what to do. The Dalmatian coast was not the best place to try and land a B-24. It also wasn't the best place to bail out.

Just after crossing the coast they spotted the small island of Pag. It is about twenty miles long and a few miles wide. That would be the last parcel of land for over a hundred and twenty miles. Hoffman rang the bail out bell, and most of the crew went out as quickly as possible. The engineer, Al Weber, recalled:

I had great trepidation about jumping out of this airplane, and Bill Weisberger was pounding on my back and I was straddled over the open bomb bay. "Okay! Okay!" And I let go."

By the time everyone else was out of the plane it had passed over the island. Hoffman crawled back into the pilot seat and turned the plane around. He set the auto pilot again and left the cockpit for the last time. As the plane crossed back over the island he jumped.

At this point in the war, the island of Pag was under joint control of the Germans and partisans. One half of the island was German, and the other side was partisan. Two of the crew landed on the German side of the island. The partisans fought a small battle with the Germans to get the two men back to their side of the island, and the entire crew was reunited. Several of the men were badly shaken,

White-Z and White-J return to Pantanella.

and there were several of the crew that had broken some bones when they landed on the rocks. Samuel Williams, the flight engineer, had hit the ground and gone over a cliff. Only the fact that his chute got caught saved him. He had broken his leg in the jump, but he managed to climb up and was sitting on the top of the cliff when several of the crew found him.

The injured crew were taken care of by the partisans as best as possible under the conditions that prevailed on the tiny island. The partisans managed to "borrow" (steal) a German E-boat and got the crew out into the Adriatic, where they were picked up by the British destroyer *H.M.S. Lauderdale*. They would make it back to Ancona within a few days.

CHICK (42-95340) had reported trouble before the group had reached the target area. The pilot radioed that they did not have enough fuel to get to the target and back to base. CHICK left the formation after the target and headed towards Switzerland. They managed to crash land, and the crew was interned. White-L (44-41084) was last seen dropping from the formation at about 1244. This aircraft and crew were listed as missing in action.

The Blue Force, consisting of eight planes, had left the base at 0855 to hit the bridge at Prejepolje, Yugoslavia. When the bombers reached the target it was covered by clouds. Unreal as it may seem, there was no Mickey ship assigned to the mission. No targets of opportunity had been given at the briefing. The planes turned for home with the bombs still hanging from the racks. Over the Adriatic they jettisoned the delay action bombs and returned to the field. Many of the crewmen on the Blue Force wondered why the heck they had not been given a Pathfinder aircraft and why they had not been given an alternate target. The answer to the questions on the Blue Forces' minds was simple. According to the outline of the Blue Force missions, they should not need a radar ship, since they were going to targets of a secondary nature on the list. Well, that may have been the way it was supposed to be, but if the crews were going to fly into harm's way, it sure would be nice to be able to drop their bombs, even if by radar.

It had been quite a day for the 464th. They had chalked up 100 credited missions since starting combat operations. It is true that they had been in the air more than a hundred times, but several of the missions had not received "official" credit.

That night, several parties broke out on the hill. Some of the guys celebrated into the wee hours of the night (or morning). The parties started breaking up when someone realized that there was a mission to be flown in the morning and that they just had to be a party pooper.

The crews that were scheduled to fly were rousted out of the sack early on the morning of the 17th. There was the usual pre-briefing routine of getting dressed and heading for the chow line. After packing the belly with the usual morning fare, they headed for the briefing room.

The target for the day was the Florisdorf Oil Complex at Vienna; another chance to face the deadly guns that surrounded that city. The Operations Orders called for a 0700 take off. The bomb load would mixed, with some delayed and others that would explode on contact. Several of the planes carried propaganda canisters to spread the word that Hitler's Third Reich would soon be kaput.

Lt/Col. Poff led the first of 29 ships into the air. One plane aborted on the ground due to a broken starter on an engine. During rendezvous with the 465th there were several very close calls when the 460th cut inside the course line. Quick work by Col. Poff kept the groups separated enough to avoid collision.

The weather at take off was good. That began to change as the formation flew over the Italian spur. Here, the clouds became solid overcast. Over the Adriatic, the planes from the 47th Wing were off course and headed towards the 464th formation. Again, the group had to maneuver to avoid collision. As the group crossed the Dalmatian coast the clouds broke for a while, then started closing in again near the Dinaric Alps.

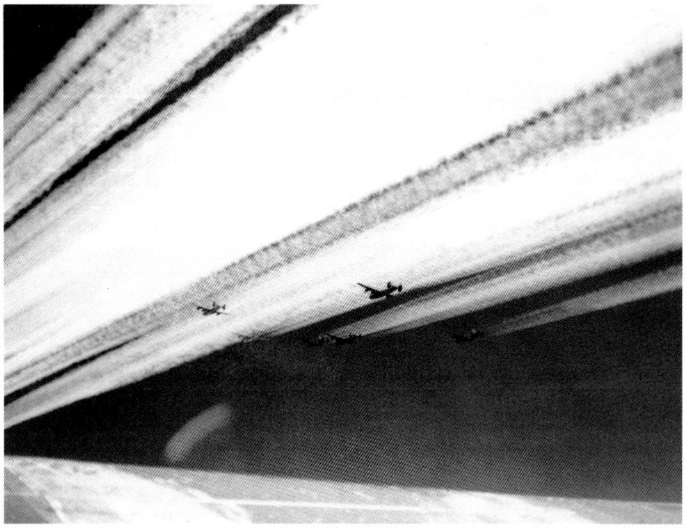

Vapor trails on the way to the target.

Cloud cover like this usually meant a radar run over the target.

The bombload hitting the target. This B-24 is caught by the strike camera over the target.

By the time the formation turned at the IP it was Mickey run time. The radar had been lowered and was giving good returns on the target from about 50 miles away. There shouldn't be any major problems finding the target .

Two minutes before the target flak appeared above the undercast. It was not quite the usual Vienna brand of flak, but it was still heavy enough to cause the pucker factor to increase. Even if it wasn't the usual flak, it would still be a long six minutes before the group would get out of it.

The final correction was made for range to target and the bomb release line was crossed at 1144. Almost 50 tons of RDX was dropped toward the target. Since the target was covered by clouds the results of their efforts could not be judged.

The return flight was flown as they had been briefed that morning, except for several minor changes to avoid weather. By the time the planes appeared over Pantanella, the overcast had broken to just a few scattered clouds.

Three planes had taken minor damage from the flak, and neither of the planes would be out of action for very long. White-S (42-51736) landed at the 460th base because they were low on fuel. After getting enough gas to fly, they returned to Pantanella later that afternoon.

On the 18th the group was scheduled to hit the Udine Campoformido Airdrome. The bomb load was a little different this time, as each plane carried clustered fragmentation bombs. This mission would be led by Lt/Col Moore, 777th Commander. Two of the scheduled planes aborted on the ground due to mechanical problems.

When a mission was getting underway the hardstands and taxi strips were a mighty dangerous place. There were heavily laden B-24s lumbering like big silver elephants towards the runway. Each of them had four deadly propellers whirling around in an invisible blur. That meant that on this morning there were 116 whirling blurs of instant death on the taxiways.

Sgt. Ben Derman had noticed that his chute was missing before the lead plane left the hardstand. He got out of the plane to get his chute. As the plane taxied down the strip, Derman cut across country to catch his plane at the next stop, and he didn't correctly judge the speed of the oncoming Liberator. The grim reaper pointed his cold bony finger to claim his prize. Sgt. Derman was struck by the whirling outboard propeller of his plane and died instantly.

The 464th was delayed while a spare gunner was found to replace Sgt. Derman. As a result the 465th took to the air while things calmed down a little for the 464th. After a fifteen minute pause, the planes were underway again.

The 29 planes of the 464th finally got into the air, formed up, and met the Wing. For a change, nature was allowing the fliers to fly in unclouded beautiful weather all the way to the target.

At the target the planes met some token flak for about four minutes. Several Me-109s were spotted about 5,000 feet below the formation. The gunners called out the fighters' position in case they turned to attack. The German fighters crossed the bombers' path at a 90 degree angle and never made a move to intercept the bombers.

At 1115 the cluster bombs fell from the bellies of the B-24s. With their deadly cargo gone the planes bobbed upward, then settled back for the trip home. Over 58 tons of frags had been delivered to the Airdrome.

Strike photos showed that the target had been hit pretty well. Several aircraft were hit in their dispersal areas. At least one hangar had been pulverized by the frags, and the runway had also taken a few hits.

By 1350 the last plane was back on the ground. Except for the horrible accident on the taxi strip, the mission had been a milk run. Only two planes had been hit by flak, and they would be ready to fly again by morning if they were needed.

Those who had witnessed the death of Sgt. Derman had been horrified by the quickness of the event. There had not been time to yell a warning. Even if someone had yelled, it would have been drowned out by the sound of the engines. The men could only be thankful that the Lord had stepped in and let the reaper only claim a single victim for the day.

Col. Schroeder stood in front of the 31 crews at the morning briefing on the 19th. The target was the Linz Benzol plant at Linz, Austria. He announced to the group that he would be in the lead plane. Although it was not that apparent, there was an undertone of trepidation.

The group was off and flying a 0740 that morning. Form up was a lot easier when the sky was clear over Italy. Rendezvous with the 55th Wing was on time. The 460th and 485th lagged behind the rest of the Wing until the formation was near Vis.

For a change, the crews did not have to worry about the weather. Scattered clouds dotted the route, but nothing like it had been on previous missions. The crews could concentrate on the mission and not worry about the weather.

At the IP, the bombers turned towards the target and began the bomb run. The target was clear of clouds, so the lead bombardier set his bombsight up for a visual run. The German smoke pots were putting out a pretty good screen, but the wind seemed to be blowing in just the right direction to clear enough of the target to continue the visual run.

About 30 seconds before release, the flak opened with an accurate barrage that was too close for comfort, and several planes took hits from the first bursts. Ahead the flak looked even thicker. There was nothing that could be done except to fly towards the bursting shells and hope the chaff would help.

The release point was attained at 1154, and almost 57 tons of RDX fell towards the target. At the same moment, flak they could walk on was all around the formation.

Yellow-Y (42-50843) was hit in the nose compartment. The blast damaged the nosewheel and wounded the navigator, but they were able to stay with the formation. Flak scored hits on sixteen other planes in the group before they could clear the flak ring. None of the hits appeared to be serious, and all of the planes were still in formation.

The flight back was filled with tension as crews worked to repair broken hydraulic lines or severed control cables. Several of the planes had taken damage in the fuel tanks or transfer system and were swetting out the fuel supply.

Yellow-Y radioed the leader that they were going to head for Bari so their navigator could get medical help. They managed a pretty good landing without a nosewheel at that base. The rest of the planes came on towards Pantanella. Racecard tower had a pretty lively time getting the formation sorted out and into the pattern. By 1515 the last of the ships was rolling out amid the clatter of the PSP runway.

November 20th found the men awakened early for another mission. Officer's briefing was at 0520 that morning. At the briefing, the fliers were told that the target for the day was the Blechhammer South Oil Refinery. When the target was revealed, there were several low moans. Someone muttered, "Yeh, Blechhammer! Hit the IP, bomb the target, and rally left to Russia!" Stations was at 0705; that way the group would be ready to taxi at 0720.

Lt/Col Goodyear lifted his B-24 off the runway at 0730, right on schedule. He was followed by another 27 B-24s from the 464th. The group formed up and passed over Andria at 0825; so far they were on time for the mission.

The 460th and 485th were late for the second day in a row. They lagged behind about 12-15 miles until almost the first turn point. Finally, the entire 55th Wing got it together and headed for Germany.

At about 1129, Black-L (42-78590) reported that their #2 engine was running rough and they would have to shut it down. They also said that they were aborting the Primary Target, but would try and hit a target of opportunity on the way back. Ten minutes later they toggled their bombs on flak batteries near Gyor, Austria.

When the wing leader reached the Pathfinder IP at Zuckmantel he decided that a visual bomb run could be made. At this point the entire Wing made a 360 degree turn and changed course enough to make a run from the visual IP at Ober Glogau. The new axis of attack was 72 degrees, and the bombing altitude would be about 22,000 feet.

From their position behind the 465th the flightcrews of the 464th watched their sister group fly into the flak blackened sky near the target. Several of the pilots saw the 465th's lead plane take a direct hit. The Liberator shuttered under the impact and flames erupted, but the plane held steady on the bomb run. The pilot, Lt/Col. Clarence Lokker, fought the controls as the fire spread. The fire

The 464th as they rally for home.

spread and the left wing buckled. Lokker gave the signal to bail out as the wing ripped away, and the Liberator started its death dive. Several of the crew, including Lokker, were able to jump clear before the plane exploded. The Liberator directly behind flew through the fireball and was hit by the left landing gear from the burning plane. Several of the crew bailed out when they believed that their plane was on fire. With two engines out that plane headed for the Russian lines.

Another plane in the lead box also took a direct hit from flak and started down out of control, with fire streaming back for over 300 feet. Several of the crew were able to bail out of the stricken plane before it hit the ground. The 465th had lost three planes to flak and they had not dropped their bombs yet.

The crews of the 464th watched their sister group take it in the teeth. The flak had scored too many times on the 465th's formation. The 464th was the next group in line, and they would also have to fly through the deadly flak that lay just ahead.

As the 464th approached the IP, the bombardiers complied with the briefing flimsy for the third and final time before the target. With winter just around the corner the temperature at 24,000 feet hovered around thirty below. To prevent the bomb doors from freezing or getting sluggish, the flimsy had noted "Excrecise bomb bay doors at least three times before IP."

Between the IP and the target the navigator on Red-J (42-51886) accidentally hit the salvo lever, and about a half a ton of bombs spilled from the racks and punched through the doors. Another B-24, White-U (44-48880), dropped their entire load during the turn at the IP when the select lever was pushed due to a huge jolt caused by prop wash. Needless to say, someone on the ground had a very nasty surprise when the bombs came raining down.

Flak greeted the 464th's arrival near the target. It was just a few scattered bursts at first that gradually built up to five minutes of good old intense and accurate flak. Some of the bursts were a lot bigger than some of the crews had seen for some time.

Bombs away crackled over the intercoms at 1228 as over 58 tons of 500 pound RDX bombs began their journey to the ground some 22,000 feet below. Most of the bombs would explode on impact for the initial destructive blow. Over 25 % of the bombs were fuzed to detonate anywhere from six to seventy-two hours later.

The group rallied right towards Skoczow and began the long flight back to Italy. The 464th was out of the flak zone within a few moments of the rally. Granted, they had been in the flak for what seemed an eternity, but everyone had made it through. Maybe the gunners on the ground had been satisfied with shooting the hell out of the 465th and figured they could give the 464th a break.

Strike photos revealed that the group's aim was off. There were several dozen hits almost 3,500 feet northwest of the briefed MPI. This area was identified as a labor camp for railway repair crews. Other bombs fell in the wooded area about a half mile from the refinery. In all, the results were classified as "well, we came close."

As the group headed home, several Me-109s passed under the formation heading back towards Blechhammer. They were about 5,000 feet below the formation and made no attempt to attack. For some of the replacement crews it was the first time they had even seen an enemy fighter. The "old hats" were glad to see the fighters headed away from the formation.

STEVEONOVICH (42-51625) was in dire trouble. Just before the IP they lost the #3 engine. Copilot Tony Schneider recalled:

We turned short to pick up the group after the group's swing over the target area. Unfortunately, we passed over some flak batteries that nailed us and caused the failure of #2 engine. Our bombardier, Gerald Welstad, had salvoed the 500 pounders carried that day, but with only #1 and #4 operating we were left behind as the group turned for home. Needless to say we were losing altitude constantly, and the crew began to throw out everything that was not nailed down. They even joked about throwing me out, because as copilot I was not necessary and was excess baggage. Coming down over Czechoslovakia and Austria, we were fortunate to have an escort of two little friends in the form of P-51s. They stayed with us until we broke the Adriatic coast and then had to depart because of fuel levels. We headed for Vis, but did not make it because #1 ran away. With only #3 engine operating we went down fast. We hit the water at 120 mph at 800 fpm descent. The tail broke and sank immediately. Matthew Arlington (Pilot) exited through the broken canopy. The forward fuselage was completely submerged. Only the back of the wings and broken fuselage at the waist window were above water.

Most of the crew managed to get out of the sinking plane. Flight Engineer James Hurst may have been trapped by the top turret breaking free and pinning him in the sinking wreckage. He was never seen after impact. The eight survivors were picked up by two Yugoslavian fishing boats.

Thanksgiving 1944, with turkey and all the trimmings.

Red-J returned with her bomb doors flapping in the slipstream. Crew Chief John Graham had his work cut out for him that evening. It would take quite a while for the ground crew to get the rollers lined up in the slots and get the doors aligned properly.

The group stood down on the 21st due to bad weather moving in over the usual targets. The day off gave most of the men a chance to work on their pet projects or write a letter to the folks back home.

Operations Order #261 alerted the 464th for a mission on 22 November. The primary target was the rail yards at Munich, Germany. The orders called for the 26 planes to be loaded with 500 pounders. As always, the fuel trucks arrived and filled the tanks to the bottom of the caps. Belts of ammo were strung into the guns in case the German fighters showed up. The ground crews also made sure there was lots of chaff to throw into the slipstream.

The lead plane left the runway at 0720 that morning. Just to show the men that he could do it, Brig/Gen. George Acheson, Commander of the 55th Wing, was the formation commander. The 55th Wing CO had a habit of flying along with the groups from time to time just to see how each of the groups under his command functioned under combat conditions.

From the start, weather was a problem for the men flying in the planes. The 464th got into formation without a problem. The 465th did not make the wing form up, and so the 464th circled three times between Andria and Canosa. At 0822 the 464th slid in behind the 460th and followed them out over the Adriatic. The 485th and 465th finally caught up with the formation over the northern Adriatic. At this point, the 464th assumed the lead for the mission.

Over the Dinaric Alps the weather turned sour. Clouds reached up to 20,000 feet, and the farther the formation flew the higher the clouds billowed. BIG FAT MAMA (41-29453) lost the formation in the clouds and turned back towards Italy. 42-78612 also lost the formation. They both dropped their bombs on a bridge at Amaro. FAST NUMBER (42-95337) from the 779th lost the 464th, but was able to find the 460th and continued the mission.

As the formation approached the IP the clouds were topping out at over 26,000 feet. The wing leader abandoned the Primary Target and turned the formation towards the alternate at Salzburg.

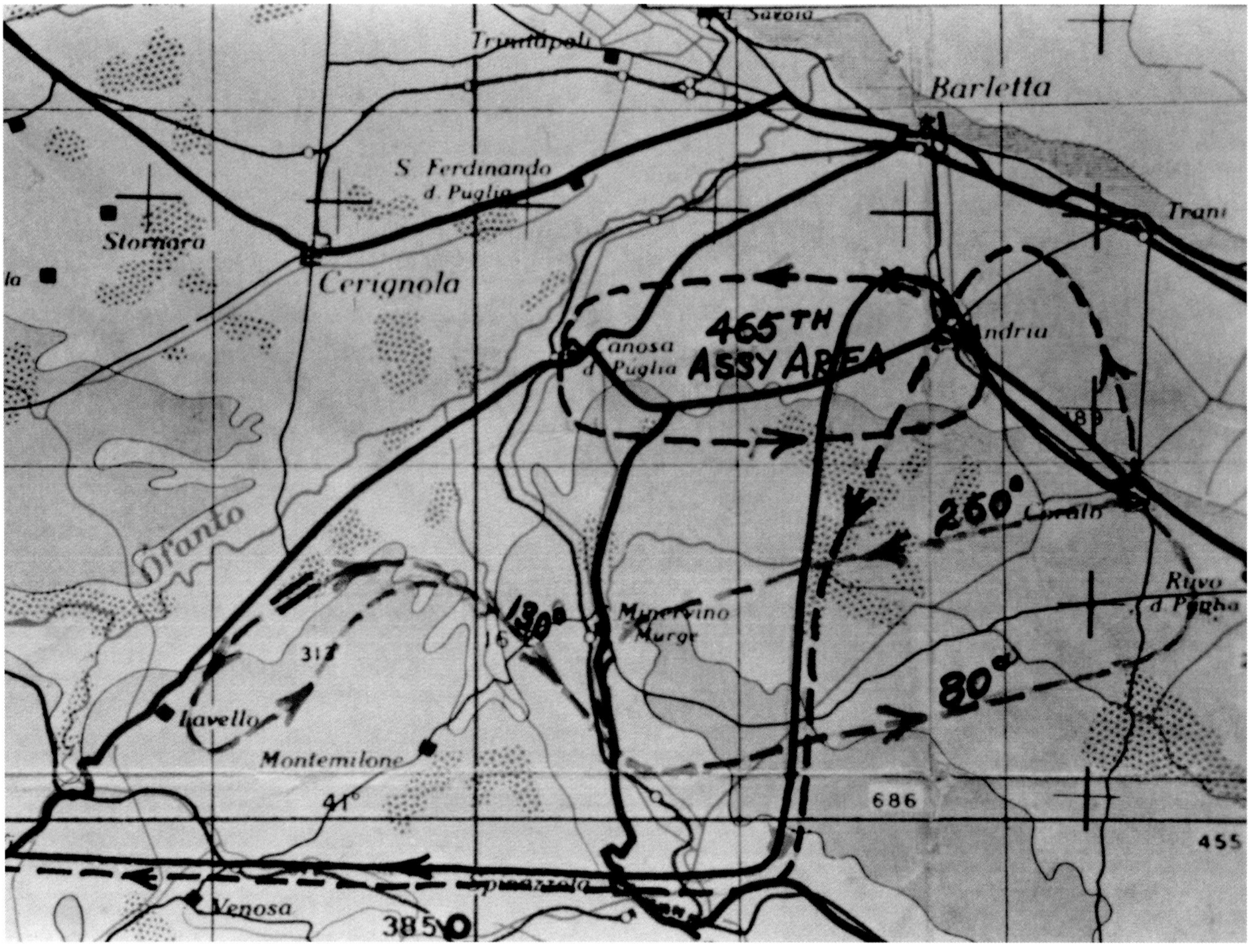

Map of the 464th and 465th form up areas.

At the IP for the alternate, the group turned towards the target. At this point the two attack units of the 464th were separated by almost five minutes. Flak met the first unit at the target just before release. The second unit was in flak from the turn at the IP.

Over the target the flak continued to hammer away at the oncoming B-24s. Thankfully, the gunners on the ground were not coming very close at this point. At 1224 the first attack unit released about 14 tons of bombs from approximately 18,000 feet. Five minutes later the second unit arrived and deposited another 20 tons from over 27,000 feet.

Strike photos showed that there were some hits in the rail yard and buildings near the yards. Several bombs strayed into a residential area between the main station and the Salzach River.

The planes returned by the briefed route with several minor turns and corrections to get around the bad weather. The formation was back home by 1510 that afternoon, and all of the planes returned. One had minor battle damage, and one crewman had taken a minor wound from flak.

The 464th stood down on the 22nd to celebrate Thanksgiving. For the last several days the rumor mill had been overactive. The rumors were that real turkey and all the trimmings were going to be served at the mess areas of the squadrons. Someone was heard to grumble that even if there was real turkey, the cooks would find a way to either mess it up or include Spam.

For once, the rumor mongers were right. The posted menu for Thanksgiving dinner was the traditional American feast of turkey and almost all of the trimmings. Those that got the straight poop were in the chow line as soon as they could get there. On this particular day the chow line seemed even longer than usual.

Now, the exact number of turkeys that were consumed by the men of the 464th is lost to history. Rest assured, to feed almost 2,300 men it would take quite a few gobblers. Granted, there were some canned turkeys, but the frozen turkey was straight from the USA. Imagine the logistics of getting frozen and canned turkeys from the United States to Italy for the 464th. And it was not just turkey for the 464th. Almost all of the bomb groups in Italy had

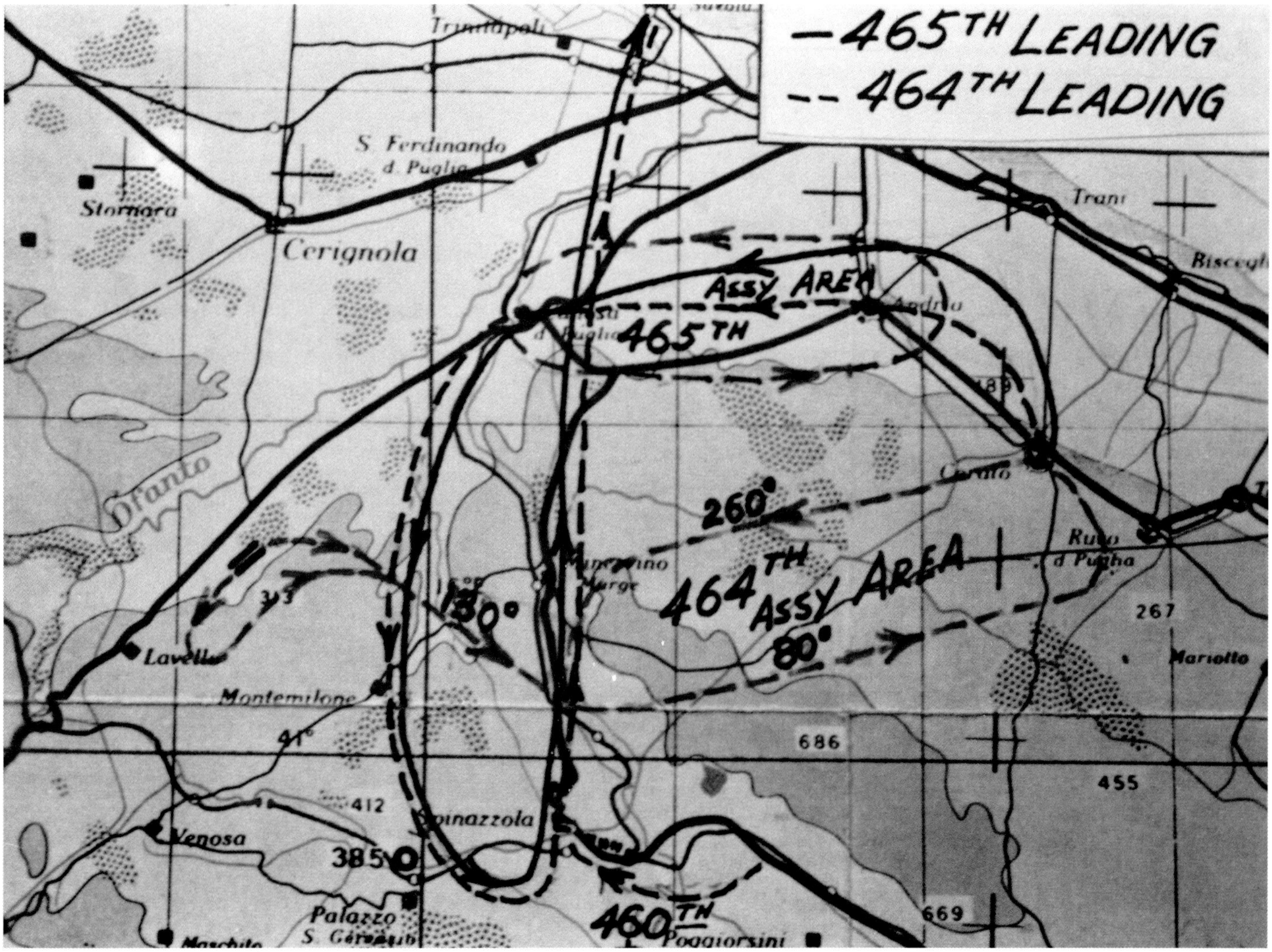

Map showing the alternate form up area and route to wing rendezvous.

turkey on the menu. On top of that, add to that as many of the Infantry outfits as possible and you have a real logistical nightmare. The men of Air Transport and Supply had broken their backs to see that Uncle Sam's men had a taste of home on this special day.

The cooks did themselves proud that day. The men had one of, if not the best meal that they had consumed since leaving the states and arriving in Italy. With Thanksgiving as a model, the men of the 464th looked forward to seeing if the cooks could equal or outdo themselves at Christmas.

The 464th took the 24th off so that the big meal from the day before could digest properly. Actually, the group did not fly because of weather. Some of the guys milled around the mess area hoping that there were some leftovers, or maybe a turkey sandwich,but alas, no luck!

The 464th tried another Lone Wolf mission on the 25th. This one was different from the others that had been flown, as it would be a night mission. Each of the planes would be on their own and were to drop only if the target was covered with clouds.

The first plane, White-F (42-95613), took off at 0040. The next was White-B(44-49032), which left at 0048. The last plane off the ground was Red-Y (44-49048). Due to mechanical problems this aircraft did not take off until 0122.

Of the three planes to take off, only the first one made it to the Primary Target. The Mickey operator picked up the target from about 70 miles away. At the IP, Capt. Joe Shymanski turned the plane to 040 degrees and started the bomb run. At 0435 they released their 8 500 pounders and headed for home.

Red-Y diverted to an alternate target at Innsbruck. They had problems with the radar at the alternate, and it was clear enough to make a visual run, even at night. Since there wasn't any flak, they released their bombs and headed home.

White-B also hit Innsbruck. They dropped their bombs at 0442 from 23,000 feet. Since their radar was working they made a radar run, then ran for home. All three planes were back at Pantanella by 0730 that morning, just in time for breakfast.

Mother nature prevented the group from flying any further missions for the rest of the month. Even if the weather had been good over targets, the 464th could not get off the ground. There was fog, rain, and wind at Pantanella. Even with weather problems the group had managed to fly fifteen missions during the month. Thirteen missions had been canceled or recalled because of the bad weather conditions that prevailed over European targets.

One of the most notable missions was the one flown on the 16th of the month. It was the 100th mission since the group had arrived in Italy. Because of the low mission rate, weather, and the effect that the Allied bombing was having on the German war machine, the loss rate for the group was the lowest for any month so far, with only six planes lost to enemy action.

During the last few days of the month word came down from 55th Wing that none of the flight crews were happy to hear; the mission quota criteria had been changed. Under the new directive, the men would have to fly 35 sorties. Now, this may sound good to some. After all, until now you had to fly 50 missions before you could go home. Now for the rub. Under the old system, one could get double credit for a mission if it was a long haul, like Ploesti, Vienna, or Linz. Now that was out, and you had to fly 35 effective sorties into the Third Reich before you could go home. No more double credit for any of the targets. The flight crews grumbled, and many thought it wasn't fair for the rules to be changed. For the ground echelon it did not matter. They would be in Italy for the duration, no matter how many months it was.

A survey of the base showed that almost everyone figured the cold weather was there to stay and so were they. Over 75% of the living quarters had some kind of heating stove to try and keep the occupants warm.

On top of everything else, the men could now proudly wear the Distinguished Unit Citation ribbon on their uniform. November had been quite a month, and hopefully December would have better weather so the planes could get into the air and get the war over with as soon as possible.

December 1944

The same crummy weather that had been over Europe during the last few days of November was still there on December 1, 1944. If the weather section and nature didn't start cooperating, it would take forever to bring Hitler's Reich to its knees.

On 2 December, the Operations Orders from the 55th Wing called for a big one. The target was the oil refinery at Blechhammer South. It was not only a long haul, but they could expect a lot of flak, as well.

At 0750 Lt/Col. Reddell took off in the lead plane. He was followed by 35 more overburdened B-24s. The 464th formed into three attack units and headed for the Wing rendezvous. Three planes aborted on the ground.

The Wing get together was fouled up by local weather conditions. The 464th was over Spinazzola at 0904, on time, but the 460th was nowhere in sight. After two orbits of the area the formation

A crowd gathers around Red-J after she returned from the 2 December mission.

headed for the Adriatic. The 460th finally showed up and was leading the Wing by the time the Yugoslavian Coast was crossed. By this time four planes had aborted because of mechanical problems.

Weather during the flight to the target was marginal. About 25 miles inland over Yugoslavia the cloud cover was 10/10 strato cumulus topping out at about 10,000 feet. After crossing into Hungary the clouds broke to scattered. Just north of Vienna the clouds moved back in again.

As the formation got closer to the target the clouds increased. The Mickey men had already turned on their magic scopes. So far most of the navigating had been by radar, so the equipment had been fine tuned already. If the weather continued, the bomb run would also have to be made by radar.

About 25 miles from the target the clouds appeared to be opening up just a little. At the IP, the clouds really started to thin out. The group turned to a heading of 80 degrees and began the run to the target at 23,000 feet. Fifteen miles from the target the clouds broke, and Blechhammer lay below, in clear view of the oncoming Liberators.

About two minutes from bomb release the first angry bursts of flak appeared. The planes held a steady formation and entered the inner ring of flak defenses. Within a matter of moments, the sky around the Liberators was filled with black, red, and white dumbbell shaped clouds of bursting steel. Several of the planes were already taking hits from the flying shards of hot steel.

At 1245 the bombs began to fall from the racks. Over 70 tons of RDX bombs were released towards the refinery. Over 15 tons of bombs carried were the infamous delay action fuzes. Several leaflet canisters were also released to spread propaganda messages to the people below.

Coming off the target, the group rallied for home amidst exploding intense and very accurate flak. They had been grinding through the flak for about three minutes and still had roughly four minutes to go before they would be out of range.

Yellow-L (44-49328) had the left wing punctured by flak. The #1 engine was damaged and had to be shut down. The #2 engine was running ragged, but was still turning and putting out power to stay in the air. Yellow-H was wounded, but for the time being, still within the safety of the formation.

Yellow-H (44-41231) had taken hits, and the #2 engine was damaged. 42-78452 had been badly hit by flak and left the formation, but they were finally able to move back into position in the rear box and continue towards home. Yellow-H was last seen near Szony, Hungary, when it left the formation under control. 2/Lt. George Maheu and his crew would be listed as MIA.

As Red-J flew through the flak, an 88mm shell exploded within inches of the right waist area. The blast killed gunner Emile Michaud, who was manning a waist gun. The other waist gunner, Robert Davis, either bailed out or was blown out of the nearly severed waist by the blast. Control cables were cut, and the Liberator started to wobble all over the sky. Wingmen scattered away from Red-J to avoid midair collisions.

On the flight deck, Pilot David Eppley and copilot Noel Wood fought the odds for control of the badly wounded Liberator. They finally managed to gain some control by using the auto pilot. On top of the damage to the waist area two engines had also been damaged, but they were still usable for the moment.

The flight back to Italy was filled with tension as flight crews watched the gas gauges and tried to repair as much battle damage as they could in order to stay in the air and make it back to Pantanella.

Over Yugoslavia, Yellow-L left the formation with both engines on the left side out. Lt. Charles Stanley knew the plane would not make it all the way across the Adriatic. He rang the bail out bell, and the entire crew left the faltering Liberator. They would manage to evade capture and return to the group in January. This was the second time that this crew had been shot down on a mission to Blechhammer.

Results of a direct hit from a 88mm flak shell on Red-J.

Aboard Red-J, the situation was serious. The tail section was hanging by just a few panels of aluminum and stringers. The flight engineer, Ralph Madera, managed to splice some of the control cables. Exactly what he used is lost to history. Legend has it that he used his shoe laces to complete the job, while others say he used arming wires from the bombs. Either way, the cables held as Red-J limped towards home.

As the planes neared Pantanella, Racecard tower became a beehive of activity as frantic calls for landing priority came over the air. In the tower, Philip Turner (778th) was busy helping sort things out. He recalled:

The depressing sound of voices calling for medical personnel to meet the planes because of injured or dead crew members.

42-78452 landed at Gioia del Colle. The crew would return. The plane would be repaired, then flown to Depot 52 for major repairs before returning to the 464th in January.

Warren MacDonald's Liberator had taken some battle damage over the target. There were holes in the right wing and fuselage. One of the engines had been shot out, and two of the remaining three started to act up as they approached the field. The radio operator, William Brown, had taken a flak wound in the elbow. MacDonald called Racecard tower for priority to land. He was told to get the hell out of the pattern and land on the 465th's runway; there was a plane behind him that was in real deep trouble.

The crew of Red-J was still fighting the odds on getting back. After an epic flight, the pilots could see the friendly outline of the hills and the runway at Pantanella. Tony Schneider recalled:

Because our crew had not been re-outfitted as of yet after the Monday, 20 November '44 ditching (Blechammer South also) I was tower officer that day, and when the red very signals blossomed above the aircraft that had requested an emergency approach, I grabbed the binoculars and focused on the oncoming B-24. The aircraft was almost cut in half at the waist windows. The turtle back was cut badly, and I was fearful the fuselage would buckle when it landed.

In an outstanding display of airmanship, Eppley and Wood managed to bring the Liberator down with two engines out and the tail swaying like a swimming fish. They did not try to taxi the plane to their hardstand. They just pulled her off the runway onto one of the taxi strips and shut the remaining engines off. Medical crews met the plane and started taking the dead and wounded off and moving them to the field hospital. The rest of the crew piled out, shaken and numbed from their ordeal.

One waist gunner was killed, and one either bailed out or was blown out by the impact.

Crew chief John Graham met his plane as she rolled to a stop. He could not believe what his eyes were looking at. That morning he had sent the crew off in a good looking B-24, and they brought back a piece of junk—but they had brought it back. Graham recalled:

She was a mess. Above the waist she was nearly cut in two. The wings were full of holes. Fuel tanks had been hit, but the self sealing feature had worked. Some of the holes were big enough to put my fist through. I don't ever want to see the carnage that I saw in the waist area again. There was blood and gore all over the place. Like I said, I don't ever want to see something like that again. We did not even tow her back to the hardstand, we just took her down to the boneyard and used her for spare parts. She only had sixteen missions.

On 3 December the weather over Europe made the 464th revert to Lone Wolf tactics. Red-Y (44-49048), flown by Lt. Phil Savage, Jr., and crew left Pantanella at 0733. They were followed by White-W (42-95613), flown by Lt. Ray Beaubien and crew at 0741. The scheduled target for the two Lone Wolf Liberators was Linz, Austria.

As the two planes neared the target area they heard radio traffic from other B-24s that were in front of them. It seemed that the weather over the target was clear. Since the Lone Wolf was only supposed to attack a target that was cloud covered, the two ships turned for the alternate at Villach, Austria.

Red-Y reached the alternate and released two tons of bombs at 1110. The radar had been tuned in for some time, but they were having some trouble getting good returns of the target because of the mountains that were in the area. At the last moment, the target was spotted through a hole in the cloud cover and a visual bomb run was made.

White-W attained the target and released another two tons of bombs by radar. This plane did not have any trouble with the radar and got good returns on the scope despite the mountains.

Both planes rallied and returned to their home base later that afternoon. The results of the mission could not be judged because of the cloud cover. All they could do was give the 464th two effective sorties as a score for the day.

Nature provided bad weather in the form of rain on the 5th. The local weather, combined with a low pressure area over target areas, caused the mission to be called off before the engines were even turned over. With no mission to fly, the flight crews rode back up the hill to their quarters for the rest of the day off.

That night there was a meeting of the Christmas for Kids committee. Plans for the big event were starting to gel. A lot of the men were giving donations of money from their pay, along with candy bars and other goodies that were coming over from the States. Warren MacDonald recalled the evening of 5 December:

The flight notice board outside the 779th's Squadron Headquarters listed our crew as up for tomorrow's mission. We had "stood down" three days since the Blechhammer mission on the 2nd. Was our plane ready yet? It had taken considerable damage that day. Also, who would be our Radio Operator-Gunner? "Brownie" was still in the hospital.

On the morning of the 6th, the crews were up and standing in the chow line early. The briefing was the usual how the mission was going to be flown stuff. Col. Schroeder told the boys that he would be in the lead ship. One of the last details covered was possible fighter attacks. Most of the newer crews kinda winked and shook their heads. A lot of them had not seen an enemy fighter yet. Warren MacDonald recalled the briefing:

At briefing we were told that the principal target was the marshalling yards of Bratislava, Czechoslovakia—on the Danube—and the secondary target was another marshalling yard nearby. At some point, it was said that I was to fly a plane from the 778th Squadron. This was followed by identifying information—probably "White Zebra"—but I missed it due to the murmuring that rippled across the room. I don't believe the unofficial name of the plane, "Green Hornet," was mentioned. Even if it had been, it would have meant nothing to me.

MacDonald's crew arrived at the HORNET's hardstand and got ready for the mission. MacDonald climbed aboard and looked at the Form 1. He was more than amused to find that there were no write ups on the Form 1. That was something that he had never seen before.

Take off was scheduled for 0715 that morning. It was delayed for over 20 minutes by a take off accident with the 465th. Roy Wehmen (778th) had been assigned as Airdrome Officer for the day. This was one of the other duties that could be assigned to copilots on days when they were not going to fly. He recalled:

I had paid little attention before, but found the flat building over on the 465th side was the control tower. Handed a clip board, my instructions were "List every plane that actually lifts off the runway for the mission." No problem.

It seemed that the job could best be done by going near the end of the runway. Waiting the first take off, I walked down the steel mat to establish a good place to do my job. When I stepped off the mat, I found the earth soggy wet with water standing on top of the soil; my feet would sink into the ground, and I knew that standing there in the oozy mess was not for me. I chose to step up on the very edge of the steel mat. As always there were delays, so I finally decided to have a seat on the steel mat, and as the planes started their take off, I sat there properly recording the designation letters as the wing tips passed over my head. Why not?

As the minutes passed, the 465th was in the process of making their take off. One of the big silver birds came towards me, and for some reason the nose lifted and settled back to the runway, causing the nose wheel assembly to collapse and the nose of the plane to go down the steel mat. The sparks from the metal nose looked like a July Fourth fireworks display. The plane was carrying 10-pounder cluster bombs, and one of the clusters broke apart, so the 10-pound babies were dropping out and bouncing alongside the grinding metal like stones skipping on the water, all coming straight for me. I was not correct in saying that the mud beside the steel mat was too soft to walk on. I ran several hundred feet across that oozy mess without making tracks before I stopped to look back and see that the plane had come to a stop without burning. Airdrome Officer can be an interesting assignment.

Because of the delay in getting off the ground, the wing rendezvous was changed a little to make up some time. The entire wing was over Andria at 0830. Everyone got into position and then headed out over the Adriatic.

The 464th was scheduled to have 32 planes on the mission. LITTLE WILLIE (42-51178) aborted on the ground. During runup, the #4 engine started running rough. As the magnetos were being checked there was a 400 rpm drop, and the crew taxied the ship back to hardstand. At about 0927, Black-L aborted when they lost oil pressure on an engine. 42-51152 had a runaway prop on the #4 engine. The copilot hit the feathering button and pulled the power back, trying to control the prop. After several attempts at controlling the runaway with the feather button, he gave up and shut the engine down. Both aborts would jettison their bombs into the Adriatic.

An escort force of about twenty P-38s showed up at about 1050. They were above the formation, criss crossing the bomber stream so they could stay within striking distance in case the Luftwaffe showed up.

THE GREEN HORNET was also having some trouble. Warren MacDonald wrote:

Damage extended almost to the top of the fuselage.

Just after bomb release on December 6, 1944. Target is below the two small clouds of smoke.

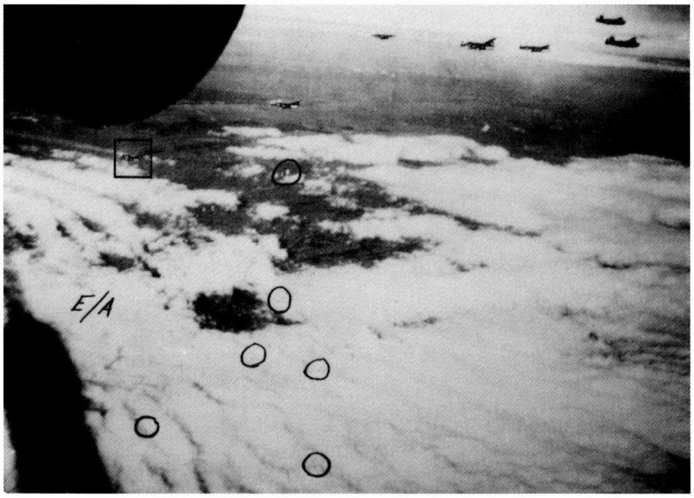

Rally right! The 464th under attack by Me-109s (circles). One B-24 (square) is smoking from the #2 engine.

The straggler is believed to be THE GREEN HORNET going down after attacks by Me-109s.

In the aerial battle the 464th claim several Me-109s destroyed.

THE GREEN HORNET burning in a field near Bucany, Czechoslavakia.

THE GREEN HORNET, December 6,1944.

Local villagers watch as THE GREEN HORNET burns.

White-J was shot down moments after THE GREEN HORNET.

Soon we were at 12,000 feet over the Adriatic, and it was time to check the guns, with all that noisy chatter and shaking of the plane. First "Manny" in the top turret let me know that only one of his guns would fire; then "Matt" (Sgt.Garrow) in the ball turret reported that the turret would swivel, but neither gun would fire. Jim (Sgt. Miller) said the tail turret was working ok, and Walt (Sgt. Kubic) said the same for the nose turret. "Griff," now at his right waist gun window, and Joe (Sgt. Koster) at the left waist window reported both guns working fine.

On top of these problems, THE GREEN HORNET was having trouble with all four superchargers and burning fuel at an alarming rate. MacDonald also noticed that the plane did not fly right. She was impossible to trim properly:

It was as if the plane was being dragged or shoved—like a wagon with a flat wheel. Later I would find that no amount of rolling the trim tabs would eliminate this feeling.

"Mac" would have been justified in aborting the mission, and MacDonald probably would have if he had known the full history of THE GREEN HORNET.

As the planes arrived near the target area the weather started falling apart. The primary target and both alternates were socked in with total cloud cover. The wing leader signaled for the entire wing to attack the rail yards at Devinska Nova Ves, Czechoslavakia. This was a target of opportunity a few miles northeast of the primary target at Bratislava.

The 464th reached that target at 1115 and released over 61 tons of bombs. Three planes were unable to drop at the target and finally hit targets of last resort. As the group rallied for home, several token puffs of flak were seen low and behind the formation. It seemed that the bombers had caught the flak gunners napping.

The 464th rallied to the right and took up a heading of 90 degrees to get around Bratislava, since there were a lot of heavy guns there. The men also recalled that there were two airfields in the area that were supposed to house several squadrons of Me-109s.

With the changes in the targets the fighter escort had drifted away from the bomber stream. At this point the 464th and 465th could not see a P-38 anywhere in the sky. The two groups were naked against any determined attack by enemy fighters. They had

White-J crash site just southwest of Malzenice, Czecheslovakia.

Four crewmen were killed in the crash of White-J on December 6, 1944. This site is very close to the site of THE GREEN HORNET's final resting place.

not seen any fighters for a few missions, so maybe the group would get out of the area without any problems.

At 1125, an alert tail gunner in "Dog Box" spotted some black specks above the formation. At first glance they appeared to be the escort. A second good look, though, showed that they did not have the twin booms of a P-38. They were single engined Me-109s. The intercom crackled:

"Bandits, six o'clock high!"

"How Many?"

"About 15 or 20! Shit! Here they come!"

Across Charlie and Dog Boxes, power turrets whined as the gunners swung around to meet the onrushing threat from behind the formation. The rest of the formation heard the alert, and the gunners stood by their guns, ready to defend their ships when the 109s came into range.

The first attack was made by seven fighters from behind and almost level with Dog Box. As they closed to within range of their guns, the wings and noses began to flash like strobes. White puffs of exploding 20mm shells dotted the sky. The first wave rolled over and dove under the formation in an attempt to decoy any escort into following them—what escort!

In the lead plane Col. Schroeder could hear what was going on behind him in the second attack unit. It was obvious the 464th needed help as quickly as possible.

"CRABTREE, CRABTREE! This is LONGSTICK. We are under fighter attack!"

The frantic call went out over the escort channel, but there was no reply. Again the call went out. This time the Col's earphones crackled, and he heard, "Hang on, we're on the way!"

The second wave of 109s queued for the attack, this time in pairs and coming straight up from behind the formation. Well out of range of the bombers' defensive fire, they started pumping 20mm shells at the "furniture vans."

The gunners on the Liberators were ready, and they poured a steady stream of defensive fire towards the attacking fighters. Empty shell casings fell from the big "fifties" like rain and clattered to the floor. The planes shuddered under the recoil of the guns, while the smell of cordite hung like a morning dew. The gunners were putting up a good fight, but the fighters were still getting through, and at the moment were winning the battle.

LITTLE ROCKET (42-50962) had taken several hits from flak on the way to the target. The electrical system had been shot out, and there was no power to the turrets. Borrowed Bombardier Charles Houlihan recalled, "We were a sitting duck!" The first wave of Me-109s hit LITTLE ROCKET hard, and she was starting to fall apart at the rivets. An engine caught fire, and the wings were riddled by cannon fire. The second attack finished LITTLE ROCKET off. Houlihan could see that the ship was doomed and bailed out of the nosewheel door. Four other men of the crew cleared LITTLE ROCKET before she exploded in a ball of fire and tumbling debris.

One of the crew from LITTLE ROCKET drifted down in his chute and landed in the Danube. He was rescued by local towns people. Radio Operator Gordon K. Swygard had been able to clear the burning wreck on the way down. One of the crew recalled that his chute appeared to be on fire. His remains were never found. It is possible that he landed in the Danube also and was lost. The pilot of THE GREEN HORNET, Warren MacDonald, wrote:

I could see Billy's face in the astrodome over the navigator's table, looking to our rear. Over the intercom he said, "Multi Me-109s. They're cutting White Howe (LITTLE ROCKET) to ribbons; it's going down, they're blowing up." I turned the wheel over to Andy and looked left and back to see plane parts and smoke.

Jim, in the tail turret, cut in with, "Mac, there's sixteen of them coming in waves of four." I heard his guns firing as Joe called, "Number two engine's on fire." I pulled off my oxygen mask to get better visibility and looked at the flames from the rear of that engine, then cut off its throttle. Then I tried to feather the #2 propeller, but there was no change; it just windmilled. Tracer bullets were going past my window.

On top of the engine fire, exploding 20mm shells had riddled the tail turret, killing the gunner, James Miller. Cannon fire had also hit the ball turret, mortally wounding Matt Garrow. The waist area was riddled, and a fire started in the bomb bay. The same cannon fire that had killed the tail gunner cut the elevator controls. MacDonald wrote:

Andy yelled, "Mac, do something, I can't hold it." We had lost elevator control, and the plane was sharply climbing. We both pushed on the wheel as hard as we could. This slowed the climb, but we had gone up to about 23,000 feet. I tried to activate the automatic pilot but got no reaction. Then came the final blow, with Joe Koster calling, "Mac, the bomb bay is on fire." I then pressed the bail out buzzer and called over the intercom, "Bail out, boys!" I asked Andy to stay so as to help me keep the plane as level as possible while the others got out. Manny also stayed nearby.

Tim, Billy, and Walt dropped out fairly quickly from the nose hatch. Then some terrible news came from Joe in the rear. "Mac, I

AWOL, the half-coyote dog that became a legend in the 464th.

thing Jim's dead." I asked him to double check, and he came back with, "He's dead, and I think Matt is, too." Again, I asked him to double check. "He's dead," he said, followed by, "and Mac, Griff is wounded and can't stand up and get his chute on." I asked if he could snap his chest pack on and get him to the hatch door, pull the ripcord, and drop him. He agreed to try and was successful.

Then I told Andy and Manny to get out. When Andy turned loose of the wheel, I could not hold it forward on my own and it came back hard against my chest. The plane went up sharply again, and apparently went into a wing over and then into a flat spin

I was still in the seat when the altimeter read 9,000 feet and the plane was passing through a cloud bank. I struggled out from the force of the wheel by twisting enough to grab the edges of the armor plate and pulled myself on out to the flight deck. I noticed my cigarettes and hat but decided quickly to leave them and climb out the top hatch.

THE GREEN HORNET fell in a flat spin until she pancaked into the ground near the village of Bucany, Czechoslovakia. The old war horse had flown a lot of missions, and she had taken more than her share of flak damage. THE GREEN HORNET had the dubious distinction of having three tail gunners killed while serving on her. Perhaps she should have been retired from combat. Crushed like a bug, she burned, leaving a pyre of smoke to mark her final resting place.

White-J (42-78682) had two engines blazing as a result of the fighter attacks, and Robert Stevens (pilot) gave the bail out signal. The crew began to hit the silk. Robert Penman (engineer), Robert Edwards (nose gunner), and Howard Shanfield (ball turret) had either been killed by gunfire or were trapped in the falling Liberator. Their remains were found in the wreckage. The tail gunner, Edward Roslefake, managed to jump but was too low for his chute to open in time to stop his fall. Five survivors were captured. Thomas III (navigator) managed to evade capture with the help of several local villagers. He would return to Allied hands in 1945.

The P-38s finally came to the rescue, and the Me-109s dove for cover. The P-38s were in hot pursuit and managed to bag a Messerschmitt, but the damage had already been done. The 464th was given credit for seven enemy fighters shot down by the aerial gunners. German records reveal that nine fighters were lost that day for this particular area.

The formation had been badly mauled by the German fighters. After the Me-109s had broken off, the nerve of the crews was about ready to snap. As the 464th approached Lake Balaton they spotted an Me-262 jet about 3-4 miles east of the formation. Immediately the pucker factor increased by 100%. The German jet made no effort to attack the formation.

The flight back to Pantanella was long and tense as the crews sweated it out. Other planes had been hit by the 109s. Fuel lines had been hit, along with hydraulic lines and other internal systems critical to keeping the planes in the air. Amidst the formation, feathered props were the group's cockade.

Yellow-M (44-10566) had left the formation before the target. Walter Freeman, bombardier, recalled:

We lost #3 and #4 before the target. Both were feathered. We never made the target. I salvoed the bombs to try and lighten the load.

There was solid undercast below, and we did not know exactly were we where. I did not know if we could get over the mountains as the pilot rang the bail out bell.

I went out and could not remember if you were supposed to count to three or ten before pulling the rip cord. I saw the tail of the plane go by and pulled the rip cord. The chute opened, and I swang once and hit the trees.

It was snowing, and there was almost six inches of snow on the ground. I started walking and I found a parachute. I followed the tracks, and pretty soon five of us were together. Pretty soon we saw people looking at us, and they took us to the wreckage of the plane and turned us over to the partisans. They took us to a house. The next morning they gave us a big bowl of scrambled eggs. There was a man sitting in the corner of the room watching us eat. Finally, he said, "Where in the States are you men from?" His name was Jovan Mizdrak, and he had been a streetcar conductor in Philadelphia.

When we left, I asked him if there was anything he needed. He wanted black pepper. When I got back to the States after the war I sent him two pounds of black pepper.

There were four empty hardstands that night at Pantanella Hill. The crew chiefs from six other planes would have a lot of battle damage to repair. The deadly encounter with the Luftewaffe had been the first major attack on the 464th since 24 August. Although the German Air Force was down on its knees, the air battle of 6 December proved that the Luftwaffe was not down for the count just yet. Thankfully, this would be the last major fighter attack the 464th would endure from the Luftwaffe.

Christmas dinner being prepared.

The strike photos were disappointing. They showed six hits on the tracks on the east side of the yards. There was a heavy concentration on the east edge of the yards, while the rest of the bombs landed in a residential area. There were also about 30 bombs in the March river just east of the yards.

The 7th found the ground crews patching planes from the previous day's mission. In view of this and bad weather, Lone Wolf tactics were employed for the mission scheduled for the 7th.

Yellow-A (42-52070), flown by Lt. Philip Savage, Jr., and crew from the 777th, left Pantanella at 0236. White-W (42-95613), flown by Lt. Forrest Robbins and crew, followed at 0239. Their target was the marshaling yards at Salzberg, Austria.

Both planes climbed through the overcast that hung over the hills at Pantanella and flew towards the line of departure. Out over the Adriatic, both planes began climbing to bombing altitude and turned towards the north into the night.

Clouds reached upward to about 16,000 feet from the Adriatic to the Alps. Hurdling the mountains, the Lone Wolves could see that the clouds were starting to break a little. From here on they would have to keep an eye on the weather. If the clouds broke, they would have to divert to a cloud covered alternate target.

When White-W reached the turn point for the Primary Target, the clouds ahead were next to nothing. Believing that the Primary would be clear of clouds, the decision was made to turn for the first alternate target at Villach, Austria.

White-W reached the target area and found clear weather. They already had the radar up and running, so they continued to make the bomb run using corrections from the radar scope. Flying at 24,000 feet on a heading of 180 degrees, over two tons of bombs were released at 0510. Several of the bombs hung up, but fell from the racks when the bombardier pulled the salvo lever.

Several bursts of flak lit up the night sky like a flash of lightning, but they were inaccurate and low. Even so, the brilliant red bursts were close enough to momentarily wreck the night vision of the pilots and scare the living daylights out of the rest of the crew.

Turkey and all the fixins for Uncles Sam's 464th.

Shortly after bomb release, the crew spotted a large spot of flame on the horizon coming from behind the plane. It approached at a very high speed towards the lone Liberator. White-W took some evasive action. The flame was a brilliant red-orange. After about three minutes, the flame went out as suddenly as it had appeared. Was it a jet, an Me-163 rocket plane, or could it have been a rocket fired from the ground?

Yellow-A hit the IP for the Primary and turned for the target. At 0540 they dropped their RDX from 24,000 feet on a heading of 120 degrees. Five sighting corrections were made during the bomb run.

This crew could see several spotlights casting a yellowish glow in the clouds below. The searchlights could not penetrate the clouds, so the Liberator turned for home without being seen.

The flight back to Italy was almost routine. One of the crews reported seeing a large fire near the top of a mountain. There was no way of knowing what had started the raging inferno. Both planes flew back using the same route they had flown towards the target. The Mickey ships were back at Pantanella by 0800 that morning. After the crews debriefed they hit the sack and tried to get some sleep.

December 8 saw the launch of another Lone Wolf mission. The same two crews from the night before were rested and left Pantanella at 0155. The two Mickey ships climbed through the overcast and crossed the line of departure near the Italian spur.

Two hours out, the radar on Yellow-A failed completely. Lt. Savage aborted the mission and turned for home. The bombardier salvoed the bombload into the Adriatic.

White-B (44-49032) flew on to near Arzburg. Both the Primary and first alternate were found to have clear weather, so Lt. Beaubin turned away and took up a heading for Villach, Austria. The radar was working perfectly, and the target was bright in the scope. At 0524, the release point was reached and 8 500 pound bombs fell from the racks towards the undercast.

The only problem that the crew encountered was that they could not broadcast a bombing report., as the Germans were jamming the airways with music and patriotic speeches. As if anyone on the ground was awake at that time of the morning!

White-B flew home without any other problems and was back at the hardstand by 0730 that morning. The crew hit the sack again after debriefing and some breakfast.

The missions on 9 and 10 December got off the ground and climbed through the low hanging stratus clouds. On both days there was trouble getting the group together in the low hanging cloudy muck, adn on both days the recall signal was sent to the Wing before they reached the Yugoslavian coast.

These were disappointing attempts at flying missions. It was dangerous enough to fly in clear weather, but this was ridiculous. Take off, form up, and start to the target, just to have to come back and try to find the field in the clouds and rain with a full bomb load. Who came up with these crazy ideas? Whoever it was surely did not have to try and fly in those conditions.

The December 10 edition of *The Tower* hit the hardstands as it did every Sunday afternoon. As usual, it was full of news from the 464th. Now, it is a well known fact that where there are G.I.s there are always examples of "man's best friend." This particular example had joined Lt. Sharron Waggoner's crew at Casper, Wyoming, during training. She was just a pup at the time she heard the call to duty. Her pedigree was not exactly up to U.S. Kennel Club standards. She was the result of a one night stand between a mongrel and a coyote. Her new owner was Sgt. Vance Myers, the ball turret gunner. She finished training with the crew and went overseas to Italy to serve her country and have further adventures. Her name was AWOL, and she became a legend in the 464th.

As a legend, she was accorded a front page article in the paper. AWOL hardly ever missed a mission briefing. She was either inside, or being chased around the outside of the briefing area by all of the male dogs in the compound. At times, the commotion they put up drowned out the briefing officer. She attended the USO shows, and according to the article nearly always stole the show. Arden Mattice from Waggoner's crew recalled:

She was kind of gray and black, and everyone said she looked like a coyote. She had more of a high pitch yelp than a bark. Another point of interest was that we always had other stray dogs around the base because they could find food there. But AWOL would have no part of the canine association, not even when she was in heat.

AWOL was always at the hardstand with Waggoner's crew to see them off on a mission. After the plane was gone she would make her rounds of the mess halls, then return to the hardstand, find her usual place to lay down, and wait for her crew to return. She greeted them with her wagging tail, and then it was off to the chow line with Meyers to get a bite to eat.

After Waggoner's crew completed their missions AWOL stayed on in Italy, and she found a new friend that would keep her supplied with goodies from the mess hall. Finally nature did catch up to AWOL during one of her romantic periods. It was rumored that a male dog named Shotgun finally cornered the wily female, and the result was a single pup named Malfunction. The full life of AWOL is lost to history. It is very possible that some of the dogs that live in the area where the old Army base was are descendants of that wily legend, AWOL.

On the 11th, the weather over Europe looked good enough to try another mission. A total of 30 planes left the base at 0830 to bomb the South Ordnance Depot at Vienna. The mission was under command of Lt/Col. Goodyear, while the second attack unit was led by Lt. Richard Price from the 779th. Weather at take off was fair to partly cloudy, so form up and wing rendezvous were fairly easy.

There were four aborts due to mechanical problems along the way. White-B (44-49032) had a problem with the oxygen system. They had flown long enough to be near a target of opportunity and dropped their bombs.

The formation turned at the IP and headed for the target. Several crews spotted an Me-262 jet fighter at about 27,000 feet. There were two P-51s chasing it, but it was pulling away and left the Mustangs hanging in the clouds.

The first few moments of the bomb run were controlled by radar. The clouds parted, and a visual run was made from 24,000 feet. A slight turn to the right was needed to put the formation in position. On a heading of 41 degrees, the 464th reached the release point at 1237.

As the 57 tons of M-17 Incendiary bombs headed towards the target, the flak appeared near the 464th. It shortly became intense and accurate. The bursts were coming in salvoes of four, all around the Liberators.

The group rallied, and the flak followed them. Within a few more moments the salvoes were bursting four, then eight at a time. The gunners on the ground were not putting up barrages, they were tracking the bombers. Some of the bursts left large rings that looked like large black Cheerios. It took about seven minutes to clear the flak. So far, everyone was still in formation as the group headed home.

Just east of Bratislavia, FAST NUMBER (42-95337) left the formation. It was last seen at roughly 1310. There was no visible problem. Sgt. Matthew Streit would be the only crewman returned to Allied control after the war. The exact cause of the loss remains a mystery.

The flight back to Italy was almost a carbon copy of the trip to the target. A couple of times the group was close enough to flak guns so that the batteries would take a few pot shots as the group flew over, though none of the planes took any hits from the flak during the return flight.

The planes returned to Pantanella around 1520, and two ships fired red flares as they approached. They landed first and were met by medical teams to treat the wounded. The injuries were not serious, but they still warranted a Purple Heart.

Thirteen planes returned with battle damage from the flak. Only one plane was damaged enough to remain grounded for more than several days. It still meant that the sheet metal boys would have work to do patching the holes.

The 464th went back to Lone Wolf tactics on 12 December. Operations Order #281 called for four radar ships to hit the oil refinery at Blechhammer South. This was a high priority target, and as such had to be hit until it could no longer produce oil products for the German war machine.

The first B-24 left the runway at 0725 and was followed by three more Mickey ships. It was a long hard climb through the overcast, but the planes finally broke through at about 8,000 feet.

Shortly after take off it became apparent that the weather was going to play havoc on the mission. Near the line of departure, multilayered clouds ranged from 8 to 20,000 feet. With the danger of mid-air encounters in the clouds, a decision was made for each plane to proceed alone towards the target.

Yellow-A (42-52071) reached the target area, and the radar navigator picked up the target from about 40 miles away. At the IP, the ship turned to 125 degrees and began the bomb run. The Mickey operator gave the bombardier several sighting angles and course corrections. At about ten miles from the target they made a 3 degree correction and were lined up for bomb release.

At 1114 the bombardier called bombs away as he released 6 500 pound bombs towards the oil complex. The cloud cover prevented seeing if any of the bombs hit or even came close to the target. As Yellow-A left the target area, flak erupted in their wake. Since it was low and to the left, it was safe to say that they had caught the German gunners resting.

Red-H (42-50533) had flown all the way to the target area. It appeared that the clouds were starting to break at the Primary and Alternate, so the pilot turned the plane towards Italy, aborting the mission.

White-B (44-49032) arrived in the target area. They also saw that the weather was clearing. They turned towards the second alternate target, Morarska Ostrana Oil Refinery. At the IP, the target was giving good returns in the scope, so the Liberator turned towards a heading of 87 degrees and started the bomb run. They crossed the release point at 1102, and 6 500 pound bombs dropped towards the target.

Several bursts of flak dotted the sky ahead. Moments later, White-B was bracketed by three bursts. One was close enough to put some extra holes in her aluminum hide. Thankfully, none of the crew were hit by flying steel.

Black-Y (44-49402) also turned away from the Primary target. They headed towards Graz to try and put some of the railway rolling stock out of action. The radar worked perfectly, and the target was picked up on the scope as the turn at the IP was made. The run to the target was made from 20,000 feet on a heading of 260 degrees. The Mickey operator and bombardier were busy on the intercom with corrections and sightings.

Black-Y crossed the release point at 1201. They dropped their bombs towards the undercast and turned to the left for home. They were well out of the flak zone before the first burst dotted the sky behind them.

All of the planes returned to Pantanella without any problems until they called Racecard Tower. The returning planes were advised that the base weather was ugly. There was solid overcast and light rain. As the planes came in, they broke through the clouds at about 3,000 feet and spotted the runway. As they touched down they kicked up a rooster tail of spray from the wet PSP.

The weather at Pantanella went from bad to worse. The skies opened up, and the rain came down with a vengeance. It came in buckets, straight down. There was nothing to do but cower in the tents and listen to the rain fall. Not only was it raining, but the temperature started to fall. Up and down the hill there were puffs of smoke as the men lit their 100 octane stoves to try and keep the tent (casa) warm.

The 464th returned to full group operations on the 15th. Twenty-eight aircraft were scheduled to bomb the Amstetten marshaling yards. During engine start, White-W (42-95613) suffered a broken supercharger governor and aborted on the ground. The crew grabbed another plane and tried to catch the formation but couldn't.

The group formed into two attack units. Lt/Col. Gilson would lead the mission, and Lt. Bedford May would lead the second unit to the target. The 464th was about three minutes late getting to the Wing rendezvous area. While the 464th may have been late, the 460th did not even show up for the mission.

At 0935, Black-A (42-51856) aborted the mission when they lost the #4 supercharger. The crew dropped their bombs into the Adriatic. Ten minutes later BONNIE-ANNIE-LAURIE (42-51760) lost the #3 engine and aborted. 42-51644 aborted after losing oil pressure on #2 and #3 engine. They released their bombs into the Adriatic at about 1228.

Except for minor changes to avoid weather, the mission proceeded according to the briefing. Clouds continued to billow upward to 17,000 feet at times. Within the 464th formation, the four Mickey ships had lowered their radar units and were checking the equipment. They were able to identify the target at between 35 and 40 miles out, and the operators gave corrections to put the group in line for the IP.

At the IP, the group turned towards the target. The intercom was alive with range to target readings and course corrections. The last range reading was about five miles from the release point. That five miles fell behind the group very fast. At 1114 they reached the target. The Liberators heaved upwards as 34 tons of extra weight fell from the formation.

The bombers rallied for home. They had not seen a fighter, except for the 20 or so P-51s that were escorting the formation. Better yet, there had not been any flak at all. The flight back was a repeat of the flight to the target. All of the planes made it back to Pantanella and were back at their hardstands by 1440.

The morning of the 16th found the 464th going through the usual preparations for another trip to German occupied Europe. Ground crews had the planes fine tuned to human perfection. Wing tanks were topped off, and the 500 pounders hung from the racks waiting to be delivered.

Capt. Joe Skymanski would lead the mission. Since it was his first mission as leader, Lt/Col. Goodyear went along to help if needed. Lt. Ken Machado would lead the second attack unit to the target.

The weather in the form up area wasn't too bad. After reaching the spur it became partly cloudy, with scattered cumulus ranging up to about 10,000 feet. By the time the formation was north of the Alps the clouds were almost solid up to about 12,000 feet.

At the Primary target area, the wing leader informed the rest of the wing that his PFF equipment was out and that he was turning for the alternate target. With the wing lead heading for the alternate, the 464th had no choice but to follow.

As the group neared the alternate, eight Me-109s approached from 6 o'clock. They banked away, then moved to 3 o'clock and stayed about a thousand yards away from the formation. Suddenly, they turned away without attacking. Maybe they thought that the 464th's formation was too big a nut to crack.

The 464th reached the IP for the alternate, which was the Pilsen Skoda Works. At the IP they turned to a heading of 30 degrees and started the flight to the target. Within a few moments of turning flak appeared in the sky in front of the group. Perhaps the Me-109s had shadowed the formation and radioed information to the flak gunners .

The bomb release line was reached at 1317. Thirty-three planes reached the target, and 29 of them toggled a total of 14 tons of bombs with delayed action fuzes and another 43 tons of regular fuzed bombs. Planes that did not release at the target either dropped later or returned with their bombs.

The formation had been in the flak for about five minutes, and that was more than enough time for several of the planes to take hits from the flying shards of exploding shells. So far, all of the planes were still with the group.

The flight back was tense for several reasons. First, many of the planes were getting low on fuel because of the extra mileage flown to skirt the weather, then flying to the alternate target. Weather was also a concern, since it was causing more course changes. There were also planes with battle damage.

42-78514 from the 777th was last seen leaving the formation near the Italian coast at the west edge of Lake Lesina. 44-49334 (777th) ditched in the Adriatic. Air sea rescue was called in before the ship went in. After seven hours of searching Gunner Hugh McGough was still missing. The rest of the crew was picked up.

Four planes had landed at other bases because of low fuel, but they refueled and came back to Pantanella. The rest of the planes landed at home plate. Two planes had taken enough flak damage to be grounded for several days, and one crewman went to the hospital with injuries from flak.

On 17 December the 464th was up and ready for another mission to the Third Reich. The Operations Order called for 31 bombers to hit the oil refinery at Blechhammer South. Blechhammer was always one of the more infamous targets, with lots of possible flak and always the chance of fighters. This was the begining of the 15th Air Force's "Big Week" against oil targets.

Lt/Col. McKenna left the runway at 0815 in the lead plane. The other planes trundled along the taxiways and got into position to take off. The planes took off at the usual thirty second intervals.

As Black-F (42-78618) taxied towards the runway, the taxi strip crumbled under the weight of the heavy B-24. The Liberator bogged down and blocked the taxi strip. Try as they did, the crew could not get the mud caked BLACK FOX to budge from the mire. The last five planes in line were late taking off because they had to turn around and taxi back in the other direction, then taxi back on the other strips until they reached the end of the runway.

Because of the weather conditions the 464th borrowed the form up area of the 460th. Rendezvous with the rest of the wing was accomplished with difficulty because of the local weather conditions. Three planes of the 464th aborted before reaching the spur.

The weather on the way to the target varied from solid undercast to large broken patches. From Lake Balaton to the IP the clouds were scattered. Because of the changing weather conditions, radar was used to navigate towards the target. The target was picked up on the radar scopes before the group reached the IP. As the group turned towards the target at the IP it was decided to make a radar run on the oil refinery.

At the release point, 25 planes toggled almost 50 tons of RDX towards the refinery. Damage could not be scored because of a cloud bank that crept over the target at the last second. The group rallied for home as flak spotted the sky with black clouds of flying steel. It was intense, but the Germans' aim was way off. It seemed to follow the clouds of chaff that the gunners were throwing into the slipstream.

On the way home Lt/Col. McKenna advised the Deputy Leader to take over the formation lead. His aircraft, RITZ (44-49073), was last seen leaving the formation with the #3 engine streaming a heavy ribbon of smoke. The rest of the flight back was almost mundane. The crews broke out their flight lunches and tried to eat and relax a little. The engineers kept their eyes on the fuel gauges to make sure there was enough 100 octane to keep the fuel hungry Pratt and Whitneys turning.

By 1615 the last of the planes had made it back to roost at their hardstands, but there were two empty revetments. Black-J (42-78671) had taken off that morning and was last seen about ten minutes later. They never made form up and never returned to Pantanella. Black-J had become lost during form up. They managed to join the

The Holiday feast for the men of the fightin' 464th.

461st Bomb Group and made the mission. The 461st was attacked by Fw-190s from II/JG300. During the air battle five Liberators were shot down, including Black-J from the 464th. Pilot James Creekmore and his crew managed to get out of Black-J and became guests of the Germans.

RITZ, with Lt/Col. McKenna and Lt/Col. Reddell, was also missing. This was a heavy blow to the 464th. Lt/Col. McKenna was flying his first mission of his second tour of duty after returning from leave in the United States, and Lt/Col. Reddell was flying his last mission before going home. It had been a cruel twist of fate on that cloudy fateful day. Most of the crew would return to Allied control after the war.

Although still in a state of shock and dismay over the loss of two high ranking officers on the previous mission, it was back into the wild blue on the 18th. The briefing that morning was quiet and subdued as the men listened to where they were headed—Blechhammer!

The first plane left the runway at 0720. Lt/Col. William Moore, Jr., was leading the group. Twenty-nine more planes left the base at specified intervals. The group formed up and headed towards the rendezvous area in two attack units. The 464th followed the 465th to Spinazzola and joined the 55th Wing. As they arrived, another group (460th) came out of nowhere at the same altitude and dead ahead on a collision course. The 464th and 465th pulled a hard turn to avoid the oncoming 460th. The next few moments were full of maneuvers that would surely give a few gray hairs to the young fliers.

Four planes aborted the mission for mechanical reasons. MICKEY (42-52526) from the 778th had an engine catch fire. The crew pulled out of formation and landed at Vis at about 1030. Their arrival was radioed back to 15th Air Force, and then Pantanella was advised as to the situation.

Another 464th ship was having trouble. Clayton Ryder was flying his first mission with his own crew. He had two missions under his belt with other pilots for indoctrination. He wrote:

We had been climbing to get above the weather. The formation was having trouble hanging together. At times the soup was so thick that we could not see our own wingtips. We were at 15,000 and climbing when my #1 engine ran away. We were over the Yugoslavian coast. The engine was thrashing like a cement mixer. I tried to feather the propeller but couldn't, and finally we cut the ignition."

With the bad situation in hand for the moment, Ryder aborted the mission and headed home. They dropped to about 10,000 feet and jettisoned the bombs into the Adriatic. Ryder recalled:

About that time my #2 engine started smoking. I knew if we tried to make Italy we would all be dunking in the Adriatic. My navigator gave me a heading for Vis. I remember sweating so much while fighting the runaway prop that I had soaked through not only my T shirt, uniform, and flight suit, but my Mae West life vest, as well.

The crew was able to get the ship down on the small island and "watched other planes land on their return from Blechhammer that afternoon."

Clayton recalled:

A few days later, I received a V-Mail from my uncle, Earle Ryder, apologizing "for the poor performance of one of our engines." That was because he was with Pratt & Whitney Aircraft, Harford, CT. Actually, he was the very first person hired when the company was formed in 1925.

The lead plane picked up the target on the radar scope about 45 miles out. The scope was giving very good returns for the bomb run. The group turned at the IP and tightened up for the actual bomb run. The Mickey operators called range and course corrections to the bombardiers. Five miles from release the last range reading was taken.

At 1158, 25 planes reached the release line. They toggled over 50 tons of General Purpose 500 pounders. After a few seconds the bombs were swallowed by the undercast. There would be no accurate way of scoring where the bombs landed, so the results would remain unknown.

Several bursts of flak filtered through the formation just after bombs away. As the group rallied for home the intensity of the black swirling puffs increased until it was almost covering the sky. After about three minutes the flak tapered off as the formation flew out of range.

The route back to Italy was almost as it had been briefed. The formation was a few miles either way of the route because of clouds and rain showers. The planes were back at the base by about 1517. Five of the Liberators were ventilated by flak.

The 19th found the crews of 27 planes up, fed, briefed, and ready to fly by 0700. Operations Order #294 called for the 55th Wing to hit Blechhammer. What, again? We just went there yesterday!

Lt/Col. Goodyear lifted the lead plane off the runway at 0740. Twenty-five more planes managed to get airborne. Two planes aborted the mission before take off because of mechanical problems. The group would fly the mission with two attack units. The second unit would be led by Lt. Harry Heiman from the 779th.

The mission went according to plan until the Wing got near the target. At this point the radar equipment on the lead plane failed. Lt/Col. Goodyear signaled for the Deputy Leader to take over the formation. By the time Capt. Charles Foote attained the lead the target had been missed.

The wing leader radioed the 464th and advised them to hit the alternate target. The group turned and headed for the alternate. Forty miles from the target the radar in Capt. Foote's plane froze up. The second attack unit leader's radar was also on the fritz.

Since the 464th had no radar to use for finding the target the entire group turned for home with their bombs still hanging from the racks. On the way home several of the planes jettisoned their bombs into the Adriatic to conserve fuel.

When the planes landed at Pantanella, a quick nose count found 44-49369 from the 776th missing from the hardstand. They had reported by radio that they were low on fuel and had an engine out. They were going to try and make it to Vis. The crew and plane would be back at Pantanella on Christmas Eve.

Speaking of Christmas, the holiday was just around the corner. According to the Christmas for Kids Committee, almost everything was ready for the big day. For the last several weeks the men of the 464th had been dropping their extra goodies into the collection boxes. Many of the men gave money from their Army pay to help the coffers grow towards the goal.

In the 776th mail room, Ed Grochowski was busier than a one armed paper hanger. With the holiday season approaching like a P-51 on a low level buzz job, he and all of the other mail clerks were really "hoppin." One of the most important things for a soldier overseas—next to chow—is mail from home. During this season it was more important than ever, as men thought about home and family.

Packages from all over the States were arriving in Italy, marked 464th Bomb Group, APO 520. They contained everything from cookies and fruit cakes to new socks. Every day, men would wait like small children on Christmas morning to see if there was something in the mail sack for them.

The mail clerks, like Ed, seemed to enjoy playing Santa for the men of the 464th. The smiles from the guys receiving mail and packages was a little icing on the cake. The saddest part of their job was returning mail that had arrived for the men that were listed as MIA.

The group was scheduled for a mission on 20 December. That morning 22 planes managed to get off the ground. Five planes aborted on the ground because of mechanical problems. Those that made it into the air formed up without a hitch.

After form up the 464th made two circuits of the form up area looking for the 465th. The 465th and the rest of the 55th Wing were nowhere in sight. Since the group was already airborne, they fell in line with the 47th Wing and continued.

Three B-24s aborted the mission after getting in the air, and three more planes returned early when they lost the formation in the deteriorating weather. Over the Italian spur thunderheads towered up to over 30,000 feet. The clouds really looked "cumulonasty."

The 47th Wing and the tagalong 464th made a Mickey run on the fourth alternate target at Villach. The seventeen planes of the 464th made their attack from 24,000 feet on an axis of 312 degrees. At 1212 the group released their bombload of over 33 tons of RDX towards the undercast and hoped that the target was in the path of the falling bombs. The group rallied for the return flight to Italy. Weather on the journey home was a repeat of the same nasty clouds, and the formation had to make several detours to skirt some really bad looking weather.

When the group got back to home base the weather was closing in at the field. Visibility was down to 3-5 miles because of low clouds and haze. Fourteen planes managed to get down before the men in Racecard tower had to shut the field down. Three planes landed at the 459th Bomb Group's base at Gulia, about 15 miles from Pantanella.

The weather that had shut the field down settled in for the next few days. The skies opened up, and the falling rain turned the base into a quagmire of mud. The group was alerted for missions, but they were never able to get off the ground to fly. The rain turned to snow, then back to rain. It was a given that, until the weather system moved out, the 464th would remain bogged down on the ground.

The weather imposed stand down gave the men of the 464th a chance to finish getting ready for Christmas. Some of the casas were sporting trees with homemade decorations. Even if the men were far away from home, there was still an air of anticipation about the upcoming holiday and the true meaning of the day. There were some "scrooges" in the group, but most of them were busy "bah, humbugging" about the weather instead of the season.

The weather was still bad when Christmas Eve arrived. The men of the 464th began to celebrate the season, and celebrate the men did, in many different ways. That night there were all kinds of activities on Pantanella Hill. The various clubs were alive with concerts and shows. Chaplain Eastwood held a candlelight service, and Chaplain McCahey celebrated mass for the Catholic boys.

In the 777th area, the spirits were flowing like water. Someone was firing off what appeared to be fireworks. One of the bursts scored a direct hit on a nearby latrine, causing a small fire. It was a good thing that the latrine hadn't been occupied when the intense and accurate "flak" hit.

Some of the men in the 778th Communication section were playing midwife to a dog named FLAK. During the evening she gave birth to eight pups, all of which were of the Heinz 57 variety. They were happy to report that mom and pups were doing well.

The Christmas Eve issue of *The Tower* was full of the latest news from around the hill and hardstands. There were a lot of articles about the Christmas season and the meaning of it to those who were in the process of celebrating the season.

Earlier that afternoon, Chaplain Eastwood and the men serving on the Christmas for Kids committee had completed their mission. They delivered 37 pairs of pajamas to the young ones at the nearby children's hospital. Then, over a thousand small Italian children packed the city theater in Canosa to watch a variety show and open small gifts of candy, other goodies, and well needed clothes. The joy on the faces of the children and orphans of the area was more payment than anything else the men could have received.

Christmas morning dawned cold and wet. Now, believe it or not, there had been a mission scheduled for the day! The crews were briefed and trucked down the hill to the waiting planes. After the usual preflight routine the men began to wait for the "green flare." They waited and waited. When they got tired of waiting, they stood around, smoked a Camel, and waited some more. Waiting was bad enough, but this particular morning it was cold, and the rain was falling from the Italian sky. Finally, the flight crews were happy to see the "red flare" fired. The mission was called off.

The rain dampened the spirits of the men a little. How the men of the 464th celebrated the day was about as diverse as a group of almost 2,000 men could be. A lot of the men used the time off to catch up on sleep, while others attended services at the Chapel. Some of the men exchanged small gifts with their buddies. It was not much, maybe a couple of packs of smokes or perhaps a pair of socks. Some of the men shared cookies or fruit cake that they had gotten from home. But the gifts that were exchanged came from the heart, and that's what counted.

A strange yet familiar odor drifted across the hill. Not since Thanksgiving had the men of the 464th been treated to the smell of turkey being cooked in the mess halls. That afternoon, the chow lines seemed to be even longer than usual as the men waited for their turn to have a real Christmas turkey dinner and the trimmings.

Most of the men would agree that the cooks had done themselves proud again. Oh sure, some of the turkey came out of a can, but most of it was good old whole gobbler that had been brought over to Italy so that Uncle Sam's fighting men could have a taste of home.

Late that afternoon, word came down from Wing that the group was scheduled to fly in the morning if the weather was good. The armament and ordnance crews trudged through the mud and started loading the planes with "gifts for the Reich." It was a cold and miserable job in the falling rain. So much for peace on Earth, good will toward man, even for a single day.

On the morning of the 26th, the group was ready to fly again. The target was the Odertal Oil Refinery. Twenty-two planes were scheduled for the mission, but two planes aborted on the hardstand. 44-41339 started her take off roll and was just getting up to flying speed when the #2 engine started acting up. The pilot pulled the power off, and the plane coasted to the end of the runway.

The rest of the planes took off and formed into the standard twin attack units. The mission leader was Lt/Col. Gilson from the 779th. The second unit was under command of Lt. George Krynovich of the 778th.

The group got formed up without a hitch. They passed over Bari at 0900, right on the button, but the 460th was nowhere in sight. A lot of the fliers wondered what the problem was with the 460th. They were late or did not show up most of the time. They caused a lot of problems coming into formation from the wrong direction, and when they were mission lead group they always seemed to fly either too fast or too slow.

By the time the fighter escort arrived at 1000 four planes had aborted the mission with problems. THE FLAKMAN (42-95332) had taken off late due to a mechanical problem. They could not find the 464th, so they joined another group for the mission.

For once, the weather was not a problem for the bomber formations—just a few scattered clouds here and there. Up ahead, it looked like the target would be clear. The Mickey operators had dropped their radar units and were busy tuning the sets just in case the weather fell apart.

A group that was ahead of the 55th Wing radioed that the Germans were using smoke pots on the ground to try and hide the target. The message pointed out the surface winds were blowing the smoke across the target and a visual run was minimal.

The Mickey men picked up the target at about forty miles out just in case. As the group turned at the IP, the target was coming in clear on the scopes. Range and course corrections flashed from Mickey to bombardier. The last range reading was at eight miles. At the last moment a two degree correction was made.

The bombs started falling from the racks at 1224 as the planes reached the release point. A total of 38 tons of bombs cascaded towards the ground. Hopefully, the bombs would find their way to the smoke covered refinery.

Pilot's eye view of Pantanella field after returning from Vis, December 1944.

The group had been greeted by a few bursts of flak near the target. For the record, it was intense and inaccurate. That might be what the records reported, but the flak had been accurate enough to damage five planes.

As the planes rallied for home, Black-F (42-78618) was last seen leaving the formation with the #3 engine smoking. Observers reported that the engine had been smoking before the target.

At 1245, Lt. Jesse Grange radioed that his #1 prop was running away and they only had 450 gallons of fuel left in the tanks. HELL'S BELLS (42-51953) turned to a heading of 85 degrees and headed for the Russian lines. Six of the crew would return to Allied control in January.

When the formation arrived over Italy, several planes radioed Racecard tower with requests for landing priority since they had wounded on board. Two planes were met by the medical crews to treat a couple of minor flak injuries. The rest of the planes lined up and came in without any major problems.

Bomb strike photos from tail end charlie showed a good break in the clouds and a clear view of the bomb pattern. For the score card, it would have been better if the overcast had hidden the results. Over a hundred bombs had hit in open country three and a half miles northwest of the intended target!

The mission flown on 27 December can be summarized as confusing. The Operations Order called for 33 planes to attack and destroy the marshaling yards at Maribor, Yugoslavia. The mission got off to a bad start. BONNIE-ANNIE-LAURIE (42-51760) ran off the taxi strip. One of the main tires was shredded, and the plane got stuck in the mud. An outboard prop hit the ground and bent the tip before the pilot could shut the engine down.

That left 32 planes for the mission. By 0920, most of the planes were in formation and headed towards Bari. BIG FAT MAMA (44-41213) flew through some prop wash, and the crew momentarily lost control of the Liberator. By the time they had control again, the 464th was nowhere in sight, so they tacked onto the 485th and continued towards the target. This particular BIG FAT MAMA was the second aircraft to use that name with the 464th, though this ship was a newer silver Liberator compared to the olive drab original.

Weather over the Adriatic was not a problem for the bombers. As the formation crossed the Yugoslavian coast clouds began to close in, but cleared again by the time the planes crossed the Drava river.

At about 1117, the Deputy Lead Red-Y (44-49048) lost oil pressure on the #2 engine. The engine was shut down and the prop feathered, and the plane signaled they were aborting the mission. That left the formation without a Pathfinder. A few minutes later, Lt/Col. Goodyear was informed that the bombsight and autopilot on his ship were on the fritz. With no bombsight and the Deputy Lead ship gone, Goodyear either had to abort or get the second attack unit into the lead position.

A quick radio call to Lt. Robert Wood, leader of the second attack unit, provided the answer to the problem. Just before the turnpoint at Popovaca, Wood turned the second unit towards the target while the first unit continued to the turn point. This put the second unit in the lead for the bomb run.

The reorganized 464th hit the IP, then turned towards the target on a heading of 284 degrees. The sky was almost clear of clouds, so the bombardiers had a clear view of the rail yards below. Just short of the target a few bursts of flak greeted the oncoming Libera-

Forming up for the mission on December 28, 1944.

tors. The German gunners were tracking the formation with gunfire. Some of the bursts were close, while most of them were "high and to the right."

Bombs away came at 1158. Over 50 tons of 500 pound bombs rained towards the target, and the group rallied to the left and headed for home. After about three minutes the group flew beyond the range of the flak. None of the planes had been hit. Don Sherard was flying his sixth mission that day. He recalled:

On the morning of 27 December, the duty officer came into our tent in the dark, shined a flashlight in my eyes, and gave me the news that I was scheduled for a combat mission. It was bad enough to be awakened in this manner, but when I sat up, my cot cover ripped and I fell through it onto the ground. During the mission we lost our number three engine, Bahnsen feathered it, and we returned on the other three. Our ship was designated as Black S (Black Sugar), and I think that it was the nearest thing to a wreck that we flew in all of the time we were overseas.

Sherard had no way of knowing the history of Black-S. She was an old war-horse, one of the few remaining original aircraft in the group. Black-S did have a lot of hours on her airframe, and they were tough hours of flying through flak and fighters. Sherard had no way of knowing that this old B-24 even had a mid-air collision. Black-S was also know as BIG FAT MAMA, the same B-24 that Robert Wingfield had flown on the group's second mission, when he brought it back with the rudder of another B-24 impaled on the nose turret. By now, she probably was getting close to being a wreck, but she was still flying; more importantly, she brought her crew home.

By 1523 that afternoon all of the planes were back at their hardstands. This included the plane that was AWOL with the 485th. They made the entire mission and dropped their bombs. Their score was included with the 485th's score.

Bomb strike photos showed that the 464th had upped their bombing score. There were hits on the tracks and rail cars. A large secondary explosion was seen on a train about halfway through the yards. This was believed to have been a train that was loaded with ammunition or some other kind of explosives.

In all, it had been a strange mission. It had taken some last minute ad-libs to accomplish the mission. While it had not been a milk run, it was better than flying in the clouds and hoping that the bombs hit the target.

On the morning of the 28th, the weather was clear and the fliers were ready for another mission. The orders called for 27 planes of the 464th to take a crack at the oil storage dumps at Roudince, Czechoslovakia. With Lt/Col. William Moore in the lead ship, the group took to the air at about 0815. All of the planes took off and formed up. The second unit was under command of Lt. George Groteluschen from the 776th.

For a welcome change of pace, the weather was downright nice for the flight to the target, with the clouds that were in the sky remaining scattered and well broken. It afforded the crews a wonderful aerial view of the snow covered Alps as the planes droned over the peaks.

So far the mission was a milk run. At the IP, the planes turned and met no resistance at all. The 464th was over the target at 1224. They dumped their lethal load of almost 50 tons of 500 pounders and rallied for home.

Just after the rally point a barrage of flak appeared in the sky, very close to the formation. Seconds later, another barrage erupted within the formation. BONNIE-ANNIE-LAURIE was too close to the flying shards of steel and took several hits, though it did not appear to be anything serious. Two other planes collected some extra holes, but everyone was still holding their position in the formation.

BIG FAT MAMA (center) after the mid-air collision on December 28, 1944.

Coming back, the group started running into bad weather about 30 miles north of Ancona. After a few minutes it seemed to clear a little. Hopefully, the group would be out of it by the time they reached the hill.

Just north of the spur, BONNIE-ANNIE-LUARIE started having problems. Flak had punctured the fuel tanks, and a lot of fuel had been lost. She was now running out of 100 octane to keep the engines running. Lt. Donald Matreia knew they would not make it all the way home. The hapless Liberator started down through the clouds.

Ditching a B-24 is risky at best, regardless of what the flight manual may say, and weather in the area was not the best. A 2,000 foot ceiling and scattered areas of rain lurked in the area where the plane was last spotted.

The other B-24s continued towards Pantanella and broke out of the clouds into good weather just south of the spur. From there on it was smooth sailing.

Bomb strike photos showed at least eight direct hits on the railway sidings, and a buried storage area was plastered by about two dozen hits. A pump house was blown to bits by several direct hits. About three dozen bombs landed in open country just to the east of the target.

The last of the returning planes were on the runway by 1544 that afternoon. The crews were trucked up the hill to the interrogation shack. Most agreed that if they had not run into the short period of flak, it would have been a milk run.

The 55th Wing called the 464th with bad news. BONNIE-ANNIE-LAURIE had indeed gone down in the Adriatic just northwest of Barletta. Lt. Robert Miller, Jr., and Cpl. James Smith, Jr., had been picked up. They were injured and were at the 61st Station Hospital. The body of another crewman had been recovered. The rest of the crew were killed and apparently went down with the wreckage.

The flight crews of the 464th were rousted out of their racks for another mission to German occupied country on the morning of the 29th. The weather was holding, so 15th Air Force was trying to get as many missions in as possible before nature went over to the other side again.

At 0905, the first of 26 planes left the runway. SPARKY'S HOT BOX (44-48768) aborted on the ground because of a broken collector ring on the #2 engine. The 464th's target for the day was the rail yards at Verona Porto Nuova, Italy.

Form up was accomplished in Area #2. The 464th had to make a couple of 360 degree turns before the lead group of the wing was in position. As usual, the 460th was late and did not make it into the formation until the 55th Wing approached the control point.

Everything was going according to the battle plan so far. As the group crossed the Yugoslavian coast the snow capped mountains could be seen ahead. As always, it was a beautiful panorama.

The grim reaper was following Dog Box in the 464th formation. At about 1120, near Villach, the reaper pointed at the Liberators and beckoned.

44-40503 and BIG FAT MAMA (44-41213) came together in the air. BIG FAT MAMA had her entire tail section broken away. The plane went out of control, did a split-S, and spiraled towards the ground. Aboard the diving plane the men were pinned and unable to move towards the escape exits. Copilot William Wilson, Navigator Charles Ames, and Bombardier Frank Bochm were finally able to overcome the force of the dive and clear the falling plane. They pulled the rip cords and their chutes opened, while the rest of the crew went in with the plane.

Aboard the other plane there was a life and death struggle to gain control of the bucking Liberator. After surviving the damage, the crew of the bent plane headed for Vis. They were able to make an emergency landing, but their flying junk heap would never fly again.

BIG FAT MAMA (center) on the way down.

The rest of Dog Box had scattered when the collision occurred, and it took a while for everyone to get back into position and settle back down to the business at hand. The 464th reached the target and released 55 tons of bombs at 1247. The crews were in for a treat, since they actually saw the bombs hit the ground. Photos showed a hit on a train that was just pulling into the yards from the south. There were also hits on rolling stock and the station.

The group flew through flak for about three minutes after the target. It was low and outside the formation and caused no damage to any of the planes.

Except for the collision of the two B-24s on the way to the target, the mission had been an easy flight. The planes arrived back at base at about 1610 and started to peel off for landing.

Weather closed in again, and the group did not fly any more missions for the rest of the month, or the rest of the year, for that matter. Besides, with the new year coming, who wanted to fly? Almost everybody was thinking about parties more than they were thinking about the war.

The Tower hit the hardstands on New Years Eve. The paper was full of news from up the hill and down the valley. There was an article about the success of the Christmas for Kids program. There was even a "Help Wanted. Ten More Voices for the Chapel Choir."

That night there was more rabble rousing than ever at the base. Several of the guys, bolstered by ample amounts of liquid courage, proceeded to find out who could drag whom the farthest through the mud. At the various clubs there was standing room only, that is, if you could still stand. More than one member of the 464th had trouble navigating back to the tent that night.

December would go into the monthly reports as better than some and not as good as others. The group had flown 17 missions for the month and had amassed a total of 645 tons of high explosives delivered to the Germans.

The 15th Air Force had mounted a campaign against oil during December. The primary target was synthetic oil production and its main byproduct, aviation fuel. During "Big Week" the 15th dropped over 1,414 tons of bombs on the refineries at Blechhammer alone. The 464th made five trips to Blechhammer during the month. By the end of the month, six of the major synthetic oil refineries were out of business for the moment.

With winter upon the group, almost every casa and tent from the top of the hill to the hardstands had some kind of heating stove. Granted, a lot of these were very crude and a few of them blew up. What can you expect when the only fuel around was 100 octane aviation gas?

Hopefully the weather would break and the local Italian workers would get back to work on the indoor movie hall and gym. It would be nice to see the movie inside instead of shivering under the clouds, or bunching together in the briefing hut.

January 1945

News Years Day dawned cold and clear. Weather over Europe was too bad to even think of flying a mission. In view of that fact, the 464th had not been alerted for a mission. Capt. Orton and the rest of the weather wizards had issued a forecast for cold. Just how cold would it be? They also said that the skies would be partly cloudy, with a slight chance of light rain later in the day.

White-H just after take off over snowy Italian countryside.

With all of the parties that had been held the night before, it was a good thing there was not a mission scheduled for the first day of the new year. Granted, there were more than enough "self inflicted" hangovers that morning, but then, News Years Eve is a time for celebration, right?

For those who could make it to the mess area, the noon meal featured another round of turkey. What, again! Imagine, trying to choke down another meal of turkey and all the trimmings after a night like the one they had just finished. Actually, turkey was better than C-Ration soup on a qweezy stomach.

After the mess halls had fed those that could make it and the mess kits were all washed up and "cleaned in the pea soup looking water," the men settled into the routine relaxation (oh really) of the afternoon.

Later that afternoon, the skies turned gray, just like the weathermen had predicted. Then the gray turned dark and nasty looking. It wasn't long before the clouds started spitting a light rain. After all, the weathermen had said it was possible.

By "chow call" that evening, the rain had turned Pantanella hill into a large mud pie. The men stood in the mud line for chow and hoped that the food was warmer than the outside air. Before the last ladle of C-ration and left over turkey soup had hit the mess kits, the rain had turned to cold, wet snow. On top of that, the wind was starting to billow the tents across the hill.

Just before dark, one of the "steak and eggs" ships came back from a trip to Rome with a cargo of passengers returning from R & R. By now, the snow was coming down very hard. The plane managed to get down on the runway, but had trouble finding the taxi way to get off the main runway. The crew finally found their way to the hardstand and shut the four big Pratt & Whitneys down. They were all relieved to be back on good old Italian terra firma. They had made it back, but just barely.

There was another B-24 in the snowy skies of Italy. It was the old war horse SHOO SHOO BABY. After 83 missions, she had been stripped of her guns and turned into a hack ship. BABY was up there somewhere in the cold snowy night, trying to find her way back to Pantanella one more time. The men that were on her that night were also returning from a holiday in Naples. There were two infantrymen onboard who had bummed a ride to get back to the front.

Phillip Turner was working in Racecard tower that night. He recalled:

I could hear the pilot calling "Big Fence" for a fix so he could find the field. I had the "Arc" light turned on and was in contact with the pilot. I heard the plane come right over the tower, then there was nothing.

BABY was starting to ice up. The pilot was pulling 55 inches and 2,700 rpm, but the plane was going down. At 5,000 feet the passengers started hitting the silk. By 3,000 feet everybody, including the infantrymen, were out of the falling plane. SHOO SHOO BABY crashed about two miles from the base. True to her legend, she had always brought her crew home safely, even if she did not make it all the way home on her final flight.

In the morning, the men of the 464th awakened to an Italian winter wonderland. White partly covered Pantanella Hill and the surrounding countryside. Off in the distance, smoke still drifted skyward from the crash site of SHOO SHOO BABY. It was cold, white, and miserable. Everyone was anxious to get the stoves fired up to take the chill off the casas.

It would take several days to clear the runway, hardstands, and taxiways of all the snow so the group could get back into the air. Makeshift snowplows were rigged to help the graders move the tons of snow so that the 464th could move around. Getting up the hill from the hardstands was a real adventure. It seemed that any vehicle that tried to climb the hill would get about one foot forward for every six feet backwards.

By 3 January the weather had warmed enough to melt a little of the snow, and the graders had cleared the runway and taxi strips enough to move the planes around if needed. It was just in the nick of time, too. On the afternoon of the 3rd, 55th Wing sent down an Operations Order for a mission on the 4th.

On the 4th, the 464th managed to get 28 planes into the cold winter sky for a mission to the Bolzano rail yards. The mission was under the command of Col. Schroeder. The weather at take off was marginal, with a 5,000 foot ceiling over the base. The planes climbed out and disappeared into the murky gray clouds. After being in the soup for about 1,500 feet the planes broke out into clear sunny skies.

The weather really messed up the briefed plan for form up. Col. Schroeder was called by the 55th Wing and told to use Area 4. Then, he was told to use the regular form up area above the clouds. Then, the Wing told him to change again and use Area 4. Col. Schroeder had a few choice words about making up their minds sometime before the war was over.

Form up was finally made just south of the spur, and the 464th was joined by the 465th at this point. Everything appeared to finally be working itself out. There was one problem, however; Charlie Box was not with the formation. Just where in the Sam Heck was Charlie Box?

Charlie Box had formed up in Area 4 as per radio instructions, and they headed for Sansego to find the group. At Sansego, Charlie Box made two orbits without spotting the rest of the group, so they turned and headed out over the Adriatic still looking for the group, or any group to tack onto.

At 1219 Charlie Box still had not found a formation to fly with. With only seven planes, the better part of valor was to abort and return to base. The major problem was that they would have to find their way back, then find the base somewhere below the clouds. The seven planes managed to find the field and land with their bombs hanging from the shackles.

While Charlie Box was trying to find the formation, the group was already heading for the target. The farther the Liberators flew, the better the weather got. At the IP, the lead ship turned and the group followed. It would not be a long run, just long enough for the flak gunners to find the range.

Just before the release point, the flak had developed into the intense and accurate variety. It almost seemed that the nasty looking black clouds were tracking the formation on the bomb run. The flak kept getting closer and closer to the planes.

Without warning, the lead plane went into a skidding turn to the left. Several pilots thought that it had taken a flak hit, and they were right. It wasn't enough to bring the Liberator down, but the plane and one crewman were wounded.

The unexpected turn meant the group had to compensate by turning sharply back to the right. The axis of attack was now 220 degrees, and the lead bombardier worked frantically to salvage the bomb run. At the last second it looked good from his view through the bombsight.

At 1305 the lead plane's bombs spilled from the racks. The bombs from 18 other B-24s started to fall until a total of 36 tons of 500 pound bombs were on the way to the ground below. 42-51563 did not release over the target. They had taken a flak hit that damaged the bomb racks to the point that they would not release. They would later jettison the load by hand.

The flak followed the 464th past the rally point. Planes throughout the formation were taking hits, but so far no planes had taken a mortal wound.

The formation came back along the route they had been briefed to follow. Coming home, the weather was just the opposite of what it had been going to the target. The further south the planes flew, the better the weather became. Near the spur, Col. Schroeder radioed the Deputy Leader to take the boys the rest of the way home. He was going to divert to Bari so his wounded crewman could get quick medical attention.

Twenty planes pulled into the pattern at about 1530 that afternoon. Most of the planes got squared away for landing, and Racecard tower kept shuffling the deck to get all of them except one down on the runway. One of the ships was having trouble getting the gear down. Flak had cut the hydraulic lines, and the crew was trying to hand crank the gear into place. The problem was that the crank was stiff, and it seemed to take hours and a lot of beef behind the handle just to get the crank around once,let alone the required thirty to get the gear down. Short of gas and wearing blisters from the crank, the crew finally locked the gear in place, and the B-24 landed at 1650.

A lot of men had been watching the drama in the sky over Pantanella hill. With the aerial show over, the men started counting holes in the planes. Twelve planes had collected flak damage during the mission. One of them would be on the hardstand for a couple of days before she would be ready for another mission.

Crummy weather moved back over Europe. For the next three days the rain turned to snow, and cold temperatures prevailed across the Italian boot. Pantanella hill was blanketed with a coat of winter white. Most of the men tried to make the best of it, and snowmen starting popping up all over the hill. One of them was complete with uniform and all the accouterments. He even sported a pair of Captain's bars on his collar. One of the more popular games was to roll a big snowball against the door of a tent and trap the occupants inside. With a lot of wet slushy snow on the ground there was a lot of the inevitable pelting each other with round balls of slush or snow.

Col. Schroeder, at the suggestion of 55th Wing, came out with an interesting directive. If the men could not fly, they could train. With that, the gunners started trudging down to the skeet range. Other crew positions went to their respective training areas to refresh their memories on how to do things according to the book. Didn't the Army Air Force remember that most of these men were graduates of the University of Combat?

On the 8th, the weather looked like it just might be good enough to get off the ground. Never mind getting back on the ground after the mission. The important thing was to get the mission into the air and worry about landing later. Lt/Col. Gilson led the first of 28 planes into the air that crisp morning.

Just after form up and rendezvous with 55th Wing, Deputy Leader Lt. Harry Heineman declared an emergency. The problem was obvious, as fire was streaming from the #2 engine of Black-Y (44-49402). The flight deck crew pulled the fire bottles, and the flames flickered for a moment. Within a moment or two the flames were back with a vengeance. The flames were licking back across the wing and spreading. The bombardier salvoed the bombload as Lt. Heineman rang the bail out bell.

One by one, the crew of the flaming Liberator jumped into the slipstream. As Lt. Heineman was getting ready to join the rest of the crew in the cold sky, the fire died and went out. Heineman climbed back into the left seat and flew the plane back to base. After calling the tower and letting them know what his situation was, he landed the plane without any further problems. One crewman was injured when he hit a stone wall on landing and was taken to the hospital. One of the other chutists was missing.

As the formation got closer to the target, the clouds became thicker and thicker until the planes were over a solid undercast. Unless things changed in a hurry, it was going to be a radar run to the target.

At about 1130, the 464th got word from the 55th Wing lead ship that, because of weather, the target was changed to the marshaling yards at Villach. The 464th made a turn to 110 degrees and headed towards the new target.

The radar scopes swept the area ahead, but Villach was nowhere on the returns. The operators checked the equipment, and it was working fine. The PFF operators could clearly see Klagenfurt on the scopes, so the 464th headed towards Klagenfurt.

Twenty-seven planes of the 464th arrived over Klagenfurt at 1158. 14 planes released 28 tons of RDX bombs. Charlie and Dog boxes did not release. In the lead plane the radar was not working on the bomb run. At 26,000 feet the leader of the boxes could not see the other planes drop because of thick vapor trails obscuring the view. These 13 planes would bring their bombs back to Pantanella.

After the planes returned, most of the crews agreed that it had been a milk run. No flak and no fighters, with only half the bombload delivered. That is, if they had hit the target. Oh well, at least half of the planes woul not have to be loaded with bombs for the next mission.

Wrong again, as the 464th stood down because of weather. Since it was dangerous to have bomb laden B-24s sitting around, the bombs had to be taken out of the planes and placed back in storage at the dump. Another wonderful job in the snow and cold after having loaded them in the cold and snow!

The clouds moved in again; actually, they never really moved out. The weather was rotten over targets, or the weather was rotten over Italy. Anyway you sliced it, the weather was just plain miserable.

If it looked like the weather over a target was improving, the group was alerted for a mission. At HQ, the men would start cranking out the paperwork. Mission plans were formulated, briefing summaries compiled, and routes plotted. Sometimes it boiled down to Able, Baker, and several other plans in case the group had to divert to an Alternate or targets of last resort.

Out at the hardstands, the ground crews made sure the planes were ready. The fuel tanks were filled to the top. Bombs hung on the racks, and ammo was placed in the guns for the mission. Every system was checked and rechecked. All of this was done outside, on the wet, cold, miserable hardstands. Time after time the men went through all of the pre-mission preparations only to have the mission called off.

On Sunday the 14th, the ninth edition of *The Tower* came out. For those who had missed the USO show on the 5th, there was a recap of what was presented. In the "778th Spotlight" there was some good natured fun poking by awarding Sgt. Merlon Bailey the D.C.C., which stood for Distinguished Cle-Trac Cross, for duty beyond the call of an Electrical Specialist. The paper also had news of a blessed event. It stated that AWOL had given birth to a single female pup last Monday. Both mother and daughter were doing well in Tent #53 in the 776th enlisted area.

Other reporters paid homage to the cooks of the 777th about the soup that had been served not once, but twice during the last week. The ingredients, as far as could be determined, were corned beef, peas, potatoes, and only God and the cooks knew what else.

Speaking of the cooks. Some of the men looked forward to the meals as a game. In some of the mess areas there were pools to come up with the type of "mystery meat" that would be served. Clayton Ryder from the 777th recalled:

Our mess sergeant was great, considering the limitations placed on him. He planned to open a restaurant after the war, and claimed he knew how to cook spam 46 different ways!

Another section mentioned Sgt. Jack McCray of the 779th. It seems that he had been aboard the Deputy Lead plane on the 8th and had to bail out. Now, the newsworthy aspect of the adventure was the fact that it was his third nylon let down from a B-24. As he bailed out he remembered thinking, "What...again?" After his chute opened, he landed and muttered, "Thanks God...Again!"

On top of all the news tidbits, there was the upcoming movie schedule for the week. The featured films were listed as "Step Lively," "G.I. Shorts," "Mr. Skeffington," and "San Diego I Love You." Due to the bad weather, the movies had moved from the outdoor area to the briefing room. It seemed that the movies were making their way through the 15th Air Force. Just last week, the men of the 451st had enjoyed "Mr. Skeffington" at Casstellucia. Now, if Special Services could just find a way of getting some good hot buttered popcorn, or maybe some dots or red hots, then the movies would be more like back home.

The weather looked good on the 18th, so the flight crews ate and went to the briefing. The mission was Plan Able, or was it Baker to...let's see, ah well, one of those targets we talked about during the last several days. The weatherman, Capt Allen Orton, promised partly cloudy skies for take off and form up.

The crews trucked—actually slid—down the hill to the hardstands. They checked the planes, had a smoke, and waited, and then waited some more. The clouds moved in, and white "partly cloudy" started to drift from the sky. The crews had another smoke and shuffled about trying to stay warm. The partly cloudy turned to mostly cloudy, and the crews waited some more.

Finally, the crews saw the red flare arch through the white flakes; the mission was scrubbed. Now, all they had to do was struggle back up the hill in the snow and maybe catch a few minutes of sacktime. That night, there was another concert like there had been every night for the last week. They were put on by the local Italian musicians. Those who attended agreed that the con-

White-H climbing towards form up.

certs were pretty good. At least the concerts took their minds off the snow, cold, food, and combat for an hour or so.

There were other things the men did for a diversion. If they had time on their hands they could always go up to the club and sit around and play cards or get a drink of grapefruit juice and brandy or whatever the club had at the moment. "Steve" Stephenson recalled:

Lucky were the people that got to sit around and listen to Smokey Howlin play his banjo. Smokey was a truly gifted entertainer. We were all starved for entertainment, and he could sure make that banjo talk and sing. He seemed to love playing, and did not find it hard to get an audience when he played. One of my favorites was "Under the Double Eagle."

Another diversion was playing cards in the tents or at the club, as was mentioned. Some of the card games became almost marathon in nature. There was cribbage, pinochle, wist, and the favorite, poker. Clayton Ryder recalled, "I can still see Col. Moore raking in the chips at the poker table, warning the rest of us, 'If you get caught bluffing, you lose!'"

On the 19th the group actually got the green flare for the mission. Maj. John Nance led the first of 28 planes into the air at 0850, and the planes formed into the usual two attack units. The entire group passed over Spinazolla on time at 1016.

Over the Adriatic, the clear skies started to become cloudy. By the time the 464th approached the Dalmatian Coast, the clouds were getting thicker by the second and billowing to over 15,000 feet.

42-51563 had aborted the mission shortly after take off when the left main gear kept creeping out of the well. Just after crossing the Dalmatian coast, 44-49696 had the #4 turbo go out. Then, seconds later the #4 prop feathered itself—or was it the Gremlins again?

At 1151 the wing leader advised the formation that they had been over the primary target and both alternates. They were all covered with solid undercast and other clouds ranging upwards to over 26,000 feet. At the time this message was heard, the 464th was approaching multi layered clouds that were building to over 28,000 feet. Reluctantly, the 464th turned away and headed back home with their bombload still on the racks.

On the morning of the 20th, the weather wizards told the men at briefing that if they could get over the clouds south of the Alps, they should be in clear skies over the target. Well, at least it sounded hopeful.

At 0810 Lt/Col. Moore took the lead plane into the air. By 0830, the last of the 27 planes was in the air, heading for the form up area. Both the 464th and 465th were forming up at 10,000 feet instead of the usual 8,000. At briefing, the crews had been told they would be climbing out fast to try and get over the weather. As the ships climbed out a lot of the bombardiers opened the bomb bay doors so they wouldn't freeze shut in the cooler air.

Over the Adriatic the formation continued to climb, then turned a little to skirt some clouds at about 24,000 feet. About this time, the cold temperature at this altitude started playing havoc on the various systems on the Liberators. Three planes aborted when the oxygen system started to leak. These planes turned away and dove for lower altitude.

One plane lost a turbo and could not stay with the formation. Then the #3 prop ran away. On Black-M (42-51264), the engines were not putting out enough power to stay with the formation. On 44-49731, the oxygen system froze and two crewmen passed out. The plane left the formation and headed down fast looking for richer air.

Just before the Key Point, the 464th had reached 28,000 feet. They were 1,500 feet higher than the rest of the 55th Wing. The clouds topped out at 25,000 feet. The 464th leveled off and headed for the target. For once, the weathermen were right; once the group got past the heavy clouds, the tops of the clouds started getting lower. Soon there were actually breaks in the clouds. The closer the group flew to the target area, the better the weather became. As they approached the IP, the bombardiers cycled the bomb bay doors again to make sure they would open over the target.

The weather may have improved, but it was still rough going. The extreme cold at altitude made the controls stiff, and the pilots had to work overtime to maintain position in the formation. Another problem was frost forming on the windshields. Pilots were constantly trying to clear the plexiglass of enough frost to see ahead. On top of that, it was downright cold in the planes. The outside air temperature was reported at -50 degrees centigrade (-58° F). Now, that's cold! As a matter of fact, that's colder than a January morning in Minot, North Dakota, believe me!

At 1251, the group arrived at the release point over the communications installations near Linz. Most of the planes released from 28,000 feet on an attack heading of 110 degrees. Several planes could not release because of frozen racks.

When the group turned at the IP they met a few scattered bursts of flak. On the plane flown by Glenn Smullins' crew they were having trouble, and they could not stay with the formation for the bomb run. They turned away from the mission and were nailed by flak. The crew would recall the mission later:

We got hit in the right wing, and the wing tank started leaking gas. We had about 250 gallons of gas in that tank, and we started transferring the gas out of there. Then we lost the number four engine. The electrical system in the nose was out, the nose turret oxygen went out, and Tom Shorney had to get out of the turret. Glenn Smullins gave the order to salvo the bombs! "Get the bombs out or we are going down," was the order. Tom McConnell, the bombardier, tried to open the doors to salvo, but the doors would not open. Smullins pulled the pilot's salvo lever, but it failed, too. Shorney rushed back to the flight deck to get an oxygen outlet and saw Tom McConnell and Orlando Perry out on the bomb bay catwalk, tripping the bombs out of the racks by hand and dropping them onto the doors, expecting the doors to tear off. It took several of the bombs laying on the doors before the doors gave way. The bombs piled up, and Perry and McConnell were kicking them on the doors to get the bombs and door to fall away.

At first, the doors hung straight down after they were broken open, and flak holes in the doors were quite visible. The force of the wind soon pulled the doors off. After we kicked the bombs out, the little oxygen bottles that were supposed to last about five minutes had lasted longer than that. Perry had put his arm under a bomb to move it out of the racks and get it to fall. He was still holding it when it started to go down, and he thought he was going to be pulled through behind the falling bomb. He still says he will never know what kept him there, the Lord had to be with us.

Just after bombs away the rest of the formation was bracketed by flak, but it was low and off to one side of the formation. Most of the men felt they were pretty safe way up there at 28,000 feet. It did not take long for the gunners on the ground to compute a correction. Within moments the flak was finding its mark, as the planes started taking damage from the flying shrapnel. The flak stayed with the group past the rally point. The 464th would be in the flak for a total of over 6 minutes. With battle damage and wounded aboard it was going to be a long cold flight home. Don Sherard wrote:

Snowmen: Theodore Hemett, Emmett Denaway, and Alfred Flanagan January 1945.

January 20, 1945, was one of the worst days that I spent while overseas. We were scheduled to fly Black Uncle (THE FLAKMAN), which was an excellent airplane. It was so cold that the propeller governors were frozen. We were lucky to make it to Aleona, Italy, a fighter field. The flak was intense, and we got a direct hit in the number two engine, so Bahnsen had to feather it over the target. We received 42 flak holes in the airplane without anyone being injured. I attempted to call Bahnsen on the intercom, but he did not answer me. It was necessary that I be in radio contact with him during the bomb run and immediately after I dropped the bombs. Finally, I called the copilot (Schiffel) and asked him if Bahnsen was all right. He told me that flak flying through the plane had cut Bahnsen's headset wire, which was not over a half inch from his face. After landing, we discovered that there were pieces of flak stuck in the copilot's pedals; a blast of flak knocked out the window in front of my bombsight, and flak came through over the navigator's table and missed him by approximately twelve inches. The radio operator, John Trabucco, was in the process of putting his steel helmet on his head when a piece of flak flew over his shoulder, hit the helmet, and knocked it out of his hands. We were fortunate that no one was injured or killed and that we were able to land safely.

The bomber stream had to deal with the same weather on the way back. They had to stay above 28,000 feet to get over the clouds, and that meant it was cold! By now, the planes had been at altitude for several hours. The Liberators were cold soaked through and through. Frost continued to build up on the plexiglass, making it hard to see out. Controls were even more sluggish than before. On top of that there was battle damage to contend with. And just how do you keep a wounded man warm at that altitude? In the plane flown by Glenn Smullins, the crew was still having problems. They recalled:

In the back of the plane Ray Quick, the ball gunner, had been hit in the ankle by a piece of flak about the size of a little finger. It entered end ways with most of it sticking out. When Tom McConnell finished with the bombs, he went to the back to give Quick first aid. The radio man, Ed Mahoney, had wrapped Quick in the emergency blankets and had the first aid kit in his hand. McConnell unzipped Quick's boot to examine the injury and decided to stuff bandages into the boot and then zip it up. If we had taken the fleece lined boot off, his foot would have frozen.

We returned to Pantanella by ourselves with three engines. We threw out everything that was loose in the plane to get over the mountains. Just before we landed we cut off the number one engine and landed with the two inboard engines. We could not land on the runways because there were wrecks on both runways, so we landed between the runways. We had the engines running from one tank of gas, which was all that we had. We stopped at the end of the runway. The Colonel was there and said, "move that damned airplane!" Perry yelled back, "You move it! There isn't enough gas to soak up a handkerchief!" Smullins did accelerate number three engine to get to a tarmac, and it conked out. That was as far as we could go.

The planes began to leave the heavy clouds behind as they neared the spur. As soon as possible, the planes began to descend to lower altitude and warmer air. Four planes broke away from the formation and headed for the nearest base to land.

Black-Q (44-49314) was flown by Maj. John McNeely. He had been Deputy Leader for the mission. Over the target they had been hit by flak. They were low on fuel, and the #1 engine was out. They pulled into the pattern at Torretto, home of the 484th and 461st, trying to make a landing. On the downwind leg #3 and #4 coughed as the fuel lines ran dry. McNeely brought Black-Q in on one engine, wheels up, and bellied in. The crew emerged shaken and bruised, but alive. Black-Q was declared Class-26.

At Pantanella the battered formation let down for landing. Near the base, 44-41339 suffered engine problems, and the crew bailed out rather than try an emergency landing in the crippled plane. Four of the crew were injured during their nylon let down. Before leaving the cockpit the pilot had set the auto pilot, and even with engine problems the plane made the Adriatic before it went into its final dive.

After the other planes landed, a survey showed that 14 of them had taken hits from flak. Four planes were damaged enough to ground them for several days, and six of the returning crewmen were taken to the hospital for treatment of minor injuries from flak.

BAD PENNY (42-78488) from the 779th was listed as missing. The daily report had no information regarding the plane or crew. That was understandable in view of what had happened. Robert Rose was flying his second mission that day in the right seat. The pilot, Clayton Morrison, was giving Rose his orientation to combat flying. Rose would recall:

We went into some clouds, and when we came out there wasn't another plane to be seen in the sky. We finally found another group and joined them. We got hit by flak. The #3 engine was damaged, intercom was shot out, and the radio equipment was hanging by the wires. A piece of flak hit my left hand and bent my wedding ring. Then the #1 prop ran away. After the target we could not keep up with the formation, and pretty soon we were flying alone. The plane started to ice up, and we were having trouble controlling it.

We finally got out of the clouds enough to see that we were over land. Morrison said we should bail out. The engineer went back and told the guys in the back to bail out. I went to the bomb bay to bail out and met the bombardier (Milton Espenshade, Jr.). He asked me if you jumped head first or feet first. I pushed him out, then followed. I pulled the D-Ring and nothing happened. I had not pulled it hard enough. I pulled it again and the chute opened. I lost my G.I. shoes that were fastened to the harness. I could see other chutes from our plane and yelled at them, but it was like yelling in a vacuum. I landed in a manure pile, and suddenly there were people all around me.

Rose had met up with some of the partisans. After some difficulty in communicating, they realized that Rose was an American. Then they were more than friendly. Most of the crew would return. Nose gunner Albert Hayes and Navigator Walter Baldwin were unable to bail out, perhaps because of frozen nosewheel doors, and were killed.

Yellow-A (42-52070) was also missing. This plane had mechanical problems that forced the crew to bail out. They would all make it back to the base within a few weeks.

One other plane had failed to return to the hardstand. Black-L (42-78590) had aborted the mission before the target. Coming back the crew had to shut down the #1 engine. As the plane got near the base another engine was lost, and the pilot ordered the crew to bail

Oxygen tank and bomb fin stove made by Rod Binger helped take the chill off the 779th casas.

out. Eight of the crew jumped from the plane at a dangerously low altitude. Five of the men who jumped were killed because their chutes did not have time to open. The pilot and copilot rode the plane in and were seriously injured in the crash. One of the men who had jumped was Robert Rose's regular bombardier, Lt. Sam Breslawski. With Rose and crew down in Yugoslavia and the bombardier killed, there was only one occupant in their tent that night.

It had been a long, hard, and very cold mission. Some of the crewmen were more than ready for their ration of combat booze to help warm the innards and calm the frayed nerves. A lot of them hoped that they would not have to take a B-24 that high again for a while.

When Don Bahnsen's crew brought FLAKMAN back to Panatella, crew chief Lester Hacker could not believe his eyes. The plane had 42 flak holes to patch. There were also pieces of flak imbedded in her innards that had to be picked out. The plexiglass bombardier's window would have to be replaced. On top of everything else, Hacker would have to check the propeller governers to make sure they were ok, which meant a lot of work for him and his assistants. But, that was what they were there for, to keep 'em flying.

It had indeed been quite a cold mission. Too cold and rough for some of the men who had flown the mission. These men were not used to the rigors of flying combat. As a matter of fact, they were not even flight crew. They were part of what was known as an exchange program between the infantry and the air force. The idea was to let infantrymen fly several combat missions with the bomber force and collect a few more points towards discharge. The idea sounded good. As a matter of fact, the infantrymen enjoyed the "easy" life of the "flyboys" while they were on the ground. They had a nice warm tent to sleep in every night and warm meals to eat. It sure beat the life they had been living in a foxhole. That is, until they were thrown aboard a B-24 and sent out to hit a target. After a mission like the one the 464th had just flown, they were more than ready to call it quits and head back to a nice warm foxhole.

Old Man Winter moved back over Europe and the southern part of the Italian boot. The sky above Pantanella clouded over and opened up with rain, then snow, and then more rain. This kept up until there were over six inches of cold wet snow covering the base.

It was a strange bit of fate that the groups of the 55th Wing were grounded at this time because of the weather. No one in the high command could have known that because of the geography of the local area that this area around the Ofanto River would be one of the worst areas to build a bomber base. It is true that other groups would also be forced into standing down because of the weather. It was just a quirk of nature that the storms seemed to follow the river and dump more rain and snow on Pantanella Hill than in the other surrounding areas.

It was obvious that the 464th and 465th would be grounded until the weather cleared enough to get off the ground, so the men of the 464th made the best of things around the base. The most important thing was trying to stay dry and warm. It was during this time that there was a rash of 100 octane stoves catching fire or blowing up.

Some of the guys listened to Axis Sally on the radios. Don Sherard recalled:

She upset us one day when she told us over the radio that the clock in the 464th officer's club was 15 minutes slow. We checked and she was right. It was clear that she had an informant on the base.

Indeed she did! Research has shown that at bases throughout the 15th Air Force information was being sent back to Berlin. The sources were Italians who were still hoping that Hitler would win the war. Many of these sympathizers had gotten jobs at the Allied bases and were keeping their eyes open for interesting tidbits of information, like a slow or fast clock, or perhaps a special meal. It was these little tidbits that were used for broadcast towards specific groups just to try and shake up the troops. After all, if Axis Sally knew about the clock, then just imagine what the German High Command might know about the next mission.

There were a lot of other things going on around the hill. The gunnery school was very busy. If the men couldn't fly combat, they could train. Gunners trudged to the skeet range, while others spent time in the power turret mock ups at the school. A lot of gunners practiced on the "Jam Handy." This was an interesting piece of equipment. It consisted of a projection screen and a film that showed fighters attacking from various lines of sight. It also had a mounted gun which "fired" a dot of light on the screen. The idea was to keep the dot of light on the fighter and shoot it down.

Marvin Nelson, one of the instructors at the gunnery school, recalled that every once in a while they would strike a deal with some of the ground personnel who wanted to "shoot some skeets." They loaned the gunnery school the latest movie and were able to have some time on the range. Of course, the "Jam Handy" was modified, and the gunnery school people had a private showing of the movie.

In most cases, the infamous 100 octane stoves worked well, as long as the users were careful with them and there was fuel to burn in them. The 779th was in the midst of a fuel crisis. This, of course, led to a lot of midnight requisitioning of fuel from someone else's barrel to keep the home fire burning. Those that returned to their casa and found that they had been hit by the "fuel bandit" had little choice but to go out and get some fuel for themselves by using the same midnight method.

The group was grounded for almost a week during this time period. With almost 2,500 men trudging around the base trying to stay warm and dry it is safe to say that there was more than one case of falling morale. To fight the boredom, there were a lot of snowball fights and other skull duggery going on around the hill.

The 464th lost a well known figure at about this time. Mr. Curtis Lamb, Field Director for the American Red Cross, was sent back to the States after suffering from an eye problem. Mr. Lamb had come over with the group. He had worked hard to help procure lumber and building materials for quarters and other buildings around the base. He was instrumental in getting a lot of things that most of the men never knew about. He tried to provide a lot of little creature comforts for the men. Little things like Coleman lanterns, those infamous "sinkers" (donuts), and coffee after the missions. Those that knew him felt he "was a swell guy." He would be missed.

During the last week in January a real winter storm hit the base. As always, it came up about sundown and blew all night. Lots of men spent the night trying to hold their tents down. Several of the tents took off without completing a preflight inspection or flightplan. The storm also dumped another healthy dose of white "partly cloudy" on the hill.

A lot of the guys were getting sick and tired of the snow. They may have been sick of it, but it was a fact of Pantanella life at the moment. With every snowstorm a rash of snowball ambushes would break out. One had to be careful at all times. You just weren't safe anywhere. It did not matter if it was the chow line, going to the movie, or just heading for the casa. The men soon developed a swivel neck to avoid being pelted by a dozen or so "white flak shells."

The weather finally cleared enough to get a mission into the air on 31 January. It would be a Red-Blue Force mission. Both would attack and destroy the Oil Refinery at Moosbierbaum. Red Force would be led by Lt/Col. Goodyear. He flew the lead ship into the air at 0810 and was followed by 20 more B-24s.

RUTHIE THE RAIDER (42-52537) aborted on the ground because her power turrets did not work. The crew changed to another plane, but could not find Red Force. They would later find and join the Blue Force.

The Red Force formation was out over the Adriatic by 0920, and the fighter escort from the 52th Fighter Group appeared on time. Another flight of P-38s showed up a few minutes later. At least the bombers would have fighter cover in case the Luftwaffe had enough gas to intercept them.

The 464th leaves vapor trails in the cold January skies.

The bombers flew towards the target about 20 miles west of where they should have been. This was because of cloud cover over the briefed route. The clouds ahead looked solid, so it appeared it would have to be a radar run when they got to the target.

The lead plane picked up the target about 35 miles out. There was some trouble with the radar, but the operator did some tweaking and got the problem squared away by the time the group was at the IP. Twelve miles from the release point, the group made a 2 degree correction and was centered on the bomb run.

Just short of bombs away the first black puffs of flak were spotted. It was classified as inaccurate. Don't mention that word to the crew of MARY O (42-51423), however. One of the inaccurate 88s went through the left wing between the engines. It did not detonate on impact, which was fortunate for the crew. Copilot Tony Schneider recalled:

#1 and #2 engines quit immediately, and we dropped out of formation and flew down the Danube above an overcast, hoping the Russian aircraft would shepherd us to a place to land. The gunners said that two fighters came up through the undercast but they made no attempt to lead us. We asked Joe Damkowski, the navigator, "Where are we?," and he replied, "I can't see the ground, and besides, we ran off the maps I have anyway."

The crew faced a hard situation; they could bail out, or ride the plane down and through the clouds, hoping there wasn't a mountain in the way which would really ruin the day. They voted to bail out. With about eight minutes of fuel left in the tanks, the crew bailed out. They came down near the village of Schaundorff, where they all linked up with each other. Tony Schnieder remembered:

With #3 and #4 pulling max power, the C-1 autopilot would not hold the aircraft level. To level the plane we reduced power so we could get to the bomb bay. After arguing with Matt about who would bail out last, I moved aft to find the bombardier standing on the catwalk, looking down at the open bays. After receiving no answer to the question "Are you going?" I put my foot in the middle of his back and pushed him out. Some of the gunners found him, fainted with his chute draped over a haystack. Fortunately he stayed conscious long enough to pull the "D" ring.

Two members of the crew had broken a leg in the jump. It would take a while, but the entire crew would journey through Romania and back to Allied control.

MARY O had managed a pretty good crash landing in a nearby field. The Russian soldiers told the crew that the plane was in fairly good shape except for bent props. Since there was no way of getting the plane fixed and back into the air, the crew didn't go to the plane to look at it.

Bombs away was called at 1317. Nineteen planes reached the target, and 16 of those dropped over 30 tons of bombs towards the undercast. Those that were not able to drop would either drop on targets of last resort or dump their bombs in the Adriatic.

The 464th rallied and headed home. The route home was almost a carbon copy of the route to the target. Near the island of Vis,

Heading home and leaving the flak behind.

White-Z (44-49653) left the formation and started down. It was later reported to have made a landing at the emergency field on that small island. The rest of the planes were back over the field by 1515.

The 21 planes of Blue Force had left Pantanella at 0910. By the time they were over the Adriatic they had been joined by the lost Red Force Liberator and a fighter escort from the 332nd Fighter Group. The men in the planes were always very happy to see the red tailed Mustangs of the 332nd.

Two planes aborted the mission and turned back to Italy. About an hour from the target, the radar unit in the lead plane failed. Lt/Col. Moore surrendered the lead to Lt. Arnold Klimpel flying White-W (42-95613)

Blue Force arrived at the target and released another 36 tons of bombs at 1409. There were a few bursts of flak dotting the sky, but none of it was even close to the Blue Force formation. Since there was solid undercast, no bombing score was credited for the mission.

The Blue Force rallied for home. Now that the bombs had been delivered, Lt/Col. Moore took over the lead for the trip home. Like the Red Force, the trip back was a carbon copy of the trip to the target. Blue Force made it back to the field by about 1630.

With the mission for the day over, those that felt like it sloshed up or down the hill (depending on where you were) to the briefing hut to take in the evening showing of the latest "flick." As always there was a delay, and so the men started the usual catcalls. "Hurry up, start the movie, the I-ties are here!" When the title "Summer Storm" danced onto the screen there were even more whistles and calls expressing the hope that at least summer would arrive.

January had been the most miserable month in all apects since arriving in Italy. It was cold, wet, snowy, and downright boring. And for some of the men, those were the better memories of the month. The group had been able to fly only five missions, and one of those had been scored as ineffective because the group had turned back before reaching the target area, thus no credit was given for that mission.

The month was hard on everyone. Almost every day, several mission plans had been prepared and briefed, only to have the mission called off. Crews were baffled by trying to remember what the Primary target was and the five to seven alternates or last resort target.

Because of the stand downs and weather, the gunnery school had kept busy. The boys fired over 19,000 rounds on the skeet range during 22 days. Forty-eight crews had spent an hour or more on the "Jam Handy," while 980 gunners took an hour to refresh their memory on the six turret mockups.

And then there were the ground crews at the hardstands. There were no hangars to work in; after all, that was a luxury that the men at Pantanella never hoped to have. Everything from loading fuel to changing an engine was done outside in the snow, rain, and teeth chattering cold.

Granted, it was not -20 degrees out, but it was still cold out there on the hardstands. Try changing a flat tire on your daughter's car at night in the rain at a warm 32 degrees and you may get a small appreciation for what these men did out on the hardstands. Believe me, I have and feel greater respect than ever for the unsung heros of the hardstands.

On January 30, 1945, Adolf Hitler made a radio broadcast to the people of Germany. It was full of his usual rhetoric. He called for the German people to fight on and achieve the final victory over the Allies. He demanded that they fight to the last for the "Fatherland." It was strange that in one breath he called for victory and in the next he was calling for the people to fight on to the very last. Perhaps his mind was really going after all. This would be the last radio broadcast Hitler would make. The planners and clerks at Group Headquarters offered the following:

Oh Lord, give us the strength to continue to prepare and brief three plans each night. May we be able to present nine targets to the combat crews so they will be able to remember them clearly and not get mixed up on axis or rally. May we do our best to keep our many miles of flak routes from running into each other. Give us control of our inner selves so as to act in a manner of an Officer and Gentleman when all three plans are stood down when the weather man gets through briefing. Give us, oh Lord, more escape and food kits, so that when the maximum efforts and normal efforts and three ship element missions are set up at the same time that we will have enough to go around. Please, oh Lord, desist from adding Dog and Easy plans in place of Able and Baker after they have been prepared.

Most especially, Lord, give us some good bombing weather, with one plan, let it remain for one month so that we may do our job and get this over with. Amen.

6

Finishing Off the Reich

February 1945

It looked like the weather prayer that the Headquarters men had put in the month end report had worked for the 464th. The weather over Europe looked pretty good on February 1, 1945. At 0805 that morning, the first of 41 B-24s lifted off the runway for a mission.

Just after take off, something went wrong on Yellow-N (44-49363). The pilot called an emergency to Racecard tower. The plane circled the field and landed, using the entire runway. The rest of the planes continued to take off after the emergency was over.

The planes of the 464th formed into three attack units. The group was led by Col. Schroeder. The 465th had gotten off the ground and was on time for the form up of the two sister groups. They both headed for Wing rendezvous and met the rest of the Wing on time. With the 465th in the lead for the wing and the 464th second in the bomber stream, the formation headed out over the Adriatic.

When the formation reached the area of Split, Yugoslavia, the wing leader signaled for a change in route. The weather had closed in over the Primary, and he had been advised that the Alternate was open enough to make an attack. In order to get everyone going in the right direction the formation made a 180 degree turn and several circles until everyone was in line on the new course.

Over the Dinaric Alps the clouds broke apart, and the weather ahead looked even better. The formation had climbed to 19,000 feet, and everyone was in their briefed positions. For once, almost everything was going according to plan.

After flying about another hour, the lead plane of the formation could see clouds building ahead. It looked like a real storm system brewing. As they got closer, the leader could see that the clouds were billowing up to over 30,000 feet.

Word was received by the Wing leader that all prospective targets were socked in, and the formation was cleared to hit any target of opportunity or return to their respective bases. The 464th aborted the mission and headed back towards Italy. The formation flew through some clouds that had moved into the area, but nothing serious was found on the way back.

Most of the planes brought their bombs back to the base. Several of the Liberators had jettisoned their loads into the Adriatic when they started having mechanical problems on the way home.

The bad weather that had scrubbed the previous day's mission had moved south and was now over the bases in southern Italy. Missions would be planned, only to be called off for the next several days. Across Pantanella hill there was a general feeling of displeasure towards the weathermen. It always seemed that the weather section was blamed when the mission was canceled. Didn't they know about the clouds and storms that were over Europe? After all, they were the weather wizards!

It must be pointed out that the weather patterns over southern Europe can become very complex. Add to that the fact that the area of operations for the 15th Air Force is noted for being a region of high precipitation during the winter. Then, throw in the strangest weather patterns for the last 25 years and you have a real forecaster's nightmare. The winter of '44-45 would go into the record book as one of the worst winters in Europe in recent memory.

The weather broke, and the 464th was ready for a mission of 5 February. The target for the day was Regensburg, Germany, a real bladder buster. The first of the 42 scheduled planes was rolling down the runway by 0825. By 0845, the last plane was in the air and heading for the form up area.

The group formed into three attack units led by Lt/Col. Gilson. There was some trouble getting the wing together. Several of the formations had problems keeping the right spacing, and the 460th seemed to be bunched up and out of line most of the way over the Adriatic.

Three planes of the 464th returned early with mechanical problems. 42-51563 aborted with #1 engine out because of a fuel line being clogged. They pulled into the pattern at 1245 and touched down on the PSP. As the plane rolled down the runway, one of the landing gears folded and the ship skidded to a stop. The crew was unhurt, but the plane was going to need a lot of sheet metal work to her belly before she would fly again.

As the formation approached the target, they found it covered with clouds. It would be a radar run without a doubt! The target was picked up on the radar about sixty miles out. It was bright in the radar scope, and there was no problem identifying it.

When the group turned to a heading of 282 degrees at the IP, the Wing was still bunched up. The 464th was forced into a wide turn for the bomb run. This put the group a little out of position, but they corrected for it within a few minutes.

At 1258, the 464th was over the target and hit the release point. Seventy-one tons of bombs fell from the planes and started the long drop to the ground. Several of the planes were unable to release because they had problems with the racks. Several photos were taken at the release, but no score could be estimated because of the clouds covering the target.

The 464th rallied for home without seeing as much as a flak burst. As they turned, they could see that the group behind was catching all kinds of flak. The 464th had been at the right place at the right time to avoid the flak for a change.

Heading home, the crew of RUTHIE THE RAIDER (42-52537) was having problems. When they took off that morning the cylinder head temperature on one of the engines had been dangerously high. As they climbed out into cooler air, the temperature settled down. Over the Adriatic they had a small fire in the ball turret, but the crew got that problem under control and made it to the target. Bombardier Fred DeMatteis recalled what happened next:

After bombs away, the top turret gunner was filling his oxygen bottles when he heard the tail gunner yell that he saw a jet plane. The gunner jumped into the turret, spun it around without disconnecting the oxygen bottles, and pulled out all the oxygen lines to the nose. This good news was conveyed to the nose gunner and myself, so we had to leave the nose and proceed to the flight deck.

While the nose gunner and I were retreating to the flight deck and out of touch with the intercom, the pilot issued orders that he was leaving the formation and proceeding to Switzerland. On the way to Switzerland, we flew over Innsbruck and got shot up pretty badly. For whatever reason, the navigator lost his cool and gave the pilot a heading which took us over the Alps and over enemy held Italy, where we were told by the pilot to bail out because our fuel tanks had evidently been punctured by enemy fire over Innsbruck.

Instead, he found a large snow covered field and decided to crash land the plane, and did a spectacular job in doing so. It turned out to be a deserted German airfield that was full of bomb craters covered with snow. The wheels collapsed, and we slid to a halt with a few injuries. While changing our boots and preparing to become prisoner, a man came running across the field waving his arms and yelling in Italian.

No one understood him, but we decided to follow him. In a small farm adjacent to the field they had two horse drawn wagons. He made us jump into the wagons, covered us with hay, and got us out of the area to another farm. That night, an English major who was helping organize the partisans visited us. He told us that he would try and get us to France, even though the mountains were piled high with snow.

After a harrowing 59 days of climbing mountains and hiding from the Germans, the entire crew would return to Allied control. Don Sherard recalled the mission on the 5th:

We lost number one engine over the target, and as we left the target area Bahnsen feathered it. About an hour later, engine two failed and Bahnsen feathered it, leaving the plane flying on engines three and four, which were the two engines on the right side. At this point Bahnsen directed Rice to transfer fuel from the tanks feeding engines one and two to the tanks for engines three and four. Bahnsen ordered the crew to lighten the plane as much as possible to try and maintain sufficient altitude to clear the peaks of the Alps on two engines.

The rest of the formation flew back to Italy along the briefed flight plan. As they crossed the Adriatic, it looked like another frontal system was moving in from the west. The planes of the 464th approached the field for landing and kept their weather eye on the approaching clouds. By 1645 that afternoon the planes were down and headed for their hardstands. That is, all except a couple of the Liberators. One of the missing planes was trying to make it back the hard way. Don Sherard wrote:

We were able to clear the Alps, and Bahnsen then directed the crew to prepare for ditching. At this point, Kephart gave Bahnsen a bearing to a fighter strip just south of the American and British lines in Northern Italy. Fighter strips were generally much shorter than bomber strips. As we approached the strip, we could see a crashed fighter burning at one end of the field. In order to line up with the runway, it was necessary that Bahnsen bank to the left into the side with the dead engines, and then he dove the plane at a sufficient rate of speed to gain enough lift to level the plane on the approach.

Group S-4 and photo building, February 1945.

As he leveled the plane for landing engines three and four failed; apparently the gasoline was displaced by the plane's attitude, and he proceeded to land the bomber "dead stick." As soon as the plane touched down he locked the brakes, and the plane skidded down the runway, washed out the gear, and slid to a stop on its belly. We were all thankful to be on the ground.

Except for the loss of the old warhorse RUTHIE THE RAIDER, it had been a pretty good mission. No fighters had been seen except for the escort. The flak had not even come close to the formation. No one was hurt. Yep, a pretty good mission.

The incoming frontal system caused a stand down on the 6th. Most of the men tried to take the day off and catch up on their sack time. There were several new crews at the base, and they were busy attending the required three day "Indoctrination 101" course. As always, the gunnery school was busy trying to find enough unbroken clay pigeons so the gunners could use the skeet range.

Beginning at 0930 on the morning of the 7th, the first of 42 planes left the PSP runway. The target was the Florisdorf Oil Refinery at "Flak City" (Vienna). The first unit was led by Lt/Col. John Cornett, Deputy Group Commander. The second unit would be led by Col. Schroeder.

The group formed up about nine miles NW of the base due to the clouds in the usual form up area. The 465th and the rest of the Wing were met over the spur at about 12,000 feet. The bombers headed out over the Adriatic at about 1101.

Four Liberators aborted the mission. Red-H (42-50533) aborted after take off when both inverters failed. The plane circled the field until the rest of the planes had taken off and cleared the area. They came back and landed hot and heavy with the bombload still aboard

The clouds thinned out near the Dalmatian Coast, then got thicker over the Dinaric Alps. By the time the group approached the IP, the clouds had evaporated to just thin wisps. Towards the target it looked clear as a bell.

As the 464th approached the target they could see that the Germans had started the smoke generators on the ground, trying to hide the target from the approaching bombers. There was a slight breeze on the ground, and it was just enough to keep the smoke drifting away so that the bomb run could be made by visual means.

Just before reaching the release point the first bursts of flak opened up. At first it was light and inaccurate. The closer the group got to the target, the more accurate the flak became.

Over the target, flak scored a hit on OH U KID (42-50752). The damage was serious enough to cause the plane to start losing fuel.

The formation released their bombs at 1407 from about 25,000 and rallied for the return trip. The group reached the outer ring of flak after being under fire for about four minutes. So far everybody was still in formation. On the way home, OH U KID was last seen about four thousand feet below the formation, apparently trying to make the Russian lines.

Aboard OH U KID, pilot Merle Hoffman was having trouble with their damaged crate. He knew they were not going to make it all the way back. He was trying to let down through some heavy clouds and find a place to set down. He recalled:

We broke out of the clouds, and being a farm boy I could see corn stalks sticking out of the snow in a field. It looked like a hayfield between us and the cornfield, so I tried for the hayfield. I missed. There was a tree, and I picked up the left wing just a little bit, just cut the top right off the tree, and then we set down in the cornfield.

Everyone aboard was able to get out of the plane after getting on the ground. The locals helped the crew link up with the Russians, who in turn moved the crew from town to town until they had traveled across Hungary, and then to Arad, Romania. From here the crew was flown in a C-47 flown by a Russian crew to Bucharest. Hoffman recalled:

It was really cold out—really cold! We were sitting on board when the Russian pilot came out. He cranked the engine, started taxiing, and took off. Never warmed up the engine, never checked the mags.

Hoffman's crew was listed as MIA for the second time. While their families were worried about what had happened to them, they were having a pretty good time in Bucharest. They would spend about a month in Romania before they were able to get back to Allied control.

When the planes arrived back at Pantanella the strike photos were developed and printed. The photos showed disappointing results. The target area was completely free of bomb hits. Most of the hits were about two miles northwest of the refinery. More hits were observed on the east side of the Danube.

On the 8th, the 464th headed back to Vienna. This time the target was the industrial area on the East side of the city. At 0825 the lead ship, flown by Lt/Col. William Moore, lifted into the air. He was followed by 27 more Liberators. The 464th formed into two attack units and met up with the 465th. The rest of the wing was waiting over Spinazzola.

As the groups headed for the spur several radio calls were received from "Uphill" (Wing lead) calling for changes in the route. Instead of heading across the Adriatic the formation flew north, almost in the middle of the Adriatic. When the formation was about sixty miles east of Rimini, they turned towards Austria.

The Gremlins were working overtime on this mission. A total of seven planes aborted the mission between 0922 and 1230. When 42-95332 returned early that day, her crew chief was rather upset. Sgt. Lester Hacker's THE FLAKMAN had not aborted a mission in a long time. Now the streak of missions was broken. The crew had been scheduled to fly a different plane that morning. They had trouble with the bomb bay doors and abandoned that plane for THE FLAKMAN. They could not catch up to the formation, so they came back. Now, in view of the fact that THE FLAKMAN had not been scheduled for the mission and the abort was not because of mechanical problems, Hacker and his ground crew were not given an official abort.

Just after the group had made the turn towards Austria, about 20 Mustangs from the 332nd FG arrived to give fighter escort to the target. The flight crews always liked to have Little Friends along with them on a mission. At this juncture of the war, the Luftwaffe hardly ever had enough gas to come up and intercept the bombers. But you just never knew when they might show up.

As the 464th turned at the IP, several Me-109s and Fw-190s were seen approaching from behind the group. They were getting lined up for the attack. Before they even got close to the 464th they were bounced by the red tailed Mustangs from the 332nd. The German fighters turned away and tried to run for cover.

With clouds in the area the radar operators had already been looking for the target on the scopes. The first target returns had been identified at a range of about 45 miles. During the run to the target there were several minor corrections, until the group was on a heading of 68 degrees. At the last moment, the lead bombardier could see the target through the smoke screen and took over for a visual release. The bombardier released the first of 42 tons of RDX towards the target.

At almost the same time the target was spotted, the formation was greeted by the first flak bursts. They were just in front of the lead plane. The flak gunners adjusted a little, and within seconds the flak was not only intense and accurate, but was tracking the formation as they flew the bomb run.

The 464th rallied right and headed home. The flak followed for a few more minutes until the Liberators were out of range. The group had been in the flak for seven minutes. Several of the planes had taken minor hits, but all stayed in position.

On the way home, one of the crews spotted a lone B-17 under attack by some Fw-190s. A frantic call was made to the escorts, and within moments a flight of P-38s showed up and the Focke-Wulfes broke off and ran for home.

The formation crossed the Italian coast near the spur, each of the groups in the wing headed for their own bases. The first plane of the 464th rattled the PSP at 1505. By 1525, the last plane was down and the PSP grew quiet again.

On 9 February the 464th reverted to Lone Wolf tactics for a mission to Moosbierbaum, Austria. The first plane was Red-A (44-49589), flown by Lt. Bert Pugh, Jr., and crew from the 776th. Red-H (42-50533) was flown by Capt. Forrest Robbins' crew, also from the 776th. White-F (42-95613) took off late at 0959 when the scheduled B-24 had electrical problems. Lt. Frank Lane and his crew had to change planes.

The first two planes formed up and crossed the line of departure. By the time they reached the Key Point near Split, the late plane had joined up. About 15 miles beyond the Key Point, the three planes ran into clouds. They broke up and headed on individual flight plans.

When Red-A arrived at the IP it appeared that the clouds were breaking up at Moosbierbaum, so they turned and started for the alternate at Graz. The target was picked up about 45 miles out. The Mickey operator called corrections for both range and angle until their heading was 220 degrees. At 1255 they reached the release point and dropped their bombs towards the target.

Just before release, the plane was bracketed by flak, and several shards of steel whistled through the airframe. Tail gunner Sgt. Henry Fulghum was hit by flying steel. He was pulled from his turret and given first aid.

They rallied right and headed for home after being in the flak for about six minutes. The damage to the plane was minor. The crew would be concerned about their tail gunner until they made it back to Italy.

Red-H made a run on the Primary at Moosbierbaum. The target was picked up on the radar scope at 20 miles. After several sighting angles a final correction of nine degrees to the right put them on a course of 68 degrees. At the release point they dropped their 8 500 pounders onto the target. They rallied to the right and ran into the flak. The flak was actually classified as inaccurate, although several bursts were as close as fifty feet.

White-F had also flown to the Primary target. The target was picked up about 30 miles out. At first, the image was fuzzy. At about 15 miles, the scope cleared and the target was clear. A final correction of 4 degrees to the right put the Mickey ship on a heading of 70 degrees.

At 1225 they reached the release point and dropped their bombs from 24,500 feet. They also rallied to the right and headed home. As they raced away from the target, a barrage of flak blossomed about 500 feet behind them. Several chunks of steel rattled against the plane, but none of them came through the aluminum.

On the way home, White-F had trouble sending the strike completed signal. It seems there was a German radio station broadcast-

Chow line at the 777th, February 1945.

ing on the same frequency as the 55th Wing Headquarters, and that station affected reception between the plane and Italy.

The three planes returned to Pantanella and landed between 1500 and 1518 that afternoon. While the results of the mission were unknown, it was felt that it had been a good mission. When Red-A landed, they were met by the medics so their wounded tail gunner could be treated for his wounds.

The 464th stood down 10-12 February. The weather over Europe had closed in, and the 15th Air Force felt that even Lone Wolf missions were marginal. There was a mission scheduled for the 12th, but it was canceled before take off.

About the most important thing happening on the afternoon of the 10th was Presentation Day. Col. Schroeder presented decorations that had been approved by 15th Air Force to the men who had been awarded the Air Medal, Pruple Heart, and Distinguished Flying Crosses.

On the morning of the 13th, Col.Schroeder led the first of 20 planes off the runway at 0830. This was going to be a Red-Blue Force mission. The Red Force had no trouble forming up and meeting the rest of the Wing's Red Force. One of the planes aborted when they lost a turbo.

At the last turn point before the IP, the radar unit in the lead plane failed. Col. Schroeder was about to turn the lead over to the Deputy Leader, then that plane radioed Col. Schroeder to inform him that they had lost an engine. Col. Schroeder turned the formation towards the alternate target at Pola to try and salvage the Red Force mission.

When the planes reached the IP for Pola, they turned to a heading of 181 degrees and started the run to the target. About a minute before the bomb release, the first burst of flak appeared in the sky within the group. Several planes took hits from the first barrage but stayed in position.

At 1335 the lead bombardier hit the toggle and released the first of 34 tons of high explosives towards the naval yards 25,000 feet below the Liberators. Sixteen more planes released and then rallied right.

The planes were still grinding through the flak, which would last for several more minutes. Don Sherard, bombardier in the 779th, asked their tail gunner, Carl Henry ,if he could see where the bombs hit. Henry leaned forward in his turret as a flak shell went off just outside the turret. Shrapnel came through one side of the turret and shattered the plexiglass on the other side. If Henry had not leaned forward at that moment, he would have taken the full burst of shrapnel in his head.

The 464th had done a good job on Pola that day. The target was well covered with hits, and several sub pens had taken direct hits. A couple of bombs had landed in the torpedo storage area and created quite a secondary explosion. Several warehouses, training stations, and barracks had also felt the brunt of the 464th.

Just after the group rallied, Yellow-Y (42-50843) peeled off to the left of the formation and started going down. She appeared to be under control. The Liberator had taken several hits from flak. The rudder controls had snapped, and the rudders were flapping in the slipstream. Lt. Leonard Vaughn was able to get the plane far enough south so the crew could bail out. They would be back at Pantanella by the 17th.

The rest of the planes in the formation returned to base and were in the landing pattern by 1456. Thirteen planes had been hit by flak. Two of the planes had taken enough battle damage to be grounded for several days.

While Red-Force was flying their mission, Blue Force had been briefed for a mission to the marshaling yards at Graz. Lt/Col. Gilson led the first of 21 planes into the air at 1130 that morning.

The mission could almost be called a milk run. The weather had cleared and stayed that way almost to the target. The group arrived over the target at 1501 and released the bombload. Two planes had rack problems and could not release. They would bomb "by hand" on the way back to Italy.

Strike photos showed a good pattern of strikes right down the middle of the tracks. Several lines of freight cars were blown to bits, and several bombs hit near the choke points. The local trains to Graz would be late again.

There was some flak over the target. It wasn't accurate and lasted about three minutes. Several of the planes took some minor damage. One crewman was dinged by a piece of steel that had come through the side of the plane. If he could find the spent shard of steel, it would make a great souvenir. All of the planes returned to the base later that afternoon. Except for the minor damage on the two planes, the 464th had come through the mission in good shape.

On the 14th, the 464th again split their effort into Red and Blue Forces. Maj. Sherman Martin, Commander of the 778th, led the Red Force Liberators into the air at 0900. Twenty more planes would follow at short intervals.

The form up of Red Force went without a hitch, and the formation was in position with the rest of the wing as they passed over Spinazzola. As the bomber stream headed out over the Adriatic, the 460th pulled ahead of the rest of the wing. By the time the formation approached the Dinaric Alps, the 460th was still pulling ahead and was soon swallowed by heavy clouds.

This presented a problem for the wing. The 460th was the designated lead group for the mission. Across the 464th formation the crews were wondering just what in the hell the 460th was trying to do. The 464th continued towards the target with what was left of the 55th Wing.

As the group hurtled the Dinarics they spotted heavy clouds ahead. These were the same clouds that had swallowed the 460th. The 464th was flying at 26,000 feet. The tops of the clouds in front of them climbed upwards to 30,000 feet. Maj. Martin saw that the weather looked better to the west. After quick consultation with his navigator, he turned the 464th towards the 5th Alternate target at Villach.

Poor Villach was in the wrong place at the wrong time. This small town in lower Austria just happened to be in the middle of a valley. A valley that just happened to have a railway running through it, which happened to be a railway between lower and upper Europe. In other words, a main railway through the mountains. Ah yes, it made sense to the flight crews. It was not a strategic target, yet bottle the trains up near Villach, and maybe, just maybe, some important supplies would not get through to the German Army in Italy.

As the 464th approached their new target the weather cleared until it was almost CAVU all around the group. At the IP, they turned to 175 degrees and began the run to the target. Just before reaching the target MICHIGAN B & P WOMEN (42-50728) pulled away and started heading down from the formation's altitude of 22,000 feet. During a crew position check the ball turret gunner failed to check in, and the waist gunners found him unconscious. The ball turret gunner's oxygen mask had frozen, and he was suffering from lack of oxygen. He was pulled from the turret, and a different mask was slapped on his face. The pilot salvoed the bombs and headed for Italy. They would land at Falconara, where the gunner was pronounced dead. Sgt. William Gay would be the only casualty on the mission.

The Red Force arrived over the target at 1310 and released over 33 tons of bombs onto the target. Since it was clear, the bomb run was done by the old fashion use of the bombsight, instead of radar.

It was a good run. Most of the bombs hit in the middle of the yards and walked through the target area almost to the choke point. Several bombs hit just beyond the choke point, and several landed in the military barracks area just to the southeast of the main yard. The formation rallied for home without seeing so much as a single burst of flak. The 464th had caught the flak batteries napping.

The Blue Force had taken off at 1000 under the leadership of Capt. Joe Shymanski from the 779th. The 21 Liberators formed into a single attack unit and headed towards the 55th Wing rendezvous point. The Blue Force leader for the wing was also the 460th. This time the 460th flew at a slower airspeed than outlined in the Operations Orders for the mission. As a result the wing was bunched up, and the pilots had to constantly jockey the throttles to stay in position.

On 17 February Yellow-S crashed on take off.

As the formation got near the target, Blue Force leader was having trouble with the #2 engine on STEVEONOVICH II, alias Black-N. He signaled for the Deputy Leader to take over the formation. Things got really messed up during the change of command. The formation fell apart, and by the time they were together again some of the boxes had dropped their bombs on targets of opportunity. With things all fouled up the formation turned for home, bringing what was left of the bombload back with them.

When the planes were back at the hardstands, it looked like Ted Mouldenhauer would have to roll up his sleeves and replace the engine on BLACK-N that had caused all of the problems. Maybe, if his brother "Red" did not have much to do, he could help get the job done before morning arrived. Another sleepless night for the unsung heros that worked to keep the planes flying.

The Blue Force part of the mission could be classified as a complete failure. Strike photos showed the elements that released missed their target by over nine miles.

February 15th saw the 464th split their efforts into Red and Blue Forces again. Hopefully, things would go better than it had the day before. At 0915 that morning, Lt/Col. Moore lifted the first of 21 Red Force planes into the air for a mission to Wiener Neustadt. The low scud clouds swallowed the planes shortly after they left the runway.

Because of the low clouds, the group formed up at over 6,500 feet. The 464th hit the wing rendezvous point about three minutes late. Only their sister group, the 465th, was in sight. Out over the Adriatic the rest of the wing showed up, and the entire wing headed for the Primary with the 464th in the lead position.

The clouds that were in front of the 464th did not look that bad. There was solid undercast, but these clouds topped out at about 10,000 feet. As long as the clouds stayed below, the 464th could bomb by radar. The Mickey operator in the lead plane was having some trouble with his radar unit. He was getting some kind of interference from the radar units being used in two of the other planes.

The target was picked up on the scope near the Moos turnpoint, about 45 miles from the target. The 464th turned at the IP and started the bomb run. Everything was working fine with the radar by now. The target returns were bright and clear on the scope. The last correction was 2 degrees to the left to a heading of 122 degrees.

At 1301 the formation attained the release point, and over 42 tons of bombs began to rain towards the target. The radar men in all three elements were sure that they had hit the target as the Red Force rallied to the right for home.

The fliers couldn't believe it. There had only been a few puffs of flak during the entire bomb run. Granted, they had used a lot of chaff since they turned at the IP, but it seemed that the gunners on the ground did not even find the formation.

The flight back to Italy was a piece of cake. None of the planes had been damaged, and none had reported any mechanical problems. By 1522 the first Liberator of Red Force was back on the runway. Red Force had been treated to a milk run.

At 1015 the Blue Force started into the air to hit the same target at Wiener Neustadt. Twenty-one planes left Pantanella under the command of Capt. Shymanski from the 779th. The group flew as one attack unit made up of three boxes. Each of the boxes had a Mickey ship in the lead position.

The weather was a little worse since the Red Force had taken off. Form up was between Trani and Barletta at about 7,000 feet. The 464th met up with the 465th and 485th on time and right where they should be. The 460th was nowhere in sight (as usual) and never showed up with the 55th Wing.

At about 1255 BIG ED (41-29394) radioed that they were having engine trouble and were aborting the mission. The old olive drab war horse turned for home and landed at Bari with two engines out. DONNA DO IT (41-29594) aborted the mission after losing oil pressure on the #3 engine, and she headed towards Vis. This plane had served with the 8th Air Force and had a lot of air across her wings by the time she was transferred to the 464th.

The lead Mickey men picked up the target at a range of 45 miles. As the formation flew over the mountains towards the IP the scope returns got dimmer. The group missed the IP and overflew the turn by about 8 miles. The target returns came back clear at this point, and the group turned for the bomb run.

As the Liberators got closer to the target the scope returns were getting even better, and several range sightings and course corrections were made. About five miles from the release, a final 2 degree correction was made to a heading of 131 degrees for the actual drop.

The group reached the release point at 1403 and sent over 37 tons of bombs hurtling towards the ground below. Blue Force rallied right and headed back to Italy. Blue Force had really caught the flak gunners napping, as no one had even seen a burst of flak on the entire mission.

The Liberators of the 464th returned on approximately the same route they had used on the trip out. When they got back to Pantanella they found the base socked in tight. Racecard tower advised the returning formation that the ceiling over the base was down to 2,500 feet. One by one, the planes let down into the gray murky clouds. Somewhere down there in the swirling mist was the runway and home. It took almost an hour for all of the planes to make it down. Everyone was safe on the ground by 1650.

The 16th of February saw the 464th ready to carry out the mission outlined in Operations Order #77. It called for 42 B-24s to bomb the Obertraubling Air Drome at Regensburg. The battle plan called for the group to attack in three units, with each unit made up of 14 ships.

At 0830 Lt/Col. Moore lifted the first B-24 from the runway and into the low clouds. As the planes took off they were swallowed by the low ceiling. Each of the planes would have to climb to over 2,000 feet before they broke out into clear sky at about 5,000 feet.

The 55th Wing did not get everyone together until they approached landfall at the Yugoslavian coastline. The formation was flying in and out of clouds all the way across the Adriatic. Don Sherard recalled a close call:

We entered the dense cloud cover in tight formation. The pilot asked all crewmembers to keep a sharp lookout in all directions for the other planes. In a few minutes Bob Rice, in the upper Martin turret, calmly announced that a bomber was flying about six or eight feet above us. We looked up and could see the rivets in the belly of the plane almost on top of us. Gradually that plane moved out of sight, and we found ourselves settling down or another plane rising up immediately beneath us. We called this to Bahnsen's attention. This situation continued for five or ten minutes, but it seemed like hours. Finally we broke out on top of the clouds, and most of the planes were now widely scattered. The group again "formed up," and we proceeded on our way.

Six planes aborted the mission. Four of them aborted because they lost the formation in the clouds. With all of the planes groping around in the clouds, it was a major miracle that none of them found each other by accident.

The planes flew on towards the target. As they did, the bombardiers moved back to the bomb bay to remove the safeties from the bombs. It was a routine procedure that had to be carried out on every mission. For Don Sherard, it was not going to be routine on this mission:

I went back and removed the safety pins from the bomb rack. It was dark in the bay, and I was not aware that one of the ground crewmembers had loaded the bombs improperly, so that when I pulled the safety pin, the bands on one of the bomb clusters were released. I found myself with eight or ten loose fragmentation bombs in the bomb bay.

As an added safety feature, each of the bombs had a small propeller on its nose. When released and falling into the air stream, the propeller would spin and fall off. Once it had fallen off, the bomb was armed and would detonate upon a slight impact. There was sufficient air coming through the bomb bays to cause several of the propellers on the bombs to spin, and the bombs were therefore in the process of becoming armed and ready to detonate. I first tried to replace the bombs in the cluster while holding the propellers so that they could not spin. Being unsuccessful, I called nose gunner Daniel Jeffery, and we held the propellers stationary on the loose bombs. I called Bahnsen on the intercom, told him what the problem was, and asked him to break out of the formation, as we did not want to drop the bombs on one of our planes below us. After we had left the formation, Jeffery and I "cracked open" the bomb bay doors and dropped the bombs by hand, one at a time until the loose bombs were gone. We closed the bomb bays, double checked the other clusters, and proceeded to the target.

At the IP, the group turned towards an attack heading of 338 degrees and started the run to the target. Moments before reaching the target, several bursts of flak mushroomed off to the left of the formation. Moments later several more exploded behind the 464th.

As the group neared the target, the 465th crowded the 464th to the right of the flight plan. The 465th turned away, and the 464th corrected back to the left and continued the bomb run.

At 1317 the formation of the 464th was over the target, and the call "Bombs Away!" crackled over the intercoms. Over 72 tons of fragmentation clusters were dropped from about 24,000 feet. The group rallied to the right about three minutes after bomb release.

The flight back to Pantanella was flown as it had been briefed. Clouds caused more anxious moments as the group came in over the spur. Again, the field was covered by low clouds and the planes had to let down in the soup until they could see the ground and land.

While it was not exactly a milk run, it had been a fairly good mission for the 464th. All of the planes returned, and no one was injured. The results were questionable, since the target was covered by smoke from earlier strikes.

February 17 saw the group readied for another trip to Hitler's Third Reich. The target for the day was the harbor installations at Pola, Italy. The plan called for 42 Liberators to form into three attack units and proceed to the target with a maximum load of 500 pound RDX bombs. The mission would be led by Lt/Col. Gilson.

The mission had trouble before it even got started. Black-A (42-51856) had trouble with oil pressure on an engine. The ground crew pulled the cowling and dug into the engine innards and engine plumbing, trying to find the oil gremlin before it was time to taxi. Try as they did they could not get the oil pressure to stay up, and the plane aborted on the ground.

Lt/Col. Gilson pulled onto the runway aboard his plane STEVEONOVICH II. It was named after his son, with a bit of a Russian twist. After going through the routine final pre-take off checks, he pushed the throttles forward and started the take off roll at 1120. One by one, the lumbering Liberators followed.

As RAMBLIN RECK (44-48767) lifted off the PSP the pilot, Joe Miniter called for the gear. One of the main landing gears retracted, but the others hesitated. Then something went wrong with an engine, and the overloaded Liberator started falling back towards the ground. Miniter recalled a fleeting thought, "How are we going to get out of this." Ahead he could see an approaching farm house, and he was afraid of hitting it. Miniter had no choice in the matter. The crew on the flight deck killed the switches and issued a quick warning to the crew that, "We are going in!" The flightcrew in the front office held the wings level as they hit the ground with a resounding crunch of aluminum. The Liberator slid along the ground, the left wing dropped, and the props dug into the ground, throwing up a cloud of dust as the props bent, then broke away. The impact with the ground caused some of the bombs to come loose from the racks, and they bounced along the ground until they came to a stop. After what seemed an eternity, the sliding hulk came to a stop in a cloud of dust. The crew was shaken, but still realized that they had to "get the hell out of the plane." Miniter recalled that they literally threw the navigator through the top hatch and then followed as quickly as possible. RAMBLIN RECK was exactly that, but at least the crew was still alive.

The low clouds over the base caused problems getting the group formed up. As the 464th circled in the form up area, there were several close calls as B-24s popped up out of the clouds. Black- A (42-51856) could not find the group when she emerged from the cloudy murk. Off to the north there were some B-24s, so #856 headed for them. The B-24s turned out to be from the 461st BG. #856 transferred to the 49th Wing and flew the mission with them to Trieste.

The clouds began to break up over the Adriatic, then closed in again as the group approached the IP for the target. At the IP, the clouds broke again and the target appeared clear. The 464th turned towards Pola and set up for a visual bomb run on the harbor.

The bombsight in STEVEONOVICH II was lined up on the aiming point. Just seconds before release, the gyros in the bombsight tumbled and the sight failed. The lead element flew over the target without dropping their bombs, while the rest of the group released as they crossed the target.

Gilson signaled for the group to begin a 360 degree turn. He was then informed that only his element had not dropped their bombs. Discretion was the better part of valor, and Gilson's element returned to base with their bombs.

Even though the 464th had only dropped part of the bomb load, it was still a good mission. Strike photos showed they had scored direct hits on the dry docks and shop area. Hits were also scored on oil storage tanks and piping facilities. Several seaplanes were destroyed, and several bombs landed in the barracks area near the seaplane base.

On the morning of the 18th, 28 planes of the 464th left Pantanella for another mission. Right away, weather started creating havoc with the flight. The group had started climbing as soon as they were formed up. Weather reports from other groups indicated that the clouds were topping out at about 14,000 feet over the middle of the Adriatic.

As they crossed the Dalmatian coast, the formation was flying at over 21,000 feet. There was a lot of radio traffic between the wing leader and the other groups. The wing leader radioed that he was at 23,000 feet and the clouds in front looked like they went up over 30,000 feet. The clouds were too high to climb over with the bombload, and the wing leader aborted the mission.

The 464th made a sweeping turn of about 200 degrees and headed back towards Italy with their bombload hanging from the racks. By 1229 the first plane of the 464th was back in the pattern at Pantanella. The ineffective mission on the 18th was not officially credited by the 55th Wing, and the fliers of the 464th were upset, to say the least. They would have another chance on the 19th.

Beginning at 0740, the first of 28 Liberators took off on the morning of the 19th. The group formed into two attack units and headed for the Wing rendezvous area. The 465th and 485th were late, so the 464th pulled in behind the 460th and headed for the target. The other two groups caught up with the Wing in the middle of the Adriatic.

Just as the 464th moved into position during rendezvous, two planes aborted. White-V (42-95364) lost a fuel boost pump and was leaking fuel into the bomb bay. The situation was serious. The bomb bay doors were opened to allow the sloshing fuel to drain out into the slipstream, and the pilot turned the leaking Liberator back towards Italy.

For the first time in days the clouds were not a problem during the flight towards the target area. When the formation neared the IP they found a different problem to deal with; the winds aloft were a lot higher than forcasted. They were also blowing from the wrong direction. The Wing leader signaled to abandon the Primary and strike the First Alternate, the railway yards at Graz.

At 1217 WILLY (42-51903) lost oil pressure on #4. They left the formation and dropped their bombs on a rail line. Three minutes later White-E (42-78472) lost #4 engine and left the group. They dropped their bombs on a rail siding at 1225.

The rest of the 464th reached the IP and turned to a heading of 173 degrees for the bomb run. Ahead, the target was clear and the winds had improved for a visual run from 26,000 feet.

At 1251 the left and right index pointers on the lead bombsight merged, and the first of over 45 tons of RDX fell from the Liberators. As the bombs began their ballistic flight towards the ground, the flak shells began their journey towards the formation. As they burst close to the formation, the flying shrapnel rattled off the sides of the planes like gravel on a tin roof. Shortly the bursts were close enough to send hot steel shards through the sides of the planes.

The group rallied to the left and skirted the flak after roughly two minutes. Several of the planes had taken damage but remained with the formation for the time being. It would be a long trip back with the battle damage. Some of the planes had taken hits in the fuel tanks and were losing fuel, so the flight engineers kept an eye on the sight gauges during the trip home.

By the time the planes returned to Pantanella, four planes were reported as missing. Black-M (42-51264) landed at another base, refueled, and returned later that afternoon. SKY PIRATE (42-94823) had landed at Pecs, Hungary. Black-O (44-49751) left the formation on the way back with one engine out and two smoking. The pilot, Lt. John Damhorst, radioed that he was heading for the Russian lines. GRAVEL GERTIE (44-49394) landed at Vis because of low fuel caused by flak holes in the wing tanks.

Many a flight crew and plane owed their lives to the small island of Vis. It is about 33 miles off the Yugoslavian coast. From the small island it was just over a hundred miles to Pantanella as the Liberator flew. The runway was only about 3,500 feet long, with gravel and some PSP for its surface. If you were trying to make it back to Italy with a shot up airplane, that small piece of real estate could look pretty darn good. For many, it was a life saver.

When the strike photos were developed and printed they showed that the 464th had accomplished their mission. The target had been well hit by most of the bombs. The 55th Wing gave the group an overall score of 48% of the bombs within 1,000 feet of the aiming point.

Operations Order #85 called for 28 planes of the 464th to take off at 0840 on the morning of the 20th and bomb the Primary target. That target was the Fortezza rail yards near Brenner Pass. As always, the route to the target and back was planned to keep the planes as far away from the known flak concentrations as possible. Sounded simple on paper, however, weather would cause more than enough problems during the execution of the mission.

Lt/Col. Gilson lifted off the runway in his trusty STEVEONOVICH II (Black-N) at 0840. That would be the last time that any part of the mission would go according to the briefing flimsy.

Weather in the form up area went from marginal to bad to downright dangerous. The group had to break up, then climb through clouds until they broke out at 11,000 feet. There, they had to regroup. With planes all over the place climbing through the clouds, it was a miracle that none of them had any collisions.

Out over the Adriatic the clouds thinned for a while. At the midpoint of the Adriatic the clouds closed in, and the formation had to skirt them over the Yugoslavian Coast. Out ahead of the bombers a weather ship was checking out the conditions over the various targets that had been assigned for visits by the 15th Air Force. The weather was bad at almost all of the targets. The only one that looked hopeful was the shipyards at Trieste.

The 464th reached the Alternate Target and released over 56 tons of bombs onto the ship yards from 23,000 feet. The group rallied for home, then rallied again to the left over the harbor. The fliers figured they should see the opening rounds of flak at any

Part of the bombload broke loose and ended up here.

time. They were lucky, as they had caught the German gunners either out of ammo or napping. The 464th started for home without seeing a single burst of flak.

The planes hugged the Dalmatian coast most of the way back down the Adriatic. Near Split, the formation turned towards the spur. By the time they got back to Pantanella the clouds had broken somewhat, and the planes found large holes and let down without any problems.

The strike photos showed that the 464th had put their bombs right down the chute. Over two thirds of the shipyard had been blanketed. Three merchant ships had taken direct hits, and several piers and a dry dock had also been hit. In all, the bombing scorecard for the 464th should have good marks on it from the 55th Wing umpires.

The men of the 464th awoke to light snow showers on the morning of 21 February. The sky was covered with low clouds, and it looked like the scheduled mission would not get off the ground. By the time the men had eaten breakfast and briefed, the snow had stopped and the mission was on.

As the crews waited for the green flare they tried to stay warm in the cool Italian air. Clayton Ryder (777th) recalled:

On getting down to the flight line, a few of us ducked into crew chief Ross' tent to get warm. We knew all about mission secrecy and "loose lips," but we could not help making a few wisecracks when we saw his wooden case full of Vienna sausage tins!

At 0930, Lt/Col. Moore took off in the first of 28 planes scheduled to fly the mission. When his plane reached 3,500 feet, the low clouds enveloped the plane and it disappeared from view. Due to the low clouds in the area, the rest of the planes had to stay low and fly towards the spur. There they climbed to about 14,000 feet, then returned to the local form up area for the 464th. This extra flying time made the group a couple minutes late for the wing rendezvous.

The 464th was not the only group having trouble getting formed up. Almost every group was late. Finally the 55th Wing got everybody together, then headed for the Matzleindorf rail yards near Vienna. That is, everybody but the 460th. Again, they were nowhere in sight, except for one lonely B-24. That ship joined the 464th formation for the mission.

By the time the formation was over the Yugoslavian coast the clouds had thinned to almost nothing. As the planes flew over the snow covered Dinaric Alps, some of the men remarked how beautiful they were. Beautiful yes, but a formidable place to try and make a forced landing or bail out.

The clouds began to move in again, so the Mickey ships lowered the radar sets and started tuning them. As the group got near the IP the radar in the lead plane went out. Lt/Col. Moore signaled for the Deputy Leader to take over. Shortly after this, the gyros in the Deputy Leader's bombsight tumbled. At this point, Able 13 took over the lead at about 1340.

At the IP, MICHIGAN B & P WOMEN (42-50728) left the formation with a problem; the ball turret was jammed. It wouldn't move at all. To compound the problem, the gunner was trapped in the turret. They headed back towards Italy alone, while the crew tried to console the gunner and figure out how to get him out of his cocoon.

The group made the IP and turned to a heading of 90 degrees for the run to the target. The radar aboard Able 13 was working fine, and the target returns were clear. Several corrections were made just before the target.

About one and a half minutes before the 464th was over the target, the flak batteries sent a greeting barrage of about 20 rounds at 12 o'clock. The flak continued to track the formation as they approached the release point.

At 1350 the 464th released over 48 tons of 500 pound RDX bombs onto the target from 24,000 feet. Just as they released, the clouds thinned enough to see the ground through the low haze. The bomb path looked good.

As the group rallied to the right the flak followed. By this time, the flak was scattered to the right of the formation, then scattered off to the left. It might not have been the usual Vienna flak, but several of the planes had already been hit. The group would be in and out of the flak for a total of about five minutes.

The planes returned to Italy by the same route they had flown to the target. By the time they got back to Pantanella the weather had improved dramatically. The returning Liberators had no problems finding the field and getting down.

MICHIGAN B & P WOMEN had made it home by 1606 and landed with the ball turret down and the gunner still inside. To say the least it was a harrowing trip back, and a nerve racking landing, especially when you consider there were only six inches of clearance between the turret and the PSP. One good bounce would be all that was needed to send the turret scraping along the PSP at over a hundred miles an hour.

Six planes had taken flak hits over the target, and several would be out of commission for several days before they would be able to fly another mission. The ground crew for MICHIGAN B & WOMEN would have to have the turret specialists check out the ball turret and find out what Germlins had infested it during the mission.

The mission for the 22nd as outlined in the Operations Order was very simple on paper. It called for the 464th to put 48 planes into the air and attack the marshaling yards at Munich, Germany. The group would attack in two separate waves in a Red-Blue Force mission. From the start, the mission was Fouled Up Beyond All Recognition (FUBAR).

Lt/Col. Goodyear lifted the first plane off the runway at 0816 and headed for the form up area. At the form up area clouds prevented the group from getting together. The only area that was clear was directly over Pantanella. Imagine 24 planes trying to get into position while the next wave is taking off and trying to form up underneath. Add to this the fact that other groups were trying to muscle in on the only clear airspace for miles around, and you have a real dangerous mess.

There were B-24s all over the place above Pantanella. Groups crossed, then crisscrossed in the mounting confusion. At one point the 460th appeared out of nowhere, headed directly towards the 464th on a nose to nose course. Last second jockying prevented the two groups from coming together in a spectacular fashion.

If the form up was fouled up, then wing rendezvous was a complete disaster. Moments before the 464th had to maneuver to avoid collision with other groups from the wing. When they got to the rendezvous area, there wasn't another B-24 in sight. After several circuits of the area, the 464th turned on course for the target. Over the Adriatic one element of the 464th caught up to the formation. Near the Dalmatian coast the 464th found the 5th Bomb Wing. They were headed in the same general direction, so the 464th transferred to the 5th.

The group flew on towards Munich. As they arrived over the north part of the Adriatic, the clouds lowered and almost disappeared. Then, as they got over land, the clouds moved back in until there was almost solid undercast. When they approached the northern border of Italy, the clouds not only covered the mountains but climbed upward, presenting a wall of murky white billowing mist.

Ahead, the clouds looked like they did not top out any lower than 32,000 feet. Near San Candinto, Lt/Col. Goodyear signaled for a 360 degree turn. After the turn, the group took up a heading for Sacile, at which point the group made a left turn for a bomb run on a railroad bridge near Maniago.

Able and Charlie boxes released their bombs on the bridge. Baker Box did not release, so the formation went through another series of left and right turns until Baker Box was able to release on the rail yards at Casaren. The Red Force rallied right and headed for home.

Blue Force turned back about the same time as Red Force. They had attempted a bomb run on Udine. High clouds prevented them from bombing the target, and they turned back for southern Italy. As they turned, several bursts of flak dotted the sky within the formation. One plane took a minor hit.

When the planes got back to Pantanella the crews hit the debriefing shack. There was a lot of extra grumbling about the mission. It had been a nightmare for the navigators, trying to figure out just where the heck they were and where the hell they were trying to go. On top of all the problems with the mixed up mission, the group was charged with 30 ineffective sorties for the day. Hopefully, things would get better in the near future.

While the flight crews were off on their mixed up tour of northern Italy, the teletype at Group Headquarters clattered out Operations Order #89 for the next day's mission. The activity at the base focused on getting things squared away for tomorrow. Trucks rumbled off to the bomb dump to get the next load of RDX. Clerks typed up all the material needed to brief the crews, while others prepared the maps and other parts of the flight kits.

On the morning of the 23rd, 28 crews prepared to carry out the Operations Order. The Primary Target was the rail yards at Linz, Austria. This was always an infamous target for the crews to fly against. Next to flak city at Vienna, Linz was now second on the list of possible flak encounters.

Col. Schroeder led the first attack unit into the air at 0850. The second unit was led by Lt. George Laser (778th). Unlike the day before, the group had no problems getting formed up and meeting the rest of the Wing. It looked like the weather was going to cooperate for a change.

Close up of Yellow-S' left wing and engines.

Actually, the weather turned out to be fair to partly cloudy. Clouds remained along the route, but most of the route was clear. North of the Dinaric Alps the group was sandwiched between two layers of clouds. By the time the group arrived in the target area there was a solid undercast.

Col. Schroeder abandoned the attack on the Primary and turned the group towards the alternate at Klagenfurt. At the new IP the group turned to a heading of 298 degrees and started for the release point. Moments before the target a large hole opened in the undercast, and the bomb run was changed to a visual release.

At 1345 the lead bombsight pointers merged and the bombs were released. Each element toggled at the release point until over 61 tons of 500 pound RDX bombs were headed towards the rail yards below. As the group rallied for home, a lot of the crews were wondering what was going on. They had been over the target, dropped their bombs, and so far had not seen a single burst of flak.

The group flew back to Pantanella without a problem. Except for the fact that they had not gained the Primary Target, it had been a good mission. No flak, no fighters, and bombs on the target. What more could the big wigs at Wing ask for?

February 24 found the 464th back in action. The target was the rail yards at Udine, Italy. The mission was flown as briefed for a change. There were a few clouds, but the bomb run was made without a problem. Some flak greeted the group on the bomb run. The formation made it through and delivered over 50 tons of bombs with good results. In all, the mission was a milk run. Flak had not hit anyone, and the rail yards at Udine were a mess after the visit by the 464th.

Twenty-four crews were awakened at 0400 on the morning of the 25th. Briefing was the usual important mission details. Their target for the day was the Ordnance Depot at Linz, Austria. The men were told that there were over 392 heavy flak guns in the target area. The group had been there just the day before and had not seen much action from those guns, so maybe they could get away with it again.

Lt/Col. Moore led the group into the air at 0810 that morning, and twenty-seven more B-24s followed him into the overcast sky above the base. The group formed up into two elements at 9,000 feet because of the low clouds. The group was about twelve minutes late arriving at the Wing rendezvous point. They tacked onto the 465th and found the 485th near the spur. The 464th pulled in behind the 485th as they turned north over the Adriatic. The 460th was again nowhere in sight.

Two planes aborted the mission. THE FLAKMAN (42-95332) aborted when the #2 prop ran away. This was the second mission in a row that THE FLAKMAN had aborted. Her crew chief, Lester Hacker, was not going to be very happy about it.

The formation crossed the Yugoslavian coast near Split and turned for a direct heading towards Linz. The weather improved as the Liberators got closer to the IP, with just a few clouds here and there. Just in case the weather turned sour, the radar tubs had been lowered and the sets tuned up.

Just before reaching the IP, the crew of SHORT FAT & 4F spotted a swept wing Me-262 flash past and disappear. It was an encounter that scared the living daylights out of them. It was a good thing the German pilot was not eager to score against the American bombers that day.

At the IP the leadship, White-T (44-49250), turned the group to a heading of 110 degrees to begin the bomb run by radar. The target was clear, but the Germans were putting up a very good smokescreen on the ground. The target return on the scope was clear as a bell.

Moments after the turn at the IP the first bursts of flak were spotted. These opening rounds were accurate enough to puncture the skin on several of the planes. As the planes neared the release the flak intensified, until it was the good old walkin' stuff.

The bomb release came at 1310, and 26 planes delivered 52 tons of bombs to the target from about 24,000 feet as the flak continued to pound away at the group. The strike cameras were running, and recorded frame after frame as the bombs started to impact the ground below.

Within moments of bombs away, Lt/Col. Moore's plane was hit by flak. It wasn't a mortal hit as far as the airplane was concerned. However, the flight engineer was hit in the head by a flying piece of steel. It was a serious scalp wound, and the crew rushed to his aid.

SHORT FAT & 4F also took some flying steel. Navigator Madison Bell, Jr., wrote:

The pieces penetrated our plane 30 to 35 times. One engine was hit, and the prop had to be feathered as we left the formation for lack of power. We descended to 10,000 feet and headed back to our base.

During the rally for home the flak changed from barrage to tracking. It was still intense and very accurate, as the Liberators of the 464th continued to take hits. The group was in the flak for about seven minutes. It was the worst flak that the group had been in for a long time.

The formation finally cleared the flak, and the crews began thinking about how they were going to get back to Italy with their wounded and battle damage. The weather would not be a problem for the planes, but a lot of anxious eyes were on the fuel gauges.

Madison Bell, Jr., flying the flak punctured SHORT FAT & 4F, recalled:

We picked up more flak from Trieste, Italy, and called for air cover from the 99th Fighter Sq. (332nd Fighter Group). At this stage of the war the German fighters only attacked stragglers like us. Two or three P-51s covered us to a safe distance over the Adriatic Sea and left with these words, "Ya'll are safe now man, see yo' later."

Lt/Col. Moore left the formation as they approached the spur. He was headed for Bari so the wounded engineer could get quick medical attention. The rest of the formation headed for Pantanella and pulled into the pattern.

One by one the Liberators of the 464th landed. By 1600 all of the planes were down or taxiing to their hardstand. Thirteen planes out of the 25 had taken flak damage. One plane bellied in and would be out of commission for several days while the sheet metal crews replaced some of the skin on her belly.

The mission scheduled for the 26th was canceled because of weather over the target area. Late that afternoon, the 464th was alerted for a mission on the 27th. As always, there was a lot of activity down on the line as the planes were readied for the next trip.

The first plane of the 464th left the ground at 0850 on the morning of the 27th. Another 26 planes followed the lead ship, flown by Lt/Col. Gibson. One plane aborted before take off. The group formed into two attack units as usual. The second unit was led by Capt. Wayne Shearer from the 777th. The Liberators were about six minutes late for rendezvous with the Wing, but the group got into proper position as they crossed the Italian coast near the spur.

The flight across the Adriatic was peaceful, except for when the gunners cleared their guns. At the Dalmatian coast the planes turned north and headed for the target at Augsberg, Germany. Weather was fairly good along the flight path to the target.

After turning at the IP the group started the bomb run by radar. The weather was clear, but the 464th was one of the last groups over the target. Since the target would be covered by smoke from the other attacks, radar would have to be used to guide the 464th to the release point.

Just before the target the German gunners on the ground fired the first barrage of 88s. About 15 seconds later the shells reached 24,000 and started bursting. The group would be under attack for the next five to six minutes.

The lead bombardier was able to find the target with just enough time to finish the run visually. The group made a minor correction to a heading of 218 degrees. Bombs away was called at 1353, and 27 planes released over 26 tons of 1,000 pound RDX bombs towards the target. The group rallied left at Neuberg to a heading of 176 degrees and headed home.

Several of the planes had been hit by flak over the target. By the time the group was out of range more planes were ventilated by flying shrapnel. WILLY (42-51903) limped off the target with the #3 engine out and #4 trailing smoke, but still providing some power to stay in the air. Pilot Douglas Lambert recalled:

We lost the two engines over the target. We stayed with the formation as long as we could. When we got near Lake Constance, the #4 was smoking even more. I figured our only chance was to head for Switzerland. I had to shut the engine down, and shortly afterward we started bailing out.

The entire crew escaped the plane when it was evident that WILLY would not make it. They would be interned by Swiss officials.

The rest of the formation continued their flight back to the Italian spur, where another plane left the formation and landed at Bari. The first plane back to Pantanella was on the runway at 1640, and the rest of the Liberators landed without problems.

A total of 14 planes were battle damaged by flak. Most of the damage could be patched or repaired quickly. Three of the planes were damaged enough to be out of commission for at least a week. While the flak had not brought anybody down over the target, it had scored enough to cause the loss of one plane and crew, and caused others to be listed on the repair schedule for the next few days.

Strike photos were disappointing. The majority of the bombs landed in open country, about three miles northeast of the railway. Smoke from previous attacks covered other areas of the target, so an accurate accounting of the attack could not be judged.

The last day of the month saw the group ready to fly another Red-Blue Force mission. Col. Schroeder led the Red Force into the air at 1005 that morning. The 21 planes of the force formed up and met the wing about a minute early. Col. Schroeder flew the group

The crew managed to escape with cuts and bruises.

through a short dog leg and was in position without further problems.

The Blue Force started taking off at 1030 to follow the Red Force to the target. This part of the mission was led by Lt. Shymanski from the 779th. The 18 Liberators of this force formed up and made rendezvous with the wing.

Red Force arrived in the target area and ran into a weather problem. The Primary Target could not be picked up on the radar because of the mountains near the target. At this point Col. Schroeder turned towards the alternate target at Vicenza.

Red Force dropped their bomb load at the alternate target at 1453. Nineteen planes released from 20,000 feet. Two planes released early: one accidentally released, and the other toggled because the first plane had released.

The Blue Force arrived over the Primary and found the same problem as the Red Force. They also headed for the alternate, arriving there at 1610. This force dropped another 44 tons of bombs onto the target.

The only positive aspect of this mission was that no one was injured. The other nice thing was that the strike photos showed the rail yards at the alternate had been hammered by the 464th.

February went into the reports as one of the most outstanding months of all for the group since starting combat. The group flew 20 missions in 28 days, which added another 510 effective sorties to the group records. Over a thousand tons of explosives had been delivered to Hitler's Third Reich. In view of the month that the group had just finished, the men of the 464th were ready to get on to the next month and hopefully finish off the axis.

March 1945

After one of the best months in the history of the 464th, the flight crews started the month of March with a mission on the 1st. The Operations Order called for a Red-Blue Force mission. The Primary Target was the marshaling yards at Linz. This would be a milestone mission for the 464th. If they managed to get to the target and return, they would have flown their 150th credited mission since beginning combat operations.

The Red Force began taking off at 0945. The Blue Force was right behind, leaving at 1005 that morning. Red Force ran into some trouble finding the 55th Wing. By the Yugoslavian coast they had made radio contact and found that the wing was 12 minutes ahead of schedule. The 464th was two minutes behind the mission schedule, which put the group behind by 14 minutes.

The Blue Force formed up and made the rendezvous without a problem. This force fell in line and headed for the Primary Target at Linz.

Red-Y (44-49048) from the Red Force aborted the mission at 1237 when the oil pressure on the #2 engine was lost. This abort left the formation without a Mickey ship in one of the boxes. The Red Force was still behind the rest of the 55th Wing Red Force formation. Lt/Col. Moore was in radio contact with the Wing Leader. He was informed that the Primary target was closed due to weather and that they were going to hit the Alternate.

Three minutes before the IP for the Alternate, the wing leader radioed that he was going to climb and head for the Primary again. Lt/Col. Moore and the 464th were committed to the Alternate at this point.

The Blue Force leader, Lt/Col. Gilson, had been monitoring the radio chatter from the Red Force, so he turned the Blue Force towards the second alternate at Amstetten, Austria.

The Red Force Pathfinder radar had picked up the target fifty miles out. This formation turned at the IP and started for the rail yards at St. Polten, Austria.

The Blue Force had picked up their target at a range of 25 miles and turned at their respective IP for the bomb run. Several sighting angles and range corrections were made during the run to the target. A final 2 degree left correction put the Blue Force on a heading of 276 degrees as they hit the release point.

At 1407 the Blue Force released over 42 tons of bombs from 20,000 feet. Within seconds the bombs disappeared into the undercast, making the results unknown. The formation rallied for home as the first clouds of flak appeared almost a mile behind the fleeing formation.

Red Force had turned at their IP, and the radar operators called several corrections to the bombardiers. A final correction put the formation on a heading of 172 degrees at the release point. Red Force dropped 40 tons of bombs at 1432 and rallied for home. Strike photos would show that Red Force missed their intended target by over six miles.

By midafternoon the teletype at Pantanella was busy cranking out Operations Order #106 from the 55th Wing. The bomb load for the next mission would be 500 pound RDX bombs, which had to be loaded on the planes that were scheduled to fly the next day.

Ordnance men from the squadrons climbed aboard trucks and headed for the bomb dump to get the "eggs" for the upcoming mission. The men of the ordnance section had made the trip to the

Remains of a truck and scattered bombs after the explosion at the bomb dump March 1, 1945.

bomb dump many times as part of their daily routine. They had no idea that the grim reaper was a passenger that afternoon.

Bomb Dump #18 in the 517th Air Service Group was located about six miles from the base at Pantanella. Explosives arrived at a nearby railhead and were trucked to the dump for storage until they were needed. As with all of the bases across Italy, local Italians were hired to help at the bomb dump.

It was common practice to unload the trucks by putting them in reverse, backing up, then hitting the brake, shifting, and driving forward as the bombs tumbled onto the ground. Effective, but not exactly according to the safety manual. Lester Watkins (778th) wrote:

I was sent in a jeep to pick up a couple of cases of fuzes so we could finish our loading. I went to the bomb dump, and they were unloading 500 pound bombs from six by six trucks by rolling the bombs off the trucks directly onto the ground. The bombs still had the shipping bands on them, and when the bomb would hit the earth, they would roll around on the ground.

Ordnance men were taking off the shipping bands on the bombs and loading them onto bomb trailers for delivery to the aircraft. The fuze shack was a couple of hundred yards on up in the bomb dump area. I drove up to the shack, loaded several cases of fuzes onto the jeep, and started back to the airfield.

Joseph Santkuyl and Leo Scherlinger from the 776th were getting a trailer loaded with bombs. Joe was in the cab of the truck. Around the bomb dump were other men from the 464th and the local Italian workers loading the trailers with bombs. Somewhere, in one of the bombs, there was a flicker of light. In a nanosecond the flicker turned into a ball of white hot expanding gas. Within .0002 of a second the gas expanded 10,000 times in volume, shattering the casing of the bomb. There was a deadly flash as the bomb dump erupted in a tremendous explosion. The shock wave moved up and outward from the center, like a ripple after a rock has been thrown into a pond.

Merle Hoffman wasn't flying that day, and he was at the 779th Engineering shed when the shock wave arrived:

We were about six miles from the bomb dump when it went up. The concussion wave hit, and I thought the shed was going to go over.

Lester Watkins:

I was down the road, maybe half a mile from the dump when the explosion occurred. I felt the heat, but did not hear the noise of the explosion. My jeep wound up in the middle of a ditch on the side of the road, upright and running. I turned and saw the immense fireball rolling up into the sky. I turned around and drove back towards the explosion; all I could see was fire, smoke, and debris falling from the sky. When I arrived at the point where the explosion occurred, all the six by six trucks and trailers had just disappeared. Fires were scattered everywhere, and burning pieces of trucks were not recognizable. The largest piece I saw was an engine from one of the trucks lying about a hundred yards from the hole which the bombs created in the surface of the earth. The hole was large enough to put a small two story house into.

Joe Santkuyl:

The explosion blew me out of my truck. After getting up I began to run, and that is when I got nailed. I stopped 13 pieces of shrapnel in every place, but my buttocks, left arm, and head!

John O'Hara, Flight Surgeon (777th) wrote:

I rarely left the base except on medical business, but on this day my tentmates Dave Camera (S-2), Andy Anderson (Ordnance), Daryl McWhirter (Armament), and I were in Canosa when we heard and felt the explosion and saw the black smoke. "It's the bomb dump," Andy said, and we headed for it. We were the first to arrive. All hell was going on.

The old warhorse BIG FAT MAMA after her crash landing on March 2, 1945.

At the entrance was a group of shocked and dazed G.I.s. They said there were wounded men. Andy and I improvised a litter out of some plywood and ran in. I found a G.I. with a large sucking chest wound in his left breast and plugged it as best I could. He was in shock, and we carried him out on the liter and went back for another. By this time help was arriving, so we dressed wounds, loaded ambulances, and headed for the field hospital.

Lester Watkins:

The fuze shack was gone, but I saw three people standing where it had been. An officer drove up about that time, and he and I started toward the shack area. There were bays of 500 pound incendiary bombs burning, and every now and then one would explode and scatter thermite for 40 to 50 yards. The men in the shack were in a state of shock, but they were not injured; in fact, two of them still had fuzes in their hands on which they had been working. They said later, "We were right on the spot that the wave from the explosion hit the ground." The officer and I found one man that had all his clothes burned off except for his belt, shoes, and the collar of his shirt. They started for the field hospital with him, and they said he raised up and said, "Oh My God!" and died.

John O'Hara:

The man with the sucking chest wound (Leo Scherlinger) did not recover from shock despite blood transfusions, and the surgeon did not consider it safe to operate. I sat and watched the man die.

As Joe Santkuyl lay on the ground, he recalled seeing B-24s coming back from the mission. They passed right overhead and had no idea what was going on. There were still bombs cooking off, and the planes had to take evasive action to clear the area.

Joe was taken to the hospital, where the Doctors flipped a coin to see if they would amputate his right arm. The doctors lost the call, and Joe was able to keep his arm. Joe was lucky that day; he was the sole survivor of those who had been at ground zero.

Fifteen men of the 464th were killed in the line of duty when the dump exploded. The exact number of Italian workers killed was never accurately determined, but could have been as high as 22.

The planes of Blue Force arrived back at Pantanella at 1634, just after the bomb dump went up. They scattered as they came in over the dump, reformed, and landed. Red Force began landing at 1703 that afternoon.

The events of March 1, 1945, would go into the records as one of the darkest days in the history of the group. While the group had lost more men in combat during a single mission, "Black Thursday" would always be remembered by those of the ground echelon who had lost dear friends when the dump blew.

Bombs for the next day's mission were brought in from the rail head, and also from several other bomb dumps around the 55th Wing. Since the exact cause of the disaster was not known, the men were ordered to stay out of the bomb dump.

One theory for the explosion was the explosive material in one of the bombs had not hardened according to specifications. The gel would be highly unstable. In other words, a time bomb looking for just the right conditions to set it off. Perhaps this one in a million bomb ended up at the dump and had caused the disaster of Black Thursday.

The 464th was still in a state of shock over the horrible events of the day before. Nonetheless, the planes were ready for the upcoming mission on 2 March. Operations Order #106 called for 32 planes of the 464th to attack and destroy the North Main rail yards at Linz, Austria.

The lead ship, flown by Capt. Shymanski (779th), lifted off the runway at 0905. The second attack unit would be led by Lt. Robert Elliott (776th). Group form up was done in almost record time, and it was a good thing, too. Even though the 464th was on time, the 55th Wing lead was six minutes early. The 464th leader nudged the throttles a little and caught up with the wing over the Adriatic.

The formation continued towards Yugoslavia. At this point the lead group of the Wing started slowing down, and then they speeded

John Trabucco and Robert Kephart touring Pecs, Hungary, after their landing in HOOSIER PETE . Photo taken March 18, 1945.

up, which made it very difficult for everyone to stay in the proper position within the bomber stream. Not only was it difficult to stay in line, it was downright dangerous.

As the formation passed to the east of Brenner Pass, the lead boxes of the 464th reported two B-24s from a group ahead had collided and were spinning down out of control. The erratic airspeed of the lead group had possibly claimed two victims.

At about 1240 Yellow-N (44-49363) lost power on the #4 engine. They left the formation, but dropped their bomb load on the rail yard at Villach. At least the plane and crew would be credited with an effective sortie. At 1258 White-E (42-78472) lost the turbo on their #1 engine. They pulled out of formation and later released their bombs on the main rail yard at Reid, Austria. They would also get credit for the mission.

As the formation approached the IP, the clouds had already started to obscure the ground for long stretches. The radar units had been lowered, and the target was showing up on the scopes. At the IP, the group turned to the right and took up the heading for the target. As they turned two Me-109s were spotted ahead. Throughout the formation, the turrets spun towards the fighters just in case they made a move to attack.

A final correction to the left put the group on a heading of 159 degrees. There was less than two minutes to release. The first burst of flak appeared at 12 o'clock and at the same altitude as the group.

Within a matter of seconds the sky was filled with deadly accurate bursts of flak. It was the kind that the older crews had come to expect over Linz. For some of the newer crews, it was "some of the heaviest flak that we had ever seen up to that time." Don Sherard wrote:

....the amplifier on number two engine went out and the number four propeller ran away.... Bahnsen (Donald Bahnsen, pilot) very calmly gave a continuous series of orders to Rice (Robert Rice, Flight Engineer), who changed the amplifier on the number two engine while the flak was hitting the plane, and Bahnsen managed to control the prop on #4. The stress Bahnsen was under was clearly apparent. Even though the temperature was far below zero, ice formed around the collar of his flying suit from his perspiration. Our plane picked up fifteen or twenty holes as a result of the flak over the target without injuring any of the crew or causing serious damage to the plane.

Robert Rice (Flight engineer) from HOOSIER PETE poses with a downed German fighter and unknown local at Pecs, Hungary, March 18, 1945.

At about 1345 the group hit the release line over the target. They released over 50 tons of 500 pounders from 24,500 feet. The Liberators rallied to the right and the flak bursts followed. The group would be in the flak for a total of six to seven minutes.

The flight back was long and filled with tension. Don Sherard wrote:

Our fuel supply was extremely low, and we "sweated out" the gas supply all the way home.

All of the planes returned to Pantanella. Several made it with just enough fuel left in the tanks to taxi to their hardstand.

A quick battle damage survey showed that 10 Liberators had taken minor hits. The old war horse BIG FAT MAMA had taken some pretty heavy damage. Her main gear gave out as she came in, and she ended up on her belly. This was the same BIG FAT MAMA that had collided with another plane on the group's second mission back in May 1944. Since she was an old war horse she would not be repaired, but would instead be "put out to pasture."

The strike photos were very disappointing. They showed that most of the bombs landed in open fields about four and a half miles from the target area. The 55th wing umpires scored the 464th as "Results Poor."

The 464th did not fly a mission on 3 March due to bad weather in the local area and over prospective targets. Later that afternoon, what was left of BIG FAT MAMA was taken down to the gunnery school area for use as a ditching and gunnery trainer.

The Operations Order for the next mission came down from Wing on the afternoon of the 3rd. The flight schedule was posted so that the men who would fly could plan the rest of their day and night accordingly.

On 4 March the crews that were going to fly were up and ready to go by 0730. Down at the planes, the crews made their usual preflight checks, then put their personal equipment on the planes. It was cold, and low clouds hung from the sky. Snow showers came and went. Nothing serious, just enough to say they were having snow showers in the area. The surface winds were also kicking up and causing some problems. They were gusty, with some of the gusts hitting over 25 mph. Thankfully the winds were coming right down the runway.

The green flare arched into the sky, and the mission was on. By 0810 the first of 42 planes left the runway. One by one the Liberators would turn onto the runway, set the trim tabs, and check the mags. The four big engines roared as the throttles were advanced to the stops. Slowly at first the big planes started forward down the PSP. At about 75 miles per hour indicated the pilot would ease back on the wheel to take the weight off the nosewheel. At about 125 indicated the heavy ships would leave the runway and start the climb to altitude.

The group would form into three attack units for this mission. The flight leader would be Maj. Harry Wilson (Asst Ops Officer). The second unit was commanded by Lt. George Quay II (777th), while the third unit would be under the lead of Capt. Ken Machado (777th)

Because of the clouds and scattered snowstorms, the group had to form up just southwest of Spinnazola at 14,000 feet. Due to the weather, the 464th had some problems getting it all together for the mission.

Yellow-N (44-49363) was having problems of their own. As they climbed away from the runway for the form up area the #3 engine blew up. There was a drop in oil pressure—no warning at all, it just lost pressure and blew up. The explosion blew the cowling off, exposing the Pratt and Whitney engine to the elements.

Lt. James Lemon, pilot, and copilot Lt. Stan Dyer cut the fuel flow to the engine to try and keep the fire from spreading. Gunner Don Dickson moved to the bomb bay to try and change a fuse in hope of recovering partial engine power.

After a gallant yet futile effort, Lt. Lemon rang the bail out bell. The copilot and Don Dickson went out through the bomb bay. The rest of the crew hit the silk from the closest exit. For reasons unknown, Lt. Lemon did not make it out of the burning ship before it hit the ground in a blinding flash.

Karl Walkin's chute opened, and he floated down to the ground. The gusty wind caught his chute before he could grab the risers and spill the air from the canopy. He was drug along the ground until he hit one of the infamous Italian stone fences. He suffered a fractured skull and would be "out cold" for two weeks. Dickson and the rest of the surviving crewmen received only bumps and bruises from their jump.

Although the exact cause of the engine explosion was never officially determined, several of the crew, including Dickson, believed that it may have been sabotage. Dickson believes the possibility of sabotage because of the way the engine blew up.

Legend had it there was an unnamed Master Sergeant that was caught and arrested for possible acts of sabotage to aircraft. Now, this legend comes from at least three different groups in the 15th Air Force. One story even has the saboteur being shot just hours after his arrest. Research of 15th Air Force records and other documents reveal no official confirmation.

There is no mention of any arrest of Army Air Force personnel on charges of sabotage, and no records of any General Court Martial on these charges. This does not mean that it did not happen, just that there is no official record to confirm it.

The formation reached the target area and turned at the IP for the bomb run. The target was clear, so the lead bombardier set up for a visual run. At the release point over 74 tons of explosives were dropped towards the rail yards at Szombathely, Hugary.

The formation ran into flak for 3-4 minutes just after bomb release. It was not very intense, but accurate enough to damage four planes in the formation. The group rallied towards home with everybody still in formation.

The planes were back in the landing pattern by 1458 that afternoon. The four damaged planes would be repaired and back in action within a few days. Except for the unexplained loss of Yellow-N, the mission was considered a milk run.

The 464th stood down for the next several days. Not that they did not want to fly and get the war over with. It seems that old man winter was not exactly ready to call it quits over Europe just yet. Some of the guys were rather put out with the bad weather. They had high hopes of hitting the sand lots and playing some baseball.

The group was up and at 'em on 8 March. It was a Red-Blue Force mission to the rail yards at Verona, Italy. Red Force would launch 18 planes and 3 spares, and Lt/Col. Gilson would be in the lead aircraft. Blue Force would also send 18 scheduled and three spares. Lt/Col. William Moore, CO of the 77th, would fly the lead position for Blue Force.

The Red Force began taking to the air at 1050 that morning. There were some clouds over the base, but not enough to cause any major problems getting formed up and meeting with the rest of the 55th Wing

The journey to the target was uneventful as far as the weather was concerned. Red Force turned at the IP and headed for the target, and there was no sign of any German opposition. A few minutes before the target the group was greeted by a few scattered bursts of flak.

The 21 planes of Red Force reached the release point at 1444. As the lead ship started to release, the rest of the formation began to toggle a total of over 37 tons of bombs towards the rail yards below. The strike photos would reveal that the 464th still knew how to work on railroads. There were bomb hits on the shops and station, and a direct hit on the locomotive repair area. The group rallied for home and left the burning rail yards behind them.

Don Jeffeson (L) nose gunner, and Don Sherand, bombardier, in front of HOOSIER PETE, Pecs, Hungary, March 1945.

Blue Force had left Pantanella at 1110, formed up, and started for Verona to add more RDX to the rail yards. As with the Red Force, Blue Force had good flying weather almost all the way to the target. They hit the target area and released their 41 tons of bombs at 1506. The release was manual, since there was a problem with the autopilot on the lead plane. As the bombs fell towards the ground it looked like the Blue Force would derail a lot more trains.

There were a few scattered bursts of flak just before the bomb release. As the Blue Force rallied, they were bracketed by more flak. It was not intense, but it was accurate enough to punch holes in the aluminum skin of several Liberators.

Strike photos taken by Blue Force showed that they had also hit the target fairly well. The middle of the yards between the station and the shop areas had taken the brunt of the bomb impacts. There were also several direct hits on the locomotive depot and the storage area.

All of the planes returned to Pantanella that afternoon. Eight of the planes had taken flak hits, with one coming back with some pretty good sized holes in her. It would take several days to patch her up and ready her for the next journey to the shrinking Third Reich.

At the debriefing, one crewman who had just finished his first mission was overheard saying, "Where was the flak?" He got some pretty hard looks and several comments about the fact that he must be looking for a Section 8.

The 464th put together another Red-Blue Force mission for their trip on 9 March. The lead ship for the Red Force left the PSP at 0900 that morning. The mission leader was Maj. Wilson, Asstistant Operations Officer for the group. He was followed by another 20 planes.

Red Force from the 464th joined the rest of the Wing Red Force and set course for the spur. Over the Adriatic the formation started running into more and more clouds. Over the Dinaric Alps the ground vanished below the billowing clouds. Up ahead, the weather looked even more threatening. The formation seemed to be constantly turning to avoid the growing cloud mass. At 1243 Maj Wilson received a radio message from the Wing leader. He was instructed to abandon the Primary and bomb the fourth alternate target at Graz.

At the IP, the Red Force turned towards the rail yards at the alternate. The lead radar was working, but they could not pick up the target well enough to identify it on the scope. Red Force made two runs over the target, and still the target did not appear well enough in the scope to identify. At this point Maj.Wilson turned the formation for home with the bombs still aboard the planes.

Meanwhile, the Blue Force's 21 planes had taken to the air at 0920 to hit the same Primary target as the Red Force. Capt. William Black (776th) got the Liberators sorted out and in the boxes, then found the Wing Blue Force.

The Blue Force encountered the same weather as the proceeding force. By the time the Blue Force hurtled the Dinarics the clouds had broken a little. Further on the clouds continued to break, until there were long stretches of almost clear skies. At 1256 the wing leader came over the command channel. The call was to change the attack to the alternate target.

The formation of the 464th turned and flew towards the IP for the Alternate target at Graz. At the IP for that target they turned for the bomb run. The lead ship picked up the target on the radar and began a Mickey run. The 464th was perched at 23,500 feet on a heading of 70 degrees, just as they had been briefed for the alternate.

At 1328, the 21 planes of Blue Force attained the target and released 42 tons of bombs toward the target at Graz. As the Blue Force began the rally for home, the flak began to burst around the formation. For the next four minutes the 464th would be within the range of the guns on the ground.

The weather on the return trip was about the same as it had been for the trip to the target. Near the spur the planes flew through several rain showers. The Liberators descended to about 4,000 feet to get under the clouds as they came home to Pantanella Hill.

Five of the returning planes had been ventilated by flak, Nothing serious, just enough so that the sheet metal crews would be busy that night. As 44-49736 turned into its hardstand the gear collapsed, causing the wing to fall and the props to dig into the turf. The plane had been hit by flak over the target, and a shard of steel had gone through a hydraulic accumulator, causing a loss of fluid and pressure. The plane would be repaired, but it would take more than a few days.

Strike photos from the Blue Force showed that the bombs landed just about where they should have. Hits were scored at the choke points, and several columns of freight cars had been blown to bits. The score at the end of the mission: Blue Force good, Red Force ineffective goose egg,

During the last several days the rumor mill had been very active around Pantanella Hill. All of the rumors centered around the Commanding Officer of the 464th, Col. Schroeder. Now, depending on what side of the fence an individual stood, you either liked him, or you didn't.

It was well known that the Col. could and would, "chew somebodie's backside" pretty well. If you happened to be on the receiving end, you knew you had been chewed out by one of the best. It did not matter if it was a major or minor offense, when Col. Schroeder felt like putting someone on the carpet, he did it.

One of the men from Headquarters recalled that he was called into the CO's Office for something. The Col. was busy reaming out a Major and just kept on chewing in front of the newly arrived Sgt. When Schroeder was finished with the Major he dismissed him and started on the Sgt. with his next breath.

Now, everyone around the HQ knew that Col. Schroeder was hard to beat at organization and administration. Several of the pilots who flew with him remarked that, "he wasn't much of a flier." The main rumor flying around was that Col. Schroeder was going to be relieved as Commanding Officer of the 464th. The men around Headquarters had noted that Col. Schroeder had not been feeling very well during the last several weeks. He had actually been to the hospital in Bari several times in the same time frame.

The rumor mongers were right this time. Col. Schroeder was relieved of command by orders that came down from 55th Wing. It wasn't because he had flown his required number of missions, because a review of the records shows that he had flown only 16 mission since taking command in June 1944. The official reason was that Col.Schroeder was suffering from a flu like illness, and that it was affecting his ability to continue to command a group in combat.

The new Commanding Officer was Col. Andrew Jackson Bird. He came down from the 49th Bomb Wing to take command of the group. Col. Bird had been a commander of a B-25 outfit in the States before coming to Italy. He had started as an aviation cadet in the early 30s. He must have had something on the ball, since he rose from the rank of "first looey" to full Bird Colonel between April 1942 and August 1943.

On 12 March Col. Bird arrived at Pantanella. Although he would not officially take command of the 464th until the 13th, he was at the morning briefing, in his flying togs.

The mission for the 12th was a Red-Blue Force mission again. The target outlined in the Operations Order was the Florisdorf Oil Refinery at Vienna. It looked like the new boss had a tough target for his combat debut with the group.

Col. Bird led the first of 21 planes from Red Force into the air at 0932 that morning. The planes got into the air in record time. The first Liberator of Blue Force's 21 planes left the runway at 0942.

Both attack forces from the 460th were late arriving for wing rendezvous. Col. Bird took the 464th through several short dog legs so that the 460th could get into position. By the time the formation reached the Yugoslavian Coast everyone was in the proper formation. By the time the two forces crossed the coast, the weather was turning bad. As the mission force climbed over the Dinarics, the weather ahead looked better. In spite of improving cloud conditions the radar units were lowered to help navigate.

FLAMIN MAMIE (44-41337) from the Red Force had taken off late because of a mechanical problem. They tried to catch the formation but couldn't. The navigator managed to find a target of opportunity at Celja, and they deposited their load at 1308. From there they flew back to Italy.

The gremlins had really infested the Liberators of the 464th! A total of five planes aborted the mission before reaching the target. White-U (44-48880) managed to bomb a bridge as a target of opportunity on the way back.

About a hundred miles from the target a bank of clouds moved in. If it didn not move away the target would be covered. The radar sets had been up and scanning the ground for some time, however. At forty miles out the first target returns showed up on the radar scopes.

At the IP the target returns for Red Force were good. As the group started the run, the Mickey operators started giving the sighting angles and course corrections. A final correction put the Red Force on a heading of 202 degrees just before bomb release. The Blue Force was about two minutes behind the Red Force on a heading of 212 degrees.

A few moments before reaching the target the first bursts of flak dotted the sky around the Liberators. At first it was scattered, but the flak batteries found the range and altitude in record time. By the release point the black puffs were filling the sky with bursting steel shards.

Red Force released over 36 tons of high explosive RDX at 1348. The Blue Force added another 36 tons of bombs at 1350. Both forces rallied for home amid the bursting flak. The Liberators of the 464th had been in the flak for about 4 minutes. So far, nobody had reported taking any hits.

The flight back was almost the same as the trip to the target. There were several slight changes to skirt some clouds over Yugoslavia and the Adriatic. By the time the planes were over the base, the weather was almost clear.

The mission for the 13th found the group ready to take a crack at the rail yards at Regensberg, Germany. The 32 planes from the group got off the ground and formed up with no problems. The group made it to the target, dropped their bombs, and rallied for home. The entire mission was a milk run. The group did not see a fighter, but more importantly, they had not seen a burst of flak.

On the 14th, the group divided into Red and Blue Force for a mission to the rail yards at Nova Zomky, Hungary. There were 42 planes scheduled for the mission. Red Force leader Lt/Col. Gerald Black lifted his Liberator into the air at about 0820. The Blue Force leader was Lt/Col. Gilson.

Form up and rendezvous went without a hitch. The 460th was late (again) for wing rendezvous. They caught up with the formation as it passed over the spur. A lot of the guys in the 464th were still wondering just what was with the 460th. They always seemed

THE FLAKMAN lived up to its name by returning from a March mission with these extra holes.

Flak damage to the nose area of THE FLAKMAN.

late, and their record had not improved with the passing of time. Granted, they were the oldest group in the 55th Wing, but did they have some kind of inherent problem with getting their group together for a mission?

PENSY BELLE (42-94878) aborted the mission after having a mechanical problem over the Adriatic. The crew jettisoned their bombs into the Adriatic and came back to Pantanella.

As the two forces flew over the Yugoslavian coast the clouds started to move in and cover the ground from view. To help navigate to the target the radar units were lowered and turned on. About a hundred miles from the target the Liberators ran out of the clouds into clear sky.

As the formation turned at the IP for the bomb run they were greeted by a few scattered bursts of flak. Ahead, several of the other groups were already grinding through some pretty nasty looking flak. When the 464th arrived, the flak seemed to calm down to scattered bursts off to both sides of the group.

At approximately 1308 the Red Force hit the release point and began dropping over 39 tons of bombs. Blue Force was right behind and unloaded their deadly cargo of RDX at 1311. Both of the formations rallied for home and left the flak smeared sky behind.

The strike photos would show disappointing results. Most of the Red Force bombs hit short of the rail yards, though a small concentration did walk far enough to damage some freight cars that were on a siding. Blue Force's RDX rained down in the center of Nova Zamky itself. The Blue Force had missed the rail yards by a mile, literally.

As the planes headed home, Lt. Don Bahnsen's crew aboard HOOSIER PETE (44-49713) discovered they were low on fuel. HOOSIER PETE left the formation and headed for Pecs, Hungary. This area had just been "liberated" by the advancing Red Army. For the last several missions Pecs had been listed as a possible safe landing field for planes that were in trouble.

While Lt. Bahnsen's crew headed for Pecs, the rest of the 464th continued towards home. At about 1329 several of the planes spotted 5 Me-109s attacking a medium bomber force. Several "little friends" peeled off and dove to the rescue like the cavalry. The 109s wanted no part of the fight and broke hard for the ground to avoid the '51s.

HOOSIER PETE managed a pretty good landing on a fighter strip at Pecs. It was a pretty good landing, alright. Everyone walked away, and the plane was undamaged. Don Sherard wrote:

The Russians met us at the plane with drawn rifles and demanded identification. Our oldest crewmember, Chester Stanizewski, a waist gunner, was approximately 25 years old and sported a large black mustache. The Russian approached him with the question, "Commandeer?" It was amusing to see their reaction when they discovered that Bahnsen, our 20 year old pilot, was the commander.

The crew of HOOSIER PETE did not have much of a problem with the language barrier. The radio operator, John Trabucco, spoke Italian. Chester Stanizewski spoke almost fluent Russian. The co-pilot, Frank Schiffel, spoke Hungarian.

The Russians informed the crew that there was no fuel to be had. Since they were stuck at Pecs until they could figure a way home the crew accepted Russian hospitality for the next several days.

The rest of the 464th flew on towards home and landed around 1624 that afternoon. Except for HOOSIER PETE's empty hardstand, all of the planes returned. It was almost a milk run, with one plane missing and the rest returning without any damage.

Col. Bird greeted the men at the morning briefing for the 15 March mission. Several of the crews were somewhat surprised that the new boss was going to fly another mission so soon after taking command and flying a mission on the 12th.

Operations Order #130 called for another Red-Blue Force mission. Each force would be made up of 21 planes. Col. Bird would lead Red Force, while Capt. Walter Steves would fly the lead ship for the Blue Force.

Col. Bird lifted his Liberator off the ground at 0805. Form up was done in near record time. The weather was fairly clear, and for

Big Fence Radio Direction Trnasmitter, March 1945.

a change, the 460th was on time and right where they should have been.

Over the Adriatic the formation began to run into bad weather. The clouds were reaching up to almost 20,000 feet, and some billowed even higher. Col. Bird made several turns to skirt the high clouds. During one of these turns, four planes from Red Force lost sight of the group. When they couldn't find the 464th again, they joined the 460th's formation for the duration of the flight.

As the 464th approached the IP at Rosendorf the formation ran into heavy weather and turbulence. The wing leader signaled for the mission to the Primary to be called off and to bomb the Alternate target. The 464th turned for the alternate at Graz. As they approached the IP the cloud cover parted and the group set up for a visual bomb run. About a minute from Bombs Away, several bursts of flak bracketed the group.

Red Force reached the target and released over 33 tons of bombs at 1328. Five planes from the Red Force did not release because of problems with either the bomb doors or racks. Blue Force released over 49 tons of bombs about one minute later. Both formations rallied right, and the flak followed them through the turn.

The journey home was almost routine, and the combined formation was back on the ground by 1730 that afternoon. It could not be classified as a milk run, because nine planes had taken minor hits from flak. Another six had landed at other fields to either refuel or make emergency repairs before coming back to Pantanella.

When the strike films came out of the fixer the results looked good. Bombs had hit rolling stock, warehouses, and the choke point. A lot of bombs had landed in a large construction area just a few yards from the choke point.

When the mission had been debriefed, the crews headed back to their casas for the rest of the day. On the flightline, the crew chiefs and ground crews had already started getting the planes ready for the next mission. Some of the planes had battle damage to repair, which was the first priority. Up at Headquarters the typewriters were singing as the clerks pounded out the mission reports, bomb strike reports, and this report and that report. Since the crew of HOOSIER PETE had not returned from the mission on the 14th they were now officially declared MIA. With that official classification, paperwork was started to notify the families of the crew. Chaplain Eastwood would be busy writing letters to the families, trying to give them hope or consolation.

By now the 464th was getting so good at the Red-Blue Force missions that they tried it again on the 16th. The Primary Target for the Red Force would be the Korneuburg Oil Refinery at Vienna. Some of the newer crews wondered why there were audible moans when the curtain was pulled away from the target map. The last few missions had been pretty easy, and had no doubt bolstered the confidence of the new crews. The older crews knew all about Vienna. The Germans could always serve up a mean bowl of flak there, and after all, Vienna still known as "flak city."

Lt/Col. Gilson led the Red Force into the air at 0745. Red Force managed to get everyone tucked into the boxes without major problems. Over Andria, the Red Force fell in behind the 460th and the 485th. As the formation neared the spur, bad weather forced the bombers to climb up to get over the clouds. When the 464th broke out, Lt/Col. Gilson found himself leading the wing. Instead of reshuffling the bomber deck, the wing leader signaled for the 464th to continue in the lead position.

One plane aborted when the #1 magneto failed and the #1 propeller governor started throwing oil all over the place. The plane returned with the bomb load and landed at Pantanella at 1000.

The clouds kept forcing the formation to the right of the briefed heading over the Adriatic. The clouds would interfere with the flight until the planes passed over Zara, Yugoslavia. From here on the sky cleared, and the formation got back on track to the target.

At the IP the 464th turned to a 169 degree heading for the bomb run. At 1414 Red Force released 38 tons of bombs onto the oil refinery. Flak opened up just before the target. It was not the usual Vienna walkin stuff, yet it was accurate enough to damage five planes. Red Force rallied according to plan and headed home.

At 1242 BREEZI WHEEZI (42-78613) left the formation with the #2 propeller feathered. They appeared to be heading for Zara, Yugoslavia. Ten minutes later Yellow-H (44-49409) left the formation with the #4 prop feathered. They were also going to try and make it to Zara.

The first of the 21 Blue Force Liberators had taken off at 0805. Blue Force was under command of Lt/Col. Moore (777th). This force flew into the same kind of weather as the other mission force. Over the Adriatic the formation got lost in the clouds. They circled a few times and then found the rest of the wing.

Two Blue Force planes aborted the mission over the Adriatic, due to oxygen leaks and engine problems. One ship came back with their bombload, while the other dropped their load into the water off the Italian spur.

As the formation crossed the Dalmatian coast, the cloud deck broke to almost severe clear. Over the Dinarics the clouds were

Planes of the 464th hurdle the Alps during a mission in March 1945.

scattered and continued all the way to the target area. So far, except for getting lost for a few minutes, the group was right on track.

At the IP, Lt/Col. Moore turned the Blue Force to an attack heading of 193 degrees for the run to the target. As the formation made the turn, the gunners in the waist started kicking out their chaff. The lead planes turned on their Carpet Blinkers to try and give the German radar a big electronic "raspberry."

The 19 Liberators of Blue Force dropped over 38 tons of bombs onto the Amstetten rail yards at 1229, then rallied for home. As the planes headed away from the target there were five or six bursts of flak seen by the tail gunners in the last boxes of the formation.

The route home was flown as the men had been briefed, and the first of the homeward bound planes was back at Pantanella by 1507 that afternoon. The mission had been another milk run. Strike photos would add some cream to the milk run. The photos showed that most of the Blue Force bombs landed smack in the middle of the rail yards near the choke point. Some bombs had walked into the rolling stock near the choke point. The bombing judges were well pleased with the Blue Force results.

Another weather front had moved into the target areas within the range of the 15th Air Force. In view of that, the 464th stood down on 17 March and again on the 18th.

On Sunday, 18 March, the weekly issue of *The Tower* hit the hill. A lot of the men looked forward to the paper coming out after Chaplain Eastwood's church service on Sunday. There was always something of interest within the pages of the paper. The front page featured an article called "A Year Ago, Remember!" The article was aimed at those original members of the 464th who were still at Pantanella. It talked about the trip to Italy on the troop ships, the first night on the hill, and what it had been like in the early days of the group's service in Italy.

The last page had a column called "Chow Line Chatter." According to the article there was an officer eating at the enlisted mess. The food seemed to be a little better than usual since there was an inspection going on. It also made mention of the fact that there was hot water to rinse the mess kits in. That was better than the usual water, which had all the visions of cold pea soup.

Now, it may have been Sunday and the local paper might have come out, but that really did not mean much to the men who worked out on the hardstands. If there was even a hint of a mission in the air, the crew chiefs were at their hardstand working on "their plane." There was always something happening down on the line. If an airplane was ready to fly and the ground crew didn't have anything pressing to work on, they would pitch in on a sister ship. "Steve" Stephenson recalled:

One night someone broke a spark plug off in one of the cylinders. Usually that meant getting an Easy-Out and removing the remaining part of the plug. The Easy-Out would not budge it, and the Line Chief said to replace the cylinder. Then, Jack Shipman came along down the line—Jack was always around when someone was in trouble. "Let me see what I can do," he said. He got a hack saw blade and ground it down. Then, using the new tool, he cut through to the threads of the plug in three places. Then with a chisel he started tapping, and removed one third of the plug remaining in the cylinder. As he tried to remove the two thirds that remained, it fell inside the cylinder. The Line Chief went for a new cylinder, and Jack said, "Let him go." Then Jack put mechanical fingers through one plug hole, propped that cylinder to Top Dead Center. He picked up the part of the plug that had fallen inside with mechanical fingers, and while holding it with one hand he sawed it in two, inside the cylinder, through the other plug hole. Someone else was holding the flashlight. It was a long, tiring, and tough job. When the new cylinder arrived, Jack was blowing and washing out the filings from inside the cylinder. It was after midnight. There were many fellows in the 464th that performed such feats.

Wlliam Loughlin had finished his combat tour on 5 February, but he was still at Pantanella waiting for orders to go back to the states. In one of his letters dated 18 March he wrote:

The B-24 flies overhead. A great powerful fighting machine. Large bomb load, ten half inch machine guns which can spit several hundred rounds per minute. Now it has landed, and from it emerge 10 men of different sizes, likes and dislikes. Men who love different things, come from different towns and states. Men who went to different schools or didn't go at all. Men from different nationalities and religion. Yes, even different political parties. Yet these are men who have so much in common: a country; a uniform; a common hate of what is wrong; and a love of the air. They walk away leaving an empty useless piece of machinery behind them. Tomorrow these men, with their many skills working as a team, will bring power and life to that machine again.

The 464th was scheduled for another mission to the rail yards at Muhldorf, Germany, on 19 March. According to Operations Order #140 it was going to be another Red/Blue Force mission. The 42 scheduled planes would be divided into two attack forces of 21 planes. The Red Force would be led by Capt. William Black, Jr., the flight leader of the 776th. Blue Force would be commanded by Capt. Howard Brown, flight leader of the 778th.

In formation and headed for the target.

Capt. Orton gave the fliers a fairly good weather report at the briefing. According to his forecast, the weather would be pretty good over Italy. He also said that they would find a few clouds over Yugoslavia, but it should not be a major problem for the mission force.

As the planes were taxiing towards the runway, the main gear on THE FLAKMAN (779TH) gave way and the plane spun around as the props caught the dirt along the taxistrip. Her crew chief, Lester Hacker, could not believe his eyes as his beloved B-24 came to a halt in a cloud of dust. She was pretty banged up, but Hacker thought he and his crew could get the kinks out of her and get her back into flying condition.

For once, the weather people had gotten all the isobars plotted in the right spots. The crews were treated to good weather at take off and across the Adriatic. The worst weather that they found were a few scattered clouds over Yugslavia, right where Capt. Orton had said they would be. The group hurtled the Dinaric Alps and saw a few more scattered clouds. After the Dinarics the clouds were widely scattered.

Red Force hit the target at 1254. They toggled 50 tons of bombs towards the rail yards from 18,000 feet. Blue Force followed with their 52 tons a minute later, and both forces rallied for home without seeing a burst of flak.

Bombing scores were obscured by heavy smoke from the fires started by bombs from earlier groups. There were some large concentrations of hits on sidings and on the tracks to the northwest of the station. While the actual results could not be observed, the bombardiers felt they had hit the target pretty well.

The crews were awakened, fed, and briefed on the morning of the 20th. Another Red-Blue Force mission was scheduled. Col. Bird was at the briefing and informed the crews that he would lead the group on the mission. Blue Force would be under the command of Lt/Col. Gilson from the 779th.

Col. Bird led the Red Force into the air at 0920 and headed for the form up area. When the last plane of Red Force was airborne, Lt/Col. Gilson pushed the throttles forward and started getting the Blue Force into the air.

The form up for both forces went smoothly. Both formations were over Andria for wing rendezvous on time, but there was a problem at this point. The 460th came barreling in from the wrong direction. The lead group pulled to the right, and the 460th slid into place without hitting anyone from the other groups.

As the formation flew over the Dinarics the weather turned bad. High clouds moved in, and there was also a layer of clouds below the formation. For the moment, the bombers were sandwiched between two layers of clouds.

The 464th Red Force arrived at the IP and turned for the bomb run. Before the last box had settled for the run, the Wing leader signaled for the formation to abandon the attack on the Primary target. Col. Bird turned the group towards the right and took up a heading for Amstetten.

Red Force arrived over the Amstetten rail yards at 1259. The turn from the primary had put the Red Force on a heading of 61 degrees for the bomb run. The formation released 47 tons of bombs from about 18,000 feet. They rallied to the right and headed home without seeing any flak at all.

The Blue Force also turned at the briefed IP. As they reached the target area, the signal was given to abandon the target. Blue Force turned right. Because they had almost reached the Primary two things happened. First, they were unable to make a bomb run on the alternate from the heading which had resulted from the right turn away from the Primary. Blue Force had to make a 270 degree turn back to the left and attacked from a heading of 191 degrees. The second thing that happened was that all of the extra turning put the formation in range of some pretty heavy guns, and they were bracketed as they turned away from the Primary target.

Blue Force arrived over the rail yards at Amstetten, Austria, at 1321. They released 46 tons of RDX from 19,000 feet and rallied to the left. LITTLE WILLIE (42-51178) from the Blue Force had taken flak damage during the turn. They were unable to drop their bombs because the bomb doors would not open over the target. They would finally get rid of their lethal load over the Adriatic near Vis.

The mission could not be considered a milk run. After all, they had to make a lot of corrections just to get to a target, and some of the planes had taken some fairly nasty hits from the flak. The biggest bright spot was that everybody made it back to Italy and that they had hit the target pretty well according to strike photos.

By the time the planes returned to Pantanella, Lester Hacker and his crew had gotten THE FLAKMAN hoisted off her belly and the bad gear had been locked into place. They towed her back to the hardstand and surveyed the damage. It had a bad landing gear, a badly bent prop, and lots of crumpled aluminum on the belly. THE FLAKMAN was a mess, but Hacker and his crew started cleaning it up and getting ready to repair their ship.

The target for the 21st was the airfield at Neuberg, Germany. The idea behind this mission was to hit the German airfield and

LITTLE WILLY (42-51178) from the 776th headed for the target, March 1945.

nearby plant where they were making the dreaded Me-262 jet aircraft. The "Hollywood Air Force" (8th) had hit this target several days before. Now the 15th would try and finish the job.

The ground crews had 32 planes ready for take off at 0700 that morning. Take off and form up were done in record fashion, and the formation was headed for the Adriatic by 0800. As they crossed the Adriatic there were a few scattered clouds, but nothing serious. These clouds dogged the formation until they crossed the Alps. By the time the group was near the IP, the clouds were classified as patchy.

At the IP, Capt. Foote, the mission leader, turned the 464th to a heading of 288 degrees for the flight to the target. The group arrived at the release point at 1147. When the bombsight agreed with the settings that had been computed, 62 tons of 100 pound fragmentation bombs rained towards the airfield below.

The bomb pattern looked good. The majority of the strikes were on or near the east-west runway and traveled almost 4,000 feet. Several Me-262s parked along the runway were blown to bits, and several more were badly damaged. The group rallied for home without seeing a burst of flak. For once, the mission had been flown without a sign of German opposition to the intruding Liberators.

When the planes landed, the hardstand for RAMP TRAMP (42-78692) was empty. About half an hour from the target the plane was observed jettisoning its bombload. The plane also had the #1 and #2 propellers feathered. They were last sighted about an hour after the target, below and to the right of the group on a heading of 170 degrees.

Except for Lt. William McGowen's crew being listed as missing, the mission had been a good one. It appeared that the combined strategic bombing by Allied planes was having the desired effect on the German war machine. The 464th had not fought an aerial battle with the Luftwaffe in several months. Flak for the last several missions was either absent or just a few scattered bursts.

While the group did not know it at the time, the mission on the 21st had been part of an 800 ton raid on Neuberg by the entire 15th Air Force. They had delt a death blow to the German jet plant and airfield from which the Germans would not recover. While there would be encounters with the feared Me-262 in the future, they would be rare and ineffective.

The 464th had been alerted on the afternoon of the 21st that they would be flying again on the 22nd. The flight crews had no way of knowing until briefing that the target was one of their "infamous favorites"—Vienna again!

Major John McNeely (Asst Group Operations Officer) led the first of 42 Liberators into the air at 0828 that morning. By 0847, all of the planes were in the air and forming up as planned. Three planes aborted with mechanical problems.

A lot of the fliers could not believe the weather for the mission. Except for a few scattered clouds over Italy and across the Adriatic, the weather was very good. The group did run into some headwinds after they passed over the Dinarics. It slowed the formation a little, so they had to adjust the throttles to try and keep the formation together.

When the group reached the briefed IP they turned towards the target. Within moments of the turn, the #2 engine on BONNIE-ANNIE-LAURIE (44-49194) went out. Mission Leader Capt. McNeely relinquished the lead to Deputy Leader Lt. Laser of the 778th. Lt. Laser had the lead for about 3 minutes before the target, then his bombsight started having problems. The bombardier would put in corrections to the left, and the PDI (Pilots Direction Indicator) would indicate right. As a result, the first unit leader did not release the bombs at the release point. The rest of the 464th hit the release point and the release button at 1249. Over 69 tons of 100 pound GP bombs were dropped on the Heilegensthdt rail yards at Vienna.

While the 464th was busy changing leaders, the German flak gunners were busy loading shells into their guns on the ground. Within seconds the 464th was under flak attack. At first, it was light, then it turned to intense and accurate. Within another few seconds the flak was the usual type that flak city had been noted for in the past.

Back-I (44-50332) was hit by a burst just before the target. It fell behind the formation, rolled over on its back, and started to spin. On the flight deck, Lts. Theodore Toscano and Donald Hokinson were in a life and death struggle to regain control. After falling several thousand feet they managed to gain control of the dying B-24. The plane was blazing from the wings to the tail. One crewman, George Frazier, Jr., managed to leap from the doomed ship before it rolled over on its back again, and like a dying fish spun towards the ground, taking the rest of the crew with her.

Some of the "rookie" crewmen in other planes stared in horrid disbelief. For them it was the first time they had seen a plane hit by flak and go down blazing. One minute she was there in formation, the next second she was headed down, taking some of their friends with her.

The 464th had bombed the target and lost one plane as they rallied for home. Because the bombload had been 100 pounders,

LITTLE WILLY, Bombs away!

the intervalometer had not been able to keep up with the drop sequence in 10 of the planes. Bombs were frozen to the racks or piled up on each other, and crewmen scrambled to the bomb bay to try and get the bombs out of the plane.

White-F (44-49146) had been hit in the #3 and #4 engines over the target. On the flight deck, Lt. Lyle Wilson and copilot Roy Wehmen had feathered the props and cut the fuel flow to the damaged engines. Without power on the right side, they fell from formation and headed down. Ahead were the mountains. The crew knew they would not make it over the obstacle, so Lt. Wilson told the crew to bail out. Everyone escaped the plane, but not the Germans on the ground. They were captured and were POWs for the duration of the war.

The planes returned to Pantanella and landed by 1543 that afternoon. There were 13 planes damaged by flak. None of the damage was serious, just enough to make a lot of sheet metal crews have to work late that night.

Results of the mission were disappointing considering the loss of several airplanes and crews. The largest concentration of bombs was five miles away from the target. Several smaller areas of bomb hits were almost two and a half miles away. It appeared that the last minute change of leadership over the target had thrown the group's aim way off.

On the morning of 23 March, 42 planes took off to bomb the rail yards at Gmund, Austria. The mission was under the command of Capt. Charles Foote (779th). The second attack unit was led by Capt. May (776th).

The flight crews were treated to a milk run. The weather was clear almost all of the way to the target. Only one plane aborted the mission with mechanical problems.

At the IP, the 464th turned to a heading of 304 degrees for the bomb run. The target was clear, so the bombardiers had plenty of time to set their sights on the rail yards. The group hit the release point at 1156 and sent over 79 tons of 100 pound GP bombs cascading towards the tracks below. As always when they carried the small bombs, a lot of them hung up in the racks.

On THE BAD PENNY (42-78433), 36 bombs still hung from the racks. The intervalometer would not work at all, so the entire load was salvoed on the way back.

The flight back to the base was almost as planned. There were several minor corrections to skirt some building clouds near the spur, but otherwise there were no problems. For once, the returning crews could eat their K-Ration flight lunches without worrying about the fuel remaining or whether or not someone would call out "fighters."

The strike photos added a little cream to the milk run. The group's bombs landed smack in the middle of the rail yard and continued through the choke point. The locomotive repair depot was pasted, along with a lot of hits on the tracks leading to the choke point. It was safe to say that the "old 5:15" would be very late for days to come.

Col. Bird led the first of 42 B-24s into the air on the morning of 24 March. They were going to take another crack at the German Me-262s in Neuberg, Germany. This was a target that had to be knocked out of the war. If even one of the German jets could make it into the air they could cause a lot of damage to a bomber formation. The 464th formed into two attack units with Lt. Philip Savage leading the second unit.

The fliers were given a real treat from the boys in the weather department. From take off to target the skies were clear as a bell. It was a welcome change of pace for the flight crews.

Three planes aborted the mission when they started having mechanical problems after getting into the air. Black-M (42-51264) aborted at 1115 when a cylinder in the #1 engine blew out. The prop was feathered, and the Liberator landed at Zara, Yugoslavia, for repairs.

At about 1222, the remaining 39 planes reached the target and sent over 83 tons of fragmentation bombs towards the airfield. The formation made a right rally from the attack heading of 294 degrees and headed for home. The bomb run had been a good one. The frags hit several fuel storage tanks, starting some fairly large infernos on the airfield. Other bombs landed in the workshops and hangar area. Nine of the infamous Me-262s were blown to junk, and another five were damaged.

The 464th had another milk run under their wings. The only fighters that they had seen were on the ground, and they were given the frag treatment. The boys in the air did not even see a burst of flak on the mission.

The group was back in the air on 25 March. They continued their strikes against the Luftwaffe by hitting the airfield at Prague Litanang in Czechoslovakia. The two attack units were treated to another milk run.

It may have been a milk run for most of the Liberators of the 464th, but not for the crew of Yellow-M. Although the crew did not know it at the time, they had been hit by "friendly" fire. When the gunners had cleared their guns, a single .50 cal bullet had hit Yellow-M near the bomb bay. As they approached the target they could not get the bomb bay doors to open. Clifton Callahan left his position and moved to the bomb bay. He chopped part of the bomb bay doors away with a crash ax and started hacking away at the bomb shackles with the ax. The temperature in the bay was about 50 below, and the slipstream made it even colder. One by one, Callahan was able to chop the bombs free and let them fall through the bomb bay. It took almost two hours, but finally all the bombs were gone and the plane made it back to Pantanella.

The fact that Yellow-M had been hit by friendly fire was not reported at the interrogation for fear that the gunner would be court-martialed. Clifton Callahan would not receive his Distinguished Flying Cross for over 40 years.

Strike photos showed the frags landed right where they were supposed to. Over 32 aircraft were destroyed on the ground. Several hangars had also been hit, and the runway had taken hits from the bombs, as well. The 464th was taking revenge against the Luftwaffe for the times when the German fighters had mauled the group during the previous summer and fall.

A big spoonful of cream floated to the top of the milk can that morning. A lone silver B-24 pulled into the pattern. The incoming Liberator could not call Racecard tower because the Russians had stolen the radio equipment. Some of the men thought it was a plane that had aborted the mission. As it got closer the men on the ground stared in disbelief, as it appeared to be a ghost returning from the dead. Actually it was HOOSIER PETE, with Lt. Don Bahnsen's crew coming back home! Bombardier Don Sherard wrote:

On 23 March we heard a bomber overhead. It was a B-24, and we dashed down to the airstrip. The pilot landed the badly shot-up plane with number one and four engines feathered. The tail gunner was injured. While we were there, another plane landed with the number one engine out, and he almost tore the nose off of the plane making the landing. We immediately made arrangements to get the gasoline out of the two planes for our plane.

The following morning, 24 March, we transferred the gasoline from the two crippled planes, and shortly after noon we took off for Italy. The airstrip was fifteen miles from the German lines, and you could hear the artillery fire. We took off at approximately 100 miles an hour with 40 degrees flaps and had to gain sufficient altitude to clear some two story buildings at the end of the runway. Bahnsen did an excellent job of flying, getting the plane off of the short ash-covered fighter strip and turning before we went over the German lines. We proceeded to Bari, Italy, where we went to the hospital for physical examinations and "delousing." We were then put to bed.

In the morning we took showers, washing off the louse powder, donned new clothes, and were interrogated. Shortly afterward, we took off and came back to the 464th.

On 26 March the 464th changed from airfields to railroads. The target was the Bratislava Rangier marshaling yards. At 0955 Capt. Walter Steves led the group into the air, and 31 more Liberators followed. The second attack unit would be under the command of Col. Virgil Zoller, Deputy Group Commander.

The 779th near the Dalmation Coast.

Everything went according to the plan of attack. The weather was not a problem, just a few scattered clouds along the way. At 1155 the mission leader radioed that he was having some problems with the autopilot. Capt. Steves pulled BONNIE ANNIE LAURIE (44-49194) to the side, and the Deputy Leader, Capt. Keith Cooke, slid his ship into the lead position.

The 464th turned at the IP and started the bomb run. As they turned, several crews spotted a lone Fw-190 dogging the formation, It was flying at 23,000 feet, which was the same altitude as the 464th. It stayed out of range and never made a move to attack. Within a few moments, the German fighter peeled away and headed for the deck. At almost the same moment the Focke-Wulfe peeled off the first bursts of flak appeared, right in front of the group.

Within seconds the flak was bursting within the formation and was concentrated and very accurate. Talmadge Callison was flying on BONNIE ANNIE LAURIE that day and wrote:

Things went well until we turned on to the IP. The flak concentration became heavy, and we took a direct hit on the right side of the bomb bay, with a full load of bombs. One of the control cables snapped, and our plane went out of control. Steves sounded the bail-out alarm. The waist gunners, Lawson and Buffo, went out. The pilot and I went out, and Peter Wilson, the radar operator, went out next. Johnson, Brown, and Black in the nose section came out in that order. The nose wheel doors closed as Lt. Black was attempting to clear and mangled his leg when he hit the tail section of the aircraft. S/Sgt. Skinner was flying in the top turret that day and was one of the last to leave. When he opened his chute, two panels ripped out, and he fell faster than the rest of us. His descent only took about five minutes, whereas it took most of us fifteen minutes to descend. Skinner lay motionless in the wheat field as civilians and German military personnel gathered around him. Our crew watched from the air as we floated down. Major Wilson refused to leave the aircraft and rode it down. One big explosion and a red ball of fire, and our B-24 was gone.

The formation crossed the release point at 1405. Over 69 tons of 250 pound GP bombs belched from the Liberators. The group rallied for home as the flak became even more intense and accurate. Several other planes had been hit by flak, but so far all of the planes that had made it over the target were still in formation as they headed back towards home base.

The results of the day's effort was poor. Most of the bombs ploughed through open country about a mile north of the rail yards. Several repair sheds were hit, but overall the 464th had missed the MPI by a long way.

When the planes returned to Pantanella at about 1735 the weather had turned sour. The group had flown through some haze near the spur. At the base, there was a 20 mph wind kicking up a lot of dust. When the last plane was finally down, the crew chiefs had a chance to look them over. Two of the planes had a lot of holes in

Letting down from altitude over Italy.

them to patch. Three others were damaged enough to spend at least a week on the hardstand being repaired. That night those that cared to, or had the time, trudged over to the movie hall to take in the flick. They didn't know it at the time, but they saw what would become considered a classic. The movie for the night was "Stagecoach," starring John Wayne.

The weather closed in over Europe and forced the 464th into a three day lull in flying missions. It gave the boys time off to catch up on a few things. Some of the guys had not had a chance to read the 25 March issue of *The Tower*.

The front page ran an article introducing the men to the new commander. It gave Col. Bird's background in the military, and it also pointed out that he had been the commander of a B-25 training unit back in the States. One point of interest was that Col. Bird had begun an "open door policy" so the troops could get to know him if they desired. In "Chow Line Chatter" the following appeared:

This week is also tinged with sorrow at the sickness of a leading member of our Squadron.

At take off on the morning of the 19th, FLAKMAN felt tired and gently laid down to die. The airplane doctors were called in and have hopes that the patient's life will be saved, although he will probably never again dodge the flak over Vienna. FLAKMAN is an outstanding plane of the group, a veteran of 74 missions and 898 combat hours. He has come through all these forays without losing a man, and with only one crewmember wounded. Yet seven Nazi fighters and nine probables went down before his guns. He is a tractable and well-behaved ship. Once Capt. Fowler landed him successfully with a flat tire. Another time, Lt. Bahnsen at the controls, FLAKMAN alone of all the ships in the Squadron completed a certain mission and returned unscathed.

Special credit goes to his ground crew, Hacker, Terry, and Renna. Since they received him last June 3rd they have changed 9 engines. All last June and July, FLAKMAN led the group in hours flown per month, and also the first ship to have a chaff chute, which Hacker and his boys installed themselves. For the generally outstanding record of his ship, Hacker received the Bronze Star.

It was good of FLAKMAN to lay down on the taxi strip before take off rather than while landing. A creditable end to a great combat career. We are glad to hear that he will fly again.

Because of the continued coming and going of weather fronts over the targets, the 464th reverted back to Lone Wolf tactics on 30 March. The first of four Mickey ships left Pantanella at 0833 that morning. At 30 second intervals the other three took to the air and headed for the line of departure.

Red-Y was designated as the lead plane. She was followed by White-Z (44-49688), also known as MULTO BOMB-BINO, and Red-A (44-49589). The flight to the target was hampered by clouds ranging up to 27,000 feet. The radar had been lowered almost from the start to help navigate along the route to the target.

When the lead plane arrived near the target, the weather had cleared to the point that an attack would violate the Lone Wolf concept. With that in mind, the lead plane turned towards the alternate, which was the Kapfenberg Tank Works. White-Z also turned for the same target, and both planes released their bombs towards the undercast and rallied right for home.

#688 abandoned the Primary and headed for the rail yards at Graz. The radar scope picked up a mountain peak which was identified as the target. At the last second, the mistake was acknowledged and the mission aborted.

Red-A took up a heading of 208 degrees and arrived over Graz at 1224. They were able to get a clear target return and released their bombload. After a sharp right turn they headed back to Italy.

Although there was no flak on the mission there were plenty of sightings of enemy aircraft before reaching the target area. Three Fw-190s were over Graz, but stayed about three miles away from the attacking Liberators. It was a good thing the fighters didn't attack, since there was no fighter escort and the Mickey ships would have to fend for themselves if the fighters had decided to attack.

The 464th unloads on the Marshaling Yards at Heilegenstadt, Austria, March 22, 1945.

The Fortezza, Italy, marshaling yards as captured by the strike camera, March 8, 1945.

The weather cleared enough for the 464th to get 32 planes in the air on the morning of the 31st. The lead plane would be flown by Maj. John McNeely (Group Training Officer). The group was able to form up and meet the rest of the 55th Wing without any problems.

All went well until the group was over the Adriatic. The eight planes of Baker Box lost the formation in the clouds. They could not find the 464th, so they transferred to the 485th for the duration of the mission.

As the formation approached the target area, clouds billowed in front of the group. They were nasty looking and reached up to about 29,000 feet. The mission leader decided not to try and go over or penetrate the alto-atrocious and turned the formation towards the alternate at Villach.

At the IP for Villach, the group turned to a heading of 140 degrees for the bomb run. During the run to the target, two Me-262 jet fighters flashed through the group. They were followed by five Me-109s. It was a fleeting encounter, as none of the fighters turned back to attack the 464th. The entire incident was over before the gunners in the Liberators could even call out the fact that there were fighters in the area, or bring a gun to bear on the German fighters.

The 464th arrived over the rail yards at 1258 and released 51 tons of General Purpose 250 pound bombs. As they rallied to the left several bursts of flak appeared. It was more of a departing gesture; the Germans wanted the 464th to know that they were still down there on the ground.

On the way home, Black-D lost oil pressure on the #2 engine. Then the #4 prop ran away. The plane landed at Zara. White-Y ran low on fuel and landed at the fighter base at Lesina. After a brief pit stop, she came back to Pantanella.

The month of March 1945 had been a busy one for the men of the 464th. The group had flown 20 missions. That added up to 745 effective sorties that delivered over 1,450 tons of explosives to the Third Reich.

A lot of the 464th's missions had been in support of the Russian advance. Rail yards had taken a beating from the 15th Air Force in an effort to keep the German forces from getting supplies or retreating. Airfields were also high on the target list. It was fairly obvious that the 15th Air Force was quickly running out of strategic targets and moving more and more towards tactical targets.

April 1945

A lot of the men from the 464th hit the deck at o'light hundred on the morning of April 1, 1945. It was Easter Sunday! Those that were up headed for the valley between the two hills of Pantanella. At 0530 Chaplain Eastwood and chaplains from the 465th began celebrating sunrise services.

After the service, the flight crews headed for the briefing room to get the poop on the day's mission. The target for the day was the rail yards at Bruck, Austria. The planes managed to get off the ground and head for the target without major problems

It may have been Easter Sunday, but it was also 1 April, and Mother Nature could not let the opportunity pass without playing an April Fools joke on the fliers. As the formation approached the Control Point near Lese, Austria, she conjured up some mean looking clouds that the bombers could not get over or around. The mission was aborted, and the planes returned with the "Easter eggs" hanging from the racks.

April 2 found the group trying to get off the ground for a mission to the marshaling yards at Graz. The lead ship, with Col. Zoller at the helm, left the runway at 0950. Thirty-one Liberators followed at about 30 second intervals.

Form up was accomplished without any problems, however, getting the wing together was a different story. The 465th was late, which in turn made the 464th late. The 460th was flying at their accustomed snail's pace, which left the Liberators of the 55th Wing hanging by their props. The wing was finally all together and over Spinazzola at 1110.

The 464th hit tactical targets in Northern Italy during April 1945.

Heading home after hitting German supply lines.

The formation headed towards the target. After a couple of hours of flying in formation, FLAK ALLEY SALLY (44-50350) started having problems with the #1 engine. The oil pressure started falling towards zero, and the engine had to be shut down. The bomb load was jettisoned to get rid of the extra weight as the plane headed back towards Italy.

As the planes turned at the IP, several Me-109s were spotted at about the same altitude as the oncoming Liberator formation. They made no move to attack and dove away several moments after the IP. As the Me-109s dove away, the first bursts of flak greeted the 464th. As the group got closer to the target, the flak followed and got closer to the group. Just before bombs away, the flak was getting intense and fairly accurate.

Thirty-one planes reached the target on a heading of 292 degrees. At 1345 the Liberators of the 464th released over 75 tons of high explosive RDX on the target. For once, the release was exactly at the briefed time. As the formation rallied for home the flak began to trail off, and finally the Liberators were out of range.

About an hour after turning for home the group spotted four unidentified fighters. They appeared at around the 3 o'clock position and were headed away from the formation. The fighters made no move to attack.

As the formation approached the spur they saw a B-24 crash into the Adriatic. It appeared to have yellow tail markings, so it almost had to be from the 55th Wing. A quick nose count of the group found all of the 464th Liberators in their proper place. At least the crashing plane was not from the 464th.

When the planes got near the field they broke formation and went into the pattern. One by one the planes flew downwind, base and final. When they were lined up on the PSP they lowered the flaps and pulled the power back a little. Some of the pilots used a little trick on final. They would crank in a little trim so that the nose of the Liberator wanted to come up, then they would hold the nose down with the yoke until they were ready to flare out. When they relaxed the pressure on the yoke the nose would come up and the big Liberator would flare out and settle onto the runway.

The planes were back at their hardstands by 1630 that afternoon. Nine of the 464th planes had been damaged by flak, though none of the planes had been hit bad enough to be out of commissions for more then 48 hours.

Just because it wouldn't take long to get the planes ready for the next mission did not mean that there was not a lot of work to get accomplished. "Steve" Stephenson, crew chief, recalled:

I remember changing an engine. The plane came home with a feathered engine from a mission at 4 pm. We went to early chow, and when we got back to the line the new engine was sitting on my hardstand. While the other two men on our crew started removing the cowling, I started to remove the engine from the crate. The prop man came by and removed the propeller. Soon, both the old and new engines were sitting on the ground next to each other, and we were removing accessories from the old engine and putting them on the new one. Any line personnel with a few minutes to spare would drop by to lend a hand. Any time there was a difficult or hard job to be done, Jack Shipman was on hand. The 779th was almost like a big family and friendly. Help your neighbor today, because tomorrow it may be you that needs a helping hand. At 10:00 pm we had already put in the required ground time, and the order was put in for pilots to slow time the engine in the air. This was another

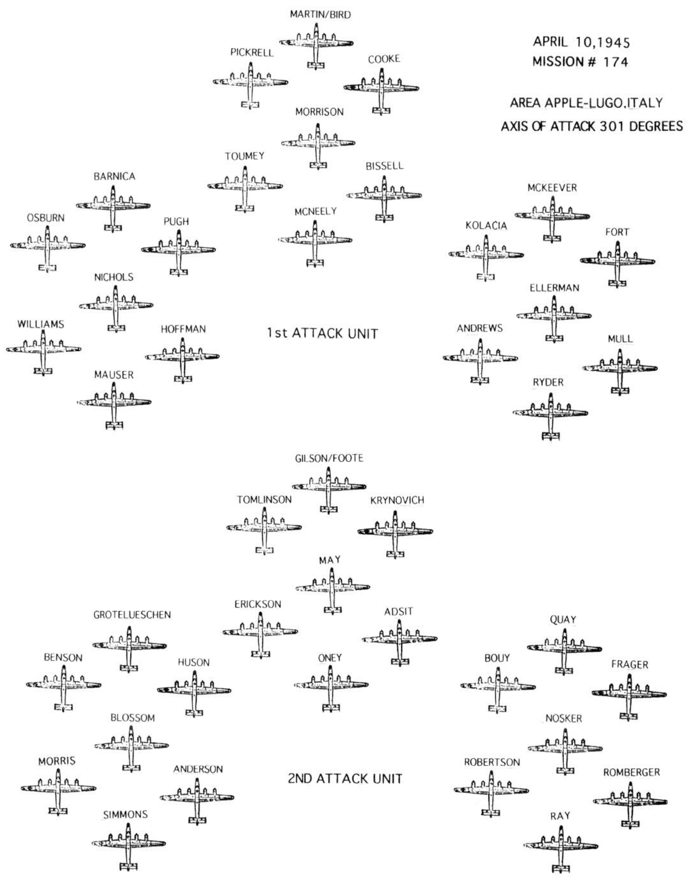

Formation diagram for the April 10, 1945, mission.

time when I was designated flight engineer. The pilots had volunteered my services. This aircraft also took off with the rest of the group at seven o'clock the next morning. I should mention that we got plenty of experience changing engines.

Strike photos revealed that the 464th had put together a good mission. There was a good concentration of direct hits on the rail yards, and the station was obliterated. Several locomotives were hit, and the choke point was well covered.

The group, as well as most of the 15th Air Force, stood down 3 and 4 April due to the weather over the continent. The stand down gave the men a chance to catch up on their sack time, letters to home, and the latest war news.

By now the Russian Army was rapidly advancing towards the west, and they were almost to Vienna. Everyone was hoping that the Russians would get there and capture Vienna so that "flak city" would be stricken from the target list. Patton's Third Army was rolling towards the east. They were taking ground faster than the Germans could retreat. In Italy, the Allied forces were pushing north and driving the German army back towards the mountains. The way things were going, everyone figured that it was just a matter of time before the war would be over. The problem was just how much time was it going to take? More importantly, how many more lives would be lost before the conflict would end?

On the 5th, the 464th was ready to fly towards Hitler's ever shrinking Europe again. A total of 38 B-24s began taking off at 0850. The first six planes were designated as a "special effort." The special effort was led by Capt. Willard Patterson (777th).

The special effort had some trouble getting together with the rest of the wing's special effort. They could not make radio contact with the 465th, although the 465th was spotted twice. The 464th circled several times, then turned towards the departure line. The 464th and 485th were able to get together near Termoli, but the 460th and 465th never showed up.

The normal effort planes started leaving Pantanella at 0907. This group was led by Capt. William Black. They formed into two attack units and found the 465th despite adverse weather in the form up area.

As the Liberators flew farther north, the weather turned from bad to absolutely alto-awful. Short of the Primary, the leaders for both attacking formations turned for the alternate target and then turned for home. Both the special effort and normal effort formations returned to Pantanella with their bombs still nestled in the bomb bays. They had gotten close to the target, but they had not been able to light the cigar.

The group stood down on 6 April due to the bad weather. A large frontal system had moved into the area and caused most of the 15th Air Force to stand down. The last several days of bad weather brought back memories of the kind of weather that the fliers had experienced during January.

On the 7th 32 planes left Pantanella at 1105 to hit tactical targets in northern Italy. The take off had been delayed by weather. Because of low clouds and fog they could not see the end of the runway. Finally, the green flare was fired and the lead plane rolled down the runway. The group would use the usual two attack unit formation for this mission. Capt. Foote was the mission leader, while Lt. George Quay would shepherd the 2nd unit.

The 464th flew as briefed to Zara, and then the weather got really stinky. The group made a 360 degree climbing turn to the right to get high enough to hurtle the clouds that were building in front of them. At about 1445, the signal "Shoehorn" was heard over the radio. The recall had been sent, and the formation turned back towards Italy with their bombloads.

The 464th was a week into April and had been able to get only one effective mission under their belts. Weather seemed to be giving the Germans another chance at escaping back towards "der Fatherland" and consolidating their defenses for a possible final stand.

On the 8th, the 464th was ready to try it again! Thirty-two planes were ready for take off at 0820. The Primary target was the rail yards at Fortezza, in northern Italy. Col. Zoller would lead, and Lt. George Laser would lead the second unit over the target.

The 464th released thier load at 1207 on April 10,1945.

Bombs on the way towards German troop concentrations.

Two bursts of flak between Black-N and her wingman.

Black-N has taken a direct hit from flak. Note the smoke and a piece of aluminum near the ball turret.

As the group approached Zara they ran into high stratocumulus clouds. A lot of the crews listened for the recall signal to flash over the radio, but the formation was able to get around the clouds and continue. The clouds broke over the Alps, and from then on it was clear flying.

At the IP, the group turned to an attack heading of 190 degrees. The lead bombardier set his Norden bombsight up for the bomb run, the drift was killed, and everything was ready for release when the dials came together.

At 1226 the bombs were released, and over 51 tons of 500 pound RDX fell towards the rail yards below. In Baker Box there was a problem with the C-1 autopilot on BABY SANDY (44-49857). This was the box leader, and they did not drop their bombs at the target. As a result, none of Baker Box released on the target.

As the other planes released their bombs the flak opened up on the formation. It was accurate, but not intense. The 464th would be in the black and white blossoms for about four minutes, and it was enough for several planes to take minor hits.

The flight back to Pantanella was along the planned and briefed route. The weather had improved, and all of the planes were back in the Racecard pattern by 1521. The strike photos showed several bombs hitting the tracks and the north choke point. The majority of the bombs were in the hills on the west edge of the yards about 3,000 feet away from the target. Results were classified as poor for the mission.

During the afternoon of the 8th a small miracle happened at Pantanella Hill. Several members of the crew of BONNIE-ANNIE-LAURIE arrived back home after being listed as MIA on 26 March, and they had a strange tale to tell to all who would listen.

After bailing out of their stricken Liberator they were captured by the German forces in the area. After being transported to several different locations they arrived at a German airfield. Talmadge Callison would later write:

As we passed by the airstrip the Me-109s, JU-52s, and Me-210s came into view. A short ride carried us to a new location with more bars. Johnston and I watched the cell door locked securely on Brown and Steves. Johnston and I were carried to our cell. Bolted in, we sat in silence on the edge of a single wooden bed for the two of us. The sun rose and set before we were fed or even given water. Johnston had been escorted to the latrine by a trustee—he was a German pilot who was locked up for going AWOL. He offered to assist in an escape plot if the four of us would arrange to carry another German with us and make him a prisoner of the Americans. This German was Bernard Kerstings, the son of a renowned industrialist. Four other Germans were enlisted to come out with us. They were trustees and had access to all of the cells. The Russians were pushing in from the east, and no German wanted to be a prisoner of the Russians. On Easter Sunday night the German trustee began his mission. Around 2 am Fredil, the German pilot trustee, opened our cell and brought three other German political prisoners who would make the trip with us. They brought us German overcoats and military hats and provided woolen socks to pull over our

Black-N' wing buckles and she begins her death spiral to the ground.

shoes. We were united with Brown and Steves. Fredil was given wine to take to the jailer and drank with him. The German pilot tongued the bottle while the jailer drank. The jailer passed out. The key to the wing exit was found in the jailer's desk. We passed through the corridor to the main entrance and out onto the road. We formed into a squad and marched down the street onto the airfield with Fredil saluting the guard as we passed. Fredil marched us up to a Ju-52 parked on a hardstand. As he flung open the door, out popped a German pilot. As he descended, he roared in a voice, surprising us, "Vot's dis?" Fredil told him that his plane had been assigned to us for a mission and that he would have to leave. Finally, the pilot turned and motioned, and an embarrassed fraulein crawled out of the plane. She wept bitterly and accused us of taking her bed in the middle of the night. Then, as we cranked the engines, the German pilot offered his assistance. We four Americans kept quiet, hoping we would not have to kill him. We taxied out on the runway, swung the Ju-52 around, and lumbered off as red lights blinked in the control tower. They were aware that we should not be taking off. We flew over some restricted areas and received some flak, but we were flying at a low altitude and the flak caused us no problems. All the German pilots were sergeants, and Fredil had flown five years in Ju-52s. As we flew over Yugoslavian partisan territory we received small arms fire. We were short of fuel and needed to reach Zara, a partisan held airfield along the Adriatic.

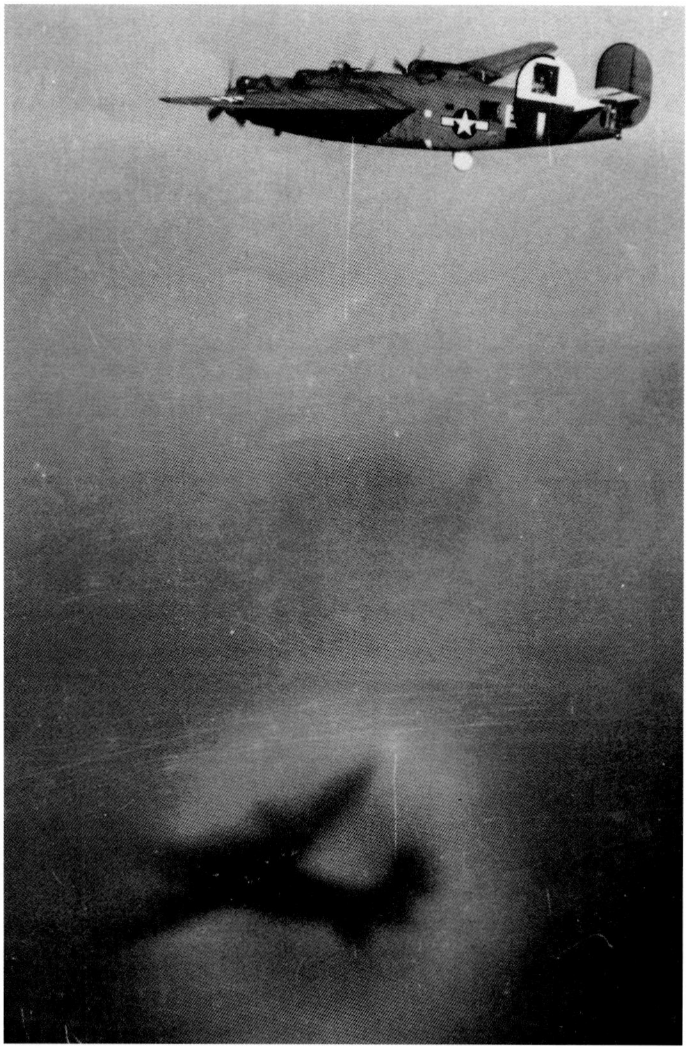

White-E casts a shadow on the undercast as she heads for Palmonova,Italy, April 14, 1945.

The escapees did not quite make Zara. They managed to put the Junkers down in a field about ten miles from Zara. Here, they met up with several partisans and convinced them that they were Americans, in spite of the fact that they were wearing German uniforms. All went well until one of the Germans said something. Then things turned very cold. Callison wrote:

We four Americans were put into one room, and the four Germans into another. The next day, interrogation of all of us began again. The American mission representative, with a T/Sgt., drove up outside and came in, made himself known to the guard at the door, and stepped inside. He informed us that he was working as a team member dropped behind the lines to coordinate activities concerning Americans. He left us four Red Cross packets and said the OSS would have our commanding officer flown over to identify us. The next day the OSS brought our CO (778th) over. He identified us, and we were released to the British, who wined and dined us along with our four OSS members, who then carried us to the Zara airstrip. We were flown back to the 464th with our CO.

The four Germans who aided in the escape, and had been promised that they would be made prisoners of the Americans, did not fair as well as the Americans. They were held in a Yugoslavian labor camp, and they would spend several years in this and other camps. For the Germans, it was a cruel twist of fate for helping the Americans escape.

On 9 April 42 flight crews headed for the briefing room. It was a special mission and required a special briefing. The 15th Air Force was in the process of changing from strategic to tactical bombing in direct support of the advancing 5th and 8th Armies in northern Italy. This direct support was coded "Operation Wowser."

The briefing officer pointed out that there would be special white marker panels on the ground to show the position of the troops. There would also be white smoke pots, and the group would tune into the SCS-51 radio beacon so they would not bomb the wrong positions. The planes could not release before or after a specific time.

The planes would be loaded with 20 pound fragmentation bombs bundled together to form 400 pound clusters. Any aircraft that could not release over the target was to bring their bomb load back to the base or dump it into the Adriatic.

Lt/Col. Gilson led the first Liberator of Red Force into the air at 1120, followed by 20 more planes. Blue Force's 21 planes were led by Col. Bird.

The form up was almost a disaster. As Blue Force was getting ready to turn towards the wing rendezvous, the 454th BG from the 304th Wing was spotted on a collision course. Col. Bird led Blue

Force into an emergency hard right to avoid the oncoming group, and then hit the radio with a few choice words for the group as they passed by.

Red Force turned to a heading of 304 degrees at the IP and started for Area Apple. Below they could clearly see the marker panels, and the localizer beam was working just like it was supposed to. At 1451 the formation toggled 35 tons of cluster frags towards the German Army.

Blue Force was right behind on a briefed heading of 302 degrees. As they approached the target area light scattered flak dotted the sky. Moments before the release point, MULTO BOMB-BINO (44-49688) accidentally dropped their load. The crew of 44-49419 saw the bombs fall and toggled on their leader. At the time of release, the planes were about a mile and a half behind the forward Allied lines. It could have been an absolute disaster for the troops on the ground, but the bombs landed beyond the ground grippers; it was still considered "danger close."

The rest of Blue Force released their bombs at 1457 from about 20,000 feet and rallied to the left as briefed. The flak was moderate and was tracking the formation. By the time the flak found the group's range the 464th was out of danger.

The strike photos showed that the 464th had excellent results. The target area was well covered by the frags, and most of the hits were well within the German positions.

The mission had been a milk run. Except for the early release by two planes, the mission had gone according to the briefing. No planes had taken any flak damage, and everyone returned to Pantanella.

As the planes came back from the mission they could see a dark cloud of smoke off to the southeast. It appeared to be somewhere along the coast. It could not be a crashed aircraft, as the cloud was too large. Actually, it was the remains of the cloud of smoke from a cargo ship. For unknown reasons, a ship loaded with bombs had exploded while unloading at Bari. Over 250 Italian workers had been killed, and another 1,600 injured. The concussion from the blast had collapsed the roof of the cathedral at Bari.

TAPS echoes across Pantanella Hill for the fallen commander in chief. April 15, 1945.

Chaplain Eastwood leads Memorial Service for President Roosevelt. April 15, 1945.

The 10th was scheduled to be a repeat mission to the same Area Apple as the day before. Since it had been a milk run and the war seemed to be winding down some of the senior crewmen wanted to fly and get another mission under their belt.

The briefing was scheduled for 0635 that morning, and Lt. Jack Bosley was headed for the briefing. He had flown on the 9th and was on the schedule again. He recalled:

Major Lacey Morton, Group Navigator, stopped me enroute to "Briefing" and asked me if I would mind if he went in my place. He would merely ride in the nose turret. I said it was O.K.

The briefing was very detailed again. The mission would be almost a carbon copy of the previous mission. The briefing flimsy outlined everything the crews needed to know for the mission:

Stations 0820,Taxi 0835,Take Off 0845.
IP Cesanatico (44,12 N,12,24 E)
Axis of Attack 301 degrees

Col. Bird led the first B-24 into the air at 0845. He was followed by 20 more Liberators of Red Force. Lt/Col. Gilson would lead Blue Force over the target. As Col. Gilson taxied away from the hardstand in Black-N—alias STEVEONOVICH II—crew chief Ted Moldenhauer waved and yelled, "Bring her back in one piece, as usual."

Form up of Red Force went without any problems, but Blue Force was forced out of position by the 465th. They finally were able to get back in the right spot and continued on. The 464th would lead the 55th Wing. At 1026, Col. Bird turned Red Force to a heading of 10 degrees and left Spinazzola right on time. Blue Force was several minutes late leaving Spinazzola, but was able to close the gap within a short time.

At the Key Point the 464th turned to 297 degrees and headed for the IP. By now, the group had reached 18,000 feet. There was some haze in the area, but weather was otherwise clear. It would be a visual bomb run unless they ran into clouds.

At Cesanatico (IP), the group turned to the heading of 301 degrees for the run to the target. At this point the men in the air could clearly see the marker panels, and the SCS-51 localizer transmitter was working very well. At 1203 a single P-38 appeared off the wing of one of the B-24s flying in the Baker 23 position of Blue Force. The P-38 had red and white tail stripes on the rudders. It dogged the formation for about a minute, then peeled off to the right as the first scattered puffs of flak appeared.

The group arrived over the target and released their load of frags at 1207. According to the briefing, no bombs could be dropped before 1205. Everything was within the time limits so far. As the bombs fell, there were several more scattered bursts of flak.

Both Red and Blue Force began to rally to the left according to plan. In the nose turret of STEVEONOVICH II (Black -N), Maj. Lacey had been treated to a scenic ride so far. Granted, it was a bit cramped in the turret, but the view from up front was something to write home about. Since it had been a visual bomb run, Radar Operator Ed Walsh had not been needed to run the radar set. He had moved to the bomb bay to watch the bombs fall from the plane.

The German gunners on the ground were tracking the formation as it rallied. The flak was a little more accurate than it had been before. Either that P-38 had a German pilot who radioed the altitude, or the Germans figured the formation would turn at the same point as the day before.

On the ground a German gunner rammed an 88mm shell into the breech and slammed it closed. Another gunner pulled the lanyard, and the big 88 belched smoke and recoiled as the projectile blasted into the air.

Seconds later STEVEONOVICH II (Black-N) shuddered as the 88 mm shell hit the left wing between the #1 and #2 engines. The impact blew away several large panels of aluminum skin that drifted back into the slipstream. The shell had severed the main wing spar and fuel and hydraulic lines. The #1 engine trailed a thin wisp of smoke, then erupted in fire.

464th formation climbing out over Italy. April 1945.

Bombs away as seen from a rear element.

In the cockpit, Lt/Col.Gilson and Capt. Foote were trying to get the engine shut down and the prop feathered, but it was a futile effort. The wing began to surge upward as the weakened ribs and aluminum gave way to the raging fire and aerodynamic force.

Within a matter of seconds, the wing started to buckle near the landing gear well. More fuel sprayed from the tanks, causing the fire to swell past the waist windows to the rudders. Aerodynamic lift and the power of the two Pratt and Whitney engines on the right side did the rest. Black-N spun counterclockwise as the wing folded back. STEVEONOVICH II completed her death spiral and began her final plunge towards the ground.

Ed Walsh was thrown clear of the bomb bay as the dying Liberator fell. He was able to open his chute, but several panels had been ripped. He landed in an olive tree, breaking both of his legs. He was captured and sent to a hospital in nearby Ferrara. When the Germans retreated they surrendered the hospital to him, and he would be liberated by advancing Allied forces.

The rest of the crew of Black-N were pinned in the dying Liberator as she spun towards the ground. There was no time for them to get to bail out stations, and the force of the violent spiral held them in place until the Liberator smashed into the ground.

The entire episode was captured on film by Leland Conrad, radio operator on White-Q, flying off the left wing of Black-N. The graphic photos of the Liberator flipping over would become some of the most famous photos of the air war.

The formation flew back to Pantanella without any other problems. On landing, it was found that seven other planes had taken minor flak damage and one had taken major damage. One plane was listed as missing, but later reports came in that the plane had landed at another base.

Ted Mouldenhauer waited in vain at his hardstand. He just could not believe that his Black-N had not made it back from the mission. He had always kept his plane in tip top shape like all of the other crew chiefs. It just did not seem fair that his plane had been lost to a lucky burst of flak.

The 464th running into clouds on the way to the target in April 1945.

When the word about the loss of Black-N got around the base the men could hardly believe it. Lt/Col. Gilson had been well liked by the men. Don Sherard recalled:

We arrived at Pantanella on the night of December 1, 1944. It was dark and raining, mud was several inches deep, and it was necessary to set up our tent in the rain. When a tent is wet on both sides it does not turn water. Some of the base personnel turned out to help us raise the tent. I was particularly impressed with a fellow who had no insignia on his fatigues, but who was supervising and helping set up the tents. I was surprised later to learn that he was a Lieutenant Colonel and was out there in the rain helping us get situated. His name was Colonel Gilson, and he was our squadron leader.

Jack Bosly couldn't believe that his life had been spared because of the simple fact that Maj. Morton had wanted to fly the mission. It all boiled down to, "there by the grace of God, go I."

Thirty-two B-24s of the 464th started taking to the air at 0809 on the morning of 11 April. The target for the day was the rail bridge at Campo Di Treno. Col. Zoller, Deputy Group Commander, would lead the group on the mission. Lt. Bennie Aday (779th) would be in the lead plane for the second attack group.

The 464th and her sister group, the 465th, got together as briefed and headed for the wing rendezvous. As they were getting in line with the 460th, the 485th cut in front of the formation. For a few very tense moments it looked like there would be a lot of mid-air collisions. After everyone's tempers and nerves settled down, the formation headed out over the Adriatic and on towards the target.

At the IP the group turned to the attack heading of 130 degrees. At the target 13 planes dropped over 32 tons of bombs from 24,000 feet. Now, the mission started to get messed up. In the second attack unit the lead bombardier could not see the target because of smoke from previous attacks. Seven planes from Baker Box hit the first Alternate at Vipiteno. Another group of nine planes from Able and Dog Boxes did not release because the lead bombardier had not set the bombsight up correctly. These planes hit the 3rd Alternate.

At the Primary target the formation had been under flak attack for about two minutes, and two of the planes had taken minor damage. There was no flak encountered at either of the alternate targets. After a lot of turning and flying around Robin Hood's barn the three formations got back together near Pistoia and headed back to Pantanella. The planes were all back over home plate by 1504.

On the 12th the group went after the Panti Di Piave railway bridge with 32 planes. Major Robert Laughry, Group Operations Officer, led the first plane off the ground at 0901. The group formed up into two attack units and headed out over the blue Adriatic.

The formation ran into some building clouds and had to make several turns to get around them. At the IP the weather had cleared, so a visual bomb run was set up. Just after the IP MICHIGAN B &P WOMEN (42-50728) lost the #3 engine. They left the formation and headed back towards the base. Just after leaving the formation the crew spotted a rail road and released their bombs onto the tracks.

Thirty-two planes arrived over the briefed target at 1239 and dropped over 73 tons of bombs from 20,000 feet. Since their axis of attack was 188 degrees there was no actual turn for rally. The group just nudged the throttles a little and headed for home.

Except for some turning to get around clouds the mission was considered a milk run. The crews welcomed the fact that no flak had been seen during the entire mission. There had been several sightings of possible fighters, but none of these sightings produced any attacks.

Bomb strike photos showed several direct hits on the bridge and along the approaches to the bridge. There was also a large concentration of bombs hitting just to the west and walking about 2,000 feet towards the north.

The 464th stood down from flying 13 April. Weather over potential targets was marginal, at best. The list of targets that were considered worth a visit from the bombers had shrunk, and with

DROOPY DRAWERS returns towards Italy with a solid undercast.

Vapor tarails in the sky as the 464th flies in the cold April skies.

that in mind, bad weather did not have to cover a lot of country to make it unwise to risk flying a mission.

The German war machine was just a shadow of its former self. The Russian Army was advancing towards the west and rolling over the German Army., and Allied forces were driving towards the East. In Italy the 5th and 8th Armies were moving north, driving the tattered remains of the German Army towards the Alps.

During the afternoon of the 13th, official word arrived that President Franklin D. Roosevelt had passed away the day before. Everyone was deeply saddened by the loss of the Commander in Chief. Although Roosevelt had often stated that he hated war, he had been America's number one soldier since the beginning. Now, the Allied forces would have to finish the job without him.

April 14th the group got the green flare for a mission to the ammunition factory at Palmanova, Italy. This was a tactical target. The idea was to deprive the remaining German forces from getting more ammo to fight with.

The first of 32 planes left the ground at 0800. The first attack unit was led by Col. Zoller, while the second unit would be led by Lt. David McKeever from the 778th.

Except for a major change in the route because of clouds, the flight to the target was as briefed. When the formation turned at the IP they spread out a little so they could try and cover the entire target.

At 1124 32 planes released over 69 tons of 250 pounders from about 19,000 feet. The release looked good, and some of the crewmen could watch the bombs fall all of the way to the ground.

From their altitude the men could see the bombs hitting the ground and exploding. The main concentration of bombs walked across the entire factory and into the storage area, and there were seven large explosions. Then, all at once, there was a really big flash. Merle Hoffman recalled:

Bombs went into every one of those encasements, and the whole dump went off at the same time. Then Dembeck (Raymond, ball turret) says, "Hey, looks like a smoke ring." And then the whole crew was talking about it.

There we were, starting to get back into formation, when this concussion ring hits us. The airplane just went crazy. It took that B-24 and threw it around like a piece of straw.

The formation was buffeted as the visible shock wave from the exploding ammunition grew like a giant bubble, then smashed into the planes as it reached their altitude. Tons of ammo had been turned to dust and smoke.

The group rallied and headed home. Most of the intercom chatter revolved around the big bang at the target, and there were lots of remarks about the fact that the German soldiers would not get many bullets from that place in the near future.

Bomb strike photos confirmed what the crews already knew. They had hit the target, and boy, did they hit it! The photos showed there were direct hits on all twenty storage units. The 464th's bombing score was excellent for the mission.

The 464th put together a Red-Blue Force mission on the 15th. For a change of pace the Blue Force, under Maj. James Anderson (776th), took off at 0905 with 16 planes to hit tactical targets in support of ground troops.

When Blue Force arrived over their target it was covered by clouds. With friendly forces below, the formation did not dare release their bombs, so they returned to base with the racks full.

Red Force left Pantanella with 42 planes at 1000. Col. Bird was the mission commander for the force. The second attack unit was under Capt. August Lechner (777th). Their mission was to hit targets in Area MA-22 in support of the American 5th Army.

Weather caused problems with form up. The individual combat boxes had to form up over the Adriatic, then fly back to Bari to get the group together. From this point, they flew over to Spinazzola for the rendezvous with the rest of the wing Red Force.

In his short tenure as Group Commander, Col. Bird had already shown himself to be a rather easygoing commander. In this case, having to travel all over the place to get the group together,

The 464th heading out over the Adriatic on April 25, 1945.

Col. Bird showed that he could be a "full bird." Merle Hoffman recalled a similar incident:

We were near the form up area. Starting to go over the spur of Italy, Bird was rasing hell with somebody. See, there was this guy on the ground, and finally he said, "You tell them 'J' Bird is giving 'em hell." We called him "J" Bird. He was a good guy.

Finally, the 55th wing turned west and headed for the Italian coast. By the time the formation was near Rome the clouds ranged up to about 24,000 feet. Just after passing Rome the formation turned towards the north. The farther north the Liberators flew, the more the clouds separated. By the time the formation reached the IP, the sky was CAVU.

At the IP, Red Force turned and headed towards the target on a heading of 25 degrees. It wasn't long before the marker panels came into view and identified the forward Allied lines. The localizer beacon was also picked up on the radio. It was evident that the formation was right where they should be.

The bombs from 42 planes were released at 1404, two minutes later than the flimsy said it should be. Over 42 tons of 100 pound bombs rained towards the German troop positions below.

Almost every time the group used the 100 pounders there were problems with either the racks or the intervalometers. Bombs hung up in five planes. These would later be jettisoned on the way back to Pantanella.

Just after bombs away flak opened up on the group. It was moderate and only lasted for about 30-40 seconds, and none of it was close enough to do any damage to the formation. Still, after the lucky shot that had brought down Black-N a few days ago, it was enough to cause the pucker factor to tighten up.

Photos of the target area showed excellent results. The target area was covered by bomb strikes, and the main highway was pulverized. If the Germans were going back to the Fatherland, they would have to walk.

The mission 15 April was the high point of Operation Wowser. The 15th Air Force put 1,233 bombers into the air that day, which

PAPPY'S PRIDE from the 776th headed for Linz on April 25.

One ship in trouble and leaving a trail of smoke. April 25, 1945.

represented 98.6% of the heavy bomber force in Italy. It had indeed been a "max effort."

During the afternoon of the 15th, Chaplain Eastwood led the 464th in a memorial service for the fallen Commander in Chief. The flag at Group Headquarters was lowered to half staff in mourning for President Roosevelt. Across the base, men paused from their duties for a moment of silence, in tribute to their fallen warrior. The service concluded to the haunting sound of the lone bugle as TAPS echoed across Pantanella Hill.

Operation Wowser continued on 16 April. The 464th was scheduled to put 42 planes into the air as their part of the day's mission. The target was enemy positions in Area ST-14 in northern Italy. Col. Bird flew the lead plane for the first unit, while Capt. Lechner (777th) would lead the second attack unit over the target.

Col. Bird left the ground at 0920 and headed for the form up area. The rest of the group found the lead ship and fell into the formation without any problems. The 464th was about two minutes early arriving over Andria, so Col. Bird signaled for a 360 degree turn. As the group came around from their turn, they fell into the proper position with the rest of the arriving wing. As the wing started to turn towards the briefed heading for departure to the target, the 485th appeared out of the haze and cut the 464th off. Col. Bird hit the radio waves with some unprintable adjectives—"J" Bird was giving 'em hell again!

The weather was not perfect, but the clouds wouldn't cause a recall on the mission. After passing near Rome, the clouds started breaking up. As the bomber stream neared the target area the clouds had moved back in and were classified as scattered.

At the IP the clouds were even thicker, but the lead bombardier could see the marker panels through the breaks in the clouds. It was enough to assure a safe bomb run. The group turned to the bomb run heading of 025 degrees and started the run to the target. As the planes got closer to the release point, the clouds moved in over the target.

There was some hurried chatter on the intercom between Col. Bird and the bombardier. The briefed aiming point could not be seen through the bombsight, but enough landmarks on the ground could be identified to assure that the first unit was over the target area and could safely release.

The first unit arrived at the release point at 1327, and they toggled 45 tons of clustered 250 pound General Purpose bombs towards the increasing undercast. The second unit arrived over the target, which by now was completely covered with clouds. The ground had simply disappeared. With American GIs somewhere below the second attack unit held onto their bombs and turned for home.

The Liberators of the 464th arrived back at Pantanella by 1552. It had been a milk run for the flight crews. They climbed out of the planes and headed for debriefing. Almost all agreed that these last couple of missions had been real easy ones.

The weather at Pantanella had warmed up enough so that the ball diamonds could dry out. Several teams had been formed, and the first pitch of the season had already been thrown. There was also increased activity at the horseshoe pits around the field. It sure looked like spring had finally arrived in Italy.

April 17th dawned, and the group was scheduled for a 1000 take off. This time, they were headed for Area ST-15 to support the 5th Army's attack on Bologna. There were 42 planes on the mission list. As with other missions during the last several days, the planes would carry 250 pound bombs.

For the third day in a row Col. Bird would be in the lead plane. Capt. Lechner would fly lead for the second unit. The planes formed up in the usual area and were over Spinazzola for wing rendezvous at 1155. So far, everything was on time according to the briefing.

Everything continued to go according to the flimsy until the group reached the IP. The 464th had to make a 360 degree turn to avoid running over the second attack unit of the 465th. As they came out of the turn, a bomb group from the 49th Wing was in the way. Col. Bird had little choice but to lead the first attack unit through another 360 degree turn to the left. During the second "a la plane left," the second attack unit of the 464th made a tighter turn and pulled ahead of Col. Bird's first attack unit.

The second attack unit arrived over the target at 1424 and released their load. The first attack unit arrived and released at 1433. A total of 92 tons of bombs were delivered from about 22,000 feet. Two planes had several bombs hang up on the racks, and these were jettisoned over the water during the return towards the base.

There were a total of six bursts of flak observed as the group rallied for home. All of them were low and way outside the formation. One plane reported a possible Me-262 jet flying on a 90 degree heading away from the formation just after the bombs were released. If it was a German jet, it was a long way from the nearest known Lufftwaffe jet base.

The group flew back along the briefed route and began landing at 1615 that afternoon. DROOPY DRAWERS (44-49374) ran short of fuel and landed at Rome to refuel. After the short pit stop, they returned to home plate at 1745.

Strike photos were disappointing. Both attack units had missed the briefed MPI by over a mile and a half. There were several secondary explosions in a wooded area, so the group must have hit something volatile.

The group stood down on the 18th. The ground crews had done a magnificent job of keeping the planes in shape during the last several missions. With the Operations Orders calling for 35 to 40 planes per mission, the crew chiefs had been real busy. The fact that there had not been much damage to repair helped to keep the group's operational aircraft status higher than it had ever been.

The 464th got 42 planes into the air on 19 April for a mission to Wels, Austria. The mission leader would be Col. Zoller, Deputy Group Commander.

For reasons unexplained, the mechanical Gremlins were overactive. Six planes aborted the mission with mechanical problems. Three planes had trouble with their #1 engine, and two of the planes lost the engine due to oil pressure problems. The other had a piston ring break.

The mission was flown as briefed to the Primary target. On arrival, the target was covered by clouds and visual bombing was impossible. At this point the group turned towards the alternate, but the alternate was also socked in. Sadly, all of the listed alternates were covered by clouds.

The group was released to bomb targets of opportunity or head home. Twenty planes returned with their bomb loads. MICHIGAN B & P WOMEN (42-50728) dropped their bombs on the Roveredo di Piano airfield. Another Liberator released on a know enemy flak position. Thirteen planes jettisoned their bombs because they were getting low on fuel.

Lt. Karl Berg (779th) in the flak hole caused by an 88mm shell hitting the wing of Black-Y on April 25, 1945.

The mission had been a disappointment. The group had covered a lot of country trying to get their bombs on target—any target. More tonnage had been jettisoned or returned than had been dropped on the enemy. Since there were two effective sorties the group was given credit for the mission.

It was "try it again," on the 20th. Forty-two planes left Pantanella to hit the bridge at Rovigo, Italy. The lead plane was flown by Maj. James Norman (778th). He lifted off the runway at 0815 that morning. The planes formed into the usual two attack units, with the second unit led by Lt. John Thornwall (779th). The two units found the 465th and left Spinazzola on time at 0931.

White-E (42-78472) from the 778th aborted the mission at 1110 when the oil pressure on #4 engine fell towards zero. The flight crew shut the engine down and left the formation. They were able to get back to Pantanella and make a safe landing on the three remaining engines.

Unlike the day before, the weather was fair to partly cloudy all the way to the target. Towards the northwest, the clouds were building to what looked like 25,000 feet. It was a good thing the planes did not have to fly any farther north.

The planes hit the target at 1208. The attack heading was 50 degrees. The 464th deposited 100 tons of 1,000 pounders smack on the target. Over 98% of the bombs were "on target." As far as accuracy, it was one of the best scores the group had achieved so far.

Flak bracketed the formation as the bombs were released. They would be in the deadly black puffs for about three minutes. It was classified as moderate and accurate, and it was accurate enough to cause minor damage to three of the planes in the formation.

On the morning of the 21st, 42 Liberators of the 464th took off, formed up, and headed for Northern Italy. The mission went fine until the bombers got near Florence, where the weather started falling apart; clouds were solid, topping out at 20-25,000 feet.

There was a lot of chatter on the radio. The leader of the 485th was heard to say he was turning away from the Primary and heading for the Alternate. At the same time, Maj. R.J. Laughry, mission leader for the 464th, decided to turn for the alternate.

At about 1301, the recall signal "SPOONFED" came over the airways, and the 464th turned away from the alternate target and headed home. They were back in the landing pattern by 1449.

The planes brought back the entire 105 tons of RDX bombs that they were supposed to deliver. Unless the bombload was changed for the next mission, the Ordnance crews would not have to load the planes with bombs.

There was no mission on 22 April due to bad weather over targets. That meant that the planes would be sitting on the ground with full bomb loads for at least another full day. This situation was dangerous, as it was an open invitation for sabotage. With that in mind, guards were posted along the flight line and at each hardstand, just in case somebody tried anything.

On April 23, 1945, the 464th was given the code Yellow Force. The mission was to hit the highway bridge #2 near Padua, Italy, and the bridge at Cavarzere, Italy. The Operations Order called for 42 planes for the mission. The group would divide into two units of 21 planes each, and as such it was nearly a Red-Blue Force mission.

The first unit would be led by Maj. James Anderson, Deputy Squadron CO of the 776th. The second unit would be under command of Maj. Elmer Balzar, Commanding Officer of the 779th. The group began taking off at 0915. They formed up and were headed for the target on time according to the briefing flimsy.

At 1355 the first attacking force was over the bridge and released over 52 tons of bombs. Most of the 1,000 pounders were right on target, and there were at least five direct hits on the main span of the bridge. Both ends of the bridge were also hit, and the approaches to the bridge were obliterated.

There were still some German defenders on the ground ready to take a few pot shots at the invading Liberators. Eight to ten bursts of flak trailed the group over the target, but none of the planes were hit. The group rallied and headed back. All of the planes of the first force were back to their hardstands by 1545.

The second unit left Pantanella at 0925 and flew towards form up and then the target. The second force had a little shorter distance to fly, so they were actually ahead of the first unit as far as the clock was concerned.

At 1223 the mission lead ship spotted what appeared to be a life raft floating in the Adriatic, and Maj. Balzar radioed the rescue service the position. He ordered the crew of LADY ESTHER to leave the formation and circle the object in the water. After a fruitless search, LADY ESTHER could not get back into the formation and returned to Pantanella.

The force arrived over the Cavarzere Bridge at 1336 and dropped over 32 tons of bombs onto the target. The lead bombardier in the last box set his sight on the wrong bridge. By the time the mistake was noticed, it was too late to correct. The seven planes of the box did not drop their RDX, instead bringing almost 30 tons of explosives back to base with them.

White-J over a solid undercast on April 26, 1945.

This force also had several pot shots taken at them by the gunners on the ground. There were a about 10 bursts, all of them far enough away to cause no damage to any of the Liberators.

Forty-two Liberators of the 464th went after the rail bridge at Brondolo on 24 April. The lead ship, with Col. Zoller at the helm, left the runway at 0700 that morning. The group formed into the usual double attack units, with the second unit led by Capt. Quay of the 777th.

For the 464th the mission was a milk run, though there were several interesting events on the way to the target. The weather ship, out in front of the formation, spotted an Me-109 that turned and headed towards the B-24. The Liberator broke hard right and dove towards the ground. The trick worked, and after turning around the German fighter was nowhere to be seen.

At 1055 the 464th spotted six Fw-190s about 3,000 feet below the formation. The fighters made no effort to climb and attack the bombers. At the same time, an Me-262 was spotted flying at about 22,000 feet. The jet made no turn to attack, either. It was evident that the heyday of the German fighter force was over.

The 464th turned to a heading of 104 degrees at the IP and headed for the bridge. At 1107 the formation released over 105 tons of bombs and turned for home as the flak began to burst about 2,000 feet below the formation.

The weather for the trip home was beautiful once the planes were over the Adriatic. By 1300 the planes of the 464th were in the pattern and making the PSP rattle.

On 25 April the group turned their attention to hitting rail yards again. The Primary target were the yards at Linz, Austria. "Yippee, Linz," always an old favorite! Thirty-two planes were scheduled for the mission. At 0845 Maj. Laughry lifted the lead plane off the runway. One plane had aborted on the ground.

In the form up area, the 31 planes sorted themselves out and formed into two units for the flight to the target. The second unit was led by Capt. Elton Clark (776th). By 0948 the group was over Andria and set course for the target.

Clouds behind them, the 464th nears the home field on April 26, 1945.

At 1110 42-51563 aborted the mission because the oxygen system was leaking. They flew back to Pantanella with their full bomb load and landed approximately at 1230.

Since the mission was a long haul to Linz, fighter escort arrived at 1130. The 30 P-38s would stay with the bombers just in case any of the Luftwaffe had enough fuel to get off the ground.

When the bombers reached the IP the formation turned to a heading of 154 degrees for the run to the target. Weather was clear, so the bombardiers set up their Nordens for a visual run.

At about 1319 the Germans greeted the 464th with the first bursts of flak. At first it was scattered, but as the formation got closer to the target the barrages got closer to the 464th. At 1321 the 464th crossed the final mile of airspace to the target and released over 72 tons of RDX towards the railyards below.

While the bombs were falling the flak intensified and became very accurate. The Germans were using big guns to fire at the 464th. Many of the crews believed that the Germans were using 105 mm guns. The flak batteries were also firing phosphorous shells at the rate of one to every other regular shell. Most of the phosphorus shells were bursting about 500 feet above the formation.

Black-Y (44-49402) took a direct hit from a shell in the left wing. The shell went through the wing without exploding on contact. Although crippled, the plane stayed in formation as the group rallied for home.

As the group passed beyond flak range, all agreed that it had been a long five minutes. It had been some of the worst flak that the fliers had seen in a long time, and Linz had once again lived up to its reputation.

The flight back was filled with tension for the crew of Black-Y. It appeared that the flak shell had missed the main spar. After what happened to Black-N over Lugo on the 10th everyone had his chute on, just in case the flak-torn wing started to buckle.

White-Y (44-49415) from the 779th landed at Zara when they ran low on fuel. Both plane and crew would return to Pantanella next day.

The planes began to arrive and land at Pantanella at 1605. When Black-Y rolled to a stop, the crew piled out to look at the large hole in the wing. It was large enough for a man to sit in and dangle his legs through. The plane was towed directly to the boneyard.

Compared to recent missions this had been a rough one. Seventeen planes returned with minor flak damage. Another plane besides Black-Y had sustained major damage and would be out of commission for several days.

For the last several days the men of the 464th had kept their eyes on the latest news from the front. The 5th and 8th Armies were driving the Germans north towards the border. The problem the Germans faced was there very few ways of getting back to Germany. Thanks to Allied air interdiction the roads, bridges, and railways were smashed. Patton's 3rd Army was driving east like a steamroller, while the Russian Army had entered Berlin and was now fighting the German resistance building by building.

Almost everyone figured it would not be much longer before the Germans would have to throw in the towel. The rumor mill was already working with, "I know a guy in supply who talked to Lt. So-in-so, who said he heard it from a cook, who overheard someone say that the Germans had offered to surrender to the British and Americans, but not the Russians."

On the afternoon of 25 April, Operations Order #216 arrived at the Headquarters of the 464th Bomb Group. The order called for 32 Liberators to attack tactical targets near Malcontenta, Italy. The usual routine began as the men started getting everything ready for the mission on the 26th.

The next morning the crews that were scheduled to fly were up and ready for the mission. At 0855 Col. Zoller led the group into the air, and the two attack units formed up and headed for Wing rendezvous.

When the 464th arrived at Andria the 454th BG (304th Wing) had invaded the 55th Wing's airspace. Since they were about 2,000 feet lower than the 464th there was no real danger, and the 464th departed for the target on time.

The 464th flew the route as briefed to the Rimini area. At that time they received a radio call from the leader of the 460th, who was near the target. The 460th was going to abandon the Primary and head for the alternate. The 464th turned right and headed for the alternate. At the IP, the group turned to 274 degrees and began the bomb run, but clouds prevented the group from dropping their bombs. Clouds to the north prevented any possibility of hitting any of the other alternates, so the group had no choice; they rallied left and headed home with their bombs still hanging from the racks.

The planes encountered clouds on the way back until they got to Rimini. Then the weather broke, and the planes had clear flying all the way back. The formation was in the pattern for landing at 1412.

The flight crews were disappointed that they had not hit the target and had to bring their bombs back. If weather was better, they could always deliver the bombs on the next mission. According to the rules set down by 15th Air Force and 55th Wing, the 464th should not be given credit for the mission. For some reason, now lost to history, the 55th Wing listed the 464th as having completed the mission and thus it was given credit. The mission for April 26, 1945, would go into the books as the 187th mission for the 464th.

The bombs they had brought back were not delivered the next day, as weather remained bad over northern Italy. On top of that, the German Army was falling apart and in full retreat. At this point, there was no real reason to fly a mission. Strategic targets were almost all neutralized, and only tactical targets remained—and to hit those, the weather had to be almost perfect.

The men of the 464th did not know it that day, but the ineffective mission on 26 April would go into the records as the last combat mission of the war for the 464th Bomb Group. The group had flown 19 missions during April, and they had delivered over 1,100 tons of bombs to targets that were assigned. The missions of Operation Wowser had helped to break the back of the German resistance in northern Italy. The real bright spot for the group was that the bombing scores for the month had been excellent. The 464th had the highest bombing accuracy for the 55th Wing. The final score for the month showed an average of 60.1% of all bombs within 1,000 feet of the Aiming Point.

It had been a good month for the 464th. Losses on combat missions had been very low, and bombing accuracy was the highest it had ever been. The war was almost over. It was just a matter of time until they could all leave sunny Italy and head for home. Well, at least that was what they had planned. But then there was something about "the best laid plans of mice and men...."

When the Russian Army entered Berlin, Hitler and some of his staff had retreated to a bunker for safety. During the last several days he had not dared venture out onto the rubble filled streets of Berlin. On April 30, 1945, the Russians were only several blocks away from the entrance to Hitler's bunker. Some time after 3:30 pm, Berlin time, Hitler took the coward's way out and shot himself.

Letting down near Pantanella. April 26, 1945.

7

Multulto Finito

May - Project Green - Coming Home

May 1, 1945, found the group being briefed for a mission. Although everyone figured flying missions were over, it seemed that they were going to have one more mission, just for good measure, and the crews were ready to go. At the last minute, the word came down from wing headquarters that the mission was canceled, and the group stood down from flying.

On the 2nd there was no alert for a combat mission, and that was fine with the flight crews. Most of them would take the day off, though there were several planes scheduled for routine flights to check out repairs that had been carried out during the last several days.

44-50471 was one of those scheduled for a routine flight. The plane had undergone work on some of the flight instruments and had to be checked out to make sure everything was done according to the manual. Lt. Robert Ray, Jr., would be the pilot and take a skeleton crew along for the flight.

Just after take off, one of the engines started acting up. It coughed, then belched a cloud of smoke, and Lt. Ray tried to gain enough altitude to turn back to the field for an emergency landing. The sick engine failed completely, and the B-24 started living up to its reputation of gliding like a brick. They were still too low to bail out, so the crew had to ride her down. The plane went out of control and slammed into the ground about five miles from the base.

Jack Bosley ready to go home. May 5, 1945.

Two of the crew were killed in the crash, while the other three emerged injured and were taken to the hospital. It was a cruel twist of fate that the reaper would strike and claim his last prize after combat flying was over.

At Pantanella field everybody figured that it was just a matter of time before the official word would come down from the top that the war was over. Everybody was sure that they would be headed back home within a short time. The big question was just when that was going to be. In good old Army fashion, it boiled down to "hurry and wait" for the word.

With almost 2,500 men milling about the base, Col. Bird had a problem on his hands. Since the group was not flying combat missions, there was a lot of time on the men's hands. Somehow, Col. Bird had to keep them busy. The solution was simple; they could fly practice missions in the local area. While some of the boys were out flying, the ground crews could work on the planes and make sure they were ready for the long trip back to the States, or England, or the Pacific. No matter where they were going to go, the 464th would be ready for their next duty assignment.

At 0241 on Monday, May 7, 1945, General Alfred Jodl signed the instrument of surrender for the German forces. The ceremony took place in a ramshackled school in the city of Reims. It was a simple surrender. Supreme Allied Commander General Dwight D. Eisenhower was absent from the formal ceremony. General Jodl simply signed the surrender at a plain wooden table and was ushered out. With Jodl's signature, 2,076 days of armed conflict in Europe came to an end. The war in Europe was over!

News of the victory spread across Europe like wildfire. Within hours of the formal surrender the teletype at Headquarters rang, then started clanking out the message that the men of the 464th had

Ready for the vicorty celebration at tent #22.

been waiting for. It did not take long for the news to travel from casa to casa, then down the hill to the hardstands. The bell in the base chapel started ringing to punctuate the good news.

It was the day that the men of the 464th had waited for a long time to hear, and there was only one thing to do at a time like that—celebrate! The war was over, and the men had to celebrate the fact that they had accomplished their mission and were victorious.

All kinds of parties broke out across, over, and around the hill. A lot of the boys had been saving their combat ration of booze for just such an occasion, and now it was time to put it to good use. Those that had not been saving the amber liquids managed to find a source for spirits. Vino, booze, and beer flowed like water. Boys will be boys at a time like this, and no celebration is complete without fireworks. Flares arched into the Italian skies from various locations around the base, and there were all kinds of expression for the moment.

After a day or so of celebrating the parties died away, and the men who had overindulged were trying to recover from their self inflicted wounds. With all of the celebrating, it would take a few more days for the heads to clear enough to think about other things at hand.

Now that the war was over, almost everybody was trying to figure out just when they would be moving off of Pantanella and home to the good old USA. Home meant just one thing, discharge from the Army. Now, in order to bee discharged you had to have enough service points. The men started to total up their points towards discharge. Time in service was so many, overseas time counted, and combat flying gave the fly boys an edge over the ground crews. Some of the guys figured that they had enough to get out and pin the "Ruptured Duck" on their lapel. All they had to do was convince the Army to get them out of Italy and back home.

Other than party, there wasn't much to do at the moment. Some of the men who had been in the service longer than the rest of the men received their traveling orders. As they left for home there were hard goodbyes and a promise to "look you up when I get back." While some left, others joined the 464th. During the last several days of April the group had taken on some men from the 98th Bomb Group. That group had been ordered back to the States, and some of the short timers were reassigned to the 464th.

Some of the men passed the time by playing softball, or pitching horseshoes. Others continued to work in their "Victory Gardens." If nothing else, the local Italians would have some fresh veggies when the group finally packed up and moved out. Since warmer weather was at hand, some of the men went down to the Ofanto river to take a dip or try to catch one of the native fish.

On 13 May the men of the 464th were still at Pantanella. A lot of them got up and abled off to church to give thanks for the end of the war. Then it was off to chow and back to the tent. Since it was Sunday the latest issue of *The Tower* was out, and the columns were full of items about the war being over.

During the last few days the rumor mill had been pretty busy with spreading the "straight poop" on just where the group was going to be sent. It seems the most informed sources believed that the flight crews would be sent back to the states, while most of the ground echelon would be sent to South America. Few of the men who had served on the ground could believe that the Army would dare do such a thing as that.

In the "Chow Line Chatter" column there was mention of all of these rumors. The column started, "Is Lt. Cole's rumor true? Are we going to Trinidad? Red Moulderhauer is all for it. He's been there before. You live in real barracks, he says, and work on the ships in hangars. It's not too hot, as there is a cool breeze from the sea. But, the mosquitoes are poison." The article went on to talk about the local sights and the fact that there was plenty of rum. It concluded by stating that "We probably won't go there. Or will we ?"

The days continued to come and go. The men were getting "itchy" to get movin'. Moving to almost anywhere that was even a mile or so closer to home, that is. They had a lot of time on their hands. Don Sherard recalled that they had to attend ditching drills

Victory in Europe demanded a party.

and spent time in the link trainer even if they were not pilots. Basically, anything to keep busy.

On 20 May another week had passed and another issue of *The Tower* was out. It would be the final issue of the group's paper, and this time it was subdued in its content. The staff seemed to know that it would be the last issue, and as such, it was full of memories and goodbyes to the men of the group.

In the "Spirit of 76" column there was yet another quip about where the group was going:

With rumors piled on rumors and some verified by the natural course of events, it doesn't require too much stretch of the imagination to see us moving out of here soon. The latest we've heard about the name "Trinidad" that has been so much bandied about is that its a code name for New York. Believe it?

Chaplain Eastwood wrote his last message to the boys he had come to know and love:

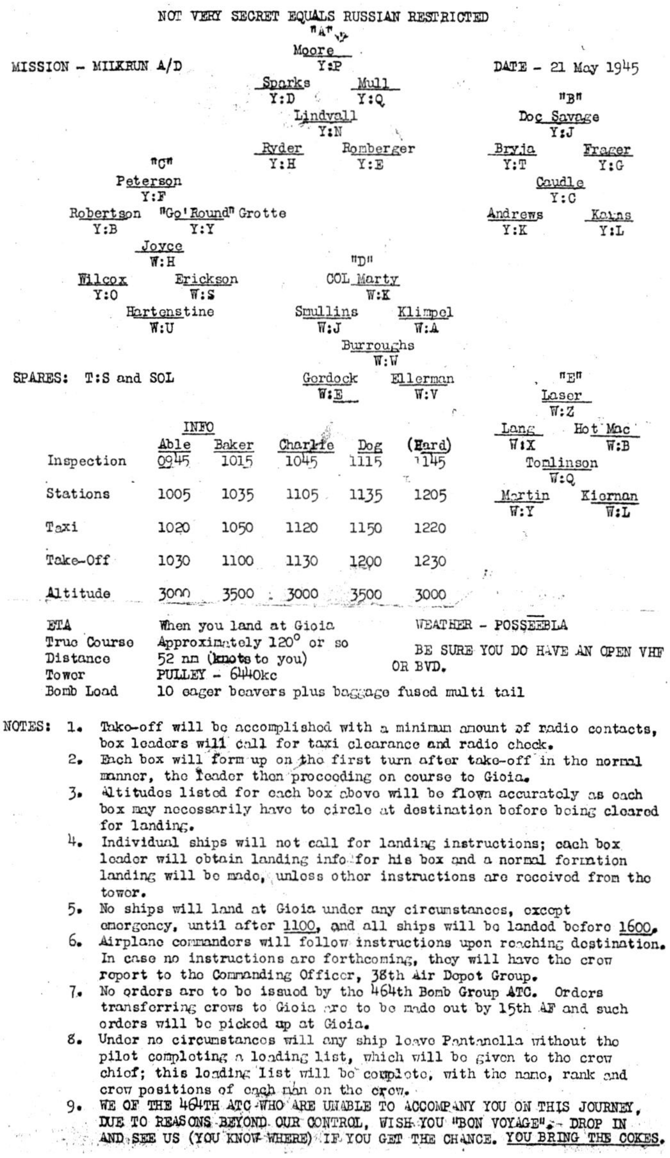

NOT VERY SECRET EQUALS RUSSIAN RESTRICTED

MISSION – MILKRUN A/D

DATE – 21 May 1945

"A": Moore Y:P; Sparks Y:D; Mull Y:Q; Lindvall Y:N; Ryder Y:H; Romberger Y:E

"B": Doc Savage Y:J; Bryja Y:T; Frager Y:G; Caudle Y:C; Andrews Y:K; Kains Y:L

"C": Peterson Y:F; Robertson Y:B; "Go'Round" Grotte Y:Y; Joyce W:H; Wilcox Y:O; Erickson W:S; Hartenstine W:U

"D": COL Marty W:K; Smullins W:J; Klimpel W:A; Burroughs W:W; Gordock W:E; Ellerman W:V

"E": Laser W:Z; Lang W:X; Hot Mac W:B; Tomlinson W:Q; Martin W:Y; Kiernan W:L

SPARES: T:S and SOL

INFO

	Able	Baker	Charlie	Dog	(Hard)
Inspection	0945	1015	1045	1115	1145
Stations	1005	1035	1105	1135	1205
Taxi	1020	1050	1120	1150	1220
Take-Off	1030	1100	1130	1200	1230
Altitude	3000	3500	3000	3500	3000

ETA — When you land at Gioia
True Course — Approximately 120° or so
Distance — 52 nm (knots to you)
Tower — PULLEY – 6440kc
Bomb Load — 10 eager beavers plus baggage fused multi tail

WEATHER – POSSEEBLA

BE SURE YOU DO HAVE AN OPEN VHF OR BVD.

NOTES:
1. Take-off will be accomplished with a minimum amount of radio contacts, box leaders will call for taxi clearance and radio check.
2. Each box will form up on the first turn after take-off in the normal manner, the leader then proceeding on course to Gioia.
3. Altitudes listed for each box above will be flown accurately as each box may necessarily have to circle at destination before being cleared for landing.
4. Individual ships will not call for landing instructions; each box leader will obtain landing info for his box and a normal formation landing will be made, unless other instructions are received from the tower.
5. No ships will land at Gioia under any circumstances, except emergency, until after 1100, and all ships will be landed before 1600.
6. Airplane commanders will follow instructions upon reaching destination. In case no instructions are forthcoming, they will have the crew report to the Commanding Officer, 38th Air Depot Group.
7. No orders are to be issued by the 464th Bomb Group ATC. Orders transferring crews to Gioia are to be made out by 15th AF and such orders will be picked up at Gioia.
8. Under no circumstances will any ship leave Pantanella without the pilot completing a loading list, which will be given to the crew chief; this loading list will be complete, with the name, rank and crew positions of each man on the crew.
9. WE OF THE 464TH ATC WHO ARE UNABLE TO ACCOMPANY YOU ON THIS JOURNEY, DUE TO REASONS BEYOND OUR CONTROL, WISH YOU "BON VOYAGE". DROP IN AND SEE US (YOU KNOW WHERE) IF YOU GET THE CHANCE. YOU BRING THE COKES.

Briefing flimsy for the final flight towards home. May 21, 1945.

Friends We Won't Forget

As we prepare to leave this hill and Italy, it is natural to spend a little time in reminiscence, recalling some of the scenes and faces that have come and gone during our days of labor here together. I find that many of my most vivid memories are of men who gave their lives or who are reported missing. News that they were to return no more seemed to engrave some word or action of theirs indelibly upon my memory. Tonight, those scenes and actions keep coming back to me.

Col. Bonner greeting us when we first arrived—Charlie Gibbs, James Hinson, Roy Wilson, Charles Mills and the rest of the crew joking about seeing me in chapel, for it was a dark Sunday morning and they were sure it would be a stand down—Bert Hayes smiling and waving as he taxied his plane towards the runway—Martin Neuhaus talking to some friends the night before his fiftieth mission—Jesse Ward, Ralph Baker, Robert Wise, Paul Bunnell and others on their crew joking and laughing as they waited for take off—Raymond Bloxsom playing ball with some of us down by the river—John Sevey putting finishing touches on the Officer's Club—Benjamin Folsom, Radler, Kidd, Taege, Fowler and Friendlich and White feeling like a family laying a brother to rest as they stood at the open grave of their nose gunner, Cluade Orrell—Robert Hornbaker singing "Benneth the Cross of Jesus" at a morning service. Don Garniss, John Durisko, Earnest Hindle and John Rankin sitting together in chapel on Sunday evening—James Lemon saying a prayer as he knelt to take communion—Gale Butler telling of his children and plans for the future—Owens, Sample, Shields, Powell and all the others hard at work linking ammunition and Welsh telling me of his wife's ill health as he worked with fuses—James Gilson sitting in my office writing some words of comfort to parents of one of his men. George Wall telling me on that last morning he believed he would make the thirty-five—Charles Foote promising to send an enlisted man to rest camp—George Setser talking about his mail and Weldon Burton saying, "We'll sure be back in time to dedicate that chapel."

What precious memories they are, for they are of men who have purchased our blessings and opportunities. Our future is made sacred by their sacrifice. As we move on to other tasks may these memories stir within us a deep and burning desire to live for others as these our fellow soldiers have sacrificed for us.

By May 21st, things were starting to get hectic around Pantanella Hill. Word had come down from the top that the aircrews would be departing for the States within the next several days. For the flight crews that meant "start packing for home." For the crew chiefs it meant they had to make sure that their ship was ready for the long trip back across the pond. The ship had to be in tip top shape for the trip; after all, the lives of the crew would depend on how well they did their job one last time. Perhaps, this was the most important final check that they would make on their ship. Their plane and crew were going home.

Ground echelon moves out towards their Project Green assignment via trains in Italy.

On the morning 22 May, 37 crews attended a special briefing for the next mission. The briefing flimsy was rather strange for the mission. The mission was listed as "Finis," and spare ships were listed as T:S and S.O.L. Bomb Load—10 eager beavers, plus baggage fused multi-tail, Target- YOUR WIFE or BEST GIRL, Weather...Undoubtedly.

The first of the planes took off at 1030 and headed for the regular form up area. As each box was formed up they flew back over the field for one last pass in review. From Pantanella the individual boxes flew down to Gioia del Colle and landed. The first leg of the trip was a total of fifty-two nautical miles.

At Gioia the men waited for their individual flight orders back to the States. They exchanged their military script for good old United States currency and got ready for the trip across the pond. As the orders came in the flight crews would head out to their assigned aircraft and begin the preflight checks.

Since these planes were headed home a lot of them were loaded with extra equipment. This equipment, for the most part, was a lot of junk that the military wanted to transport back to the States. It was not only junk, it was extra weight for the planes to carry back across the ocean.

A lot of the pilots complained about the extra weight that they were supposed to carry back with them. They were told that it was an order. The solution was simple. When they took off, they flew out over the water and dumped the extra baggage into the water, claiming a malfunction had occurred and they had to do it or lose the ship.

The route that the planes took was from Gioia to Marrakech by way of Tunis and Oran. The flight was about eleven hours if the weather along the way was good. After reaching Marrakech the planes and crew usually rested overnight. The next leg of the trip home was a hop to the Azores.

From the Azores it was a long flight over the Atlantic to Gander, Newfoundland. This was another long haul, and every bit of it would be over water. The crews hoped that the planes would not have any problems, since there wasn't any place to get out and walk.

Donald Bahnsen's crew had been assigned Black-M to take back to the States. Bombardier Don Sherard recalled the flight to Gander:

We flew through one weather front and saw a large number of icebergs. As we approached Newfoundland the weather began to close in, and it was raining. On this flight Kephart did an exceptional job of navigation. We were required to maintain radio silence, so it was necessary that he navigate the full distance of the crossing. The coast of Newfoundland is heavily timbered, dotted with lakes, and crossed with rivers, so it is difficult to pick out any distinctive landmarks. As we neared the coast it was necessary to reduce our altitude to approximately 500 feet to stay under a heavy cloud cover in the hard rainstorm. Kephart had done such a meticulous job of navigation that he was able to identify the mouth of a particular stream. He stood between the pilot and copilot, giving them directions and following the stream until he could point out the end of the runway in the rainstorm."

This crew would spend another three days at Gander before the weather would clear enough for them to continue.

Merle Hoffman and crew were also on their way back to the States. They were flying Red-R and had left Italy at the same time as Bahnsen's crew. Hoffman recalled:

We took off at Gander Field, Newfoundland. By the time we picked the nose wheel off the runway we were in weather. Raining! We flew from Gander to Portland, Maine, without seeing our inboard engine, and the B-24 leaked. I had these high boots on and was just sitting there with water running down into my boots.

Liberty Ship used to take the 464th to Brazil.

When they approached Bradley Field, Hoffman and his crew beheld quite a sight:

I bet there were 5,000 people. It was Memorial Day, and they were standing there outside the fences waving their little flags, and those battle weary planes were a coming in over their heads. I bet I wasn't 10 feet above their heads. Why they let those people out there I do not know. We were coming in one every 30 to 40 seconds. You know, if one of those old things had trouble, they could have wiped out a lot of people.

Don Sherard:

On May 30th we took off from Gander for Bradley Field, Connecticut. We encountered two weather fronts, and Bahnsen had to fly on instruments for four or five hours. In one of the fronts, ice formed on the leading edges of the wings and on the propellers; however, there was not enough to become dangerous. When the ice started breaking up and coming off of the propellers, it sounded like a machine gun when the pieces of ice hit the fuselage. We broke out of the weather over Portland, Maine, and it was exciting to see our country again.

When Black-M landed at Bradley Field they were about to finish a very interesting part of their mission home. Don Sherard wrote:

To a certain extent air crews owed their lives to the crew chiefs, who were the ground mechanics that inspected and kept the planes in repair. One of the chiefs was very much attached to a mongrel dog that he had, and before he left Italy, he asked us if we would take the dog with us as a stowaway on our plane. He said he would meet us in the States and pick up the dog. We allowed the dog (whose name was FLAK) a free run of the plane while we were in the air, but when we were on the ground we locked him in the lower ball turret, hoping that he would not be discovered. When we landed at Bradley Field the crew chief met us while we taxied in. We let the dog out, and the two had a reunion. Bringing pets into the country was strictly prohibited, but I doubt that the dog would have been carrying any more diseases than his human counterparts.

From Bradley Field most of the returning planes were shuttled on to Hunter Field, near Savannah, Georgia. If the crew had not already been busted up, they parted company with each other at Savannah and headed to their respective homes on leave.

Back in Italy, the ground grippers were also busy getting ready to head back across the Atlantic. By the end of the month most of the men had packed up their allotted baggage and had been moved to Gioia del Colle for processing and staging. A lot of them had already gotten the "sad word" that they were not going to the States. Instead, they were headed for Trinidad under what was called PROJECT GREEN.

Some of the men of the 464th were left behind at Pantanella to tear the place apart. Everything that was military was taken apart and packed away for the trip back to the States aboard ships. Across the hill and valley that had once been a thriving Army base were now just piles of lumber and other rubbish.

When the last truck left Pantanella and turned off the lights, so to speak, it did not take long for the local Italians to move in and salvage anything that the Americans had left behind. They made quick work of what was left, and within a matter of days it would have been hard for the men of the 464th to recognize their former home away from home.

Depending on just what their job was in the Army Air Force, the men of Project Green were transported to Trinidad by various means. "Red" Moldenhauer was one of the lucky ones. He and some of the men left Italy and flew to Marrakech, then on to Casablanca. On 15 June they boarded a C-54 transport and flew across the pond to Natal, Brazil. From there they flew on C-47s to Waller Field, Trinidad.

The rest of the men of the 464th that didn't fly were loaded aboard the U.S.S. *Lyons* at Naples harbor and transported to Trinidad. The 464th was no longer a bomber outfit; they had been transferred to the Air Transport Command.

Project Green was put into effect as a means of bringing the military home from Italy. Most of the men coming through Trinidad were wounded or had a higher priority assigned to them to get home. There was also a lot of equipment that had to be brought home. Since there were a great deal of airplanes coming in, there had to be qualified men there to service and repair them, which was the reason that the men of the 464th had been sent to Trinidad.

The men of Project Green settled into a rather hectic, yet at times humdrum life. They worked on the planes to keep them in good shape. When they were not working, a lot of them would travel about and see the local sights—and what sights to see. There were sandy beaches, and the water seemed crystal clear. It was not terribly hot most of the time, since the sea breeze came in and kept it tolerable. During their off time they could always go into town and get a good "rum and Coke."

In June, the paperwork had finally found its way out of the dark halls of the Pentagon. Under the provisions of General Order Number 3507, the 464th was awarded a Distinguished Unit Cita-

A C-46 on the rain soaked field in Brazil, July 1945.

Local river transportation on a Brazilian river, July 1945.

tion "for outstanding performance of duty in armed conflict with the enemy." While most of the men who had served with the 464th in Italy did not know it, they were now entitled to wear a cluster to their Distinguished Unit Citation. It had been awarded for the group's mission of 24 August to Pardubice.

With the war effort now concentrating on the Pacific there was little need to retain many of the heavy bomb groups that had flown in Europe. It would just take too long to retrain the whole group into the B-29. According to the Pentagon, there were enough B-29 groups already activated to do the job in the Pacific. In view of that, many of the groups that had served in Europe were now deactivated, and the 464th was no exception. On July 31, 1945, the 464th was deactivated as an active military unit.

In August 1945, on a small island in the Pacific, a lone B-29 headed for Japan. The single bomb that the B-29 dropped would speed the end of the armed conflict in the Pacific. After the atomic bomb was used on two of its cities the Japanese Empire called it quits, and the war in the Pacific was over.

When news of the end of WWII reached the men that were still serving under Project Green they were more elated than ever. The end of the war in the Pacific meant that they would soon be going the rest of the way home to the States. Since there had been parties after the war was over in Europe it was natural that the men celebrate the final victory.

Shortly after the end of the war the men of Project Green were alerted that they would be returning to the States fairly soon. Just how soon was a matter of question to the men. The war was over on both fronts, and they wanted to get home. A lot of the men had to wait until mid-September before their orders came through.

Most of the men of the 464th pinned their "Ruptured Duck" on their lapel and traded their Army kakhis for moth balled civvies. Their service was over, and it was time to get on with their lives. Some stayed in the military and made it a way of life. Either way, they were proud of their service and the group they had served with.

The heritage of the 464th Bomb Group was transferred to the Air Transport Command, and ultimately the Tactical Air Command on February 1, 1953. The actual designation would live on as the 464th Troop Carrier Group, and they would now fly the C-46 and C-119. The group would continue to serve on under TAC and finally be transferred to the Military Airlift Command after the cold war. Under the new designation the heritage of the 464th lives on at Pope Air Force Base in South Carolina.

Every two years the men of the 464th Bomb Group Association get together at a host city, somewhere in the States. They come together to renew old friendships and spin "war stories" about the days when they were part of the group. Each time they meet, their ranks have been thinned by the passing of comrades. There are empty chairs, as there were empty tents after a hard mission. In their own way they remember those that are no longer with them. Perhaps it is a raised glass, or a tear, perhaps a chuckle. No matter how they do it, it is done out of respect for a brother at arms.

There will never be another 464th Bomb Group. There will never be another Pantanella Hill. The memories of those hectic, horror filled days of combat in WWII are fading with the passage of time. While those memories fade from sight, it is only hoped that a member of a future generation will take the time to read what is written in this history of the 464th Bomb Group and remember what those brave men did to preserve the freedom and democratic way of life that we have come to love. Hopefully, after reading of their sacrifices that young person will close the cover and say "God bless the men of the 464th."

464th Photo Album

A Typical Mission

Getting ready to climb aboard their ship for the mission.

A B-24 taxies towards the runway.

A radar "Mickey" ship leads the line up.

The countryside reverberates with the sound of engines getting ready to take off.

Black-U lifts off the runway.

Form up complete, a nine ship element flies over Pantanella.

Wing rendezvous.

Over the Adriatic the formation tightens up as a Liberator moves into the slot.

At the Key Point the formation heads towards the target route.

White-T viewed from the cockpit of a sister ship.

Vapor trails in the cold skies.

At the IP the group begins the bomb run to the target.

White-D flies through flak as the group approaches the target.

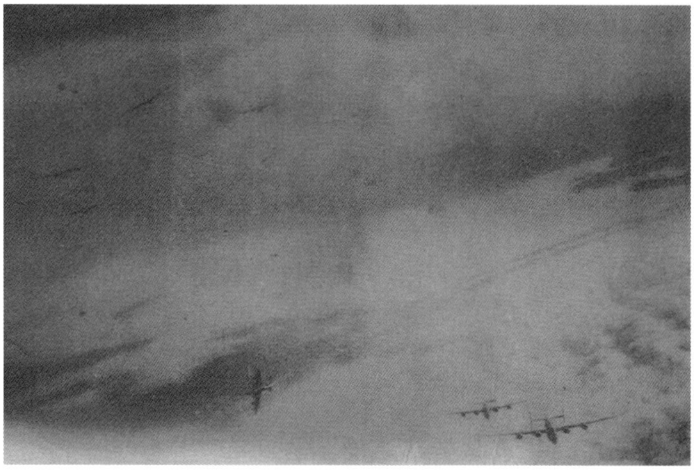

A B-24 hit by flak pulls out of formation.

As she falls a wing rips away.

Flak; DANGER CLOSE!!

Bombs Away!

BIG WHEELER DEALER unloads over the target.

Heavy flak follows the group as they begin the turn off of the target.

The flak follows the group during the rally.

The 464th heads home after hitting the target.

A Me-109 makes a pass looking for stragglers.

Red-F casts a shadow and halo on the thin clouds below as she heads home.

As the group arrives home they break away for the landing pattern.

One by one, the planes come home to Pantanella.

An empty hardstand of a ship that didn't come back. Hopefully, that's her landing in the background.

The planes that made it back taxi to their hardstands.

Glad to be back on the ground, the crew gets ready for the ride up the hill to interogation.

A plane crashes as she comes home. Part of the crews had to be cut from the wreakage.

Interogation: Reliving the mission for the daily mission report.

Pantanella in Pictures

Aerial view of Pantanella Field. The twin hills are in the left forground. 465th BG in forground with the 464th just beyond. The 464th hardstands in the center, twin runways, then the 465th hardstands. View is looking towards the west.

Hardstand area and end of the 464th runway. 779th in the forground. Looking towards the east.

Opposite end of the runway. 776th area in forground. Looking towards the west.

Above Right: The twin hills of Pantanella. 464th in forground. Runway and hardstand area to the left,out of the photo.

Right: Pantanella Hill looking south. Photo taken while flying over the runway.

Pantanella Hill looking towards the runways. Note the ball diamond in the middle left of the photo.

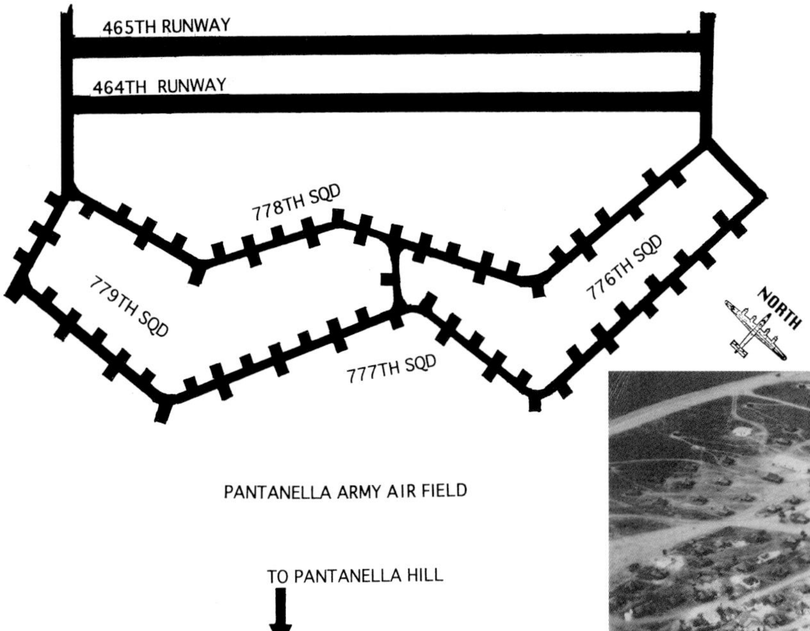

Diagram of runway and hardstand area for the 464th.

Looking down on the 464th. 776th Officers Mess at the lower left. Chapel at the center of photo. Two long buildings at the right are mess halls.

Commanding Officer's Quarters.

Group S4 and photo lab, February 1945.

Group Headquarters and Briefing Room,February 1945.

Group Theater and Gym under construction.

Outdoor Theater (left) Chapel and Dispensary in background.

Chapel, showing rear facade.

Bell Tower and dedication on front of Chapel.

Worship Service.

Chapel decorated for Christmas 1944.

Relaxing in the 778th Officers Club.

778th Officers Club bar.

Interior of the Club. Ping Pong table in the background.

Little Casa on the hill.

One of the casas in the valley near the hardstands.

777th Squadron street on the hill looking north, October 1944.

Race Card Tower during the fire in early 1945.

A nice warm (?) shower.

A no privacy privey.

Chow hounds line up at the 777th mess area, February 1945.

Constant Training Kept the 464th Sharp

Link trainer area.

Getting some ground time in the Link trainer.

Bombardiers had a chance to keep the razors edge sharp.

Gee Navigation mock up and trainer.

Right: H2X "Mickey" trainer.

464th Gunnery School

Capt. J.S. Edwards, Officer in Charge.

Original Gunnary School Personel. L-R. Marvin Nelson Capt. Edwards, Lawrence Stephens.

Rear L-R. Marvin Nelson, Fred Littlepage, Bean, Waddill. Front L-R Capt. Edwards, Lawrence Stephens.

Lawrence Stephens points out turret operations to students.

Marvin Nelson explaining details of turret operation.

On the skeet range.

Bean going over .50 cal gun details with students.

Marvin Nelson explaining electrical circuitry for the Martin upper turret.

Turret mock ups.

The "Jam Handy."

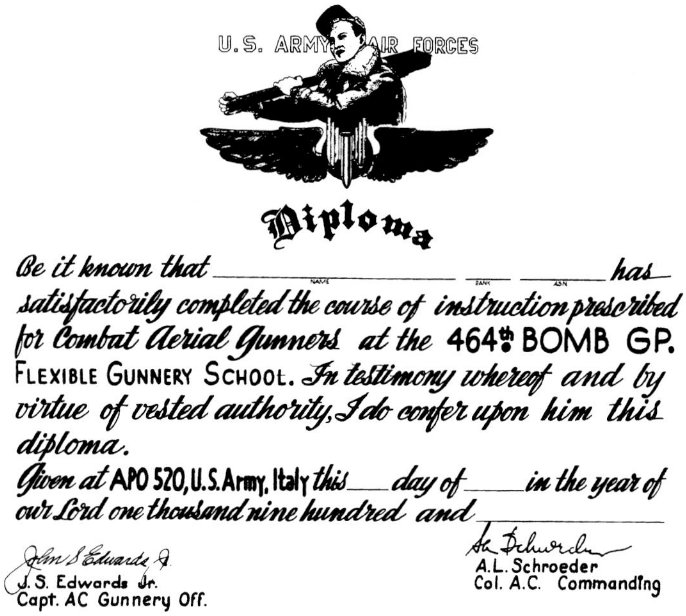

U.S. ARMY AIR FORCES

Diploma

Be it known that ______ ______ ______ has satisfactorily completed the course of instruction prescribed for Combat Aerial Gunners at the 464th BOMB GP. FLEXIBLE GUNNERY SCHOOL. In testimony whereof and by virtue of vested authority, I do confer upon him this diploma.

Given at APO 520, U.S. Army, Italy this ____ day of ____ in the year of our Lord one thousand nine hundred and ______

J. S. Edwards Jr.
Capt. AC Gunnery Off.

A.L. Schroeder
Col. A.C. Commanding

464th Gunnery School Diploma.

Unsung Heroes that "Kept 'em Flying"

Inside view of the damaged plane.

Above Left: Planes came back with incredible battle damage. This Liberator bellied in. Her ground crew started working to get her operational again.

Left: They will put a new belly in the Liberator and get her back in the air.

L-R. Marshal, Robert King, Rod Binger. "Sunny Italy—NUTS"

Unidentified groundcrewmen.

Ground crew who kept THE SKIRT PATROL mission ready.

Line Crew 777th Sq, May 1945.

THE GREEN HORNET and her crew.

Mason Alexander beside his ship.

William Veron (center) and his ground crew.

Working on the big Pratt & Whitney engine.

Instrument Specialists checking out the pitot tubes on a Liberator.

John Ernst crew chief of THE SULTAN.

Where did the rest of the plane go!

777th Armament Section. Pocatello Idaho, Jan 1944.

Left: 779th Ground Crew personel.

Opposite: Checking out the #4 engine on a 464th Liberator.

L-R John Pohed, Richard Shores, "Red" Moldenhauer, Steve Schwich, and Fred Riggs, Dec 1944.

Ground Crew for LITTLE ROCKET.

778th Engineering Section, June 30, 1944.

Far right M/Sgt Tom Scott (777th), other unidentified.

Herman "Red" Moldenhauer and brother Ted Moldenhauer (779th) June 22, 1944.

Turret specialists working on a Sperry ball turret.

Jack Shipman (779th).

They will have the turret back in the ship for the next mission.

Sgt. "Lee" Miller crew chief, LITTLE ONE.

"Fig" Newton, crew chief.

Down on a hardstand; Interesting entry way to the shack in the background.

Getting ready to change the #1 engine.

Lonnie McMichael crew chief of BOOZIN SUSAN.

L-R Steve Stephenson, Ray Perlow, and Art Brinkerhoff. Front: Lonnie McMichael. (779th)

Engineering Section 777th.

L-R Rear. Sgt Dudley, William Barron, and Willis Burke. Front: John Olive, John Graham, and John Booth.

William Barran and John Graham work on their motorcycle project.

John Graham crew chief PISTOL PACKIN MAMA.

L-R. Esteus Coldwell, Frank Ross, Chet Mendyka, Lavere Hanson, and Ken Righardt from the 777th pose after changing an engine in 4 and a half hours to set a record that was written up in Stars and Stripes.

Faces of the 464th

Col. A.L. Schroeder, 2nd Commanding Officer of the 464th.

Col. A.J. Bird Jr. Final Commanding Officer 464th.

Lt/Col. Charles McKenna Deputy Co. & Col. A.L. Schroeder

Capt. Foyle Beasley. Group Comm Officer, Jan 1944.

Capt. Kyle Spiller Jr. Group Nav. Jan 1944.

Capt. Royal Cato, Group Bombardier Jan 1944.

Capt. S.F. Martin, Operations Officer 778th.

Maj. Morris, 776th Adjt.

Maj. Weldon Burton.

Capt. Lacey Morton, Group Navigation Officer.

Capt. Myron Mershon, Operations Officer 776th.

Capt. Dave Camera, Public Relations Officer.

Lt/Col. Clarence Poff.

Father McChahey celebrating Mass.

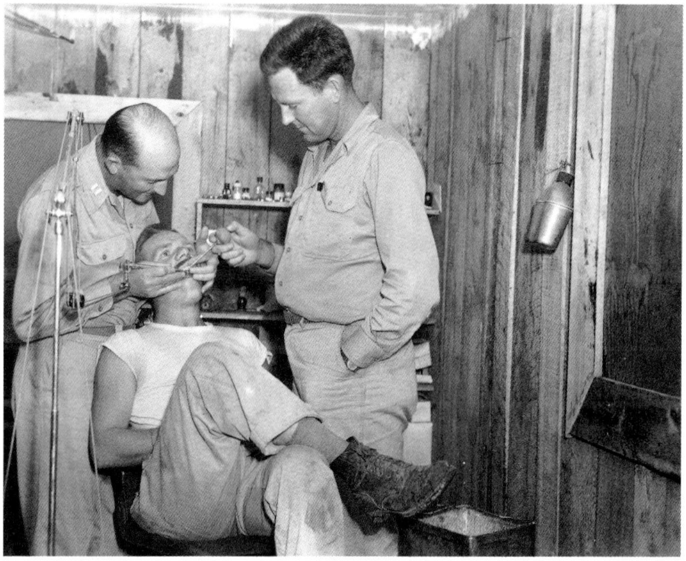

Dr. Russel, Dental Officer.

Staff Officers of the 777th, June 1944.

Capt. William Shoemaker.

Capt. Raymond Drake (Left), first to finish 50 missions in the 464th. Man on the right is unidentified.

Phillip Turner, Race Card Tower operator.

John "Doc" O'Hara, Flight Surgeon 777th.

L-R: Tony Schneider, Gerald Welstad, Matt Arlington, and John Gottschauk—Tent#22.

Robert Riccardini, 777th.

Ray Quick, ball turret gunner from Smullins crew, doing his laundry.

Tom McConnell (Bombardier) and Geroge Marshall (Nav) from Smullins' crew in front of their tent.

William Gilfillen, 464th HQ.

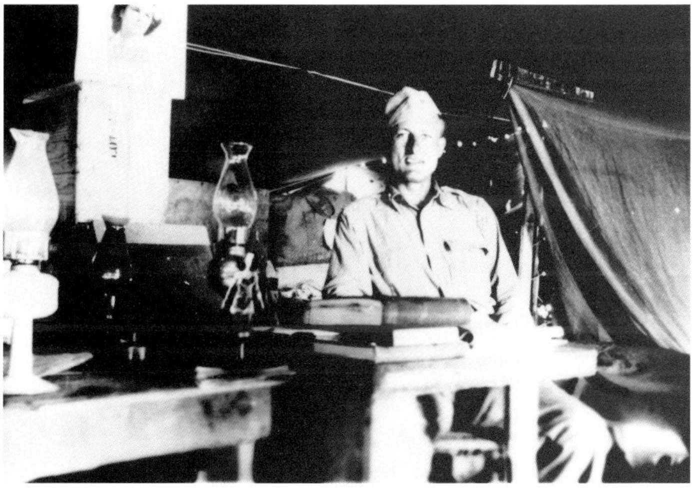

William J. Meier, 778th.

T/Sgt Huff, Orderly Room Clerk 776th.

Al "Friso" Tostado.

Lewis Janky (May's CP) relaxes in tent #22.

M/Sgt H.O. Peterson.

Franciscus, 776th Orderly Room Clerk.

Vance Edwards, 776th Orderly Room Clerk.

Robert and Ralph Newberry, Cooks Enlisted Mess 776th.

Lt. Lynn Davidson, KIA February 29, 1944.

Robert Wingfield (L) and Robert Holcomb(R) getting ready for a mission.

James Fisher, Tailgunner 778th.

William Maxson 779th.

George Beato.

Mike Yurusta—one of the first members of the 778th to finish 50 missions.

Donald K. Waldron, pilot 777th, September 1944.

Albert Danoff (Nav) and Don Weir (Copilot) 777th, September 1944.

Francis R. Holley, KIA July 7, 1944.

Standing L-R: James Trent, Bill Miller, Frank Morgan, and James Sealora. Front L-R. Edgar O'Brian, James Holmes.

Billie Silkwood.

\Rear: William Fears, George Stockinger. Front: Ellis Loree,George Krynovich

L-R James Dlinder, Rick Ferris, and Leonard West, Part of SLEEPY TIME GALS original crew.

Washing the mess kits, Pantanella 1944.

L-R Maj. George Carney, 464th; Capt Potter, 5th Army; Lt. Tutle, 5th Army; Maj. Hansen, 5th Army; and Lt. McCowen, November 13, 1944.

2/Lt. Charles Stanley.

Flight Crews of the 464th

Left: Back L-R E. Burroughs, Herschel Higdon, Geroge McMillian. Front L-R Morris Apsel, Harry Player, Elmer Griffiths, Robert Flammer, Howard Farling, Robert Hoskinson.

Standing L-R. Dean Lovitt, Wally Roberts, Howard Drollinger, Ed Horst. Front: John Chmelin, George Kroll, Jerry Long, Ed Aubray, Tom Beyer, John Holzapfel.

Rear L-R: James Miller (KIA), Walter Kubic, Matthew Garrow (KIA), Joe Kester, Bill Brown, Manny Vierce. Front L-R. Elmer Anderson, Warren McDonald, Bill LaCoss, Ken Timmerman.

Rear L-R: Joe Kolacia, Chalres Benchiere, Chales Lamerding, Jerome McGrath. Front L-R Robert Babcock, James Cott, John Margaroli, Williiam Douglas, Francis Villians.

Top L-R Ray Borg, Tom Carrothers, Rex Bryant, Gene Jalin. Middle L-R Robert Wagner, Ziehm Warner. Front L-R Wilton Albott, Robert Kelly, Burt Landberg, John Anderson.

Rear L-R Howard Huggins, Robert Johnson, Charles Tarver, Robert Garlock. Front L-R Gerald Bartung, Dale Tues, Ralph Seva, D. Gregary, Eddie Barsegewski, Hugh Wintermeyer.

Standing L-R Ken Bailey, Byron Lockren, Howard Natt, John Taylor, Eugene Mensinger. Front L-R Robert Weinberger, Leslie Owen, Victor Montgomery, Don Tate, Peter Doelder (KIA).

Rear L-R John Bertaux (KIA),Chester Kiolbasse(KIA) Charles Gustina (KIA), Mardy Fried (KIA). Front L-R Matthew Streit, Joe Guadagne (KIA), Anthony Aiallo, Richard Peterson, Fernendo Ronel (KIA), Darwin Carlson.

Rear L-R. Lenny Mates, Jim Bantes, Norm Smulley, Howard Ellerman, Jerry Felzica. Front L-R Jake Yonguorgt, Al Bogner, Wally Hieblmeier, Gene Taylor.

Front L-R Fowler, Klika, Kaufman, Ciprian. Rear L-R Nethercott, Fuller, King, Rosenbaum.

Rear L-R Charles Fowler, Rex Edwards, Harry Helion Jr., Ed Merling. Front L-R Mike Galvan, Tom Stephenson, Rudd Spints, Gene Lorent, George Allen, Vito Jicobbi.

Rear L-R Bruce Cato, Robert Rector, William Hartler, Dwight Baker. Front L-R Russel Kynoch, Robert Blazek, Glenn Blackburn, Joe Caporali, Frank Ramsey, Alvin Peterson.

Rear L-R James Moumaw, Clyde Huff, Carl Nelson, Walter Ralph. Front L-R Henry Benner, George Culliton, Earl Borland, Ron Passmore, Thomas Gray, Ray Crandell.

Rear L-R William Myers, Joe Hillis, William Lane, Joe Pohl. Front L-R. Charles Martin, Ed Luhaney, Ivan McKirgan, Charles Coffman, Dudley Snyder, Don Croy.

Standing L-R D Nan, W Laughlin, Chalmers, Mylan. Front L-R John Hare, Ralph Carver, Richard Nicholson, William Pratt, John Benson, William Hedge.

Rear L-R Don Gillian, Sherman, Vincent Iaccino, Frank Kinberger. Front L-R. William Titus, Joe Suels, Harold Harer (KIA), John McGovern, James Maxwell, Veriel McFall.

Rear L-R Robert Cunnignham, Richard Witt, William McGowen, John Fassnacht (KIA). Front L-R Ray Hadden, Merton Haigh (KIA), James Hutchinson, John Krogestadt, John Lensdorf, Lyndle Clark.

Back L-R Vern Johnson, Willis Gregory, Martin Rose, James Richardson. Front L-R John Barnaba, Fred James, James Coaney, John Traunicki, Geroge Harris, Frank Lanza.

Rear L-R Reneiky, Morgan, Sealara, Sheffield, Kauffman, Poore. Front L-R O'Brien, Homes (?).

Front L-R Saunders, Baker, Aylesworth, Hired, Turner. Back L-R Stein, Feldt, Shutts.

Lt. Marshall's Crew.

Capt. Black's crew.

Rear L-R. Matthew Arlington, Anthony Schneider, John Gottschalk, Gerald Welsat. Front L-R. Ed Erickson, Harry Mamaux, Ray Mancell, James Newton, Mack Peterson.

Top L-R Charles Simonelli, Richard Ayelsworth, Earl Hird, Bob Baker, Ernest Turner. Bottom L-R Richard Williams, Albert Fehdt, Archies Stein, Gordon Shutts, Robert Sanders.

Standing L-R Paul Schad, Art Greshemer, Harry Blau, Stanley Schiller. Front L-R Sam Lasky, William Drosckeg, Carl Zkiab, Jack Teller, Riney Hay, Charles Cope.

Standing L-R Gerald Hill, Don Matveia, William Rogers, Robert Miller. Front L-R. Frank Young, Norman Allison, Joe Kelly, Clayton Taylor, James Smith, Wallace Durbin.

Back L-R Roland Thomas, Francis Smith, Stanley Woodsen. Front L-R. Carl Clavelli, Len Petska, Brakke Locker, Ernie Neal, Dick Johnson, Frank Starling.

Back L-R Anthony Manning, Lewis Perkins, Lloyd Aclin, Francis Marley. Front L-R Neil Spain, Floyd Umfleet, B. Pezion, George Ullom, Bob McCormick.

Top L-R William Fayle, Gerhard Heinicke, Edwin Jana, George W, Robert Chesser. Bottom L-R Gordon Knowles, Dunlop Hollinger, Ray Linneman, Robert Nethercot, Harry Knowlton, Crew Chief Miller.

Lt. Burrough's Crew.

Top L-R Dale Guthrie, Robert Wolfe, Clayton Conners, William Schnieder. Front L-R James Kennedy, Silvo Antonacci, William Weber, William Cornell, Elwood, Ward, Bernard McCloskey.

Back L-R Glenn Smullins, HenryBeck, Thomas McConnell, Geroge Marshall. Middle L-R. Edward Mahony, Orville Baker, James Shodney. Front L-R. Orlando Perry, Ray Quick.

Standing L-R. William Fayle, Gerhard Heinicke, Edwin Jane, Geroge Wall, Robert Chasser. Front L-R Gordon Knowles, Dunlop Hollinger, Ray Linneman, Robert Nethercott, Harry Knolton, Miller.

Front L-R Conlon Price, Ferris, Shank. Rear L-R Wolfe, West, Williams, Morrison, Brissette, Allinder.

Back L-R Paul Kuhns Jr, Maurice Frost, Joe Hartman Jr, Richard Graham. Front L-R. W. Hazelwood, John Bergstrom, Gerald Fairbanks, James Hoopey, George Ragsdale, Rudolph Mariseal.

Capt. J.D Kibler (front 2nd from left) and crew.

Back L-R. George Laser, Wes Olson, Robert Johnston, Melvin Edelstein. Kneeling L-R. James Carrizales, Joe Burdilis, Harold Smith, Bernard Fox, Vince Cerilli, Art Marrese.

Front L-R Glenn Huttquist, Jasper Davis, Floyd Haupt, Charles Martin. Rear L-R. William Droschkey, Don Heydon, John Rogers (KIA), Wilber Tri, Carl Zkiab, Charles Kilarski.

Back L-R. Kramer, Rossini, May, Howard, Johnson. Front L-R. Smith, Brutosky, Huber, Euth, Sebring.

Top L-R Ray Beaubein, Frank Senff, Bill Dulligan, Bob Perlman. Bottom L-R. George Hubbard, Robert Hardin, Martin Shaw, Paul Nielson Jr, Walter O'Keefe Jr, William Fiore.

Rear L-R. Don Waldron, Don Weir, Albert Denoff, Jack Abrams. Front L-R David Scefflier, William Terry, John Woods, Russell Reimer, Ben Delson.

Rear L-R Ken Leahy, Jacob Johnson, Boyd Clary, unknown. Bottom L-R. Thomas Carey Jr, Robert Andrick, James Easter, Charles Haugh Jr, Dan Coughlin, Etienne Brouillette.

Back L-R Howard Ellerman, Robert O'Keefe, Earl MaDougall, William (?). Front L-R. Toivo Ollikainen, Emil Michaud, William Cook, Fred Probst, Deney Ouellette, Francis Rochetta.

Rear L-R. Robert Elliott, Frank Kelly Jr, Dave Frideu, Don Steinke. Front L-R. Leo Stein, Ken Younger, Lesmon Lehue, Dave Preller, Laverne Coleman, Forrest Matthews.

Rear L-R Jesse Franklin, Cliff Jorgenson, Tony Brom, Sid Richardson. Front L-R. Claude Kelly, Ed Voight, John Patashus, Clark McQueen, Frank Barnes, Roger Paine.

Top L-R. Roland Thompson, Francis Smith, Stan Woodman. Front L-R. Carl Clavelli, Len Petska, Brakke Lockler, Ernie Neal, Dick Johnson, Frank Sterling.

Sherman Martin and Crew.

Rear L-R Dale Morlan, Joe Stachouski, Fred Klingberger, ?, ?. Front L-R Lousteiner, Day, Johnson, Purell, Likins, Gouzales.

Back L-R Feldt, Williams, Stein, Shatts. Front L-R. Aylesworth, Baker, Hird, Simonelli, ?, Turner.

Standing L-R. Robert Ray Jr, George Setzer, Orin Lloyd, William Cook. Middle L-R. Joe Sucie, Robert Gerren, Rex Phillips. Front L-R. Francis Cook, Jack Powell, Delbert Whitney.

Rear L-R. Robert Gorder, Ernest Eckels, Geroge Doverspike, Rea, Murdock. Front L-R. Ernest Bolduc, Clifford Carberry, Robert Frame, Herbert Armetiage, Joseph Sullivan.

George Sowa's Crew (777th).

Top L-R. Raymond Borg, Tom Carrothers, Rex Bryant, Gene Jolin. Middle L-R. Robert Wegner (KIA), Warner Ziehm. Front L-R. Wilton Abbott (KIA), Robert Kelly, Bert Landberg, John Anderson (KIA).

Rear L-R Horace Mull, Dubo Harper, Dan Skurka. Front L-R. Ted Lawrence, Robert Gooden, Robert Larson, John Crane, Charles Tindell, Maxwell Taunton.

Rear L-R. Lloyd Witkind, John Oney, John Goodyear, Dave Smith, Glen Galloway. Front L-R. Albert Clark, Frank Ondrosek, Joe Vallejo, Bob Ringel, Jack Bentley.

Leverett's crew and their ship.

Standing L-R. George Quay, Robert DeLawder, James Phillips, Walter Freeman. Kneeling L-R. Ted Bator, Clifton Callahan, Alex Spires, John Dersch, Ernest Hardy, Herman Roberts.

Rear L-R. Clayton Ryder, Harry Menke, Thomas Brinson, Howard Tannenbaum. Front L-R. Leonard Octzel, Charles Lucas, Jack Owen, Charles Delfino, Leroy Price, Charles Hanson.

Standing L-R. Robert Vetten, Dan Barrilla, Walter Crowell, Denman Cloudt, Robert Dawkins, Wilber Cooper. Front L-R. James Hammonds, John McGovern, Al Pires.

Top L-R. Mullen, Brandt, Jane, Moorehead. Front L-R. Fayle, Knowlton, Beeson, Zolynski, Folby, Knowles.

Rear L-R. Huggins, Robet Johnson, Charles Tarver, R. Garlock. Front L-R. Bartrug, Tuer, Ralp Seva, Don Gregory, Ed Barsczenski, Chet Wintermeyer.

Emmett Drake (arrow) and crew.

Standing L-R. Ken Bailey, Byron Locken, Howard Nott, John Taylor, Eugen Mensinger. Kneeling L-R. Robert Weinberger, Leslie Owen, Victor Montgomery, Don Tate, Peter Doelder.

L-R Bill Smith, Geo Martin, Bill Morel, Bob Hettish, Al Reader Charles Simmons, Ira Shrader, Charles Cunningham, Fred Scalise John Marks.

Standing L-R. Dean Lovitt, Wally Roberts, Harold Drollinger, Ed Horst. Front L-R. John Chmelier, George Kroll, Jerry Lory, Ed Aubrey, Tom Beyer, John Holzepfel.

Top L-R John Bertaux (KIA), Chester Kiolbassa (KIA), Charles Gustina (KIA), Mardy Fried (KIA). Bottom L-R. Matthew Striet, Joe Guadagne (KIA), Antony Aiello (KIA), Richard Peterson, Fernando Rangel (KIA), Darwin Carlson.

Back L-R. Don Bahnsen, Frank Schiffel, Robert Kephart, Donald Sherard. Front L-R. Robert Rice, John Trabucco, Paul Staight, Danial Jeffery, Chester Stanizewski, Carl Henry.

Rear L-R Robert Elliot, Frank Kelly Jr., David Friden, Don Steinke. Front L-R. Leo Stein, Ken Younger, Leamon Lehue, David Preller, LaVerne Coloman, Forrest Matthews.

Rear L-R. William Cafarelli, Tom Cory, Henry Cox, Olan Long, Leland Conrad, Krough. Front L-R. George Falcone, Sam Berkowitz, John Tomlinson, Cecil Potter.

Rear L-R George Krynovich, William Fears, Ellis Loree, Geroge Stockinger. Front L-R. Robert Hemmeger, Hubert Gallagher, Olin Mullinax, Arvon Richardson, William Henry, Charles Brockman.

Rear W. Campbell, R. MacClemmy, H. Glaze, A. Hudeck. Front L-R. E. Manson, W. Robb, R. Loichinger, M. Mates, A. Michels, J. Ritter.

Rear: Ned Cartmille, Merle Weik, John Lewis, Guy Howard, R Marcum. Front: Joseph Lidiak, John Rucigay, Tom MacDonald, Robert Denison.

Rear Richard Manning, Lewis Perkins, Lloyd Aclin, Francis Morley. Front Neil Spain, Floyd Umfleet, Willard Griffen, Ben Pizion, George Ullom, Robert McCormick.

Rear L-R: August Eckles (KIA), John James (KIA), Edward Maloney (KIA), Ervin Dunham (KIA), Eugene Jekniewicz (KIA). Front L-R. Ralph Robinson (KIA), John D'Amore, That Watson (KIA), Edward Ivan (KIA), Felix Gleason (KIA).

Rear L-R: Vernel Johnson, Willis Gregory, Martin Rose, James Richardson. Front L-R: James Barraba, Fred Jones, James Cooney, John Trawicki, George Harris, Frank Lanza.

Aircraft Profiles/Maps

FLAKMAN 42-95332 Black U Returned to the states after the war. Flew 93 missions.

Lady Esther 42-50500 Black L Returned to the states after 71 missions.

EASY MAID 42-50796 Black Q Lost to enemy action August 27, 1944.

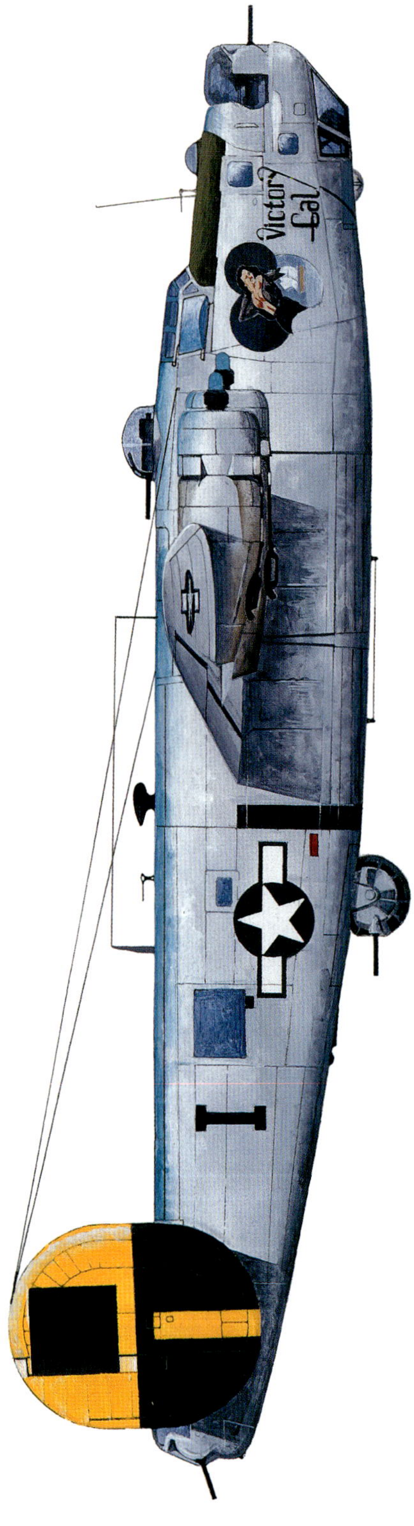

VICTORY GAL 44-40965 Black I Damaged and written off after explosion of Black-o on August 21, 1944.

HOME FOR CHRISTMAS 42-52437 White E Didn't make it back in time for Christmas, but she did return to the United States.

GREEN HORNET 42-52504 White Z After a long string of missions she was lost on December 6, 1944

LITTLE ROCKET 42-50962 White H Lost to enemy action December 6, 1944.

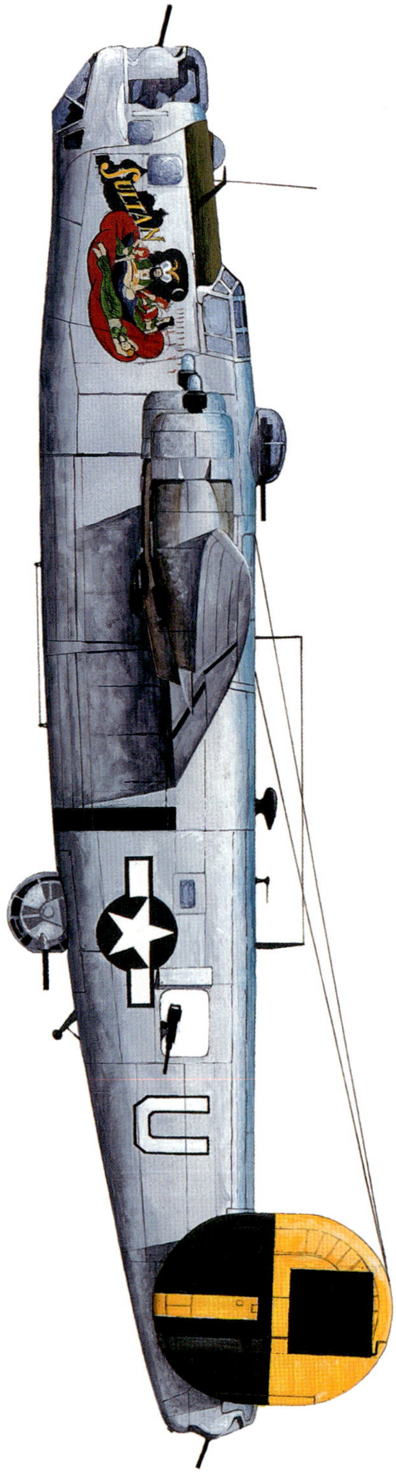

SULTAN 42-95348 White U crashed on take-off August 27, 1944

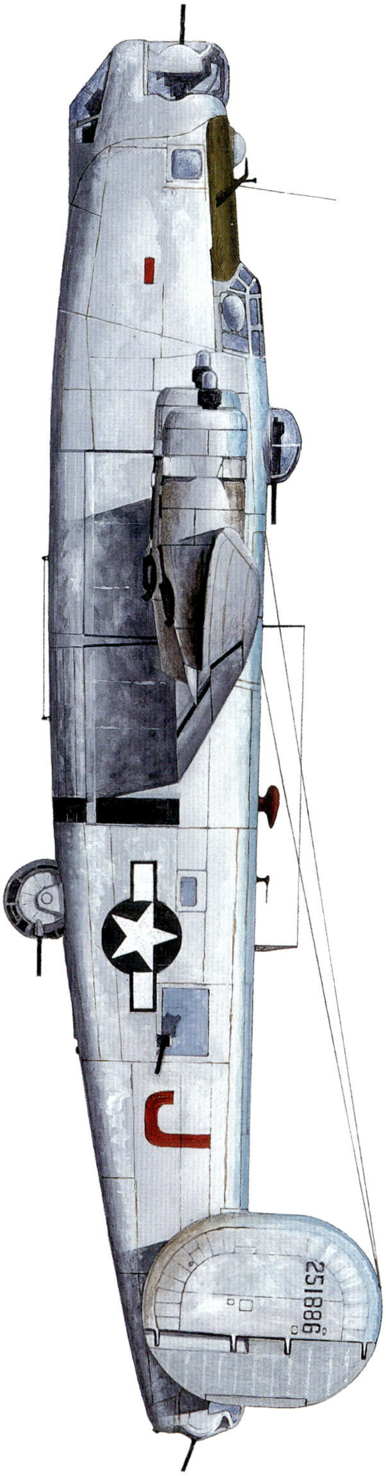

SKIRT PATROL 42-78096 77th Bomb Sq. Transfered to another group.

Red-J 42-51886 Salvaged after being hit in the waist by an 88mm shell on December 5, 1944.

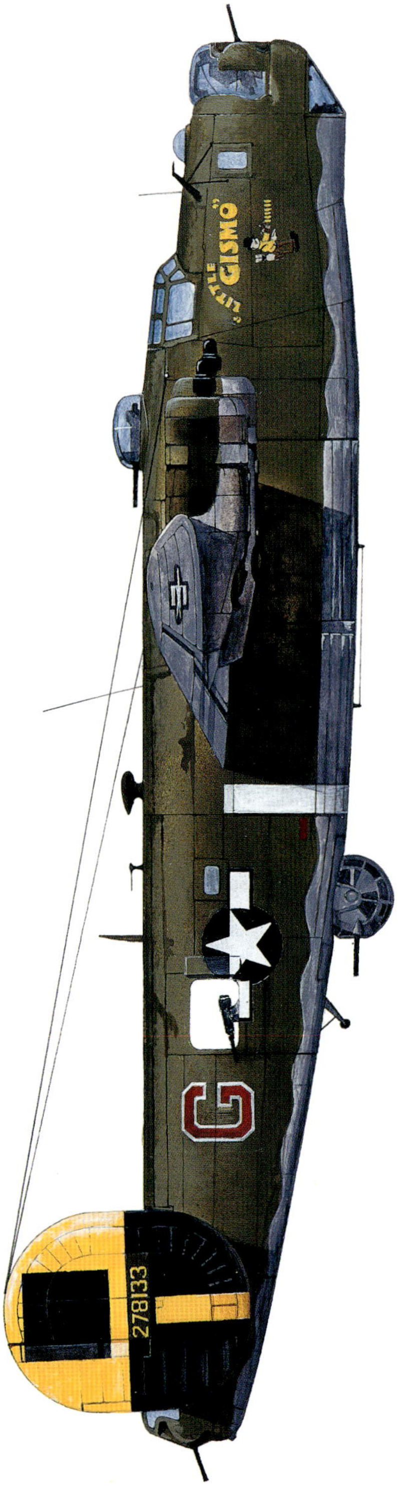

LITTLE GISMO 42-78133 Red G Lost to enemy action June 6, 1944.

LITTLE LULU 42-52479 Red L Lost to enemy action August 24,1944

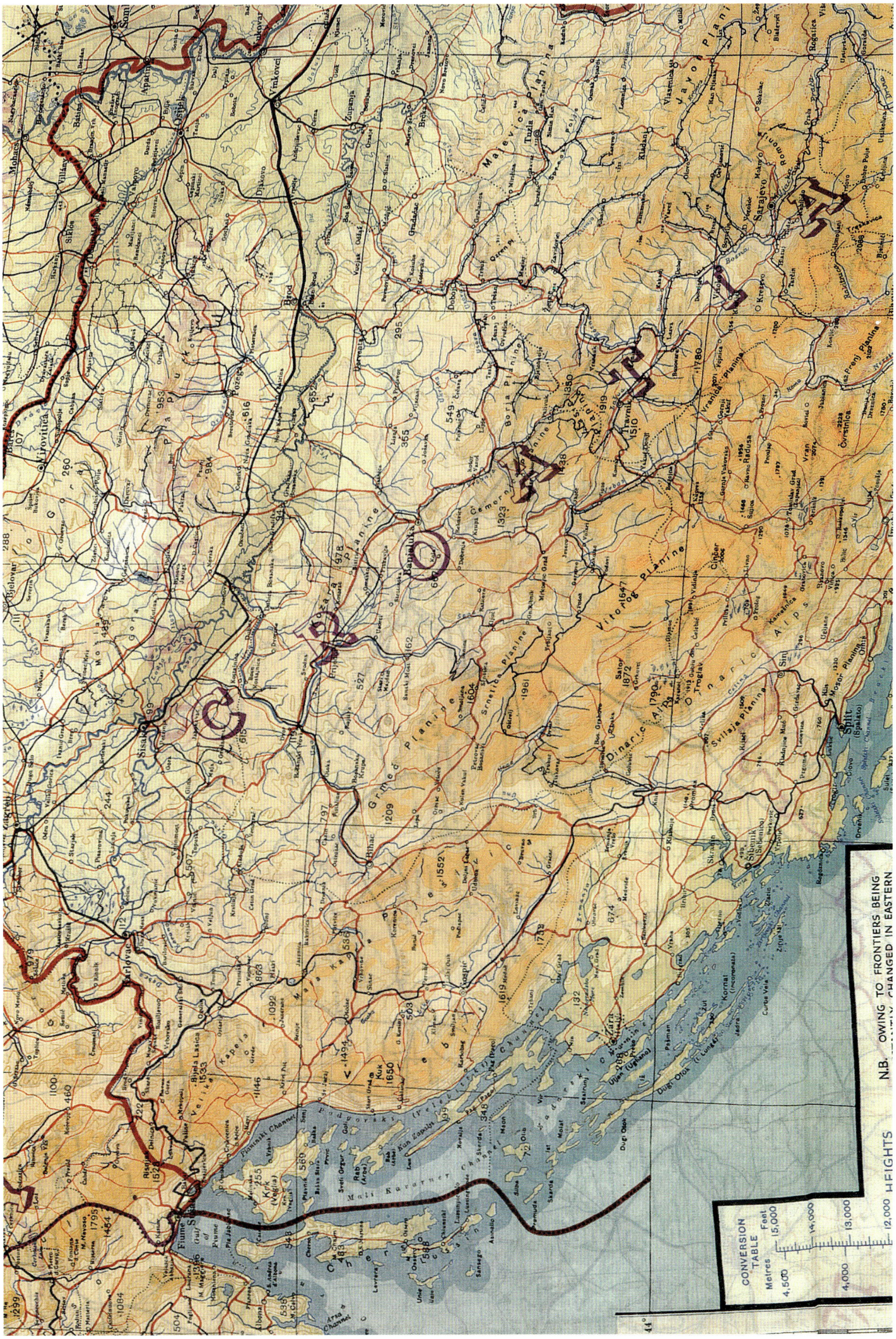
N.B. OWING TO FRONTIERS BEING
CHANGED IN EASTERN
CONVERSION TABLE
Metres
Feet
HEIGHTS
Sarajevo
Split (Spalato)
Bihać
Sisak
Fiume

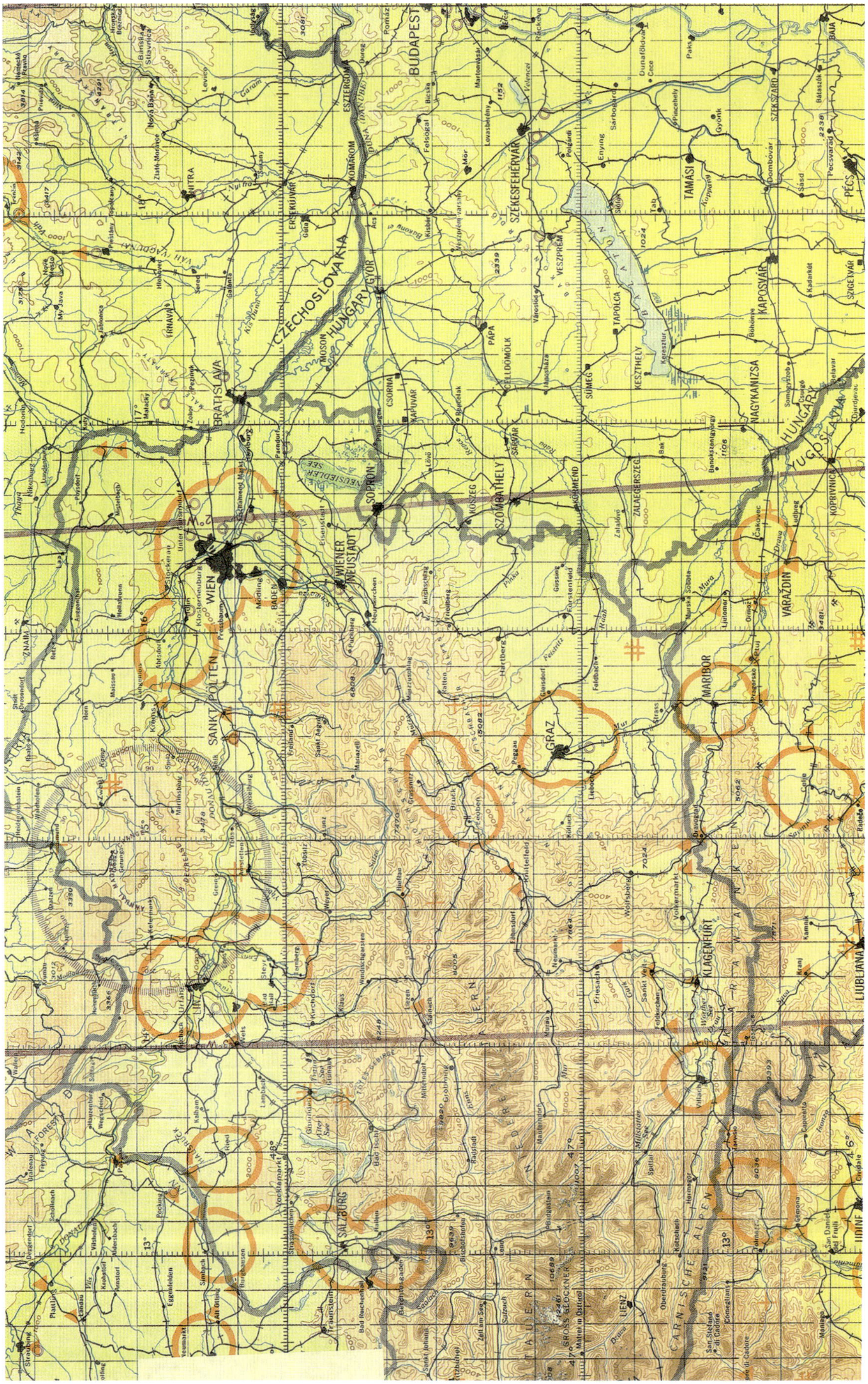
BUDAPEST
CZECHOSLOVAKIA
HUNGARY
YUGOSLAVIA
BRATISLAVA
WIEN
WIENER NEUSTADT
SOPRON
GYOR
KOMAROM
NITRA
SZEKESFEHERVAR
VESZPREM
PAPA
TAPOLCA
KESZTHELY
NAGYKANIZSA
KAPOSVAR
TAMASI
PÉCS
SZOMBATHELY
ZALAEGERSZEG
VARAZDIN
MARIBOR
GRAZ
SANKT PÖLTEN
KLAGENFURT
LJUBLJANA
LINZ
SALZBURG
LIENZ
UDINE

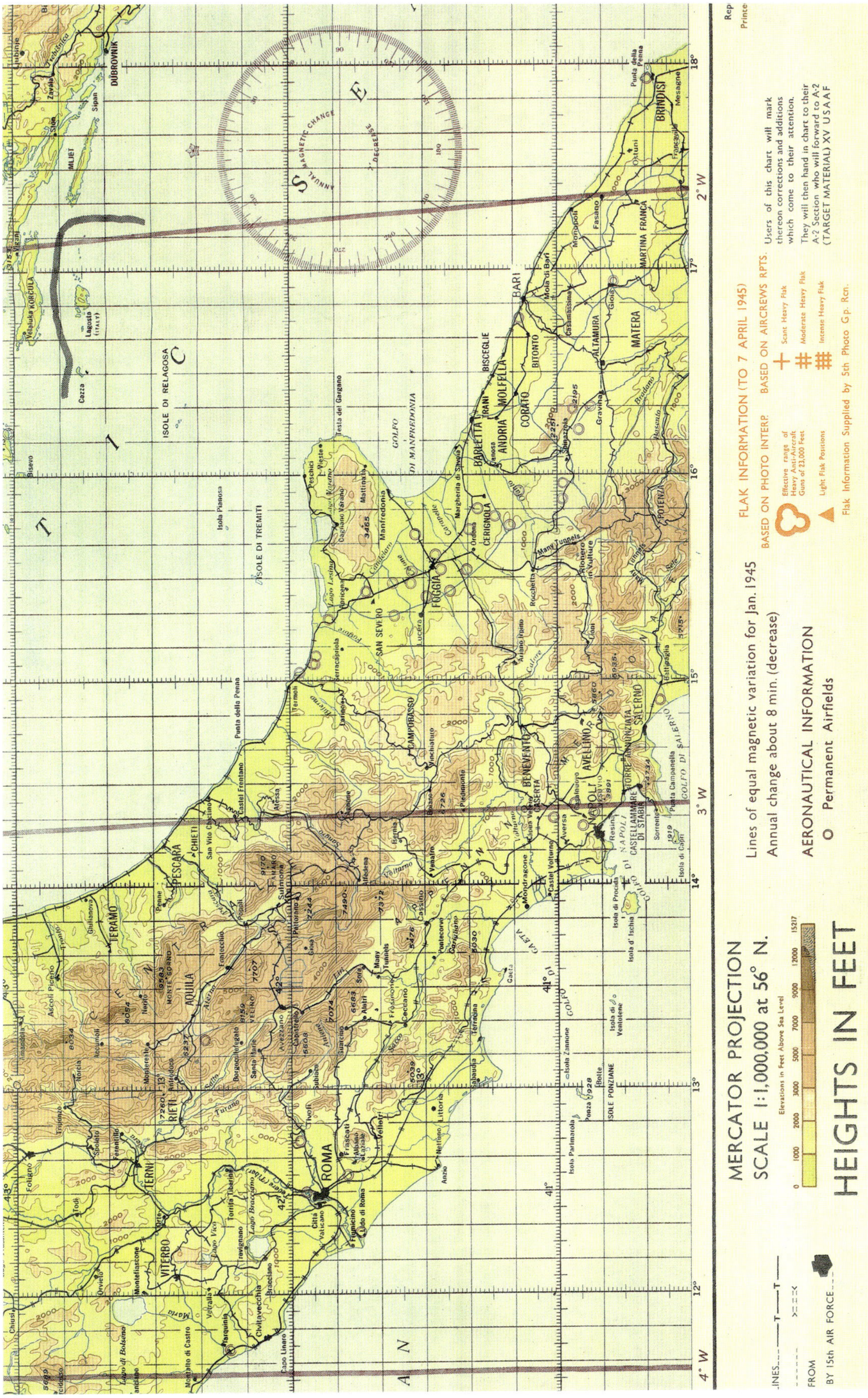
MERCATOR PROJECTION
SCALE 1:1,000,000 at 56° N.
HEIGHTS IN FEET
Lines of equal magnetic variation for Jan. 1945
Annual change about 8 min. (decrease)
AERONAUTICAL INFORMATION
Permanent Airfields
FLAK INFORMATION (TO 7 APRIL 1945)
BASED ON PHOTO INTERP.
BASED ON AIRCREWS RPTS.
Flak Information Supplied by 5th Photo Gp. Rcn.
Users of this chart will mark thereon corrections and additions which come to their attention.
They will then hand in chart to their A-2 Section who will forward to A-2 (TARGET MATERIAL) XV USAAF
BY 15th AIR FORCE
ROMA
NAPOLI
FOGGIA
BARI
BRINDISI
PESCARA
SALERNO
BENEVENTO
AVELLINO
CASERTA
VITERBO
TERNI
RIETI
AQUILA
TERAMO
CHIETI
CAMPOBASSO
SAN SEVERO
CERIGNOLA
ANDRIA
BARLETTA
TRANI
MOLFETTA
BISCEGLIE
CORATO
BITONTO
ALTAMURA
MATERA
MARTINA FRANCA
POTENZA
DUBROVNIK
ISOLE DI TREMITI
ISOLE DI PELAGOSA
GOLFO DI MANFREDONIA
GOLFO DI SALERNO
ISOLE PONZIANE

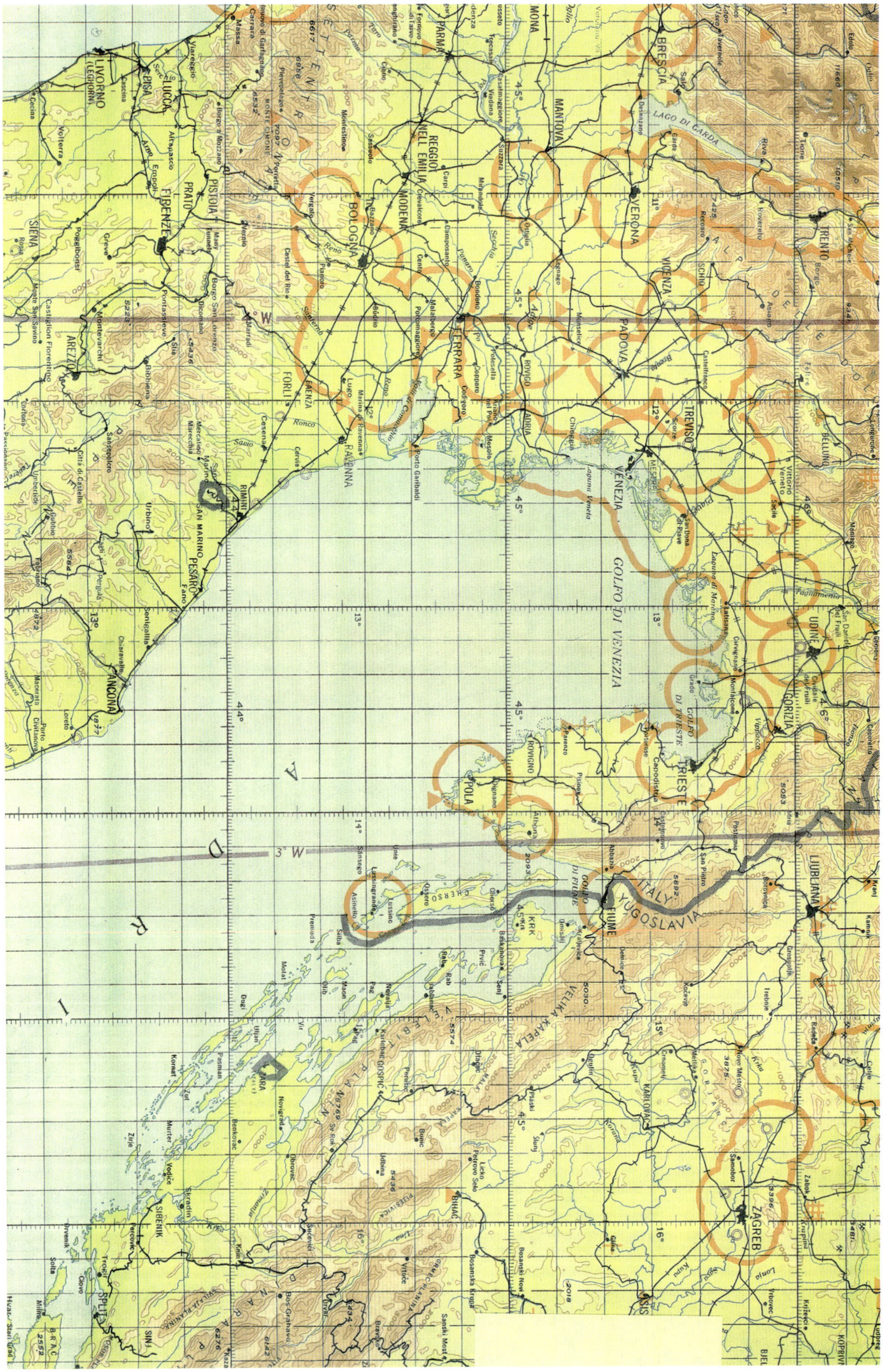
LIVORNO
PISA
LUCCA
PISTOIA
PRATO
FIRENZE
SIENA
AREZZO
PARMA
REGGIO NELL EMILIA
MODENA
BOLOGNA
FERRARA
FORLI
FAENZA
RAVENNA
RIMINI
SAN MARINO
PESARO
ANCONA
MANTOVA
BRESCIA
LAGO DI GARDA
VERONA
VICENZA
PADOVA
ROVIGO
ADRIA
TREVISO
VENEZIA
TRENTO
BELLUNO
GOLFO DI VENEZIA
UDINE
GORIZIA
TRIESTE
POLA
ROVIGNO
FIUME
ITALY
YUGOSLAVIA
LJUBLJANA
KRK
CHERSO
ZARA
SIBENIK
SPLIT
KARLOVAC
ZAGREB
BIHAĆ
GOSPIĆ

Appendix A:
Missions of the 464th Bomb Group

During their 12 months of combat flying the 464th Bomb Group took to the air on many different occasions. Several lists of missions indicate that the group flew 210 missions. The following list of combat missions is compiled from 55th Bomb Wing records and indicates the missions for which the 464th Bomb Group was given Official Mission Credit. It is interesting to note that several Red Force/Blue Force Missions were given credit for each mission, while other Red Force/Blue Force Missions were only given credit for one mission. It is also interesting to note that the 464th was given credit for the last mission flown on April 26, 1945, in view of the fact that it was an ineffective mission and should not have been credited according to mission criteria.

MISSION #	DATE		TARGET	TARGET TYPE
1	T	5-2-44	Parma, Italy	Marshalling Yards
2	F	5-5-44	Podgorcia, Yugoslavia	Troops
3	SAT	5-6-44	Craiova, Rumania	Marshalling Yards
4	W	5-10-44	Wiener-Neustadt, Austria	Aircraft Factory
5	F	5-12-44	Reggio Emilia, Italy	Marshalling Yards
6	SAT	5-13-44	Parma, Italy	Marshalling Yards
7	SUN	5-14-44	Treviso.Italy	Marshalling Yards
8	W	5-17-44	Piombino, Italy	Marshalling Yards
9	T	5-18-44	Ploesti, Rumania	Concordia Vega Refinery
10	F	5-19-44	Faenza, Italy	Marshalling Yards
11	M	5-22-44	Valmontone, Italy	Marshalling Yards Troop Concentrations
12	T	5-23-44	Valmontone, Italy	Town of Valmontone
13	W	5-24-44	Wiener-Neustadt, Austria	Wollersdorf Air Drome
14	T	5-25-44	Givors, France	Marshalling Yards
15	F	5-26-44	Lyons, France	Lyon La Nouche R/R Yards
16	SAT	5-27-44	Nimes, France	Marshalling Yards
17	M	5-29-44	Atzgersdorf, Austria	Amme-Luther-Seck Aircraft Components Factory
18	T	5-30-44	Vienna, Austria	Neudorf Flugzeugfabrik and Acbroach Components Factory
19	F	6-2-44	Cluj, Rumania	Marshalling Yards
20	SAT	6-4-44	Turin, Italy	Marshalling Yards
21	M	6-5-44	Ferrarar, Italy	Marshalling Yards
22	T	6-6-44	Ploesti, Rumania	Oil Refinery
23	W	6-7-44	La Spezia, Italy	La Spezia Harbor Oil Storage and Refinery
24	W	6-14-44	Petfurdo, Hungary	Oil Cracking PLant
25	F	6-16-44	Vienna, Austria	Oil Blending Plant
26	THUR	6-22-44	Bologna, Italy	Marshalling Yards
27	F	6-23-44	Giurgiu, Rumania	Oil Installations
28	SUN	6-25-44	Balaruc, France	Oil Refinery
29	M	6-26-44	Vienna, Austria	Florisdorf Oil Refinery

30	T	6-27-44	Blechhammer, Germany	South Synthetic Oil Plant
31	W	6-28-44	Bucharest, Rumania	Prahova Oil Refinery
32	SUN	7-2-44	Budapest , Hun gary	Marshalling Yards
33	M	7-3-44	Belgrade, Yugoslavia	Shell Oil Depot
34	W	7-5-44	Toulon, France	Submarine Docks and Pens
35	THUR	7-6-44	Porto Marghera, Italy	Oil Storage
36	F	7-7-44	Blechhammer, Germany	North Synthetic Oil Refinery
37	SAT	7-8-44	Vienna, Austria	Florisdorf Oil Refinery
38	T	7-11-44	Porto Marghera, Italy	Oil Storage
39	W	7-12-44	Nimes, France	Marshalling Yards
40	THUR	7-13-44	Mantua, Italy	Marshalling Yards
41	F	7-14-44	Mantua, Italy	Marshalling Yards
42	SAT	7-15-44	Ploesti, Rumania	Oil Refinery
43	SUN	7-16-44	Wiener-Nuedorf	Aircraft Engine Factory
44	W	7-19-44	Allach, Germany	Aircraft Engine Factory
45	THUR	7-20-44	Luftschiffhau, Germany	Zeppeline Works
46	SAT	7-22-44	Ploesti, Rumania	Americano Oil Refinery
47	T	7-25-44	Linz, Austria	Herman Goering Tank Works
48	W	7-26-44	Vienna, Austria	Zwolfaxing Air Drome
49	F	7-28-44	Ploesti, Rumania	Astra Romano Oil Refinery
50	SAT	7-30-44	Budapest, Hungary	Duna Aircraft Factory
51	W	8-2-44	Genoa, Italy	Harbor and Dock Installations
52	THUR	8-3-44	Friedrichschafen, Germany	Manzell Aircraft Works
53	SUN	8-6-44	Le Pontet, France	Oil Refinery
54	M	8-7-44	Blechhammer, Germany	North Synthetic Oil Refinery
55	W	8-9-44	Budapest, Hungary	Tokol Air Drome
56	THUR	8-10-44	Ploesti, Rumania	Astra Romano Oil Refinery
57	SAT	8-12-44	Sete, France	Gun Emplacements
58	SUN	8-13-44	Sete, France	Gun Emplacements
59	M	8-14-44	St.Tropez, France	Gun Emplacements
60	T	8-15-44	Donzere, France	Highway Bride
61	W	8-16-44	Ober Raderach, Germany	Chemical Works
62	F	8-18-44	Ploesti, Rumania	Americano Oil Refinery
63	SUN	8-20-44	Czechowice, Poland	Oil Refinery
64	M	8-21-44	Nis, Yugoslavia	Air Drome
65	T	8-22-44	Korcheuberg, Austria	Oil Storage (Vienna)
66	W	8-23-44	Markersdorf, Austria	Airdrome
67	THUR	8-24-44	Pardubice, Czechoslavakia	Oil Refinery
68	F	8-25-44	Prostejov, Czechoslavakia	Air Drome
69	SUN	8-27-44	Blechhammer, Germany	South Synthetic Oil Refinery
70	M	8-28-44	Szony, Hungary	Oil Refinery
71	T	8-29-44	Meravska, Czechoslavakia	Ostraya Industrial Targets
72	F	9-1-44	Szajol, Hungary	Marshalling Yards
73	SAT	9-2-44	Supovac, Yugoslavia	Railroad Bridge
74	M	9-4-44	Bronzola, Italy	South Marshalling Yards
75	T	9-5-44	Szob, Hungary	Railroad Bridge
76	W	9-6-44	Nviregyhaze, Hungary	Marshalling Yards
77	SUN	9-10-44	Vienna, Austria	Diesel Caterreiche Saurerwerke
78	W	9-13-44	Oswiecim, Poland	Synthetic Oil & Rubber Plant
79	SUN	9-17-44	Budapest, Hungary	Shell Oil Refinery
80	M	9-18-44	Szob, Hungary	Railroad Bridge
81	W	9-20-44	Hatvan, Hungary	Marshalling Yards
82	F	9-22-44	Munich, Germany	Oberwisenfeld BMW Buildings
83	SAT	9-23-44	Pinzano, Italy	South Railroad Bridge
84	SUN	9-24-44	Scaramanga, Greece	Submarine & Harbor Install
85	W	10-4-44	Munich, Germany	Main Marshalling Yards
86	SAT	10-7-44	Ersekujvar, Hungary	Marshalling Yards
87	W	10-11-44	Vienna, Austria	Oil Storage
88	THUR	10-12-44	Bologna, Italy	Storage Depot
89	F	10-13-44	Blechhammer, Germany	South Oil Refinery

90	M	10-16-44	St.Valentin, Austria	Tank Works
91	T	10-17-44	Vienna, Austria	South Ordnance Depot
92	F	10-20-44	Rosenheim, Germany	Marshalling Yards
93	W	11-1-44	Graz, Austria	Marshalling Yards
94	F	11-3-44	Munich, Germany	West Marshalling Yards
95	SAT	11-4-44	Linz, Austria	Benzol Plant
96	SUN	11-5-44	Vienna, Austria	Florisdorf Oil Refienry
97	M	11-6-44	Vienna, Austria	Zeltweg Air Drome
98	W	11-15-44	Linz, Austria	Benzol Oil Refiney
99	THUR	11-16-44	Munich, Germany	West MArshalling Yards
100	THUR	11-16-44	Prejepolje, Yugoslavia	Troops
101	F	11-17-44	Florisdorf, Austria	Oil Refinery
102	SAT	11-18-44	Udine, Italy	Compofomido Air Drome
103	SUN	11-19-44	Linz, Austria	Benzol Plant
104	M	11-20-44	Blechhammer, Austria	South Oil Refinery
105	W	11-22-44	Munich, Germany	Marshalling YArds
106	SAT	11-25-44	Munich, Germany	West Marshalling YArds
107	SAT	12-2-44	Blechhammer, Germany	South Oil Refinery
108	SUN	12-3-44	Linz, Austria	Industrial Area
109	W	12-6-44	Dovisk Nova Vas, Czechoslavakia	Marshalling Yards
110	THUR	12-7-44	Salzberg, Austria	West Marshalling Yards
111	F	12-8-44	Villach, Austria	Marshalling Yards
112	M	12-11-44	Vienna, Austria	South Ordnance Depot
113	T	12-12-44	Blechhammer, Germany	South Oil Refinery
114	F	12-15-44	Amstetten, Germany	Marshalling Yards
115	SAT	12-16-44	Pilsen/Villach Czech/Austria	Skoda Works/ Rail Yards
116	SUN	12-17-44	Blechhammer, Germany	South Oil Refinery
117	M	12-18-44	Blechhammer, Germany	North Synthetic Oil Refinery
118	T	12-19-44	Blechhammer, Germany	South Oil Refinery
119	W	12-20-44	Villach, Austria	Marshalling Yards
120	T	12-26-44	Odertal, Germany	Oil Refinery
121	W	12-27-44	Maribor, Yugoslavia	Marshalling Yards
122	THUR	12-28-44	Roundnice Czechoslavakia	Oil Tankage & Sidings
123	F	12-29-44	Verona, Italy	Porto Nuova Rail Yards
124	THUR	1-4-45	Bolzano, Italy	Marshalling Yards
125	M	1-8-45	Klagenfurt, Austria	Marshalling Yards
126	SAT	1-20-45	Linz, Austria	Communications
127	W	1-31-45	Moosbierbaum, Austria	Metal Works
128	M	2-5-45	Regensburg, Germany	Winter Harbor Oil Storage
129	W	2-7-45	Florisdorf, Austria	Oil Refinery
130	THUR	2-8-45	Vienna, Austria	Southeast Industrial Area
131	F	2-9-45	Moosbierbaum, Austria	Oil Refinery
132	T	2-13-45	Graz, Austria	Marshalling Yards
133	T	2-13-45	Pola, Italy	Casting & Forging Works
134	W	2-14-45	Villach, Austria	Marshalling Yards
135	W	2-14-45	Vienna, Austria	Schwechat Oil Refinery
136	THUR	2-15-45	Wiener-Neustadt, Austria	Sorting Sidings
137	F	2-16-45	Regensberg, Germany	Oberstraubling Air Drome
138	SAT	2-17-45	Pola, Italy	Harbor Installations
139	M	2-19-45	Graz, Austria	Marshalling Yards
140	T	2-20-45	Trieste, Italy	Ship Yards
141	W	2-21-45	Vienna, Austria	Matzleinedorf Rail Yards
142	THUR	2-22-45	Maniago, Italy	Railroad Bridge
143	THUR	2-22-45	Casasa, Italy	Railroad Bridge
144	F	2-23-45	Klagenfurt, Austria	Marshalling Yards
145	SAT	2-24-45	Udine, Italy	Marshalling Yards
146	SUN	2-25-45	Linz, Austria	Ordnance Depot
147	T	2-27-45	Augsberg, Germany	Marshalling Yards
148	W	2-28-45	Vicenza, Italy	Marshalling Yards
149	THUR	3-1-45	St.Polten, Austria	Marshalling Yards

150	THUR	3-1-45	Amstettin, Austria	Marshalling Yards
151	F	3-2-45	Linz, Austria	N. Main Rail Yards
152	SUN	3-4-45	Szombathely, Hungary	South Marshalling Yards
153	THUR	3-8-45	Verona, Italy	Troops
154	F	3-9-45	Graz, Austria	Station & Freight Yards
155	M	3-12-45	Florisdorf, Austria	Oil Refinery
156	T	3-13-45	Regensburg, Germany	Marshalling Yards
157	W	3-14-45	Novezamky, Hungary	Marshalling Yards
158	THUR	3-15-45	Graz, Austria	Marshalling Yards
159	F	3-16-45	Amstettin, Austria	Marshalling Yards
160	M	3-19-45	Muhldorf, Germany	Marshalling Yards
161	T	3-20-45	Amstettin, Austria	Marshalling Yards
162	W	3-21-45	Neuberg, Germany	Air Drome
163	THUR	3-22-45	Heilegenstadt, Austria	Marshalling Yards
164	F	3-23-45	Gmund, Austria	Marshalling Yards
165	SAT	3-24-45	Neuberg, Germany	Air Drome
166	SUN	3-25-45	Prague, Czechoslavakia	Letnany Air Drome
167	M	3-26-45	Bratislava, Czechoslavakia	Rangier Rail Yards
168	F	3-30-45	Kapenburg, Austria	Tank Works
169	SAT	3-31-45	Villach, Austria	Marshalling Yards
170	M	4-2-45	Graz, Austria	Station & Rail Yards
171	THUR	4-5-45	Verona/Ora, Italy	Recall Mission Credited
172	SAT	4-7-45	Campodazzo, Italy	Recall- Mission Credited
173	SUN	4-8-45	Fortezza, Italy	Marshalling Yards
174	M	4-9-45	Lugo, Italy	Targets- Area Apple
175	T	4-10-45	Lugo, Italy	Troops
176	W	4-11-45	Campo Di Trens, Italy	Troops
177	THUR	4-12-45	Ponte Di Piave, Italy	Troops
178	SAT	4-14-45	Palmanova, Italy	Ammunition Factory
179	SUN	4-15-45	Casarsa , Italy	Support-5th Army
180	M	4-16-45	North Italy	Support-5th Army
181	T	4-17-45	North Italy	Support- 5th Army
182	THUR	4-19-45	Wels, Austria	Reveredo de Piano Air Drome
183	F	4-20-45	Rovigo, Italy	Road Bridge
184	M	4-23-45	Cavarzere/Padua, Italy	Road Bridges
185	T	4-24-45	Brondolo, Italy	Railroad Bridge
186	W	4-25-45	Linz, Austria	Marshalling Yards
187	THUR	4-26-45	Malcontenta, Italy	Targets N. Italy

Appendix B:
The Last Full Measure

Survival in combat is not a matter of being the best pilot or gunner, it is a matter of luck more than anything else. Perhaps a better way to put it is, "There but for the grace of God go I." For those who survived, there was the question why them and not me? Why did one gunner make it and the gunner standing right behind him die? Why did one man get out of the burning plane and the other nine did not? There is no logical answer to these questions. We can only look at the names of those who gave the last full measure and remember their sacrifices.

Chaplain Eastwood wrote in his last article for *The Tower* about Friends We Won't Forget:

What precious memories they are,for they are the men who have purchased our blessing and opportunities. Our future is made sacred by their sacrifice. As we move on to other tasks, may these memories stir within us a deep and burning desire to live for others as these our fellow soldiers have sacrificed for us.

Name	Date	Squadron
Abbott, Wilton L. T/Sgt	10-13-44	778
Abrams, Jack L. 1/Lt	10-13-44	777
Adams, George E. S/Sgt	8-7-44	777
Aiello, Anthony J. Sgt.	12-11-44	776
Alderman,Fredrich j. Sgt.	1-20-44	777
Alfano,Edward J. S/Sgt	5-27-44	777
Allen, Roy A. Sgt.	10-13-44	776
Allison, Norman W. Cpl	12-29-44	778
Anderson, John G. S/Sgt	10-13-44	778
Anderson ,Lawrence T/Sgt	8-7-44	777
Anderson ,Theodore A. 2/Lt	8-9-44	778
Arigone, fernando J. S/Sgt	7-8-44	777
Ayer, Herbert J. Sgt.	11-11-44	777
Bailey, Joseph W. T/Sgt	8-27-44	778
Baird, George C. Sgt	7-16-44	777
Baker, Ralph T. 2/Lt	5-27-44	777
Baker, Robert L. S/Sgt.	8-22-44	779
Baldwin,Walter L. 2/Lt	1-20-45	779
Beck, John E. S/Sgt.	5-25-44	777
Berceli, Stephen J. Sgt	11-15-44	779
Bertaux,John F.1/Lt	12-11-44	776
Bielak, Joseph F. Cpl	3-1-45	778
Bloxson,Raymond A.S/Sgt.	8-24-44	776
Bogacz,Clarence L. PFC	3-1-45	778
Bokoff,Phillip Y.2/Lt	3-27-45	776
Bolash,Cyril W. S/Sgt	5-10-44	778
Bonds, James E.Jr . Cpl	10-13-44	777
Bonner, Marshall. Col.	6-26-44	HQ/Commander
Bottoms,Charlie L. S/Sgt	7-28-44	777
Boyd, Raymond I. S/Sgt.	10-29-44	779
Breslawskii,Sam.2/Lt.	1-20-45	779
Brett,Eric L. 2/Lt.	5-10-44	778
Brooks, Sheldon Capt.	10-29-44	779
Brown, Edward C. T/Sgt.	5-25-44	777
Brown, Kenneth C. Sgt.	10-16-44	776
Bruce, Fredrick W. Cpl	3-1-45	778
Bugaisky, Louis S/Sgt.	5-27-44	777
Bunnell, Paul m. T/Sgt	5-27-44	777
Burton, Weldon K. Maj.	10-29-44	779
Butler, Gale R. Sgt.	3-1-45	778
Campbell, Ronald Jr. S/Sgt.	7-22-44	776
Carpentier, Anthony P. Sgt.	6-6-44	777
Caryga, Peter Sgt.	11-15-44	779
Cato, Royal F. Maj.	10-29-44	779
Cellamore,Nicholas Sgt.	10-17-44	779
Chesser,Robert L.Capt.	5-25-44	779
Chojnacki, Walter C. 2/Lt.	10-13-44	777
Chucta,William H. S/Sgt	7-16-44	777
Claeys,Donald F. S/Sgt	6-26-44	777
Clough, Jack C. Sgt.	1-20-44	777
Colabella,George Cpl	12-11-44	776
Conners,Clayton E. 2/Lt	7-22-44	777
Cook, Fred H. Sgt	7-30-44	776
Cook, Kenneth. Cpl	10-13-44	777
Cope, Norman S. S/Sgt	4-10-45	779
Corbett, Rueben E. T/Sgt.	7-15-44	778
Crabtree, Robert S. 2/Lt	11-15-44	779
Creswall,Ory E. T/Sgt	7-5-44	776
Cuddington, Gerald A. Sgt.	1-20-44	777

Culp, Melmeth . Sgt	6-6-44	778
Cummings, Joseph T. 2/Lt	2-29-44	778
Cunningham, Calvin E. 2/Lt	11-15-44	779
Czseniuk, John A. S/Sgt	10-29-44	779
Dallmeyer, William F. 2/Lt	2-29-44	778
Daniel, Alfred W. S/Sgt	5-2-44	779
Daniels, Thomas. S/Sgt	5-2-44	779
Dansereau, Frank B. S/Sgt	12-17-44	779
Davidson, Lynn F. 2/Lt	2-29-44	778
Degman, Edward J. 2/Lt	10-17-44	779
Dempsey,Edward 1/Lt	3-27-44	776
Derman, Ben S/Sgt	11-18-44	
Dickason,Larry H 1/Lt	10-29-44	779
Dirnbauer, Robert M. S/Sgt	10-29-44	779
Dodd, John J. S/Sgt	5-25-44	779
Doelder, Peter S/Sgt	7-26-44	776
Dombrowski, Walter T/Sgt	5-7-44	776
Dominetto, Joe S/Sgt	7-7-44	777
Downey, Kenneth M. Sgt	11-17-44	777
Draney, Edwin J. S/Sgt	5-25-44	778
Dranoff, Isadore S/Sgt	1-20-45	779
Duelberg, John H. T/Sgt	7-16-44	777
Dunham, Erwin G. 2/Lt	8-24-44	776
Durbin, Wallace B. Cpl	12-29-44	778
Durisko, John A. 2/Lt	5-25-44	779
East, Wayne F. S/Sgt	6-2-44	779
Eddy, Charles W. Sgt.	1-9-44	776
Edwards, Robert C. Sgt	12-6-44	778
Ehlers, Theodore D. 2/Lt	3-22-45	779
Elliott, Jack E. T/Sgt	7-7-44	778
Ely, George Jr. 2/Lt	6-5-44	776
Esslinger, William G. S/Sgt	5-2-45	
Every, Medwin C. S/Sgt	5-25-44	779
Farguhar, Raymond,Jr. 1/Lt	10-16-44	776
Farris, Wylie T. S/Sgt	7-15-44	778
Fassnacht, John C. 2/Lt	10-17-44	778
Fenley, Frank R. Sgt.	10-17-44	779
Fiekins,Leroy W. Sgt.	2-29-44	778
Filicsky, Theodore V. S/Sgt	7-8-44	779
Finley, Joseph A. 2/Lt	10-13-44	777
Floyd, William J. Jr. S/Sgt	8-9-44	778
Folsom, Benjamin A. 1/Lt.	7-15-44	778
Foote, Charles H. Capt.	4-10-45	779
Fowler, Raymond D. S/Sgt	5-15-44	778
Freundlick, Harold D. S/Sgt	7-15-44	778
Fried, Mardy J. 1/Lt	12-11-44	776
Garniss, Donald S. 2/Lt	5-25-44	779
Garrow, Mathew J. Sgt	12-6-44	779
Gay, William S/Sgt	2-14-45	777
Gebhardt, Fredrick C. Cpl	9-10-44	779
Gein, Carl A. Jr. 1/Lt.	5-25-44	778
Gibbs, Charles R. Jr. 2/Lt	5-7-44	776
Gilbreath, Earl O. Sgt	6-6-44	778
Gillum, Leon C. Sgt.	1-17-44	778
Gilson, James H. L/Col.	5-10-45	779
Gleason, Felix	Sgt.	8-24-44
776		
Graham, John b. 2/Lt.	10-17-44	779
Green, Earcel H. 2/Lt	7-7-44	778
Griffin, Walter S. S/Sgt	7-28-44	777
Grissett, Robert T. T/Sgt	5-25-44	777
Grzesik,Stanley S/Sgt	8-24-44	776
Guadagne,Joseph J. Sgt.	12-11-44	776
Gulledge, Roy L. 2/Lt	7-7-44	778
Gustina, Charles F. F/O	12-11-44	776
Guthrie, Dale F. 2/Lt	7-22-44	777
Haigh, Merton W. S/Sgt.	10-17-44	778
Hamlin, Paul Jr. S/Sgt	5-25-44	778
Harcher, William J. S/Sgt.	5-25-44	778
Harding, Ellison Cpl.	10-13-44	777
Hardy, Kenneth W. S/Sgt.	8-24-44	779
Harer, Harold W. S/Sgt	8-27-44	778
Harries, Donald W. 2/Lt.	1-20-44	
Hayes, Albert C. Sgt.	1-20-45	779
Hays, Bert R. Jr. 2/Lt	6-6-44	779
Hedges, Richard A. 2/Lt.	1-9-44	776
Henderson, Ray G. S/Sgt.	6-6-44	778
Henneberry, Paul Jr. 2/Lt.	7-28-44	777
Hickson, Robert E. S/Sgt.	8-7-44	777
Hill, Gerald G. 2/Lt.	12-29-44	778
Hindle, Earnest C. 2/Lt	5-25-44	779
Hinkley, Richard C. T/Sgt.	8-24-44	776
Hinson, James E. 2/Lt.	5-7-44	776
Hoffman, Deneal Sgt.	5-25-44	778
Hoffman, John F. Sgt.	10-17-44	777
Hogan, William V. Jr. 2/Lt	6-2-44	779
Holcombe, Foy L. S/Sgt.	7-5-44	776
Holley, Francis R. S/Sgt.	7-7-44	778
Hornbaker, Robert W. Capt.	5-25-44	778
Hoskinson, Donald K. 2/Lt.	3-22-45	779
Howarth, Louis A. Jr. S/Sgt.	5-25-44	779
Hudgins, Hershal H. S/Sgt.	5-27-44	777
Hughes, Hubert W. Sgt.	7-7-44	777
Hurst, James C. Sgt	11-20-44	776
Hurt, Clifton S. Sgt.	1-20-44	
Ivan, Edward C. Sgt.	8-24-44	776
James, Ben G. Jr. S/Sgt.	7-28-44	777
James, John H 1/Lt.	8-24-44	776
Jenoir, Robert A. T/Sgt.	5-25-44	777
Jelenweicz, Eugene Sgt.	8-24-44	776
Johnson, Beauford C. T/Sgt.	7-16-44	779
Johnson, Harold A. Sgt.	10-17-44	779
Johnston, James C. S/Sgt.	5-27-44	777
Jones, Dale W. S/Sgt.	5-25-44	777
Jones, Ellsworth D. 2/Lt.	7-28-44	777
Kahn, Abraham 1/Lt.	7-22-44	776
Kampel, Isadore . 2/Lt.	1-17-44	778
Karas, Joe E. 2/Lt	10-17-44	777
Kelly, Joseph A. Cpl.	12-29-44	778
Kennedy, James W. Jr. Sgt.	7-22-44	777
Keepers, Lonnie L. 2/Lt.	1-9-44	776
Kibler, John D. Capt.	7-8-44	777
Kidd, Alvin S. Jr. 1/Lt	7-15-44	778
King, Ralph V. S/Sgt.	10-16-44	776
Kiobassa, Chester L. F/O	12-11-44	776
Kirkpatrick, Forrest S/Sgt.	7-16-44	779
Kolzer, Joseph S/Sgt	8-7-44	777
Krammer, Norman R. Sgt.	10-16-44	776
Krug, Kenneth E. 2/Lt.	2-29-44	778
Lapinski,Stanley E. T/Sgt.	8-9-44	778

Latimer, Stanley E. Capt.	5-10-44	777
Laub, Sherman S/Sgt.	6-6-44	
Lechowicz, Walter S/Sgt.	5-10-44	777
Lee, William W. 1/Lt.	10-16-44	776
Leistikow, Elver R. 2/Lt.	10-17-44	779
Lemon, James E. 2/Lt.	3-4-45	777
Lister, William W. S/Sgt.	6-26-44	777
Loar, Glenn E. Sgt.	7-16-44	779
Lombardo, Romeo Cpl.	10-13-44	777
Lovelle, Harry E. F/O	5-25-44	777
Luchenbach, William Jr. 2/Lt	6-2-44	779
Lynch, John W. T/Sgt.	8-24-44	776
MacDougall, Earl A 2/Lt.	7-30-44	776
Madsen, Robert W. 2/Lt.	1-9-44	776
Magill, William A. T/Sgt.	7-16-44	779
Majors, Elwin L. S/Sgt.	7-7-44	778
Makey, Herman O. Jr. S/Sgt.	10-29-44	779
Maloney, Edward J. 2/Lt.	8-24-44	776
Mann, Charles N. S/Sgt.	5-2-44	779
Marchacos, Louis H. S/Sgt.	5-7-44	776
Mattlin, Robert G. 2/Lt.	12-29-44	778
Matweia, Donald E. 2/Lt.	12-29-44	778
McBeth, Wendel L. T/Sgt.	8-9-44	778
McCarty, Robert F. Capt.	5-25-44	777
McCaslin, Robert B. 2/Lt.	6-6-44	776
McClosky, Bernard Jr. Sgt.	7-22-44	777
McCowen, Walter W. Jr. 2/Lt.	9-8-44	778
McGough, Hugh J. Sgt.	12-16-44	777
McGovern, Thomas F. 1/Lt	9-10-44	777
McGowan, Daryl F. T/Sgt.	6-26-44	777
McMichael, Lonnie D. Sgt	11-3-44	779
McMillian, Robert L. S/Sgt.	5-29-44	777
McNeil, Albert W. T/Sgt.	12-11-44	776
McPherson, Edwin R. T/Sgt.	10-17-44	777
Merrill, Richard M. 2/Lt.	10-17-44	777
Meyer, Leonard L. 2/Lt.	5-25-44	777
Michaud, Emile J. Sgt.	12-2-44	776
Millar, James C. Sgt.	12-6-44	779
Miller, John H. 2/Lt.	10-17-44	777
Miller, Joseph P. Cpl.	10-13-44	777
Mills, Charles W. S/Sgt.	5-7-44	776
Minerich, George M. S/Sgt.	4-12-44	777
Miller, Ruel H. 2/Lt	7-16-44	777
Montegut, Charles Jr. S/Sgt.	4-10-45	779
Morrison, Peter J. S/Sgt.	7-28-44	779
Morton, Lacey P. Capt.	4-10-45	779
Mower, Homer O. 1/Lt.	11-15-44	779
Munson, Robert C. 2/Lt.	5-10-44	778
Murphy, Francis P. F/O	1-20-45	777
Mydland, James l. 2/Lt.	7-7-44	778
Nagle, Vincent L. 2/Lt.	11-15-44	779
Nelson, Gordon 2/Lt.	4-12-44	777
Nemes, Lester PFC	3-1-45	776
Nethercot, Robert D	8-22-44	776
Neuhaus, Martin H. S/Sgt.	7-22-44	776
Newborg, William T. 2/Lt.	7-5-44	776
Nix, Joseph H. Sgt.	11-15-44	779
Oakley, Casey E. S/Sgt.	5-25-44	778
O'Leary, Robert J. 1/Lt.	4-10-45	779
O'Neal, Francis E. Sgt.	6-5-44	776
Orrell, Claude D. Sgt.	6-6-44	778
Ottinger, Roscoe L. S/Sgt.	1-29-44	779
Overholt, Norman O. 2/Lt.	9-12-44	779
Owens, George N. Cpl.	3-1-45	778
Pannone, Ralph. S/Sgt.	7-22-44	776
Parker, Andrew G. S/Sgt.	7-7-44	778
Parker, William J. 2/Lt.	10-17-44	779
Parrish, Rodes S. 2/Lt.	5-27-44	777
Patrick, Henry C. T/Sgt.	8-7-44	777
Payne, James L. S/Sgt.	7-28-44	777
Peel, Delbert R. Sgt.	5-2-44	779
Pearce, George H.Jr. Sgt.	1-9-44	776
Penman, Robert J. Sgt.	12-6-44	778
Penrod, Donald E. Sgt.	5-10-44	778
Peterson, Richard H. Sgt.	12-11-44	776
Petrone, James J. S/Sgt.	5-29-44	777
Piska, Glen M. Sgt.	1-20-44	777
Pitzer, Richard R. 2/Lt.	1-9-44	776
Polli, Phillip 2/Lt.	4-12-44	777
Pope, Lindley C. S/Sgt.	10-17-44	779
Porter, Farmer B. 2/Lt.	5-2-44	779
Powell, Robert W. Pvt.	3-1-45	778
Pratt,Robert C. Cpl.	12-28-44	777
Price, May T. Sgt.	10-17-44	777
Pusanski, Richard T. Cpl.	12-28-44	777
Pyrum, Herman E. S/Sgt.	6-26-44	777
Radler, Anthony J. 1/Lt.	7-15-44	778
Randolph, Richard B. S/Sgt.	6-2-44	779
Rangel, Fernando B. Sgt.	12-11-44	776
Rankin, John K. 2/Lt.	5-25-44	779
Rauber, Carl T. PFC.	3-1-45	778
Rauen, Geroge M. Sgt.	10-16-44	776
Rinke, Louis H. Sgt.	1-9-44	776
Reiche, Daniel E. S/Sgt.	11-15-44	779
Reimer, Russell H. T/Sgt.	10-17-44	777
Reinecke, Lawrence E. S/Sgt.	5-25-44	778
Renz, John R. T/Sgt.	8-24-44	776
Richardson, Stanley W. S/Sgt.	6-6-44	776
Rigdon, Ray W. Sgt.	10-17-44	777
Riley, Merle E. 2/Lt.	8-24-44	779
Robbins, Thomas V. Cpl.	3-22-45	779
Robinson, Ralph. Sgt.	8-24-44	776
Robinson, William D. 2/Lt.	9-10-44	779
Rodgers, John E. Sgt.	5-29-44	777
Rogers, Robert C. S/Sgt.	4-10-45	779
Rogers, William L. 2/Lt.	12-29-44	778
Roslefske, Edward A. Sgt.	12-6-44	778
Ross, Richard H. Cpl.	10-17-44	778
Ruben, Jerrold R. T/Sgt.	4-10-45	779
Sample, Kenneth I. Sgt.	3-1-45	778
Sampson, Thomas C. 2/Lt	10-13-44	777
Samson, David H. 2/Lt.	5-2-44	779
Sanders, Robert W. S/Sgt.	8-22-44	779
Scherlinger, Lee F. Sgt.	3-1-45	776
Schlichting, Gordon Cpl.	10-10-44	778
Schondel, Raymond Sgt.	4-12-44	777
Schonfield, Howard Sgt.	12-6-44	778
Sealey, Julius M. Jr. S/Sgt.	7-16-44	779
Serra, Americo J. Cpl.	12-28-44	777
Setliff, William C. Sgt.	3-27-44	776

Setser, Joe E. 1/Lt.	5-2-45	777
Sevey, John P. 1/Lt.	8-18-44	776
Sheppard, Frank P. S/Sgt.	8-24-44	779
Shields, Harold J. S/Sgt.	3-1-45	778
Shook, Raymond W. Sgt	1-20-44	777
Schutts, Gordon D. 1/Lt.	8-22-44	779
Silberstein, Frank Sgt.	10-17-44	777
Smallbones, John W. Cpl.	10-13-44	777
Smith, Arlan W. 2/Lt	5-7-44	776
Smith, Everrtt E. Cpl.	3-22-45	779
Snyder, Dudley C. T/Sgt.	3-22-45	779
Snyder, Richard H. Sgt.	7-15-44	778
Soloff, Milton H. S/Sgt.	11-15-44	779
Solorio, Albert R. Cpl.	12-28-44	777
Sopcsynski, Dominic J. Cpl	3-22-45	779
Spiller, Kyle Jr. Maj.	10-29-44	779
Sprague, Durrant D. Sgt.	9-10-44	779
Staron, Frank J. 2/Lt.	5-27-44	777
Stein, Archie G. 1/Lt.	8-22-44	779
Sternagle, Ray D. Jr. F/O	5-2-44	779
Stillwell, Edward P. 2/Lt.	5-7-44	776
Stoddard, Ray F. Jr. Sgt.	5-7-44	776
Straw,v Richard D. T/Sgt.	7-22-44	776
Sturgeon, Shelby J. Jr. Sgt.	10-16-44	776
Suber, John C. 2/Lt.	10-13-44	777
Sucher, Peter S/Sgt.	8-24-44	776
Sulich, George S/Sgt.	3-22-45	779
Sullivan, John F. 2/Lt.	7-28-44	777
Swartz, Glen T. Sgt.	10-17-44	779
Swygard,Gordon K. Sgt.	12-6-44	778
Taege, Norman L. S/Sgt.	7-15-44	778
Tafelski, Frank S/Sgt.	5-25-44	779
Talarico, Robert A. Cpl.	3-1-45	778
Taylor, Clayton R. Cpl.	12-29-44	778
Thielen, Gerald F. S/Sgt.	5-7-44	776
Thomason, Melvin C. S/Sgt.	4-10-45	779
Thompson, Robert J. S/Sgt.	1-20-45	779
Tillman, Sylvan H. S/Sgt.	5-2-44	779
Tobey, Thomas E. Cpl.	12-28-44	777
Toscano, Theodore D. 2/Lt.	3-22-45	779
Travaglino, Angelo Cpl.	8-21-44	776
Trizza,Sam S/Sgt.	7-16-44	779
Trotter, William O. 2/Lt.	5-25-44	777
Trout, Thorton D. Jr. S/Sgt.	6-26-44	777
Ullom, George K. T/Sgt.	7-22-44	776
Vana, Clarence R. 2/Lt.	1-26-44	777
Van Tuyl, Richard A. 2/Lt.	12-28-44	777
Vogl, George A. Jr. Sgt.	1-20-45	779
Walacavage, William Sgt.	4-12-44	777
Waldman, Robert S. Sgt.	4-12-44	777
Walas, Dennis G. 1/Lt.	11-15-44	779
Wall, George R. Capt.	4-10-45	779
Ward, Elwood J. Jr. Sgt.	7-22-44	777
Ward, James C. Cpl.	12-5-44	776
Ward, Jesse D. 2/Lt.	5-27-44	777
Watson, Thad J. Sgt.	8-24-44	776
Watt, Joseph S. Sgt.	11-15-44	779
Weaver, Walter W. 2/Lt.	8-24-44	776
Weber, William J. S/Sgt.	7-22-44	777
Weger, Ralph A. T/Sgt.	10-13-44	778
Welsh, William L. Pvt.	3-1-45	778
White, James M. 2/Lt.	7-15-44	778
White, Robert C. 2/Lt.	5-12-44	777
Whittemore, Frank J. 2/Lt.	10-29-44	779
Williams, Robert A. Sgt.	10-17-44	779
Wilson, Peter 1/Lt.	3-26-45	778
Wilson, Roy C. S/Sgt.	5-7-44	776
Wise, Robert L. T/Sgt.	5-27-44	776
Wolfe, Robert H. 2/Lt.	7-22-44	777
Wong Frank PFC.	3-1-45	778
Wright, James H. S/Sgt.	8-24-44	776
Wright, Oliver 2/Lt.	6-26-44	777
Wuller, Richard Sgt.	8-9-44	778
Wygal, Lawrence 1/Lt	5-10-44	778
Young, Frank H. Cpl.	12-29-44	778

Tactical Air Command: An Illustrated History 1946-1992. Mike Hill. Never before has such a complete pictorial history of Tactical Air Command been put together. The planes, demonstration teams, and foreign units of TAC are covered in pictorial and textual detail from the the 1940s to the 1990s. Included in this excellent account are lists of the aces of the Korean War, aerial victories in Viet Nam, and air-to-air victories during Desert Storm.
Size: 8 1/2" x 11" ■ over 250 b/w, over 350 color photographs ■ 224 pp.
ISBN: 0-7643-1288-X ■ hard cover ■ $49.95

The 451st Bomb Group in World War II - A Pictorial History. Mike Hill. This new book is an illustrated history of the 451st Bomb Group in World War II. As part of the USAAF's 15th Air Force, they flew their B-24 Liberators from Castellucia, Italy to heavily defended targets throughout the Mediterranean theater of war. During their combat tour the 451st was awarded three Presidential Unit Citations for their ability to get to the target no matter what the enemy threw at them.

Size: 8 1/2"x11" ■ over 600 b/w photographs ■ 160 pp.
ISBN: 0-7643-1287-1 ■ hard cover ■ $45.00